PRODUCT MANAGEMENT

Product Management

Edited by P. Law, C. Weinberg, P. Doyle and
K. Simmonds

Harper & Row Ltd, Publishers
London New York Evanston San Francisco

Published by Harper & Row Ltd
28 Tavistock Street, London WC2E 7PN

Standard Book Number 06-318018-7 (cloth)
Standard Book Number 06-318020-0 (paper)

Typeset by Specialised Offset Services Limited, Liverpool
Printed and bound by A. Wheaton & Company, Exeter

Contents

IV Product Line Management

Introduction

'...by their fruits ye shall know them'.

Matthew, vii, 20.

The success or failure of an enterprise is determined by its performance in the market-place. However efficient its production processes, however subtly it manipulates its financial resources, if no-one wants to buy what it is offering it will go out of business. And in the market, the performance that counts is that of the products and services that the enterprise offers. This is what brings the old customers back and helps to attract new customers. Clever advertising can arouse people's interest in a product, hard selling can make them buy it — once, but they will not buy again if it has not lived up to expectations. It is therefore vitally important to have the right product strategy. Decisions about this are the most important marketing decisions that managers have to make.

In an unchanging world this would not be difficult. Once the right products had been found, they would continue to sell, and management's efforts could be developed to making minor improvements in production and marketing techniques. Nor would it be difficult to adapt to slow changes in the environment. By definition, these would not be large, and there would be time to experiment and to adjust the firm's activities accordingly. If market research showed that customers wanted a faster operating machine tool, larger motors could be purchased and fitted, or, if buyers of shoes seemed interested in a wider range of colours, various colours could be tried out, and the successful ones produced and sold nationally.

But, nowadays, firms are faced by a market situation whose chief characteristic is change. This takes place along many dimensions, but the four most important are technology, the economy, customers and competition. The technological dimension is at once the most obvious and the best documented. Where, a few decades ago, electronic devices relied on vacuum tubes the size of light bulbs, now whole circuits can be incorporated in minute chips. Computers have shrunk from room-size to pocket-size. Even writing is not free from technical change. The quill pen lasted for centuries. Its successor, the steel-nibbed pen, was followed comparatively rapidly by the fountain pen, but even then, these two lasted for

decades. The ballpoint has only been with us since the war, but is already being challenged by fibre-tipped pens. Patents used to allow time for an idea to be developed into a marketable product. But today the chances are that a competitor will get round the patent long before it runs out. It may even be harmful to patent an invention, as it gives clues to the competition as to where they should direct their research effort.

Changes in the economy are, on the whole, less predictable. The rates of growth of whole economies are carefully measured and the development of nations into industrial and post industrial societies can be predicted. An individual organization is more likely, however, to be concerned with the detailed instruments which a government uses to manage an economy. Alterations of tariffs to protect threatened industries, changes in sales taxes, manipulation of the supply of money or credit, all these can have an enormous effect on sales, and on product design. The imposition of purchase tax on tape recorders in 1968 not only distorted sales figures, but as the tax on radios and tape recorders was now the same, it was worthwhile combining them in one unit. Previously this had not been so.

Customers do not stand still either. They are better educated, they spend less time at work and they earn more than they used to. As more money found its way into the hands of teenagers a whole new market grew up around them. More married women now go out to work and this gives them increased financial independence, but less time to spend on their families and homes. Manufacturers of convenience foods and household appliances have derived benefit from this change in life-style.

Lastly, there is always the threat of competition. Firms within an industry are on the look-out for ways to improve their competitive edge, and development of improved products is one way to do this. Changes from outside an industry, such as the Xerox and Polaroid processes, can have a catastrophic effect on existing markets. Firms may band together to resist change, but this is hard to control, as the world's airlines are finding out. A large proportion of the public are quite happy to plan their movements in advance and to make their infrequent purchases of air travel at fixed, and not necessarily convenient times. They are not interested in the regular, but expensive service provided by the major airlines and are patronizing the charter operators, who provide the service that they want.

It is not just that conditions are changing, but the rate of change is increasing, too. This means that the useful life of products is getting shorter. Yesterday's innovation is commonplace today, and may be obsolete tomorrow. The implications of this cannot be avoided. No longer can an organization rely on a haphazard approach to the management of its product policy. It doesn't matter whether it launches new products every month or every 10 years. The point is that every activity from generation of ideas, through development and launch to full-scale market exploitation, must be planned. The product-line must also be examined regularly and decaying products dropped.

This book stresses the need for an analytical approach to product management. The readings, chosen from British sources wherever possible, are built round the concept of the product life-cycle. This states that a product is conceived as an idea and after a period of gestation, during which it is developed and tested, it is born. Initially, sales will be small. Few people will have even heard of it, and of those who have, not everyone will want to take the risk of trying something new. This applies not only to final consumers, but to intermediate customers in the distribution channels, and the new product is unlikely to be widely distributed in the early stages of its life. However, if it gains acceptance, sales will increase as more and more people purchase it. This period of growth is followed by maturity. It is here that complacency often sets in. The product is selling well, and managements feel that they can relax. But there will always be newcomers trying to take sales away from existing products and these must be properly managed if they are to retain their share of the market. Finally, the time comes when rejuvenation is no longer possible and the product is dropped. This is the hardest decision of all, but must be faced because ageing products can easily drain away an organization's financial and managerial resources.

The sections in this book correspond, roughly, with various stages in the life-cycle. The first section is devoted to product strategy. The articles discuss not only what business a firm is in now, but also what business it should be in 10 years later and how it should get there. The next section deals with product development. Generation of new product ideas is relatively cheap, but as soon as research and development is started costs climb rapidly. It is important that this money is spent wisely. The third section covers the market launch and early life of new products. Here, speed is the important factor, speed of action to ensure that possible weaknesses are identified very early on. Finally, management of the existing product line is described.

Each section is preceded by a short introduction, and followed by a set of study questions. These can be used in a variety of ways. An individual reader can check whether he has understood the ideas which have been presented to him, or the questions can be discussed in class. Alternatively, written answers can be called for. Two cases are included at the end of the book. An extensive list of further readings is provided for those who want to study this topic in greater depth.

Part I
Product Strategy

Introduction

An organization's product strategy is an integral part of its corporate strategy and it is difficult to separate the two. The products that are planned and the markets in which they will be offered are shaped by a firm's capabilities, and by what resources it can acquire. But the firm itself is defined by the transactions it makes with the outside world, or, in a word, by its markets. What business are we in? What business should we be in? How do we make the change? These are the questions which a strategic product plan has to answer. Levitt, in his famous article,[1] claimed that firms took much too narrow a view of their businesses. Instead of supplying products — oil or railways — they should see themselves as fulfilling needs — energy or transportation. This is fine, and needed to be said, but a slavish application of Levitt's principles can lead to nonsense. For example, supersonic aeroplanes are 'transport', but this is no reason why a railway company should go into the aircraft business, and it should think very hard before deciding to run an airline.

This point is well made in the first article in this section, by E.P. Ward. He argues that a company should sub-divide its activities into a number of 'dynamic product areas'. These should be expressed in terms of a long-term need, fluid transport, rather than a short-term solution, centrifugal pumps, but the main point is that these areas should be visualized as the cross-section of an electric cable carrying various strands or conductors. The areas can change in shape or size over time, but must remain part of the main cable. Ward also stresses the need for forward planning and this point is taken up in the second article, by Neil Hood. Companies often underestimate how long it takes to develop new products, and how much it costs. It is therefore necessary to start the process well in advance of the market launch date, and to design organizational structures and procedures in such a way that hold-ups are kept to a minimum. Hood's article reviews the many methods which have been proposed for controlling the product planning process.

The next two articles, by J.B. Quinn and P.M.S. Jones respectively, are concerned with long-range forecasting and market research. Technological forecasting, a systematic way of looking at future developments, was the buzzword of the 1960s. It has not proved to be the panacea that it was claimed to be but Quinn shows that any form of structured thinking is better than the guesswork practised by many managements today. Jones presents three case studies concerning the development of new processes and materials at Harwell. He emphasizes the problem inherent in new product development, that because a product is new, no-one has used it. It is very difficult to define what the potential markets are, and what are the important properties of the new material or service, and the initial stages of market research must try to answer these questions.

1 T. Levitt, Marketing Myopia, Harvard Business Review 38, 45 July-Aug 1960.

1.
The Dynamics of Business Planning
by E.P. Ward

Reprinted from Marketing Forum, November/December 1967, published by the Institute of Marketing with permission.

Introduction

All living organisms adapt to their environment in order to survive. A company is no exception.

But owing to the time-lag between concept and marketable product, a company must adapt in advance of its environment, take the pill half an hour before it feels the pain coming on (though with certain pains and pills, half an hour is hardly long enough). Successful adaptation in a company is therefore measured not only by the magnitude of current profits, but also by longer-term resilience, or net cash flow over a substantial period. A large dividend one year followed by liquidation in the next would give both shareholders and employees reason to complain.

A company is consequently faced by two conflicting needs: to optimize its current operations; and to make adequate provision for the future. In a manufacturing concern these aims can best be reconciled by continuity of product policy and proper emphasis on forward planning.

It follows that product planning (or, more generally, corporate planning) may be defined as a creative function of management concerned with the forward development of a company, taking existing assets, resources and experience as the basic premise and relating or adapting them to changing markets, continuously and systematically. In other words, it is a process of fitting a company to its environment, bearing in mind that the environment evolves and can itself be influenced.

Although continuity of product policy is essential, management does in fact proceed by a series of decisions, each a discrete step or change in direction. A procedure for product planning should therefore not only enable a company to respond continuously and effectively to a changing context, but should also progress by stages, of predetermined length, at the end of which decisions become due.

So many companies, conscious that they need to introduce new products, review an endless succession of ideas and opportunities, always believing the next that comes to light will be better than the last, with the result that no decision is ever taken. Unless substantial effort is concentrated on a sensibly related group of prospects that can be studied intensively, their potential can never be properly recognized or realized in a profitable venture.

Before suggesting a procedure for thinking systematically about the future in terms of present assets, it may be useful to describe the basic change in corporate situation that has made such a procedure necessary. The change has taken place so gradually that it has hardly been apparent, with the result that industries have tended to react intuitively rather than in any rational or systematic way.

The New Situation

In the first instance, a company is founded to exploit a new idea, acquisition, invention, departure or development. The object is clear: capital must be invested, men recruited, facilities built up and markets explored in order to make the most of a particular opportunity. Initially the company can afford to be singleminded. Its product policy is ready-made.

As time goes by and the company expands, new products are accumulated, in many cases simply because an opportunity happens to present itself. More men, machines, experience and other assets are assembled to service these interests, until eventually it is the resources themselves, rather than any basic product or idea, that have to be exploited.

Whereas the purpose of a company may once have been to develop some promising invention, today the object is to stay in business, however frequently products are superseded or the market changes course. No longer are facilities and skills gathered round the product; products must be found to suit the facilities and skills.

It is at this point that companies are driven to reconsider their position, returning to first principles in order to redefine their purpose, policy and mode of operations.

Here perhaps is an important distinction between the engineering and consumer industries. Most consumer products are made in very large numbers, so that plant can be designed for a specific product line and written off over a comparatively short sales life. In choosing new consumer products, therefore, only the potential market and the company's marketing resources need in many cases be considered.

The manufacturer of capital products, on the other hand, builds up costly facilities and valuable experience over a much longer period, usually optimized to a particular product mix. Since they are substantial, he cannot afford to disregard these assets when diversifying. No-one would continue to sit in a deckchair at the seaside after it comes on to rain simply because he has paid his 5p. But, having installed a large costly tape-controlled boring machine, a company would be wise as far as possible to keep it occupied, particularly since resale value will almost certainly be low.

Cyclic Regeneration

Since the cycle of product replacement is so much faster in the consumer industries, it may be possible to learn from their experience, much as an accelerated film of airport operations can reveal conditions that at normal speeds may not be evident.

Consumer product development is usually so planned that something new is always ready to succeed the product that has passed its peak. Sales forecasts help to determine at what point the new product should be launched, though it is important to bear in mind that profits may begin to fall well before there is any decline in total sales volume.

Typical curves for unit sales and profit per unit sold are shown in Figure 1.1. Following an initial boost, which is due in part to intensive promotion and experimental purchasing, the curve of unit sales droops slightly, then recovers, continuing to climb towards its maximum.

The profit per unit sold begins below the zero line during the launching period, but rises rapidly as initial costs are written-off and manufacture becomes more economic. Prices can be high, since at this stage few competitors have entered the field and the product holds a monopoly position. With the advent of competition, prices may have to be reduced to maintain the level of sales, and unit profit begins to fall long before the curve for unit sales has reached its highest point. It is the second differential, or rate at which the slopes of sales and profit curves are changing, that should be watched.

This pattern may be less apparent in the case of

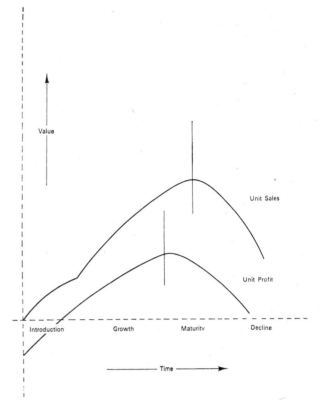

Figure 1.1 Curves of unit sales and unit profit, showing stages in product sales life. Profit per unit sold passes its peak before any decline in sales becomes apparent, and the first indicator of decline is the second differential of the unit profit curve.

industrial products, which are much more subject to individual variations, but the basic cycle of rise and decline, however irregular or extended, can still be recognized.

Ideally, products should succeed each other continuously, so that total company profit remains above a given minimum, as later curves in Figure 1.2. But with a sales life of 50 years or more, as in the case of the steam locomotive, a manufacturer may well be taken by surprise.

Identity and Role

With growing emphasis on the economic utilization of available facilities and the high rate of technical change, engineering companies are likewise beginning to think increasingly in terms of continuing product succession and review. It is therefore necessary to devise a procedure whereby a company's plant and experience may be related to emerging market needs or adapted to meet new situations. Any procedure for this purpose should assist a company to:

1 Plan its future continuously and systematically.
2 Make the most of its existing assets.
3 Keep in close touch with its market environment.
4 Make product decisions with minimum delay.
5 Exploit whatever unexpected opportunities may come to light.

The first essential in devising a planning framework is to define a company's role.

To think usefully about its development a company must have a recognizable identity, a role known and understood both by the company's employees and by the outside world, a lasting role that, as far as can be seen, will not be overtaken by events or changes in the market, in other words a dynamic corporate identity capable of adaptation. Indeed, identity must precede objectives, since nothing can have a purpose unless it first exists. Figure 1.3 shows how company identity can evolve in time.

A suitable role is the key to successful product planning and a big step towards meeting the five basic requirements enumerated above. It extends into the future, it can take account of existing reputation and experience, it provides a basis for a continuing market review, can simplify decision-making, and offers scope for 'planned opportunism'.

Bearing the company's role in mind, the management is in a position to look at current news, technical innovation, commercial developments, social, political and economic change, and ask themselves: 'What's in it for us?'

Continuing Review

Take, for example, a company that has traditionally supplied flame and explosion-proof equipment. By adopting 'aspects of safety' as a more general field of continuing interest, the company can conduct a regular review of product opportunities, focusing on product ideas consistent with its resources and experience.

The management would be aware that during recent years there has been a succession of disasters – earthquakes, breached and overflowing dams, unprecedented damage due to fire, mining accidents, losses at sea and in the air, large-scale robberies and havoc on the roads. By reviewing these events, the safety-conscious company could hardly fail to discover some product opportunities.

Such a review would be conducted on a regular basis and should allow for immediate opportunities and opportunities over the next 5, 10 or even 15 years.

Dynamic Product Areas

It is convenient to subdivide a company's overall identity into several such continuing areas of interest or 'dynamic product areas' (Figure 1.3). Essentially, a dynamic area defines a class of activities or products in functional or general terms. It should be broad enough to embrace a great number of product ideas, including possibilities not yet conceived, but specific enough to be readily communicated and to focus a continuing review or product search.

A company may have several related or even unrelated dynamic areas, which are not simply generalizations of the company's whole activity but must be carefully defined. Such generalizations as transportation equipment for a shipbuilder and entertainment for a juke-box manufacturer may be too vague to be very useful.

These areas should as far as possible be timeless, so that a company's activities may be capable of indefinite regeneration, new products being introduced within an area, as existing products become less profitable. Thus in the case of safety: whatever vicissitudes befall particular

Curves of Total Profit for Single Product Groups

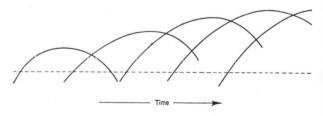

Figure 1.2 Ideally products should be introduced continuously so that total profit remains above a given level

devices, safety equipment of one kind or another will always be required.

The word 'dynamic' is used, not simply because it is a fashionable adjective, but as in 'dynamic equilibrium'. As something leaves (becomes obsolete or uncompetitive), something else enters (is introduced) to take its place. Continuous product succession (or expansion) is therefore possible within an area.

The area can be visualized as the cross-section of an electric cable carrying various strands or conductors. The area itself can change its shape or size, as new strands join the main flux or diverge from it, but it preserves an essential continuity.

Some further examples might help to clarify this fundamental concept. Any one diffusion process, evaporator, filter or centrifuge, could become obsolete; eventually it may no longer be necessary to separate fissile uranium from natural uranium. But we shall always have to separate some material from another; and equipment for 'materials separation' is a dynamic area that can last virtually for ever.

Again, any one fastener may fall into disuse; buttons may be replaced by zips, rawlplugs by anchor bolts, but fastenings themselves are indispensable and therefore constitute a dynamic product area.

Function and Image

The dynamic area is of course a term of ranging application. It might refer to the exploitation of a particular material, nickel, say, or aluminium; to a service such as conversion, including for example, the conversion of cars, private houses, factories, ships and aircraft; or even to a facility — and the necessary information sources — for buying potentially profitable companies.

It may not always be possible to express a dynamic product area in a few words, but the concept should be relatively simple. A company might for example specialize in producing 'machinery for the rolling or otherwise continuous processing of sheet and strip material, including steel, aluminium, board and plastics'.

A shipbuilder might have more difficulty in conceiving a dynamic area, consistent with his knowledge and resources. His instinct may be to consider novel forms of transport, such as hovercraft, but the field is limited and he may be better advised to expand his interest to embrace 'engineered bulk accommodation', applying his experience of packing a great deal into a small space to the design of self-contained and package

plant (mobile or static, including for example, drilling rigs) and to problems of storage, warehousing, city markets and urban market gardening, parking and congestion.

It is not suggested that any company should attempt to occupy the whole of a dynamic area; it would simply use the concept to guide its thinking and take up only the most promising ideas brought to light within it.

The dynamic area serves a variety of other purposes. It can, for example, help to direct an immediate search for manufacturing licences or associates; and has a part to play in long-term product forecasting, as will be seen later. It can also provide a company with a strong marketing image. If particular companies are widely associated with separation, aspects of safety, fastenings or conversion, any potential customer with problems in these fields will tend to turn to them for assistance or advice.

Criteria

A dynamic area may take many forms but must achieve a satisfactory balance between the too general and the too specific. Ideally it should:

1 Be capable of continued application and usefulness, irrespective of changing social, industrial and market needs. (Will it last?)

2 Be likely to embrace a large number of individual products, including many selling in growth markets. (Does it afford enough scope for seeking products?)

3 Not be limited to a single market, market area or industry. (Does it offer a sufficient breadth of market?)

4 Be simple to identify and describe and sufficiently definite to focus a product search. (Can it be expressed in a few words and readily be understood?)

5 Be in the general stream of social and industrial change. (Is it likely to yield new developments?)

6 Not be strongly associated with another company or industry. (Is it unique?)

7 Be consistent with the company's experience and image. (Does it embrace any existing products or activities?)

8 Relate in some degree to markets in which the company are already well established. (Will it provide an opportunity to use the company's present sales facilities and outlets?)

These criteria should of course be treated with some discretion. A good dynamic area may sometimes fail particular requirements.

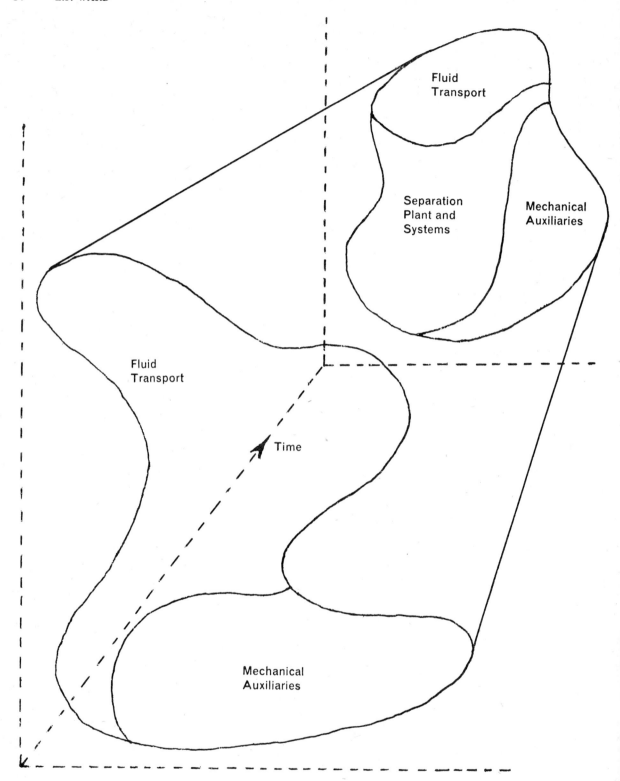

Fluid
Transport

Separation
Plant and
Systems

Mechanical
Auxiliaries

Fluid
Transport

Time

Mechanical
Auxiliaries

Figure 1.3 The identity of a company at any time may be regarded as a slice from an irregular prism, the cross section of which changes as the identity evolves.

Differentiated Assets

Where a company has no natural role or formulated product areas, a study of its resources and experience will often suggest lines of development. By thinking systematically about a company's assets and using certain guides, suitable dynamic areas can be conceived.

Assets are considered to be of two kinds: differentiated and undifferentiated. Undifferentiated assets are those common to many companies – factory space, standard tools and money. Money is universal and if a company treats capital as its primary asset when planning to diversify, it will do so in competition with every other company, from ICI to Marks and Spencer, though, during a credit squeeze, access to liquid capital may well become a differentiated asset. The differentiated assets, peculiar to a given company, form a sounder basis for a product planning study.

In undertaking a project of this kind, it is useful in the first instance to identify those assets which in combination distinguish the company from every other company. It is these assets that provide the company with any competitive advantage it may have. The market is common to everybody; a company's potential is unique.

Characteristic Table

As a preliminary, it is usual to draw up a 'characteristic table' or 'family tree', which is used to prompt ideas for product areas. A dynamic product area should transcend individual products and product groups and link as many aspects of a company's experience as possible.

The table is thus designed to provide a concise expression of a company's resources and experience, which can therefore be readily reviewed or committed to memory, and comprises three columns as follows:

1 Existing products, past products and products under consideration, though only potential products thought to be particularly appropriate should be included.

2 Details of the company's experience, assembled from design, production and research departments.

3 Sales outlets, by trades, industries and sometimes individual customers, where the customer's activities are readily identified.

Items within each column are not arranged to have any horizontal correspondence and the table in Figure 1.4,

based on a hypothetical group of four companies, is a typical example.

Trigger Mechanisms

The table may help to prompt ideas for dynamic areas in a variety of ways. A few of those that have been used from time to time are discussed below.

One approach is to take each item in turn and scan the remainder of the table to see if any relationships emerge. For example, a company might have among its products air compressors and air-conditioning equipment; be experienced in pneumatics; and supply equipment for tonnage oxygen plants. The link between these four items might suggest the product area 'air handling and processing', embracing, in addition, air conveying, air cleaning, air filtration and distillation, pressure exchangers, air-cooling, and so on.

Another method is to consider each product in the first column and endeavour to generalize it as a function. Thus a window fastener, which is a specific product, might be expanded into fastenings in general which could form a dynamic product area; car radiators into small air-cooled heat exchangers; a filter or centrifuge into materials separation plant; escalators into short-range passenger conveying.

Products	Processes	Outlets
Pumps	Dewatering	Domestic consumers
Air compressors	Crystallization	Hardware shops
Thermal driers	Control engineering	Department stores
Centrifuges	Hydraulics	Motor manufacturers
Finned tubing	Pneumatics	Garages
Evaporators	Combustion	Chemical concerns
Pressure vessels	Heat balance	Construction companies
Refrigerators	Rotation	Plant-hire firms
Filters	Reciprocation	Builders' merchants
Lightweight diesels	Structures	Tonnage oxygen plants
Domestic heaters	Soil mechanics	Mining
Window fasteners		Docks
Air-conditioning	Extrusion	Electricity undertakings
Winches	Deep drawing	Aircraft industry
Escalators	Copy turning	Research establishments
Cartridges	Broaching	Food processing
Dishwashers	Chemical milling	Sewage & water boards
Car bumpers	Complex fabrication	Education authorities
Heated towel rails	Precision casting	The Services
Immersion heaters	Powder metallurgy	Hotels

Figure 1.4 Characteristic table of products, processes and outlets. In compiling the table, special emphasis is placed on skills or knowledge in which companies have unique experience or are particularly advanced. It will be noted that there is no horizontal correspondence between different columns in the table.

Not only functions, but also applications and outlets may be generalized. Thus, a company making soap, which happens to be used for cleaning industrial premises, might extend its scope to floor maintenance and preservation generally.

Product areas can of course be based on manufacturing or technical processes, and the second column may be scanned for suitable ideas. Companies can usefully present themselves as specialists in all aspects of extrusion or control engineering, high-quality casting or soil mechanics. Particular management skills might also be borne in mind, e.g., experience in negotiating with government departments or controlling a large export programme.

Engineering principles may provide a basis for devising product areas. Thus, a company making centrifugal pumps will be familiar with hydrodynamics and rotation; in turn, hydrodynamics and rotation suggest the further product area of fluid mixing.

Framework for Thinking

Devising a company role is only the first stage. A framework for thinking usefully about a company's future must clearly involve several further stages. Also, now that identity and differentiated assets have been introduced, it is convenient to define corporate objective. The definition is formulated to be universal but capable of unique interpretation. 'We are in business to make money' is not enough — so is everybody else. The aim of any company is rather to exploit its current and potential assets in the context of present and emerging markets by supplying competitive goods and services, with competitive rewards to employees and competitive

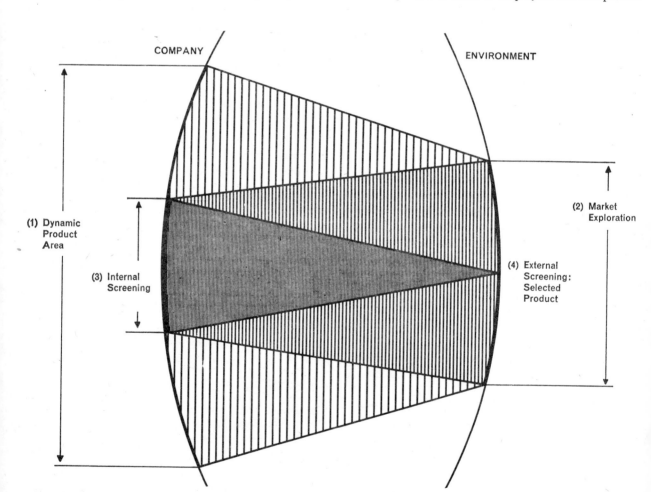

Figure 1.5 Simplified form of successive focussing, shown diagrammatically as a dialogue between a company and its environment.

returns to shareholders. Given this definition, a planning procedure becomes an almost self-evident requirement.

As already noted, the purpose of the procedure is to reconcile a company with its environment. To look at a company, scan the market and then conceive the ideal product calls for a talent that few of us possess. Something more systematic, more practical is needed.

The approach considered here may be described as 'successive focusing'. The object is to narrow the field of interest in stages; first with reference to the company and its immediate environment, second with reference to the market, third with reference to the activities of companies already serving the selected markets, fourth with reference to the scope for implementation, fifth with reference to the resulting opportunities, and finally with reference once again to the company's potential and capacity. The procedure is developed by elaboration of these stages. An abbreviated version of the process, shown as a dialogue between a company and its environment, appears in Figure 1.5.

The company's resources and experience are considered first, since it is these assets that distinguish it from every other company. Also, the whole market, present and future, is too vast to be explored in any economic way and must first be cut down to a manageable size.

Successive Focusing

Many companies will claim that they can make anything, given a first-class market opportunity, buying-in the facilities they need. In practice, an alien product can always be introduced more quickly and economically by some other company already suitably equipped.

Also, a total market study is a formidable undertaking. Presumably the whole market could be divided into sectors and their growth/time/volume characteristics calculated as in Figure 1.6. The largest fastest-growing sector (chemicals in the diagram) could then be subdivided and the most promising sub-sector selected. Meanwhile, in the most unpromising main sector (textiles), there might be a sub-sector of far greater potential than any chemical sub-sector, leading to missed opportunities in fields germane to a company's experience.

For convenience the framework is introduced as a succession of stages, but they can be regarded as a cycle and would not necessary be carried out consecutively. The stages may be called:

1 Analysis, in which the company's role would be defined, plus the terms of reference and criteria for introducing new activities.

2 Exploration, in which markets are explored in order to identify emerging market needs consistent with the company's role and terms of reference.

3 Search, in which an intensive world-wide search would be conducted to discover products already, or on the point of, being marketed, together with patented ideas, meeting the requirements established during analysis and exploration.

4 Investigation, in which additional facilities for manufacture or marketing are investigated where necessary, possibly with a view to acquisition.

5 Evaluation, in which products and facilities are assessed in order to establish the most promising combination.

6 Action, in which the information assembled is reviewed and a decision taken, to proceed, withdraw or undertake a deeper study, and any negotiations are put in hand.

These stages are discussed in detail, since they not only serve as a routine for a single product search, but also form the basis for a continuing review.

Analysis

The first stage comprises a detailed examination of the company's resources and present market environment in order to draw up a characteristic table of products, processes and outlets. Using this table as a basis, several dynamic product areas, or areas of such, are defined. Then a brief literature search and survey is carried out to determine growth sectors within the areas. During this stage, tentative check-lists and selection criteria are prepared for assessing individual products, prospective licensors and companies or agencies for possible acquisition or association. Also, existing products are investigated to check if they are being fully exploited, not only in traditional markets, but in other potential markets too.

Exploration

The purpose of a market exploration is to identify emerging or unsatisfied requirements within the product areas. In the case of 'materials separation' for example, discussions might be held with buyers and chief engineers of mineral processing concerns, oil and chemical companies, plant contractors for the food industry and other likely users of separation plant, to

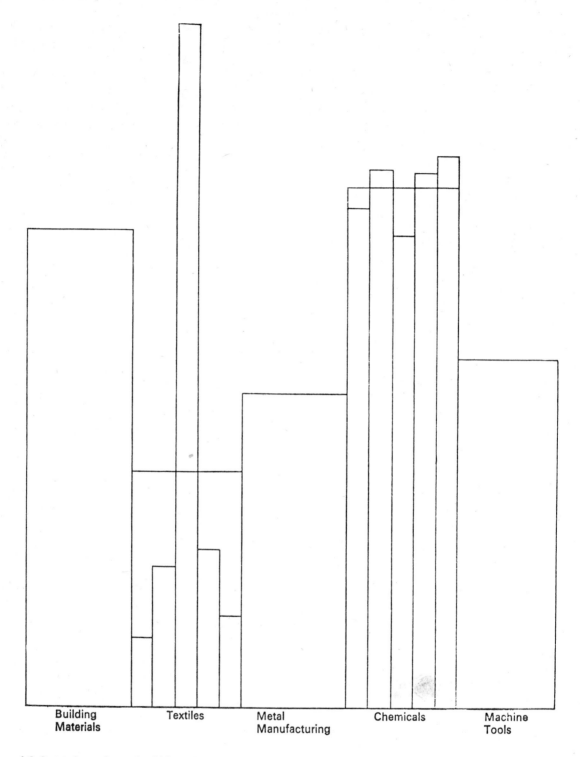

Figure 1.6 Comparison of growth within and between industrial sectors. It is seldom practical to conduct an exploration over the complete market panorama to identify potential growth sectors. Successive subdivision can also be seriously misleading, in that important opportunities may be overlooked. Vertical scale represents volume (£) times rate of growth, but the quantities do not correspond to any real situation.

ascertain: what equipment is on long delivery; what features of present equipment are unsatisfactory or what new features could usefully be introduced; and what problems in separation are not adequately solved by any equipment currently available. An exploration is not to be confused with a market survey, which is usually concerned with a single product or product group. The subject of a survey is known at the beginning; the subject of an exploration is not.

Search
Also within the dynamic product areas, a search is conducted in order to assemble a substantial list of products, perhaps a hundred or two in all, so that the probability of including a few first-class items is very high. Over the years, it is possible to build up a comprehensive register of 'product sources', listing engineers, consultants, patent and licence agencies, research foundations, development bodies and Government establishments, throughout the world, who are prepared to forward product information. Such data can then be recorded on punched cards. Another useful device is to assemble a library of exhibition catalogues, providing an up-to-date, reliable and readily accessible source of company names classified by any number of product lattices. During a search, it is also necessary to make direct approaches to manufacturers, regularly attend conferences and exhibitions, and constantly review published information, economic data, important statistics and so on. A thorough search of this kind goes a long way towards ensuring that no important opportunity is overlooked and that any product taken up is not superseded shortly afterwards. In one case a client was seeking details of dishwashers and had discovered a total of 40 different models; a subsequent intensive search revealed 40 designs in Italy alone. Information is also gathered on the performance of products in their markets of origin.

Investigation
Often the introduction of new products creates problems of manufacturing or sales capacity. Alternatively, a product may be taken up by acquisition of a company. A search for manufacturing concerns or selling agencies may therefore be carried out, usually within the same country as the company seeking to expand, but not invariably. Sometimes a company may be acquired to increase the viability of an industrial group by vertical or horizontal integration; or as a source of manufacture at some unspecified later date, when production can be

transferred to the parent company's facilities and the residual premises disposed of by resale. Generally the purpose is to supplement existing sales or manufacturing resources. Company searches are normally product oriented, since companies are prepared to publicize their products, but it is much more difficult to obtain financial information, particularly where the company is privately owned. Applying the principle of successive focusing, the first task in reducing the field is to identify companies making products of the right general character. The task of investigating a finite number of companies, selected in this way, is, of course, less formidable than covering the whole of industry.

Evaluation
All products, product ideas and companies are evaluated, using a full screening process, developed during the search and exploration stages from the checklist prepared in the planning stage. Market checks are carried out and potential competition is identified. Generally, products are screened in groups, since comparative evaluation is not only economical, particularly where large numbers of products are involved, but also tends to be more reliable than assessment of a single product in isolation.

Action
On completion of the cycle, the information assembled and analysed during the study should make a decision to proceed relatively easy. But implementation may be far more difficult. New products cut across familiar procedures, and executives, already overloaded, may regard a departure from established routine as the last straw. If the product is to be launched effectively, someone with sufficient authority to break through traditional practice must be charged with its success, usually reporting directly to the chief executive. Any negotiations can then be initiated, royalties and down-payments agreed, and a programme prepared. Decisions are required on whether sales and manufacture are to be handled by existing organizations; or whether the new activity should be isolated, with separate costing and overhead structure. The project manager must participate in resolving these issues and share responsibility for the decisions taken.

The six stages provide the core of any product study, but it may be useful to enlarge a little on the evaluation or screening stage. Anyone can choose a horse, but few can pick the winner. According to some American investigators working in the field, one product in 20 taken up in the US has proved successful. Others say one in a 100. No doubt the variation arises from differences in consumer and industrial practice and from differences in definition.

Screening Profile

A typical screening process, which has been developed over several years, is in three parts: a coarse screening using criteria assembled during the initial appraisal of a company's facilities; a second review involving information gathered from prospective associates and licensors; and a full assessment based on a standard checklist of nearly 80 factors. Again, the procedure involves successive focusing, in other words, an increasingly intensive study of a progressively decreasing field.

The checklist is divided into eight factor groups as follows:

1 Performance factors.
2 Stability factors.
3 Growth factors.
4 Assimilation factors.
5 Marketability factors.
6 Development factors.
7 Production factors.
8 Legal factors.

Legal factors, though mentioned last, are often crucial, but a product does not normally reach the screening stage unless it has been cleared in this respect.

These factors can be used merely as a checklist to ensure that no significant consideration has been overlooked or, by introducing a weighting for each factor, as a basis for quantitative rating.

Quantitative rating, however, should be treated with suspicion. No practical range of weightings can ade-

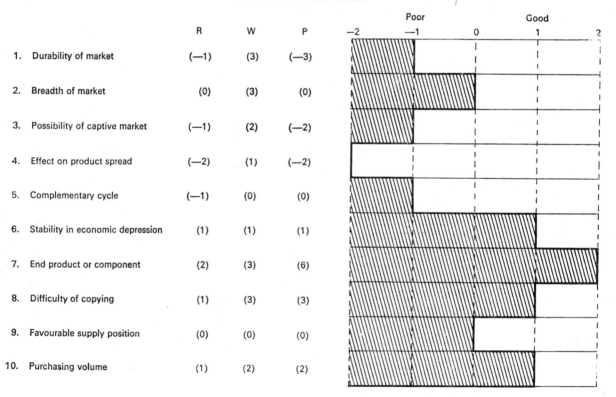

SIMPLE PROFILE CHART

		R	W	P
1.	Durability of market	(—1)	(3)	(—3)
2.	Breadth of market	(0)	(3)	(0)
3.	Possibility of captive market	(—1)	(2)	(—2)
4.	Effect on product spread	(—2)	(1)	(—2)
5.	Complementary cycle	(—1)	(0)	(0)
6.	Stability in economic depression	(1)	(1)	(1)
7.	End product or component	(2)	(3)	(6)
8.	Difficulty of copying	(1)	(3)	(3)
9.	Favourable supply position	(0)	(0)	(0)
10.	Purchasing volume	(1)	(2)	(2)

Figure 1.7 Simple profile chart for the ten stability factors. The figures in brackets represent rating (R), weighting (W) and weighted rating (P). Only unweighted ratings are shown in this diagram, but also see overall weighted profile below.

quately cover the differential importance of particular factors. For a small company, a patent suit brought by an industrial giant could be fatal; thus the weightings for the legal factors in this case would approach infinity. Also to use a quantitative process subjectively without gathering information in the field can be very dangerous. There is no substitute for fact.

A simple profile chart appears in Figure 1.7, and is concerned with a single factor group. Each factor represents one aspect of product or company stability.

Thus, if the market is durable, sales are likely to be secure for a considerable period; if the market is broad, then the decline of any particular market sector will not be critical. Products sold to associated companies would be less exposed to the idiosyncrasies of customers than those selling on the open market. If a new product adds to the product spread, has a sales cycle complementary to the cycle of existing products or is independent of economic fluctuations, it will increase the company's stability. An end product gives a company more latitude than a component; while a product with good patent cover, made by a difficult or secret process, cannot easily be imitated. If the raw materials are readily available or components are purchased in sufficient volume to command the supplier's favour, again the company will be less vulnerable.

The comprehensive chart in Figure 1.8 covers all factor groups and is based on weighted rating. The stability section corresponds to the values in the simple profile chart.

Screening, though depending ultimately on judgement, serves to eliminate the pitfalls of a purely intuitive approach. Thus, in examining American, Japanese or Soviet equipment available for licensing, it should be borne in mind that circumstances in other countries are often very different from those in Britain. Scale of operations may be particularly important.

The Russians have, for example, devised an interesting process for prefabricating in a factory the cylindrical body of a storage vessel, rolling it up into a scroll, transporting it to site, unrolling it and completing a simple final weld, thereby reducing the cost of sitework, which can be very high.

Although the method appears most attractive, a prospective UK licensee would be advised to ask the following questions. How many factories are serving the whole Soviet requirement? Is the annual demand in Britain commensurate with the cost of the necessary capital equipment? Is the thickness of plate employed consistent with Western practice and standards? Could the scrolls be readily transported on British roads?

OVERALL WEIGHTED PROFILE CHART

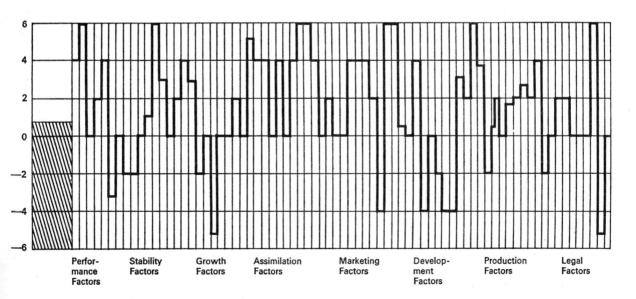

Figure 1.8 Overall weighted profile chart. Quantitative evaluations of this kind, though indicative, should be used with particular caution. Weightings and weighted ratings for the ten stability factors are shown in brackets on the first chart above.

Intuition and Opportunism

Product acquisition has often tended to be opportunist and piecemeal, and some companies have pursued diversification until control has become virtually impossible.

There has also been a tendency to jump on bandwagons. The same opportunities and prospects seem to be discussed in every boardroom: if one man's intuition leads him to select the building, road-making, quarry or construction industries as good potential markets, it is not unlikely that his competitors will be looking in the same direction. The attraction of the building industry has led several companies to venture into competition with the specialists, sometimes with disastrous results.

Interest in a particular chemical product has sometimes been followed by wholesale construction of new plants until there is excess capacity. One company is reported to have started building a polyethylene plant when other companies were petitioning the Department of Trade and Industry to prohibit dumping. On the other hand, there is a temptation to announce the construction of new plants simply to discourage the others. Information is usually a better guide than hunch.

A good market is often regarded as more important than the company's own ability to sell or make the product. Vending machines, whatever the demand, are unlikely to support the overheads in heating, space, machinery and technical resources of an aircraft factory, though a combination of products might conceivably utilize all key facilities.

Conversely, companies have sometimes rejected promising opportunities on insufficient grounds, as seems to have happened in the case of the LD process, at the time a revolutionary method of steel-making using tonnage oxygen. Products are discarded for mistaken reasons as often as they are adopted. Apparent trends can be most deceptive. Few would have foreseen the post-war resurgence of the gas industry or have believed that control systems based on fluid logic could replace electronics in many applications.

Time-scale

In screening products and product ideas, one factor of critical importance is the urgency of the company's requirement. Is it already running short of profitable work? Has it foreseen some impending technical development or market change that will affect its pattern of activity in the next few years? Or is it simply taking the precaution to plan its long-term evolution systematically?

The approach is very much determined by the situation. If time is short, then subcontracting may be the only solution, though it need not be limited to jobbing work secured from local manufacturers, who themselves may well be underloaded in times of general recession. In some cases, it is possible to secure a sizable contract from a process engineering company who are already engaged in building, say, an oil refinery, and have been let down by one of their contractors.

In the medium-term a licensing, sales, merger or joint-company agreement may be the ideal answer, though there are many pitfalls in acquiring products in this way.

Long-term planning is very much more difficult and the company is here dependent largely on its own resources. It must foresee changing requirements within its field of experience and undertake original development. In any case, licences and similar sources of developed products are only likely to be a stop-gap; and companies or countries that rely too much on licensing may find that royalty payments so reduce their margins that they cannot continue to compete.

Forecasting

In the exploration stage, some effort is made to evaluate longer-term requirements by investigation of emerging opportunities, but to forecast future product needs, over the next 10, 15 or 20 years, is far more difficult. Nevertheless, to keep abreast of change a company must attempt to do so, bearing in mind that it is easy to be mistaken.

Had we known of Fermi's experiments with uranium and graphite piles 20 years ago, most of us would have predicted that by now our power generating industry, and indeed our whole way of life, would have been transformed. We should have been wrong: as was Lord Rutherford when he declared that useful nuclear power was an impracticable dream.

The projection of current trends has little value for this purpose, just as the accountant's prediction of a company's performance on the basis of its last five balance sheets may be completely faulted by a dramatic technical development or a change in fashion. A company making razors or razo-blades, however successful in the past and vigorous today, could be put out of business overnight by the development in some entirely different industry of a thoroughly acceptable depilatory.

Trends in consumption, as recorded in statistics, are often superficial consequences of unknown circumstances, the visible portion of an iceberg that beneath the surface is melting away and may capsize at any moment. Indeed, the very existence of a trend in demand means that the demand is, to some extent, already being satisfied, and is certainly no guide to innovation. If extrapolation is the only way to make a forecast, then the basis for projection should be not the superficial effects, but their underlying causes.

These basic patterns of evolution are not easy to discern and still more difficult to project. But perhaps the problem can again be broken down into more manageable components.

Conflicting Pressures

Fundamental change springs in many cases from a conflict between resources and requirements.

Thus, growing requirements for transport and communication, imposed on limited metropolitan resources in amenities and space, lead to congestion. Congestion, in turn, may prompt the wider introduction of vertical car parks, parking meters, auxiliary crab drivers for retrieving parked vehicles, double tier roads, high-speed monorail links and pipeline urban supply systems.

Requirements are essentially a function of increasing population and may be compounded far beyond the basic rate of growth. For example, in order to communicate, two people only require one two-way channel; five people 10 channels; and seven people 21. Also, the need for multi-channel visual communication in business condemns people to concentrate in cities, further multiplying service relationships and introducing an even greater requirement for communication.

Likewise, with growing organization and prosperity, each person requires more and more accommodation, not only in his home, but in his place of work and places of relaxation or entertainment. The building industry is likely to be in business for some time to come, whatever recessions may from time to time occur.

Good long-term prospects for the capital equipment industries may also arise from a conflict between optimization and versatility in the production process. Optimum economy of manufacture may call for automatic flow-line methods, which tend to be inflexible; while at the same time, versatile facilities are needed to cope with the increasing rate of product obsolescence, particularly since with market saturation many industries are passing from the initial-sale to the replacement market.

One solution might be to introduce a three-factory system, corresponding to the three-field system. Each factory would be optimized for a particular range of products and scrapped when the products were no longer in demand — planned obsolescence of the factory, rather than the product. If this comes about, then capital goods should thrive.

This line of reasoning can often be effective in conceiving future products. Requirements may, of course, be inflated by fashion, advertising, legislation, standard of living and invention. Conversely, resources may be released by a technical breakthrough, discoveries of raw materials, or simply an operating surplus. Thus, with increasing affluence, a greater margin of national income can be spared for leisure, education, safety precautions, welfare and insurance.

Change Sectors

The principle extends beyond the simple relation between needs and raw materials, supply and demand, since the whole creative process depends on recognizing a connection between two or more hitherto unrelated factors. It should be possible to promote this effect and to develop an appropriate routine.

Once more use can be made of the dynamic product area; with the assistance of another concept — the 'change sector'.

Change sectors are those mainstreams of social and industrial change that are flowing fastest. Typical change sectors are food, territorial development, energy conversion, building, communications and production processes.

The dynamic area is peculiar to the company; the change sector to the company's environment. Thus, corresponding to dynamic areas, which represent the company's field of operations, are change sectors, which represent the company's field of opportunity. By matching one against the other, a company may discover new product opportunities.

For example, a company with separation as its dynamic area, in reviewing the change sector of power production, might alight on the removal of sulphur from fuels or sulphur dioxide from flue gases as a possible new activity.

The practical implementation of this method involves maintaining files of material drawn from the technical and daily press under dynamic area and change sector headings, and making comparisons at regular and frequent intervals.

Another technique, which we have called 'synthesized projection', is to reconcile the isolated insights of individual specialists, assembled through large numbers of depth interviews, integrating these separate forecasts into a single consistent pattern.

It may also be useful to identify what we describe as 'fixed conditions' or 'persisting points of certainty' and to use them as a framework for conjecture. Little can be certain about the future, but some things are more permanent than others. Thus, Milford Haven is one of very few deep-water harbours in Europe, and likely to remain so.

Additional aids to prediction include impending legislation, five-year plans, construction programmes and overseas investment schemes. Forecasting is difficult, but thoughtful analysis is better than blind gambling. Picking pop records before they reach the charts is an interesting exercise in judgement, but there are several aids by which it can be simplified, apart from the inspiration of an Epstein or a Grade.

Contributory Studies

Using the procedure for planning, evaluation and forecasting outlined here, it should be possible to investigate any product situation, to link a company's past experience with new and profitable activities. It may be useful to present a few brief case-histories to illustrate the way in which a number of individual problems have been solved.

Outlets by Association

One company, which in the past had been concerned exclusively with a very limited range of products, was advised to enter the building industry as manufacturers of anchor bolts for use with cartridge-actuated fixing tools. Since they had no suitable sales resources and no outlets in the building trade, it was suggested that they form an association with an existing agency already selling anchor bolts made by an overseas concern. The company did, in fact, acquire an interest in the agency and are now producing bolts in quantity. The choice of product was partly determined by the company's existing interest in firearms and it is possible that, in addition to bolts, the associated cartridge-actuated tools will be manufactured.

Side-stepping

The principle of step diversification was also applied, using the company's experience as gunmakers as a point of departure for investigating various other cartridge-operated devices — humane killers, girder punches, cable cutters, fixing tools, rock breakers, and explosive-forming, for example.

Gaps and Applications

Applications development and gap filling are other approaches. It was proposed that a company making a wide range of pumps for marine and power applications consider the introduction of screw, canned-motor and certain other types of glandless and semi-glandless pumps, with a view to securing their position in the food, chemical, oil and nuclear industries. A company producing radiators for motor cars was recommended to consider plate heat exchangers, since the company also made vehicle bodies and had access to the heavy presses necessary for forming the heat-exchanger plates.

Parallel and Series

Complementary products selling to the same customer as an existing product may sometimes be taken up, such as an accelerator pump for central heating by a company already making pressure burners. Similarly, process extension involves finding new products falling into the same process sequence as an established line. Thus, a thermal drying unit might be supplied in addition to a continuous filter.

Tool and Product

Occasionally a new production tool or process is developed which can itself be used for manufacturing a self-contained product with unique advantages in utility or price. A company might buy a machine for welding pipe helically from stainless-steel or aluminium strip, the pipe being suitable for applications where imperfections were acceptable but selling very cheaply. Or, by purchasing a Soviet gear-rolling machine, which employs induction surface heating and is said to make gears of adequate quality at low cost a newcomer might secure a foothold in this industry.

Multiple Assemblies

A company geared to manufacture and assemble in quantity might carry out a search 'by numbers'. Having prepared a list of end products made in large numbers — vehicles, machine tools, vacuum cleaners, refrigerators, traffic signals, small arms, welding equipment, parking meters, etc., — they could ascertain if there were any self-contained sub-assemblies which could be improved or were in short supply, for example, clutches, motors, switching, control devices and similar equipment.

Substitution

Manufacturers should keep their eyes open for substitution products. Where a product or a service is threatened by a strong alternative, the alternative should be considered. A company making jig borers should investigate the prospects for spark erosion; a manufacturer of rock drills the use of plasma and water jet techniques, a supplier of power generation plant the development of magnetohydrodynamics, a fabricator of light-gauge metal sheet the application of plastics, and an ironfounder the fabrication of heavy components from steel plate.

Parallel Diversification

A company planning to extend its range of products might conduct a study of other home and, more particularly, overseas concerns that have diversified from the same initial field, selecting product lines that appear to have been the most successful.

Most of these approaches are based on the logical extension of an existing product range or the wider exploitation of present assets. In a sense, they represent methods of concentration or adaptation, rather than complete diversification.

Acquisition

The favoured route to diversification has traditionally been through the acquisition of companies. In theory, it should be possible to find a going concern with good current profits and potential that can be purchased and, apart from establishing financial control, left to continue as it is. By successive acquisitions, a holding company could assemble a satisfactory spread of interests.

In practice, few companies are acquirable unless they are deficient in some way. One or more key assets is likely to be missing. It may be that a company is short of liquid capital, senior or middle management, adequate sales resources, modern equipment or a marketable product. Lack of finance alone is unlikely to be the only weakness, since, given promising human and material resources, capital can usually be raised. Conversely, money must have other assets to work upon if it is to yield returns.

Diversification, like every other area of business, has become increasingly competitive, and only by optimum acquisition in terms of complementary assets is it possible to achieve a satisfactory union. For example, in Figure 1.9, the three large squares represent companies, the smaller squares their assets. Company X has two key assets missing, say, good middle management and an efficient sales organization. Companies A and B have surplus assets, and each could help to make company X more viable. However, the union B + X is more viable than the union A + X, and hence a more competitive basis for a merger.

A miscellaneous group of companies could be controlled given three basic services: an accountancy

Missing Assets   **Surplus Assets**   **Surplus Assets**

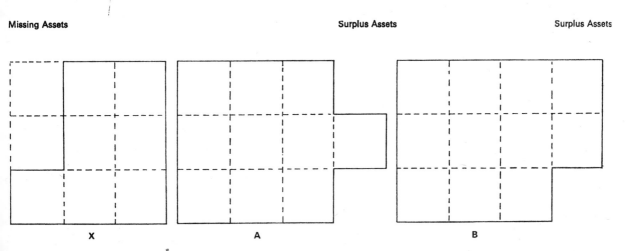

X   A   B

Figure 1.9 Today, diversification is as competitive as any other aspect of business. Diversification by acquisition is optimized when the acquiring company can supply all the missing assets of the company acquired. If X is the company acquired, the combination B + X is more viable than A + X and hence company B can afford to pay a higher price for company X. The missing assets might be good top or middle management, an effective sales force, or even a competitive product.

department to measure financial performance; a market research department to check if performance could be better; and a personnel selection department to choose new managing directors where performance is unsatisfactory.

This simple structure, though attractive, must increasingly prove inadequate, and operating relationships between member companies are becoming necessary in order to maximize return on capital or net cash flow. In other words, a group can be greater than the sum of its parts, not only through the flexible and economic use of finance, but by optimum exploitation of all available assets, irrespective of their location within member companies. Thus, some measure of inter-company trading could help to retain a greater proportion of available profit within a group, providing that it did not lead to commercial relaxation.

Human and organizational factors make it undesirable in general to submerge the identities of individual companies, but conditions can be created by a holding company such that inter-relationships are self-optimizing so as to maximize net cash flow. It is through detailed study of differentiated and undifferentiated assets that such relationships can be discovered and exploited. Size alone is no longer enough; sometimes its only property is unwieldiness.

Implementation

There are, of course, many other aspects of product planning: licence negotiation, company appraisal, industrial group analysis, investment programming, discounted cash flow, value engineering, product specification, feasibility studies, productionizing, factory planning, the costing and evaluation of research, marketing, budgeting and forecasting are a few.

Once the decision has been taken to proceed, a detailed plan and schedule needs to be prepared for implementing it, involving many of these elements. As noted already, implementation is where many projects run aground. Imposing something new on an existing structure is seldom easy. Entirely different costing, scheduling, inspection and marketing procedures may be necessary, as the aircraft component industry discovered when it tried to enter the commercial field.

There is also a natural human resistance to any departure from established practice. Busy men tend to resist change, not because they are opposed to it in principle, but because they already feel fully extended and are afraid that any diversion from their customary

routine will introduce an intolerable extra burden. This resistance must, of course, be overcome.

First, it is important to decide whether a project manager should be appointed to take the project through from beginning to end, from licensing to marketing; whether a new division of the company needs to be set up; with separate premises and staff, or whether the new product should be assimilated within the existing manufacturing and sales framework. In any case, someone should be charged with its success and left free of other day to day responsibilities.

Position for a Polymath

One new project is not enough to keep a company in business for ever. To survive, a company must be constantly awake to opportunities and, ideally, where the company is large enough, someone should be exclusively concerned with forward planning. Otherwise the future may tend to be forgotten in the press of more immediate matters. What sort of man is needed?

A product planning executive must be conscious of his company's potential, but must give the greater part of his attention to the changing world outside. Ideally, he should be a man not too encumbered with corporate tradition; he might, with advantage, be a stranger to the company who acquires his knowledge by looking round and asking questions. Rather than a deep knowledge of the company's existing products and markets, he should possess a shallower experience of a much broader market and product panorama.

Although he should be capable of ordering his thoughts logically, he should be an associative, rather than a sequential thinker — a butterfly mind controlled by strong self-discipline. (Perhaps both types are needed, reporting to a third — an integrative thinker — if associative, sequential and integrative qualities cannot be found in a single individual.)

His concern is mainly with the future, and problems of the future differ essentially from problems of the present. The present is with us and concrete; the future can only be considered in the abstract — we cannot see it, touch it or measure it, we can only think about it. Preoccupation with practical affairs has often inhibited the creative and imaginative thinking necessary for growth.

The man chosen should be capable of understanding the problems of every department   research, design, production, sales, promotion, marketing and finance. He should also recognize their scope and interests but be identified with none. The policy of any manufacturing concern is inevitably product-centred, since products are its reason for existence, so product planning necessarily embraces all aspects of a company's activity.

It follows that the product planning executive should be a senior man reporting to the managing director.

Indeed, it could be that a managing director should have two subordinates of equal status: a general manager (present) and a general manager (future). If we agree with Elliott Jaques that a man's remuneration should be in proportion to the time it takes for his mistakes to be found out, then the general manager (future) should be very highly paid.

To the general manager .(future), or director of corporate planning, would report both predominantly forward-looking company departments, namely market planning and technical research. In this way, not only would the general manager (future) gain the authority necessary to act effectively as 'counsel for the future' in the company's policy-making and direction, but he would also provide the essential link between the twin functions of technical innovation and the identification of emerging market needs, which today so often go their separate ways.

There are strictly only two sources of new products: the discovery of some property or concept for which demand could be created; and the disclosure of some market requirement which could be embodied in a suitable device. Whichever the ultimate source in a particular case, the idea must alternately be tested against the other's criteria, as in Figure 1.10. Thus, it is necessary to demonstrate the marketability of an ingenious invention; or to show that a practical machine to meet a market need can be developed at a reasonable price. In practice, a succession of tests or development phases, usually involving progressive increase in expenditure up to preproduction prototype, will be undertaken, on alternate sides of the development and marketing pivot.

Regional Development

Not only single companies, but whole industrial areas, may face a changing market environment. The development of Tees-side, for example, was based on river access to the sea and local coal. Now the coal is too expensive and the river is in many places not deep enough for modern shipping. Clydeside's dependence on one major industry has made South-West Scotland similarly vulnerable.

With the contraction of their traditional activities, these regions have to devise new product policies. But only within the regions themselves can this be done effectively and permanently, given full awareness of their differentiated assets.

So many plans for regional development depend on outside leadership – special encouragements to attract industry from elsewhere, capital injection, investment allowances, tax and rating concessions, grants, government contracts and exhortation. Valuable though these measures may be, real. vitality can only spring from within an organism. Growth must be self-generating, occurring spontaneously at every point. Some device is necessary to release this energy.

If each manufacturer and entrepreneur were alive to his opportunities, the problem might well resolve itself. Where every company has a dynamic product policy and a procedure to identify emerging market needs, growth will be organic. Companies have only to look at every changing situation in the outside world and ask themselves what it means to them.

The danger of taking the future for granted is particularly apparent on the national scale. During the American business recession in 1958, James Hagerty was press secretary in the White House. As a constant reminder, he kept a card on his desk with the following incription:

One day I sat thinking, almost in despair; a hand fell on my shoulder and a voice said reassuringly: 'Cheer-up, things could be worse.'
So, I cheered-up and, sure enough, things got worse.

Cheering-up alone is not enough. We have to make the most of our resources, systematically and unremittingly.

The Story of Specimen Industries

A Case-history

To illustrate the arguments developed in this article, it may be useful to summarize the history of a fictional concern. Perhaps it would be appropriate to call them Sample Ltd.

Origins

Set up in 1910 to package and distribute small portions of other people's produce, Sample Ltd were one of the first companies to provide an independent marketing service. Founded on a single bright idea, they gradually acquired facilities to exploit it on a national scale.

The scope was large since whatever misfortunes befell particular clients, there would always be new products to be packaged, and an insatiable demand for free samples.

At one stage, the company found that nearly half their business was in dairy produce, and the chairman, who was a keen farmer, suggested that they take up dairying as a new activity. Nobody dared disagree.

Unfortunately, once they were in dairying, they found their dairy sample customers disinclined to have their samples packaged and distributed by a company which was also their competitor. The sample business started to decline.

But the dairy business flourished and soon the company decided to manufacture dairy plant. Since they already owned 30 per cent of the dairies in the country and were acquiring more, they were not too worried about customers.

It was decided that the company needed new blood and the managing director, who was shortly due to retire, decided to recruit a personal assistant. A young man was appointed.

Band Wagon Development

He had already some experiences as a junior manager and has been to a summer school in marketing. He had also read an article by an American called Grace.

Grace had carried out a study which had shown that demand for chemicals was entering a period of rapid growth. Grace Brothers went into chemicals; so Sample followed suit. 'Cheese,' said the young executive, 'is no less sensitive to temperatures and pressures than complex chemicals, and our process experience would be invaluable.'

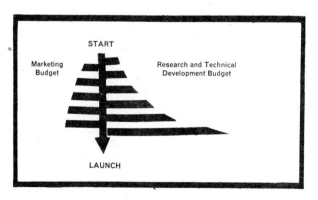

Figure 1.10 Budgeting for the development of an innovative product from idea to launch.

The founder still exerted influence and, drawing attention to the company's name, he persuaded his colleagues that Sample Ltd should specialize in producing specimen quantities of rare compounds and in the design of pilot plants.

It was about this time that Sample Ltd became a public company, but under the more imposing title of Specimen Industries Ltd. The personal assistant in due course became managing director.

He had also become a chartered engineer and ever since graduating had been fascinated by large-scale process plant. After a year or two, despite the founder's reservations, a chemical engineering company was taken over and integrated with the dairy plant department. The two sales forces were combined and a few small personal conflicts began to rear their heads.

Spread of Interest

Meanwhile, the founder's son was appointed assistant to the company secretary, who was also getting near retiring age.

The company had grown extremely prosperous and were looking for new capital outlets. 'What we need,' said the future company secretary, 'is a wider spread of interests.' So Specimen Industries started acquiring profitable companies, whenever an opportunity presented itself; whatever the activities of the companies acquired.

Specimen Industries were now one of the largest groups in the country, and it was at this point that things started going wrong.

They had assembled considerable resources in order to exploit first the original bright idea, then the products and services which had sprung from it. They had accumulated wealth and used it to acquire a great variety of interests. And now it was these assets that had to be kept profitably employed.

Opportunism

The group's evolution had been opportunist and piecemeal, and had in consequence gradually diverged from the mainstream of social and industrial change. Their activities were no longer in perfect harmony with their market environment. Specimen Industries and the requirements of society had slowly grown apart. They had also become increasingly difficult to manage.

This did not mean that their products were no longer needed, by any means. The real weaknesses were much more complex.

First of all, they were not the only company who had

recognized opportunities in the chemical industry. At the time they entered the field, the oil and chemical industries were the main topic in almost every board-room, as the building, petrochemical and gas industries have been discussed since then.

If one man's intuition leads him to select the chemical or quarry industry as a good prospective market, it is not unlikely that a competitor's intuition will guide him in the same direction.

The Same Idea
Only recently Specimen Industries had brought on stream a new phthalic anhydride plant. When the decision to build was taken, it seemed a good idea: phthalic anhydride was an intermediate in many processes – in the production of pharmaceuticals, dye-stuffs, plastics, plasticizers and other materials – so the requirement was likely to be substantial and comfort-ably spread.

Unfortunately, some 11 other companies had reached the same conclusion and the 12 plants now in existence represented an embarrassing surplus of capacity.

Growing Competition
The group's traditional activities were subject to increasing competition, both from well-established major companies and from newcomers.

The advent of young and energetic companies with low overheads into the fields which Specimen Industries had once monopolized was introducing slack, and many of their manufacturing facilities were under-utilized. Competition from abroad had likewise grown intensive.

They had sought subcontract work with only moderate success, since the whole country was going through a trade recession and companies who had at one time sub-contracted manufacture were now concerned to keep their own shops occupied.

Out of Control
In attempting to spread their interests widely, Specimen Industries had acquired a large number of relatively small companies, and it was difficult to put over a strong corporate image, even for sectors of the group. Also, in distributing the available promotional resources among so many companies, their advertising tended to be ineffective.

What is more, opportunities for inter-company trading was being overlooked and the management was not adequate in numbers or experience to control the many activities to maximum advantage, or to provide the economies of common services. Two of the companies, who had once been fierce competitors, were still at daggers drawn and through their rivalry were forcing down prices, when there was no other com-petitor in sight.

Control was attempted by allotting holding-board directors to the boards of member companies, but no such group of men could possibly encompass the range of technical and commercial experience necessary to make control effective. As a result, profits that could have been retained within the group were slipping out between their fingers and into other pockets.

Each of these problems arose from the lack of any considered group or company product policy and failure over the years to study the market systematically. .

Exchange of Views
One of the two young men who had helped in building-up the group, but had by now acquired a few grey hairs, attended a seminar on product planning. He came back with a certain desperate enthusiasm and suggested that a product development committee be formed.

The first few meetings of the committee were abortive. Most contributions were entirely negative.

'You can't make anything but resins in a plant optimized for resin manufacture', said one plant manager.

'We're just coming on load,' added another, 'and I haven't time for panel games.'

'Why can't we concentrate on selling our existing products more effectively?', remarked the sales director.

'Why not indeed,' replied the managing director. 'Let me know by Monday how you propose to set about it.'

The next meeting was worse. The chairman began by asking if anyone had any bright ideas. Everyone started looking round the room for inspiration. A young man, who had been deputed by the sales department in one of the smaller companies to attend committee meetings and had previously been in die-casting, muttered:

'I suppose we couldn't manufacture doorknobs.'
He was attacked from all sides.

'Not a chance: mostly material, no added value and look at the competition – the big metal mass production companies on one side and backyard boys with no overheads on the other. Anyway we haven't any outlets in the building industry.'

Trespassing
The chairman called the meeting to order.

'I realize the problem isn't easy,' he said. 'Perhaps we are too diversified already and need to concentrate.'

'There's no sense in entering fields where we should only be amateurs. I hear that shipbuilders are going into building; can they really hope to compete with Laings and Taylor Woodrow, Token, Turriff, Wates and Wimpey? Any new methods would surely have been spotted by the specialists, who seem pretty wide-awake to me.'

'The aircraft industry have learned that lesson,' put in the production director. 'Making slot machines in an aircraft factory is just a waste of heat and space, not to mention expensive men and machines.'

There were a few positive suggestions but no-one was responsible for pursuing them and they were soon forgotten. Two quite good proposals were turned down for no good reason, except that someone considered them outrageous.

Novelty Resistance

Not only in Specimen Industries, but elsewhere too, people pay lip-service to new products, but any actual suggestion meets a negative reaction. It is either too unexciting; or so exciting it frightens the management to death. There is a tendency to fall between two stools. A product concept that is entirely new may yield big profits but involves considerable risk. Profit margins on a product with an established market that can be measured are likely to be small. Big profits and low risks are seldom found together.

At Specimen Industries the problems seemed overwhelming.

'Perhaps we should tackle just one sector of the group at first,' suggested the managing director of a company whose activities were more mechanical than chemical. 'We shouldn't mind playing guinea pig, providing we have someone experienced in product planning, working full-time on the project.'

Eventually this proposal was accepted. Four companies in broadly related fields were to be the subject of an initial study. The managing director of one company was made responsible for the project and enjoined to maintain regular contact with his colleagues in the other

three. Otherwise, he was given a free hand: he could transfer existing staff to the study; recruit a product planning executive, with supporting staff; or call in consultants.

Acknowledgments

The original article was prepared in October 1962, while the author was employed by Martech Consultants Ltd, and since then has been progressively expanded and elaborated. Certain sections are reproduced from *The Chartered Mechanical Engineer*, January 1965, by permission of the Council of the Institution of Mechanical Engineers; and from *Metra*, the journal of Metra International. Additional material has been taken from talks and papers presented by the author for the following bodies:

British Institute of Management
Management Research Groups
University of Strathclyde
University of Sussex
Universities of Aston & Birmingham
ESOMAR
International Marketing Programme (Oxford)
APD (Madrid and Bilbao)
Ministry of Commerce (Northern Ireland)
Belfast Junior Chamber of Commerce
College of Marketing
Regent Street Polytechnic
New Product Centre
Management Centre/Europe
Management Centre (Birmingham)
Industrial Marketing Research Association
SOBEMAP (Brussels)
Minister of Technology and colleagues
Institution of Mechanical Engineers
Institution of Production Engineers

and a number of industrial companies in Britain and abroad. Much of the thinking was developed by the author while engaged in consulting work with Proplan, a member of the Metra group, and more recently with Interplan.

2.

Programmes for Product Development
by Neil Hood

Management Decision, Spring 1971. © 1971 by MCB (Management Decision) Limited; all rights reserved.

Introduction

Product development problems in many organizations appear to stem from the basic dilemma of all innovators, namely the extent to which the product change process can be successfully formalized by the erection of organizational and planning structures. Invariably the complex range of endogenous and exogenous pressures moving the company to product review are only too clear to all concerned. What is not clear is the extent to which product policy should be programmed or allowed to emerge under short-term competitive pressures. In many ways, this remains as one of the major areas of business operations which has successfully avoided the application of control techniques widely employed in other areas to solve similar problems. This article attempts to review the principal types of product planning procedures available to the decision-taker and to comment on some of the less apparent problems arising in the development of products.

Product development is defined in its widest sense for this purpose and includes the planned introduction of products, intrinsically new, or new to the company concerned, and the substantial modification of existing products. It is important for the purposes of this article that these three categories be considered as variations within the same exercise and not as discrete problems. The difference is one of degree, not of substance.

Underestimating Time Span?

One point is clear, most companies underestimate the time span of their product development programmes. This appears to be due to two principal problems which frequently occur after the high-delay initial development stages when timing problems are easily identified. First, the absorption difficulties within the structure of the existing organization, where complex sociological pressures are often obvious between the innovators and the structure. The second problem concerns the varying priority which is placed on many product modifications even after extensive initial committal and heavy investment. Product changes, for a variety of market and organizational reasons, appear highly prone to policy modifications in their planning stages. Few analysts have attempted to quantify the extent of these timing problems and in the few cases where this has happened the results are both highly complex and highly particular. Adler,[1] for example, examines 42 case-histories of basic product innovations in the consumer and industrial goods fields. Time estimation problems are emphasized in the work of both Adler, and Manning,[2] both of whom emphasize the structural problems in innovating companies.

Problem symptoms include adequate development time allowances but inadequate time for pilot market testing or decisions on correct pricing policy or effective evaluation of early market feedback. Only too frequently, the political pressures arising from products becoming identified with individuals or groups and therefore having no corporate identity, create severe problems in the flow of product development and result in many short-cuts being taken on the route to commercial launch. Perhaps this is a factor contributing to the high proportion of products which succeed only after development work has followed an initial abortive test marketing operation.

Product Development Systems

There are a wide range of studies indicating the role of formal product development structures within companies, but relatively few examining the performance of such systems or the particular management problems they pose. Murphy[3] and Chorafas[4] provide two illustrations of attempts to evaluate development systems. Irrespective of the potential effectiveness of development systems, the narrow-product horizons over which active planning occurs, the lack of commercial directives to research and development functions and the absence of overall co-ordinating authority in the formative stages, all combine to reduce effectiveness. Many firms appear to treat product policy as a fragmented activity to be handled by narrow functional departments and seem unaware of the need for a specific central decision function where specific responsibility rests for initiating the product development process and for regular monitoring of the system.

There has been a fairly strong tradition within the last 20 years[5] to imply that some type of committee organization is necessary to co-ordinate product development since only by such a joint commitment to decisions will the development process be lubricated. While the need for formalization of the product development system is widely but not universally accepted, there is still much debate as to type of system which meets the specific needs of the product, organization and market concerned. In many senses, however, the programmes reviewed in this article imply that, while organizational planning may facilitate successful new product development, there is an important sense in which the catalyst to be added to the planning system to finalize a commercial product lies outside that system, perhaps, as McCarthy[6] suggests, in the requirement that 'top management's dynamic innovating attitude be instilled into and felt by the whole company'.

Much emphasis has been placed in recent years in the role of formal planning systems in the development and control of business activity. Decision-makers wishing to apply formal systems to marketing strategies clearly require to be reminded of the limitation of such systems stemming particularly from the nature of the variables and the designed capabilities of the models. This applies equally to functional and structural models applied to marketing situations. Lipson[7] provides a basic foundation survey of the contribution of the formalists to marketing strategy and a review of the problems of conceptualization of marketing decisions.

Many product development systems are functionally biased in that they concentrate on examining the types of structure proven to result in minimum product risk and make little attempt to identify the decisions required at each stage or the inter-relations between the variables in the decision at each stage. These models directly reflect the reason for their construction, namely to direct the attention of product developers to the complexity of the stages, to the need to assure minimization of risk and development cost, and to the role that structural procedures must play in processing products through the various stages to commercial launch. Largely constructed on the basis of empirical study of a process which is both difficult and outside routine business practice, they reflect the need to minimize the risks in decision areas with high degrees of uncertainty. All attempt to identify a series of key periods within the time span from the development of

the product concept to commercialization and provide at each of these periods a set of go/no go criteria to screen off products from the development channels.

The basic literature on product development programmes is in two main categories. One, strongly empirically-based, concentrates on organizational structures and formats designed to minimize risk of premature product failure. The other, equally risk-oriented, consists of attempts to develop quantitative models for refining the process of taking new product decisions, and, in particular, the provision of methods of compatibility and profitability evaluation.

Checklist

The organizational approach is highly developed in the research work of the major management consulting organizations. Most of these programmes provide an overall framework and a series of activity checklists, which the company can use to review the need for product innovation, balance its resource base to its requirements, initiate and complete product search. Booz, Allen and Hamilton[8] provide a useful illustration of this approach. They concentrate on the identification of a set of principles in a group of companies with extensive experience in product development. From these are stressed the stages of product evolution, basic characteristics of the process, expenditure programmes at each stage, varying forms in which development could be managed and a series of critical decision areas at each phase of development. Since this type of programme structure stems from pragmatic situations, it provides at least a framework for the innovating company and at most a model for the minimization of risk in the development process. The objectives are some form of resource optimization and the provision of guidelines through processes which, even to relatively large organizations, are on the threshold of their experience. One advantage of organizational models is that they attempt to record practice in a range of companies and so provide for one of the decision-maker's basic requirements, namely a record of methods utilized by others. Even within one organization, the records of their own experience in product modification are rarely kept sufficiently accurately to enable the innovators to learn from the past problems. Further, in many cases, the time-lag between significant product changes may be long enough for staff turnover to produce a situation where new development is undertaken by staff with little experience of that company or its markets.

It is to the solution of this type of 'one-off' problem that many of the formal organizational programmes are directed. Nicolls[9] for example, attempts to identify the nature of the real strategic decisions in each case, reduce these to a minimum and test certain hypotheses at each decision stage between the concept and the commercialization of the new product. Similarly, Nord[10] identifies trouble symptoms in growth stages, postulating the existence of three critical feedback loops which provide the early warning system within a development programme. Relatively few models of this type incorporate detailed relationships between the developing product and its profitable distribution level on the market. Nord stresses the interaction between the markets' ordering behaviour and the lead time to deliver the product; between the unfilled initial orders and productive capacity; and finally between the ordering behaviour of the market and the 'capacity-acquisition' policy of the company.

Mills[11] provides a further variant on the organizational systems approach by his work on the role of market structure in the effective conduct of a new product campaign and in particular on the continuing set of interactions between developing firms, trade distributors and consumers. The ultimate determinant of the success of a product development system is argued to be the outcome of the interaction between consumer-trying and rebuying and trade stocking and restocking habits.

Key Areas

Within the overall organization of new product problems, there are certain key areas which have attracted specific attention either due to the assumed higher risk or because of the fundamental nature of the issues posed. Particularly important within the latter category is the actual period of choice of types of product to develop and the process by which that choice should be made. Rothman[12] for example, sets up a framework within which product ranges and assortment variations should be researched to ensure that each new product development balances with the existing product range. There is frequently a threshold area in product strategy when a company begins to conclude that success in its original market and with its original products can be readily transferred to an allied market area. It is particularly in this context that the importance of correct decisions on product range balance, compatibility and relative resource usage become obvious. The most common motivation for product exchange appears

to be the emergence of some of the symptoms of decline in the profit life-cycle. Many analysts tend to assume a high level of knowledge within organizations about the position of their products within a life-cycle or that the symptoms the product performance was demonstrating could be objectively and accurately attributed to cycle.

Thus, while the exercise of determining product profit plans over a period is important in that it emphasizes the need for measurement of critical product parameters, it requires considerable skill to use life-cycles as a framework for product planning. Rassweiler[13] and Clifford[14] both attempt to derive development paths from cycles, Clifford being particularly concerned to emphasize the need to treat the cycle not as an exogeneous variable but as one subject to internal modification by product policy. A further type of timing study is represented by Herrman[15], whose concern is directed to specialized types of consumer research which can identify specialized and often thin markets existing for intrinsically new products. While Herrman is concerned basically with new products it is more generally the case that product modifications of any type often require highly specific types of research methods to identify the development of embryo markets.

Much of the recent focus in research into new product development has been concentrated in the final stage of the review and planning process when, with all the basic data available in some format, estimates have to be made of expected rates of return under a series of alternative strategies. Clearly, all these strategies will involve risk in any company, the risk being a function of both the information available and the information which it was considered necessary to collect. Many of the models discussed in this section reveal the range of interpretations of the nature of new-product risk and tend to concentrate on decisions concerning the introduction of intrinsically new products or products new to the planning company. Essentially, two types of evaluation are necessary in final product decisions, the one in the areas of compatibility and feasibility of the developing product relative to existing resources and objectives, the other concerning profitability over the target planning period.

Compatibility Review

Compatibility review is one of the most worked areas in firms which regularly develop their product range, in that it is relatively simple to evaluate some of the aspects of compatibility. For example, there usually appears to be a *prima facie* case for considering the compatibility of the products to be handled by company sales force or the relationship between existing distribution networks and new products. At a more detailed level, however, there are clearly a complex of factors to be regarded in rating products for compatibility. Richman[16] and O'Meara[17] provide one type of approach to new product rating and illustrate the relatively uncomplicated framework within which decisions could be framed. All methods, however, demand microstudies of both resources and objectives which produce objectively communicable expressions of their values. Nicolson and Pullen[18] develop a linear programming system designed to aid in both planning and feasibility studies, accepting that in the long-run the major pay-off of applying the programme may be the commitment it provides to organize and analyse the company's data for usage in planning and to provide a central but neutral point of reference for functional management who may tend to operate independently.

Profit evaluation instruments focus attention on a range of factors and types of model designed to examine the expected return from a series of strategic alternatives. There is no complete review and comparison of new product decision models, although Kotler[19] has undertaken a general critique of existing model types, establishing a system by which comparisons could be undertaken and Dean[20] has examined the broader problem of applying quantitative methods to product planning. Circumstances where profit evaluations are necessary occur constantly throughout the development stages of a product. At the initial screening stages basic break-even models frequently provide sufficient indication of the overall possibilities of the product. Similarly, when preliminary investment considerations are under review, basic cash-flow models aid in the evaluation of product returns over the planned period. There are few illustrations of the detailed application of these methods to product development in the new product literature, although Disman[21] provides an example of an early adaptation of the cash-flow model to product evaluation. Both these model types, however, have inadequate consideration of the role played by different conceptions of the marketing mix in estimation of yield and profit potential, and hence lay little emphasis on the need to develop estimates of likely sales and costs under these strategies.

Kotler[22] develops a model to determine break-even volumes under alternative marketing mixes and to optimize the mix and the implied profit levels. This model is an adaptation of cash-flow and break-even models but provides little insight into the detailed operation of the specific product decision under uncertainty. Bayesian decision models[23] applied to these decisions can aid the calculation of probabilities and expected profits connected with each strategy. This method of evaluation coupled with studies such as that of Kotler[24] which provide a taxonomy of alternative product strategies, enabling more thorough optimization models to be constructed. It is important to stress that there is probably little competitive advantage in over-enthusiasm and adherence to such formal planning models of strategy. The advantage, rather, lies in the identification of the implications of alternative strategies and thus the provision of a long-term ability to anticipate product profitability.

Models

Several attempts have been made to overcome some of the basic problems of the Bayesian model, particularly those connected with the provision of probability distributions of rates of return for alternative policies. One such modified Monte Carlo simulation is provided by Pessemier,[25] although its implementation requires detailed quantified estimates of the movement of key variables such as sales, costs and investments in each year of the planning horizon. More fundamentally, such simulation models tend not to incorporate an explicit procedure for examining the relationships between existing and developing products and view many dependent variables as independent.

To tackle the problem of evaluating the company's position at each stage in the development of new products, Learner[26] and others have constructed a model (DEMON) which is based on a three-choice decision of each development stage. The objective of this system is to map an optimal path through the total information available, subject to environmental constraints. As in other cases, this model demands accurate executive specification of guiding contraints and, in a sense, can be used most successfully where a thorough information framework is already in existence. The DEMON system gives little formal attention to the inter-relationships between new products which have a direct profit relationship to existing items in the product range. Urban[27] incorporates these inter-relationships into his SPRINTER model and also considers a range of competitive reactions over the products' life-cycle. This model has similar objectives to the DEMON model and is oriented towards 'stage' decisions. The mathematical structure of the model is highly complex and thus the derivation of a solution for the best marketing mix is so difficult that Urban[28] subsequently developed a method of approximating to the best solution by simulation.

The models cited here as illustrations of the types of development in new product programmes reflect the fact that we are at present in a period of evolution in this type of model-building. Many are complex, most are directed to the resolution of relatively small parts of the overall product development problem. DEMON and SPRINTER, for example, are respectively oriented to the management of marketing research for new products and interactions between new and existing products. Crawford[29] provides another illustration of a limited objective system, in this case concerned with goal-setting for product development. Moreover, there are specific barriers on the way to developing aggregate models, not least of which are the varying types of methods by which product development is organized in companies; the method of incorporating market reaction to the product in general and competitors' reactions in particular. This is further complicated by the inadequate understanding of consumer decision processes at varying stages of the product life-cycle. Thus, while the models outlined may provide few transferable formulae for product developers, they do point to systems by which basic profit evaluations can be more effectively undertaken and by their treatment of the key parameters such as risk, information-based choices and product inter-relations, and indicate the considerations essential in estimation procedures.

Modification

Both the organizational and quantitative types of model imply advantage in formalization of the product development function. Clearly, there are some circumstances where the product type, market structure and point of initiation of the product change would not necessitate the detailed application of any of the systems discussed. It is, however, important to note that many product changes fail because they are considered to be minor and are not reviewed or programmed within any framework. It is vital thus to observe that there are common considerations in all product modifications, some of which are only placed in perspective by the adoption of a formal system of planning. Further, there are few organizations within which the substantial

modification of products is in any sense a routine. More frequently, being classified with research and development funds results in the implicit application of less detailed measures of efficiency to product development and hence past experience is often not adequately recorded. For both these types of reasons, formalized product planning offers significant benefits relative to costs incurred.

Formalizing Product Planning

One of the most common barriers against the adoption of product development planning is that the development of products is viewed as a function with a hierarchical identity and with a considerable mystique. In other words, the emphasis is on the intuitive factors in past selection of the 'correct product' and senior directors frequently consider that they should initiate all development work on such products. The controlled formalization of this function invariably provides a more effective channel for new ideas from other sources and often ensures the emergence of products which have at least an average profit performance. As with the establishment of other planning systems, they tend to require modification with experience of their application. Invariably, product planning systems are inadequately serviced since they tend to be set up to consider major product issues which occur infrequently. By default thus, organizational systems for products involving co-operation between functional departments, tend to disappear as a result of the polarization which occurs after the new or modified product is launched.

Product planning remains both one of the most contentious areas of a firm's activities and one of the most difficult to plan or control. Difficult, though for reasons of cost effectiveness and market position, critical, this function must be regulated within one of the types of system considered in this article.

References

1 Adler, L., Time Lag in New Product Development, *Journal of Marketing*, 30, Jan. 1966.
2 Manning, C.F., Principles of Product Strategy, *National Industrial Conference Board*, Oct., 1964.
3 Murphy, J.H., New Products Need Special Management, *Journal of Marketing*, 26, 4, 1962.
4 Chorafas, D.N., *An Introduction to Product Planning and Reliability Management*, Cassell, London, 1967.
5 Johnson, S.C. and Jones, C. How to Organize for New Products, *Harvard Business Review*, May-Jun., 1957.

6 McCarthy, E.J., Organization for New-Product Development, *Journal of Business,* **32**, 2, 1959.

7 Lipson, H.A., Formal Reasoning and Marketing Strategy, *Journal of Marketing,* **26**, 4, 1962.

8 Booz, Allen & Hamilton, *The Management of New Products*, New York, 4th edition, 1965.

9 Nicolls, S., Logical Procedures for New Products, *Work Study and Management Services*, Oct., 1969.

10 Nord, O.C., *Growth of a New Product*, (Effects of Capacity-Acquisition Policies), MIT Press, Cambridge, 1963.

11 Mills, H.D., Dynamics of New Product Campaigns, *Journal of Marketing,* **28**, Oct., 1964.

12 Rothman, J., Choosing the Best Product Ranges and Assortments, *Management Decision*, Summer, 1967.

13 Rasswiler, G.E., Product Strategy and Future Profits, in Berg, T.L. and Schuchman, A. (eds.) *Product Strategy and Management.*

14 Clifford, D.A., Managing the Product Life Cycle, *The McKinsey Quarterly*, Spring, 1965.

15 Herrman, C.C., Managing New Products in a Changing Market, *Journal of Marketing,* **26**, 1, 1962.

16 Richman, B., A Rating Scale for Product Innovation, *Business Horizons*, Summer, 1962.

17 O'Meara, J.T., Selecting Profitable Products, *Harvard Business Review*, Jan.-Feb., 1961.

18 Nicolson, T.A.J. and Pullen, R.D., MAPLE; A Linear Programming System for Product Planning, *Management Accounting*, Oct., 1970.

19 Kotler, P., Computer Simulation in the Analysis of New Product Decisions, Chapter 11 in *Application of the Sciences in Marketing Management*, F.M. Bass *et al.*, (eds.) Wiley, New York, 1968.

20 Dean, B.V., *Quantitative Methods in New Product Planning*, Case Institute of Technology, 1964.

21 Disman, S., Selecting R and D Projects for Profit, *Chemical Engineering*, Dec., 1961.

22 Kotler, P., Marketing Mix Decisions for New Products, *Journal of Marketing Research,* **2**, Feb., 1964.

23 Green, P.E., Bayesian Statistics and Product Decisions, *Business Horizons,* **5**, 1962.

24 Kotler, P., Competitive Strategies for New Product Marketing Over the Life Cycle, *Management Science,* **12**, 4, Dec., 1965.

25 Pessemier, E., *New Product Decisions: An Analytical Approach*, New York, McGraw-Hill, 1966.

26 Learner, D.B., DEMON: A Management Planning and Control System for Successfully Marketing New Products, *Proceedings of the American Marketing Association*, Jun., 1964.

27 Urban, G.L., SPRINTER: A Tool for New Product Decision Makers, *Industrial Management Review*, **8**, Spring 1967.

28 Urban, G.L., A New Product Analysis and Decision Model, *Management Science,* **14**, 8, 1968.

29 Crawford, C.M., The Trajectory Theory of Goal Setting for New Products, *Journal of Marketing Research*, May, 1966.

3.

Technological Strategies for Industrial Companies

by Professor J. B. Quinn

Amos Tuck School of Business Administration, Dartmouth College

Reprinted with permission from Management Decision, Autumn 1968. © 1968 by MCB (Management Decision) Limited; all rights reserved.

Introduction

What is involved in formulating a strategy? What kinds of factors must be considered in such planning? How can a management establish internal decision processes to properly develop and implement a viable strategy?

In developing a corporate strategy, it is essential to go through several specific intellectual processes. These do not necessarily require elaborate procedures nor large staff organizations. Needed formality will depend on the size, sophistication, and complexity of the company and its management group. It is the quality of thought which goes into these key analytical processes – and not their formality – which ultimately makes the difference.

The overall process of strategic formulation should follow the classic approach used by military strategists throughout history. It is best exemplified, in brief, by the development of Hannibal's strategy at Cannae.

After crossing the Alps, Hannibal had *analysed* his *situation* and *revised his grand strategy.* He had found his supply lines seriously interrupted. His troops were exhausted and needed retraining. And he had neither the equipment nor tactical support to lay seige to the series of strongholds leading to Rome itself. These considerations led to his new three-part strategy: By-pass Rome and buy time to re-equip and retrain his army. Seek needed supplies and support in the non-Latium countryside. Eventually try to draw the Roman armies into the field and manoeuvre them into situations where the legions' superior discipline and equipment were not critical. This strategy *comprised possible immediate attainment of the optimum goal* (capture of Rome) *to minimize the maximum risk of total defeat.*

Within this broad strategy Hannibal prepared for the battle of Cannae. Again he *analysed* his *strengths and weaknesses* relative to those of his opponents. His strengths were: He commanded the most superb cavalry of his time, including his cherished Numidian horse. Since the Romans were pursuing him, he could – within limits – choose the site of the battle. His relative weaknesses were: Within their accustomed battle formations, the Roman legions were superior to his foot troops. The Roman army was several times the size of his. Hence Hannibal's battle strategy was to: Select a location which decreased the legions' manoeuvreability and forced them to come uphill in cramped formations to meet the Carthaginian foot troops – *attempt to decrease the impact of the opponent's maximum strength.* Engage the legions frontally, but do not expect Carthaginian foot troops to win the day in such a confrontation – i.e., *concede that the opponent is stronger in certain respects.* Conceal the Carthaginian cavalry strength as much as possible behind the hills – *avoid excessive enemy counter-measures against the planned form of attack.* As the Carthaginian centre fails, withdraw up a pocket formed by V-shaped hills – i.e., *plan responses to opponent's gains.* When the legions 'fighting front' is most seriously engaged, out-manoeuvre and overwhelm the cavalry on their flanks and attack their rear – i.e., *utilize comparative strengths to maximum advantage.*

Hannibal inflicted on the Romans one of the most diastrous defeats in history. Some 50,000 Romans died, many of back wounds and cut hamstring muscles.

This classic of military strategy contains most of the critical elements encountered in formulating strategy for any organization. Effective formulation requires:

1 Establishing an *overall strategy* which balances organizational goals into a set that is acceptable in terms of both risk and potential gain.

2 Defining a *total posture* for the organization which allows it to meet opposition on generally favourable terms.

3 Backing-up the overall strategy with *operational plans* which maintain the intended total posture yet effectively marshal the organization's unique resources to overcome the specific opposition it encounters.

How can this actually be accomplished in a complex industrial-technical organization? Several inter-related activities are central to the process.

Relative strengths and weaknesses

As in Hannibal's case, it is essential to evaluate realistically the organization's own relative strengths and weaknesses and to relate these to the opportunities and threats in future environments. A company should make a careful periodic assessment — with or without outside help — to establish what its true competitive strengths and weaknesses are. Quantification, of course, is not always possible, but a real attempt must be made to obtain as much accuracy and objectivity as possible. Often a great deal of objective data about the company's position is readily available if management just seeks it and chooses to use it.

Two common techniques are used in analysing a company's comparative strengths and weaknesses:

1 Determining the patterns of failure and success in past company operations.

2 Developing a company profile by directly comparing its skills and capacities with those of competitors.[1]

Conceptually these pose no real problems. Actually, of course, underlying analyses can be quite complex and normally require inputs from many of the company's component divisions. Hence, corporate planning groups and top managements frequently ask component organizations to generate relative competitive position data in a strict format as a routine part of their long-range planning presentations. Such requests have the added benefit of assuring that the divisions at least occasionally analyse and justify their individual strategic postures. Corporate planning or staff groups are generally those who integrate these inputs into a total company profile. And such groups often play a major rôle in influencing top managers to discuss and act on critical features during regular long-range planning or budget preparation cycles.

Some companies seek similar results through rigorous special reviews, e.g., in the following example.

Example 1 A large divisional corporation doing business in chemical and related industries has frequently subjected itself, division by division, to full-dress audits to determine where the divisions should best seek their individual *sub-niches*. Each division is analysed in terms of how its peculiar strengths and weaknesses can best suit it to exploit recognized market opportunities and withstand competitive incursions. Senior members of corporate staff groups make these audits, but — to

further avoid axe-grinding — outside consultants are often included on audit terms. The end result of the exercise both sharpens the competitive concept of each division and also helps the corporation define its own overall *niche* better.

The purposes of such exercises should be: to identify and exploit the comparative weaknesses of competitors; to marshal sufficient resources into specific sub-areas of the company's operations to dominate them; to recognize where competitive strengths allow the company wider latitude in pricing or product policies than competitors; and to pinpoint the company's own weaknesses for more aggressive action or purposeful withdrawal. Thus, these analyses help define various niches in the competitive environment where the company — given its limited resources — can prosper despite intelligent opposition. In addition, they enable the company to concentrate internal resources into those areas where they are most needed and/or can be most effective — rather than scattering them across all areas of interest regardless of the relative opposition involved. Careful deployment of resources to exploit selected niches and to parry expected threats gives the company a unique strategic posture. This posture derives maximum benefits from the company's own strengths yet makes it as impregnable to outside attack as management's risk-taking instincts desire.

But if a company tries to match all competitors' efforts in all areas, it will assuredly fail through lack of resources. Even giant concerns such as IBM, General Motors, or du Pont occupy distinct niches in their markets and are generally unsuccessful when they attempt to move too far from their areas of established competency. Analysis of the relative postures of these concerns repeatedly has enabled smaller — as well as other giant — companies to successfully invade particular segments of their potential markets. And companies that have actually found such strategic niches rank among the most dynamic and profitable enterprises in the world. The following example is typical.

Example 2 In the mid-1950s a small drug company realized it could not hope to compete successfully with large entrenched companies either on the basis of broadscale research or intensive marketing. The company, therefore, selected two areas of high research potential — steroid and hormone chemistry — and concentrated its resources on research in these fields. For a period of five years the company spent more money than any single competitor on research in these fields, and indeed it spent more than its own total sales revenues for the period. Near the end of this period, two new products resulting from its research were so important and well publicized through professional journals that the company introduced the products through wholesalers without the high promotional expenditure programmes which its competitors normally used. The resulting high margins made the company highly profitable and enabled it to continue intensive development of its selected niche.

Future opportunities and threats

As this example suggests, merely recognizing the organization's particular strengths and weaknesses will not define a viable strategy for it. Managers must also imaginatively analyse potential opportunities and threats in the environment to see how they can best develop and exploit the organization's unique capacities and thus maintain its future dynamism. Hence, thorough strategic formulation requires careful forecasts of relevant *economic, sociological*, and *technological futures*[2] and some means of reflecting these forecasts in major decision processes.

For years companies have forecast economic, market, and financial environments. But only in recent years have many industrial-technical companies undertaken technological forecasting on a formal basis. Yet such forecasts are becoming increasingly critical for both strategic and operational planning in industrial-technical companies. Because of this, a variety of very useful technological forecasting techniques have been developed and tested in industrial environments. These now permit managers to analyse the demand forces calling forth a particular technology, its ultimate theoretical potentials and relevancy, its expected rate of progress, and its probable impact on the company and on society. Certain of these forecasting approaches are most relevant to strategic planning (see Figure 3.1).

Properly applied, such techniques[3] can help evaluate the probability and significance of various possible future opportunities and threats so that managers can make better strategic decisions. Like any other forecasts, technological forecasts cannot be expected to have pinpoint accuracy. Nor is such accuracy necessary. What managers need are range forecasts of the performance characteristics. A given use is likely to demand in the future, probability statements about what performance characteristics a given technology can provide at various future dates and analyses of the implications of having these technical economic characteristics available at such dates. Technological forecasting provides good pragmatic tools for such purposes.

But I greatly fear that the enormous potential benefits technological forecasting could provide are being undercut by a current tendency to play up its faddish aspects. The field is often obscured by unnecessary jargon. And projections to the year 2000 are much in vogue, even though little concrete action concerning the year 2000 is necessary between now and later dates when we could certainly forecast the year 2000 more accurately. I urge managers – and professionals in this new field – to concentrate more on the 3 to 10 year time horizons where technological forecasting can contribute so much to major decisions and to emphasize the pragmatic and meaningful use of these new techniques. Technological forecasting is a powerful and useful tool – as many experienced managements already know. But its utilization by other managers will be delayed if technological forecasting becomes known as a fad or fraud.

The above techniques – and their close cousins under other names – are being applied to industrial/technical strategy problems every day. Manipulation of the individual techniques is no longer the central problem. The real trick is to get managers to introduce such forecasts appropriately in their strategic decision processes. In some cases 'special exercises' backed by top level managers can be extremely effective, for example:

Example 3 the vice-president of Research and Development of TRW, Inc., asked each operating division to nominate six of its most influential and creative people to lay out what major technological advances they thought would occur (with a 50 per cent probability of success) in the next 20 years. Their first estimates were refined using a controlled feedback process, similar to the Delphi method. Final lists of projected achievements were grouped by related technologies and technical groups were asked to draw up PERT charts suggesting the most feasible paths to those end results of most interest to TRW. The top management group then held a series of meetings – in remote country surroundings – to discuss the implications of the forecasts and what TRW should do about them. These resulted in decisions to monitor some interesting new technologies and to investigate others in depth to develop possible future markets.[4]

Figure 3.1 Some technological forecasting approaches relevant to strategic planning

Demand analyses techniques

Demographic and sociological parameter analyses assess the degree to which major social trends will create new market opportunities or force the use of technology to solve certain problems. These have often been used to estimate future food, energy, anti-pollution (etc.) needs.

Conditional demand analyses evaluate under what conditions a new technology might substitute for an existing one (or be used to satisfy an identified demand), the probability of each such condition occurring, and the potential timing and value of the event if it occurs. From this, one can calculate the expected value of a particular technological advance and compare this value with the expected total cost of achieving and exploiting the advance. This technique is often used in selecting major technical programmes.

Opportunity identification techniques are extensions of marketing research methodologies used to identify the economic-technical characteristics of products or systems which could satisfy an existing or latent demand in a new way. Analytical or field investigations determine the *functional characteristics* which will make any technology viable in a given end-use. Technical people are then asked how rapidly and effectively various technical approaches could achieve the 'performance' window described by these characteritics. Costs and benefits of various approaches can then be compared.

Examination of theoretical potentials

Examining the theoretical potentials of a technology discloses: its potential relevancy to the company's technical programme; whether the technology is in its *extensive* region and hence likely to continue its progress at its existing rate, whether the technology is approaching a 'saturation level' where its rate of progress will decrease. In this latter a new case technology is likely to substitute the existing technology, if it can no longer meet the progress rate dictated by key performance characteristics in the demand function it serves. The phenomenon has been observed frequently in envelope curve analyses. From such analyses, one can estimate *when* a new technology is likely to take over, but not always the particular *type* of technology which will do so.

Parameter analyses

Technological trends can often be determined when data exists about the performance levels a given technology has been able to achieve at various past dates. When these performance levels have been measured under carefully controlled conditions in relatively similar environments, they have generally demonstrated relatively smooth and continuous progress characteristics. Progress has often been exponential (at a constant rate of growth) within the technology's extensive region, tailing-off asymptotically as saturation levels or theoretical limits are reached. Great care must be exercised in selecting the relevant progress parameters to measure and to define measurement conditions carefully. But when data about past technical programmes do exist, they should be assembled and intelligently analysed. A competent forecaster will neither use such data rigidly nor ignore them in favour of intuitive forecasts by experts.

Technological changeover points define the performance characteristics a technology must achieve if it is to substitute for another in a given end-use. Trends in performance for both the existing and substituting technology can be projected. And the performance characteristics the technology must achieve by various *future* dates can be set as programme targets for technical and marketing planning. Similarly, one can identify the nature and time of threats from technologies developing at more rapid rates than those currently utilized by the company.

Diffusion analyses predict how rapidly a technology — once in use — will diffuse in given applications. When the market consists of large numbers of individuals making independent decisions, the technology tends to diffuse smoothly in a classic curve toward eventual saturation. Numbers of people have studied these curves and concluded that their patterns are often strong enough for reliable prediction. In industrial situations where relatively few large-scale decisions dominate — as in major process substituion — diffusion curves are much more jagged, and prediction is better performed by looking at changeover criteria in individual situations.

Systems Analysis

Design simulations — like aircraft mock-ups in wind tunnels — have been used for years to predict the actual or desirable design characteristics for products. Currently computer models and computer-based video displays are being used to suggest possible and desirable designs for electric cars, conventional cars and lorries, ships, industrial processes, dams, harbours, etc.

Scenario techniques analyse potential future opportunities and threats. In this approach an identifiable trend or opportunity is used as a starting point. The analyst then attempts to establish a logical sequence of steps suggesting how a future state might evolve step by step. The primary purpose of scenario writing is not to predict the future, *per se*, but to see how various futures might evolve from certain critical decisions. However, in some cases the branches of various associated scenarios overlap to such an extent that they begin to define highly probable future opportunities or threats.

Other systems analyses can identify *functional weaknesses* in existing systems as opportunities for improvement or exploitation. Still others can investigate *hypothetical problems* of a 'what if'

nature to specify technologies needed for certain future situations like space, arctic warfare, or oceanography where the specific demands of the environment cannot be predicted. Such studies are essential precursors for designs to be placed in environments which cannot be thoroughly simulated or tested in advance.

Expert judgement

In some cases data do not exist to establish technological or demand trends. Simulation or other formal analyses are unfeasible as a basis for forecasts, and predictions must rest solely on the opinions of experts. (Examples would include forecasts of scientific break-throughs, distant future events, etc.) Under such circumstances the Delphi technique offers a means of avoiding both the potential errors of a single expert's judgement and the inordinate distortions possible when a group of experts acts in a committee environment. Delphi is an interesting tool when used properly. But it should not be regarded as a substitute for hard-headed data collection and analysis, when such steps are economically feasible.

Competitive analyses

Life-cycle models can show how competitors' actions affect the design life of a company's products or processes and suggest needed levels of defensive technical work.

Technological mapping is one of several *systematic search techniques* used to identify alternate routes to a desired end-result. Through network techniques all significant approaches to the result can be diagrammed and each competitor's position *vis-á-vis* these approaches analysed. The resulting 'map' serves as a basis for estimating future performance capacities of competitors, seeking-out attractive competitive approaches, and avoiding those dominated by competitors.

Integrated long-range planning

For most large industrial/technical companies, the most feasible and efficient time to forecast future environments — and to formulate overall corporate strategy — is during the long-range planning process. In fact, without an integrated long-range planning procedure it may very well be impossible for such companies to develop an effective total strategy. The following summary description of a real company's practice explains the procedure involved.

Example 4 An international oil company has two planning staffs (economic analysis and operations analysis) reporting to a corporate long-range planning (LRP) committee. The LRP committee consists of six members of the board of directors with responsibilities over each major operating division. It also contains corporate vice-presidents of finance, personnel, and legal affairs. In addition, each operating division has its own long-range planning staff.

In outline, the planning process proceeds like this. Semi-annually the economic analysis group forecasts all major macro-economic parameters (world-wide) for the' corporation. Operations analysis distills world-wide inputs on expected political conditions, pricing and supply trends, major technological developments, etc., and uses these with the macro-economic forecasts of economic analysis to make an energy balance forecast of corporate-wide sales, investment needs, costs, profits, etc., five years ahead. From these the corporate executive committee determines desired overall corporate objectives. These are then sent along with economic analysis' forecasts to the operating divisions. Operating divisions are asked to use the economic analysis' macro-economic forecasts as assumptions in preparing their more detailed predictions.

Operating divisions then draw up proposals showing *what* they hope to accomplish each year for the next five years, *how* they plan to achieve it, and the *resources* (capital and expense) their plans will call for. These are consolidated and reviewed at corporate levels using economic and operations analysis reports as background information. Corporate and/or divisional objectives and programmes are modified until a feasible, desirable balance is achieved. Agreed upon organizational objectives become performance criteria for each division, and capital and operating budgets are approved to support these objectives. Capital requests between formal planning periods are also reviewed in terms of their impact

on approved plans. Finally, performance reports compare actual and planned performance in terms of budgets and other non-financial objectives agreed upon.

Companies with effective long-range planning generally follow somewhat similar activity cycles. Of course, their specialized planning organizations differ from those in the example. But these are of secondary interest here. The critical point is that long-range planning involves more than just gazing into the future. Effective planning requires linking executives' evaluations and intentions about the future into: major resource allocations, important current policy decisions, and performance evaluation and motivational systems affecting executives. These in turn generally determine the company's overall strategy and the willingness and capacity of executives to support it. Therefore, an integrated long-range planning and control system can provide the following crucial steps in formulating and implementing corporate strategy.

1 Forecasting future environments.
2 Setting broad corporate objectives and policies.
3 Communicating corporate objectives, policies, and assumptions.
4 Developing proposals for divisional goals, strategies, programmes, resource needs.
5 Reviewing and consolidating proposals at corporate levels.
6 Committing resources in terms of plans.
7 Following-up and reviewing actions taken.
8 Evaluating executive performance in terms of plans.
9 Needed iteration throughout the cycle.

Each step in the sequence is critical and its importance could be amplified at length. Such detailed treatment is impossible here. But we must emphasize two basic points:

First, to produce an effective overall strategy in a complex company, the total enterprise and each of its component units need to develop integrated plans with a long enough time perspective to effectively incorporate the contributions and demands of the group with the longest necessary lead time — usually R & D. And all capital, operating, and cash budgets must be related to these plans. *Until resource allocations are tied into long-range plans, the latter will remain little more than interesting academic exercises, and co-ordinating long- and short-term commitments into a strategically balanced whole will be virtually impossible.*

But can such co-ordination be achieved without

losing the benefits of decentralized management? The answer is a resounding, 'Yes!' Decentralization does not require abdication of top management. The planning pattern suggested above leaves detailed development of plans and their implementation in the hands of operating managers, yet provides needed balance and guidance at the top level of the enterprise where it belongs. For it is only at this level in most organizations that the information, authority, and incentive exist to make the necessary compromises between various divisional objectives and to force the necessary joint action among divisions that utilize the full strength of a large company and keeps each division from simply having a small company's capacities with a large company's overhead.

Second, cold words and diagrams may make the above approach appear somewhat rigid and authoritarian. But its actual implementation must, of course, be dynamic and dominated by human factors. The process of creating long-range plans and integrating them into strategy is always evolutionary. The proposals and decisions knit together by the strategy do not suddenly leap fully blown into the minds of executives. Nor do they stand in crystalline purity as a single immutable set of long-term commitments. Instead they represent a momentary photograph of a complex operating consensus that is constantly dynamic. This consensus evolves slowly as problems change and as the political influence of individual managers and groups ebbs and flows. And it only exists because over time managerial actions have created a motivational environment that stimulates strong-minded executives to act in concert and to accept organizational objectives which — while perhaps not of their own unique choosing — offer greater benefit to the whole organization than unco-ordinated action. One cannot overemphasize the continuous personal interactions and exercises of human skills needed to achieve an operable consensus in an organization.

But superb competency in such human dynamics alone will not enable top executives to create an effective strategy. They must exercise these skills to guide action towards ends which — when achieved — will in fact have developed a strategy. Well-designed management systems can make executives' personal interactions easier and more effective. And they can extend the impact of high level interactions to those who cannot reasonably be contacted personally. The decision patterns above specify what careful planning and strategy formulation involves and demonstrate systematic approaches which increase the probability that ordinary executives will in fact accomplish those ends.

Missions in strategic planning

Nevertheless, despite well-developed corporate and divisional planning systems, many companies still find it difficult to co-ordinate activities across formal divisional lines and thus fully utilize their resources. This is especially true of industrial/technical companies. Small to medium-sized concerns cannot get their functional (marketing, production, technical divisions) to pull in the same direction. Larger companies encounter problems in co-ordinating centralized R and D, corporate development, or marketing activities with those of decentralized operating divisions. And almost all companies suffer because divisional structures create fragmentation and duplication in their scientific and technical, public relations, manpower development efforts.

Such difficulties have led some progressive companies — both large and small — to develop special 'missions' plans for strategic activities which cut across formal division lines. These plans overlay the division's normal operating and long-range plans (see Figure 3.1) and ensure that each division gives co-ordinated activities the timely and forceful attention they need for success.

The missions concept is especially useful in introducing new technologies to operations or the marketplace. Generally, such technologies must cross formal organizational lines among R & D, engineering, production, product, and/or marketing divisions. In international companies they must also cross regional lines and be modified to meet local cultural standards. In such cases missions analysis, planning, and control allow corporate managers — or programme managers — to investigate whether divisions are balancing their plans and commitments to reach the strategic goals. And the mission plan (in such cases usually a series of budgets or PERT-PERT/COST programmes, also provide a track against which the company can measure actual progress.

Almost all research, development, engineering, or plant technical programmes involve essential linkages with personnel, marketing, production, or other functional groups. In industrial-technical companies, missions planning helps ensure that scientific and technical programmes become neither isolated nor forgotten under the pressures of day to day competition. It co-ordinates personnel and resource commitments in both operating and technical units toward common goals. It makes certain that major scientific and technical programmes truly reflect operating groups' strategic needs. It forces operating groups to prepare to receive new technologies. And it provides a much-needed vehicle for information exchange and follow-up of major new technologies in their various stages of introduction.

But the missions approach is not limited to technological affairs. Division plans, commitments, and efforts to achieve other strategic goals can be co-ordinated similarly. The following example suggests several possibilities.

Example 5 A chemical company's management council (consisting of the president, executive vice-presidents, and all division heads) sets aside one meeting per month to review some strategic issue common to several divisions. The council reviews the aggregate impact of each division's (planned and actual) management development, patent exploitation, public image, government

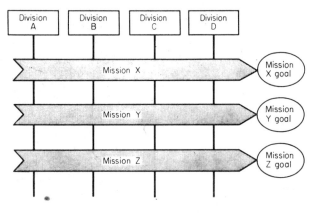

relations, recruitment, (or other) programme. In addition, when five-year plans and budgets are presented annually, each division identifies its proposed expenditures and results in each of these strategic areas, and a corporate staff group sums these for top management review. Inadequate or unco-ordinated plans in these non-financial areas are not tolerated.

Thus, missions planning and control across divisional lines can bring the full force of the corporation's resources into alignment to attack strategic problems. And it can help avoid some of the duplication, ineffectiveness, waste, and delays of unco-ordinated action.

Scientific and Technical Strategy

The missions approach and the concepts previously developed combine to provide the essential foundations for properly utilizing science and technology in an industrial concern. The scientific and technical programmes of a company exist solely to support that company's overall strategy. Research, development, engineering, and technical programmes should never be considered apart from other corporate activities. They should be explicitly integrated into the product, process, market penetration, personnel development, public relations (and so forth) missions of the company. Thus, in ranking potential applied programmes, a simple ordering in terms of *relative present value, rate of return*, or *expected profit* can be highly misleading. Within a given strategy it may be more important to invest in a low-yield project supporting division A than a higher yield project for division B. Or some research programmes – with no expected commercial pay-off – may be necessary to support broader public relations or manpower development goals.

Project selection – and indeed the whole organization and management of R & D – must be dictated by the strategic purposes the programme serves. A series of examples will demonstrate some of the many ways in which strategic considerations influence the programme content, personnel selection, and formal organization of R & D in specific industrial/technical companies.

Example 6 Company A manufactured fine chemicals and ethical drug products in the US. Its drug research group was among the world's most successful industrial laboratories. But as regulatory bodies began to delay the entry of all ethical products world-wide, the company's rapid growth-rate slowed. To decrease its dependence on a single market and to increase sales growth, management decided to diversify into proprietary drugs and to emphasize foreign markets for its existing products. It budgeted a planned loss on its proprietary division and negative cash flows on its foreign operations for a 3-year period. It then accepted development projects for either division at a lower expected rate of return than it would have accepted for domestic ethical drug products. Only by doing so could the company begin to allocate sufficient resources to these fields to achieve needed market penetrations. It further backed its strategy by adding overseas development groups to modify products to meet local needs and by hiring – or establishing relationships with – experts on the more esoteric diseases of underdeveloped areas. Since its superb ethical drug research group was quite ill-adapted to meeting the competitive requirements of proprietary drugs, a separate proprietary development group was established and staffed primarily from outside the company. The ethical research group working on domestic diseases actually decreased in size for several years, although the total technical effort grew substantially.

Chemical company B's real strength lies in exploiting highly competitive situations by applying off-beat process technology due to its unique raw materials access. The company plans to grow only in fields with large, long-run volume potentials and not in those with short-term, high-profit-margin potential and high technological obsolescence. It backs up its strategy with a strong raw-materials and process-orientated research commitment. It attempts to expand its range of technical skills slowly, but develops great depth in each skill it takes on.

These examples, from the same general industry grouping, could be amplified a thousandfold by classic examples from other industries. But these underline certain basic points.

1 There are a variety of ways in which scientific and technical commitments can be marshalled to attain company goals, depending on that company's unique strategy.

2 The scientific and technical programme is an integral part of the company's total strategy and its various components should be aligned to ensure that the individual missions composing that strategy receive the scientific and technical support they need for success.

3 A simple ordering of projects in terms of their expected profit or return by no means assures optimum use of research and development resources.

4 R & D planning and budgeting (as well as all other commitments of scientific personnel and equipment) must, therefore, be directly tied into total corporate planning and should not – as so often happens – be considered in isolation from the operating programmes they support.

Strategies for introducing new technologies

For corporate and overall scientific and technical strategies to be implemented effectively, they must ultimately be reflected in strategic thinking at the programme level – especially in introducing new technologies into the market-place or operations. The introduction of almost any significant technological change will encounter strong opposition from some quarter. But in most cases, careful consideration of strategic factors can both help overcome such opposition and ensure that the particular change involved will contribute as much as possible to company goals. Other articles have suggested ways to reduce some internal organizational resistances to changes. Here we will concentrate primarily on strategic approaches used in introducing technologies when the dominant opposing factors are outside the concern.

The first step in establishing an introduction strategy is, of course, to try to anticipate what forms of opposition the technology is likely to encounter. Strangely, even this elementary step is often overlooked when planning new product introductions. Venture analyses, PERT/COST charts, and present-value studies used to justify new technological ventures generally assume price levels, technological states of the art, competitive intensities, raw material prices, and consumer-preference patterns to be constant. Even the inclusion of simple trends in basic unit costs, end-product prices, performance characteristics of competitive products, the industry-wide production capacity $v.$ demand, (and so forth) would improve most such analyses immeasurably. And, hopefully, managers will increasingly insist on such inputs.

But is it possible for analyses to consider the *specific* counter-measures and resistances outside groups will pose? Some experience indicates that it is.

Example 7 A large chemical company's central development group constructs a very sophisticated computer model of the market for any major new product a division wants to introduce. The model, composed of component modules which can be incorporated or omitted as desired, includes inputs for relevant cost, price, and technological trends. It also includes the best available approximations of the company's customers, and (direct and functional) competitors' cost curves. Game theory analyses are conducted to see how far each competitor would rationally lower his prices to meet the new product's competition. In addition, experts from both within and outside the company are sometimes asked to estimate the most likely specific counter-measures each major competitor would use and their probable effects on each element in the model. The model is then manipulated to calculate the most likely net effort of various possible counter-measures and a 'best available' company strategy conceived.

Example 8 A smaller company selling in international markets has used what it calls the 'aggressor company' technique. The company's first experience with this technique is quite thought-provoking. It brought together its marketing and technical people most familiar with the market for a new product line and told them to assume the role of the company's strongest potential competitor. This group was then asked to devise a plan which would most effectively attack the entry of the proposed product line. So effective was the 'aggressor company' in its suggestions that its members at one stage became quite suspicious of the general manager who organized the exercise. They thought the general manager actually intended to leave the company and join the competitor. And they refused to co-operate further until he relieved their fears by specifically modifying the company's product design and marketing plans to reflect competitive action.

Game theory provides the formal mathematical framework for explicit solutions to certain strategic problems where sufficient cost and market data exist or can be approximated. But actual situations permitting the economical use of formal game theory solutions are rare. Most formal analyses must rely on simulations (or 'gaming' models) utilizing judgemental inputs and seeking solutions through multiple 'trial and error' iterations. Unfortunately, such simulations tend to be so costly to construct and manipulate that they are generally utilized only by large companies and only for major decisions. But there is no reason why every plan for introducing a new technology should not have answered certain key questions: Who will resist this introduction? Why and how will they resist it? What will be the net effect of their resistance? What have we done to overcome this resistance? Have our expected expenditures and returns been adjusted to include the effects of opposition? Careful thought on each question will tend to avoid many strategic errors without costly formal analyses.

But even with great care, no management can ever hope to foresee and cope with all the possible alignments opposition can take. How then can plans for introducing new technologies reasonably reflect strategic considerations? The basic approach has been suggested in earlier sections: analyse the specific strengths and weaknesses of both the company and the technology relative to the opportunities and threats in the environment; try to foresee the most likely specific responses opponents will make to the introduction of the new technology;

allocate resources so as to overwhelm or avoid opposition in certain key respects, while just neutralizing or ignoring it in others; and maintain flexibility to meet unexpected responses. (Note again that this is exactly the same thought process Hannibal followed in formulating his battle strategy at Cannae.)

Can such an approach be carried out in practice? Experience repeatedly indicates that it can.

Example 9 A large aircraft company was late in entering the space hardware field. After analysing the long-term needs of NASA and other nations' space agencies and carefully investigating the capacities and commitments of its major competitors, the company decided to ignore the *propulsion hardware* field where competition had developed a technology lead. Instead, it concentrated on developing a dominant position in know-how for the *payload systems* that would eventually be propelled into space. It has been highly successful.

Example 10 A small company developed one of the first non-sudsing detergents. The company soon realized it could not obtain supermarket shelf space for its product without a costly advertising campaign against some of the largest consumer products companies in the world. The company had no resources for such a flight. Instead, it took another approach. A market research group tested the product in a large housing development. There it was found that the product cleaned better than sudsing products in tumble-action machines. But more important, the product reduced machine breakdown and repair by a startling margin. Thus, washing-machine manufacturers could be induced to put a sample of the product in their machines and to distribute it through their dealers. The company concentrated its limited efforts on this unique distribution channel and avoided head-on competition with the big advertisers. Eventually, machine owners demanded the product in supermarkets and mass distribution was achieved with a minimum investment.

Of course there are myriad other examples of successful strategies for introducing products. But these few should suffice to prove that strategic thinking can be usefully extended to the programme level. Indeed, a strategic approach is always essential if limited resources are to be marshalled effectively and intelligent opponents overcome. Since resources are always limited and opponents are ever present — regardless of whether one is at the corporate, divisional, or programme level — the industrial technical manager who does not understand strategic planning courts disaster.

Conclusion

Strategic planning requires a whole new look at many of the accepted shibboleths of industrial/technical management. It demands that corporate and divisional goals be developed in a more thorough and sophisticated context and that simplistic 'profit maximization' concepts be discarded. Use of widely accepted financial techniques for performance measurement and investment allocation must be modified to reflect the over-riding necessities of sound strategy. Long-range forecasting and planning practices must be tied more directly into resource commitment and performance evaluation systems. Segmented activities in individual divisions need to be integrated to bring the full force of the corporation to bear on its major problems. And managers must learn to regard purposeful opposition as a special environmental force to be coped with explicitly in their forecasts and plans. So many changes will come hard for traditionalists. But competition will certainly enforce them in time.

Notes

[1] For a thorough treatment of one such approach see: H.I. Ansoff and J.M. Stewart, 'Strategies for a Technology-Based Business', *Harvard Business Review*, November-December, 1967.

[2] See: J.B. Quinn, 'Long Range Planning of Industrial Research', *Harvard Business Review*, July-August, 1961, and 'Technological Forecasting', *Harvard Business Review*, March-April 1967.

[3] For specific examples and amplification of these approaches see J.B. Quinn, 'Technological Forecasting', *Harvard Business Review*, March-April 1967.

[4] See: 'Setting a Timetable', *Business Week*, May 27, 1967.

[5] See: J.B. Quinn and J.A. Mueller, 'Transferring Research Results to Operations, *Harvard Business Review*, January-February, 1963.

4.

Market Research in the Novel Product Field
by Dr. P.M.S. Jones

Reprinted from the IMRA Journal Vol. 7 (1) February, 1971 with permission.

Introduction

Novel products by their very nature represent a significant advance on existing products, and market research in this field must necessarily serve a range of functions. It may be required to indicate broad guide-lines for long-range corporate planning, or it may be used to identify specific product needs and to concentrate attention and effort on potentially profitable areas. Once the concept of a specific product has hardened, the market potential can be examined to determine its economic viability and its value to the company in terms of its overall objectives and utilization of resources. As development proceeds market research is increasingly aimed at defining the product and its markets more closely in terms of its performance, design and price/demand elasticity. Finally, sales forecasts and marketing strategy must be combined to determine' optimum plant capacity and pricing policy.

In this article the emphasis will be on the early stages of market research, aimed at identifying the needs of the market and prior to finalizing the product design, since beyond that stage the research becomes more conventional.

The questions one would like to answer once the idea for a new product has been born are:

1 Can it be done, and is the proposition technically feasible?

2 Can we do it? Does the company have the necessary technical expertise, or can this be acquired?

3 Are the necessary resources available to successfully manufacture and market the product?

4 Can the product be profitably sold at a price which will assure a demand?

5 Is there a real demand for the product, or could one be created?

6 Are we capable of successfully marketing the product? What is the competition doing and how will it react?

7 How do the potential benefits compare with the apparent risks?

In some firms the market research department may be expected to confine its attention to the questions 5 and 6, with the research department having responsibility for 1 and 2, the accountants for 3, and the production department for 4. In others, and the author's own organization is among these, the whole spectrum is covered by one department, utilizing the services from other specialist groups.

For present purposes, attention will be concentrated on the purely marketing aspects covered under questions 4 to 6 and case-studies will be used to illustrate specific points. These case-studies have been modified to put them into an industrial context, although the author's organization is itself concerned with the implications of total markets for government R & D policy.

Practical Research Problems and Methods

The principle difficulty with a novel product is that its very novelty means that few potential purchasers are aware of it, or of its potential value to them. For this reason the bulk of the market survey has to be done by personal interview. The market researcher must be familiar with the technicalities of his product, its values and limitations, and he needs a fairly detailed knowledge of his respondent's business, so that he can assess and explain how the new product will benefit the potential customer. Unless he can do this he will be likely to arrive at very wrong conclusions, either because the potential customer underestimates the revolutionary changes the product could make to his business, or because he underestimates the high costs of introducing the innovation.

As usual, the first step is desk research and consultation with experts within the company itself to familiarize the researcher with the field in which he is working, and to identify the most profitable lines for further research. It will be necessary to attempt to identify the potential users of the new product and experts in the field who may be able to advise on all matters bearing on its final acceptance. It is as well to remember that the physical scientist has a vested interest in change, just as the production manager or customer has strong incentives to retain the status quo. Since it is the latter who will eventually have to accept the idea before any sales can be achieved it is their views which deserve the heaviest weighting.

Standard sampling procedures are rarely appropriate when one is dealing with novel products, because sales will not depend solely on the size of the outlet and its apparent need, but also on its attitude to innovation and risk, and these cannot in general be known in advance. Ideally, all potential sources of information should be consulted to give complete coverage, but in practice this is rarely possible. Often in the early stages the problem is not clearly defined, and only a few useful contacts can be identified. As the survey progresses the problem comes more clearly into focus, and potentially useful contacts can more easily be identified. In some instances the market for a new product may be determined by the demand for other clearly defined products and in such circumstances some form of sampling may be appropriate. The cases where this is possible can only be judged by the market researcher in the field, on the basis of his past experience.

A more detailed discussion of research methods, data sources, sampling and different forecasting techniques will appear in a forthcoming IMRA publication.

Case-history· 1 — Looking for Ideas in Profitable Outlets

The most general question the market researcher is likely to be asked is to identify new potentially profitable outlets within a defined area of the company's activities. The case to be examined is that where a garment machinery manufacturing company is interested in deciding what new product line it could usefully develop and introduce; whether there is good reason to anticipate a high demand for the product, whether there is reason to believe that such a product could be profitable, and what competing lines of development would be likely to threaten the proposed product line. Most new ideas of this sort would be likely to arise from examining existing processes and deciding that, on the face of it, a specific operation is inefficient and could be improved. One could then set about devising a machine or a gadget to produce some measure of improvement. There are two faults with this approach; it may not result in the best opportunities for development being exploited, and it runs the risk that technical progress will render the product obsolescent in a very short time. To overcome these difficulties one needs to analyse ration-

ally the needs of the consumer industry, the benefits it will achieve as a result of the innovation, and the alternative routes to improvement that the consuming industry could follow.

The garment machinery manufacturer will need, therefore, to have a good appreciation of both the structure and the problems of the garment industry itself. Certain basic statistics are immediately available. The garment industry has a turnover in excess of £600 million per annum and employs over 350,000 people, of which 93 per cent are female, with roughly one management executive per seven production workers. The output of the industry has been rising only slowly over the past decade, whilst the labour force has been decreasing. The productivity per employee has risen by some 25 per cent during this period, largely due to improvements in management and work allocation. The majority of the employees work for companies with 2 to 500 employees, but the majority of firms lie in the 25 or less employees level. The industry recruits its staff principally at school-leaving age and has a high rate of staff turnover because of its high proportion of female labour, which involves a considerable reduction in efficiency because of the skills that have to be acquired by machine operators. Labour problems are likely to be created by a reduction in the number of operatives entering the industry which will be aggravated by the raising of the school-leaving age in 1972. There is also a high level of competition from lower labour cost countries at the cheaper non-fashion end of the market. The industry has responded to the competition by exporting to those countries which have high labour costs in comparison to the UK. This cannot be a long-term solution, and to maintain its position, the industry must significantly raise productivity possibly by as much as 50 per cent over a decade. Further progress can be achieved by extending the management improvements to the remainder of the industry, but strong pressures can be anticipated for new types of machinery which would enable the garment manufacturer to get by with a reduced labour force and possibly having a lower average of skill.

From the point of view of product innovation, the answer would appear to be the increased use of mechanical aids or new machinery, and the next question to be answered is what type of machinery would command the best market. The process of garment manufacture is illustrated schematically in Figure 4.1 with current processes following the lines towards the left-hand side of the diagram. The upper group of processes relate to fabric production, and are part of the textile, rather than the garment industry, and as garment machinery manufacturers we are concerned with the lower sections of the figure. A cost analysis indicates that roughly 50 per cent of the ex-works cost of a garment is contributed by the raw material, 25 per cent relates to overheads and profit, and 25 per cent to direct labour. Of the direct labour cost 75 per cent is associated with the seaming process, and less than 10 per cent associated with cutting, pressing and finishing respectively. The most obvious area for improvement is the seaming process, and this can be divided into a number of categories. We can deduce the total number of sewing machines currently in use in the UK from a study of the employment statistics. If we can devise an improved seaming process the potential market will depend upon the productivity of the new product compared with that of existing machines, together with its versatility. Surprisingly enough, the existing sewing machines are only actually sewing for some 10 to 20 per cent of their time, with the remainder of the time being spent by the operative in handling the fabric. In the first instance, therefore, an improved seaming process needs to concentrate on the problems of fabric handling rather than, for example, increased sewing speed.

Thus, we have now arrived at a point where we have identified a potential market, and in the broadest terms the type of product that is needed to satisfy that market. Now the problem becomes a need to design and develop a machine that will satisfy some or all of the requirements of the potential market. The design engineers will have the problem of producing a solution which will enable the market researcher to go back to the potential customers and explore the market for a new specifically defined product in much greater depth and eventually to arrive at sales forecasts.

Before this is done however, there are a number of other considerations that the market researcher should look at. What are the advantages or disadvantages of sewing *v.* welding or adhesive processes? Technical comparisons of speed, cost and seam characteristics and the potential improvements of the individual processes give an indication of their relative merits. One also needs to question whether current methods of manufacturing garments will continue. The processes of whole-knitting, direct garment manufacture from fibre, or the production of disposable garments on a large scale cannot be ignored. The current state of these competing technologies must be taken into account when assessing the viability of any new product aimed at the existing

Figure 4.1 Operations in garment manufacturing processes

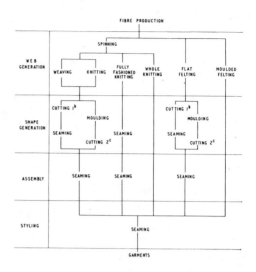

(a) 'FELTING' is used for the production of non-woven webs.
(b) 'CUTTING 1' is used for skilled cutting designed to minimize waste and to feed shape information into components.
(c) 'CUTTING 2' is used for less skilled cutting designed to separate formed components from the web.

industry. The general attitude of the industry to change, and its ability to invest in new processes will be an important factor in making this assessment.

We also have to look, and often make educated guesses, as to the actions of competing machinery manufacturers faced with the same problem as ourselves. We must take into account the implications of such competition in formulating our sales forecasts.

The degree to which fashion influences the acceptability of an innovation must be looked at in this field. How adaptable does the machine have to be, and what range of demands will be made upon it? The answer to this depends on the type of machine envisaged and the sector of the market concerned, but taken overall fashion change should not be difficult to accommodate at the large-scale production end of the spectrum, where automation or mechanization is likely to find its largest market for obvious reasons.

The market researcher must attempt to convince the potential customers that there is a need for a product which will result in a positive demand from the industry. He must also get across the conviction that the product his firm intends to develop meets the real needs and enters the most profitable area of business, and that there is no danger of early obsolescence. When all the omens are favourable, the design and development phases can be continued with greater confidence, and the whole project moves into top gear.

The analysis and detailed understanding of a consumer industry can be a lengthy business, and could well occupy one man year if undertaken from scratch. Subsequent up-dating of the statistics and keeping abreast of trends and developments is a much simpler activity, and the initial investment will prove useful in all subsequent dealings with that industry. Most market research departments will already have a lot of the basic statistics of its customer industries to hand and analysis will be much less of a time-consuming activity.

Case-study 2 – Identifying the Markets for a Defined New Material

The above example refers to the earlier stages of market research where one is looking for a product area in which to work. Once the product has been defined the market research can go into it in much greater depth. The case considers carbon fibre for which a market survey was required in order to determine what investment should be made in a R & D programme. The material had been produced on a laboratory scale, so that its properties were known, and some preliminary work had been done on scaling-up the production process, so that the costs of pilot scale production were known within reasonable limits.

The first question to be asked is, what advantages does the material have over other competing materials for which it may be substituted, and who will benefit from these advantages? That is, who are the potential customers?

The strength and rigidity modulus of a number of filamentary and whisker materials are summarized in Table 4.1. From this it can be seen that for a given stiffness or strength in a particular application a smaller weight of carbon fibre would be required than most other materials. Additionally, carbon fibre is a good conductor of heat and electricity, and also acts as a solid lubricant. The fibre itself is so fine that it has little individual strength, and to realize the advantageous properties a large number of fibres must be held together rigidly in place, so that they act in concert.

Reductions of weight for constant strength or stiffness clearly have potential value in two major areas of activity. These are transportation, where the weight of the vehicle itself can have an important bearing on fuel costs, and in self-supporting structures where the weight of the structure has some bearing on the strength to which its members must be designed. In addition there are a number of other areas of application where localized strengthening could be of value, or where current materials have serious limitations and could profitably be replaced. Each of these end-uses can be explored separately.

The aerospace industry is an obvious place to begin the study. Desk research quickly shows that significant inroads have already been made by various plastic materials and particularly by glass-fibre reinforced plastic (grp). The Trident contains 350 lbs of plastic materials, the Comet 500 lbs, and the Boeing 727 5,000 lbs. One estimate has indicated that the weight-saving to be made in aircraft by replacing aluminium alloy by structural composites could be of the order of 30 per cent. Comparison of carbon fibre with grp and aluminium alloy indicates that for components designed on an equal stiffness basic weight savings of up to 50 per cent can be achieved, and such weight savings are claimed to be worth £6 to £20 per lb for subsonic aircraft and very much more for supersonic aircraft. Thus, for subsonic aircraft the use of 0.5 lbs of carbon fibre to produce 1 lb of composite, so replacing 2 lbs of grp would be economic with a carbon fibre cost of the order of £10 per lb.

The total structural weight of aircraft can easily be determined, and fieldwork can yield design advice on the proportion of the alloys which are used in the form of unidirectionally stressed components that might be amenable to replacement by fibre composites. This in turn leads directly to the market potential for carbon fibre, though it must be remembered that major structural changes in existing aircraft are not likely to take place, and the market has been successfully proved. Thus, the market research will be concerned not only with the acceptability of the material, but more importantly the time scale of its development.

Non-structural applications in the aerospace field arise from the possibility of replacing grp composites with carbon fibre. Tables 4.2 and 4.3 show the use of grp in the UK and when the study was done in 1967 it was known that the total grp consumption had risen from 3,500 tons in 1962 to 12,000 tons in 1966 in rough proportion to the polyester market. The latest break-down figures related to 1963 and the levelling off in UK aircraft production led us to believe that the use of grp would not have continued to increase after 1963. The possible market for carbon fibre composites was, therefore, taken to equate to that quantity needed to replace the best estimate of current grp usage in aircraft.

Table 4.1 Properties of metals, whiskers, fibres and composites

	Ultimate Tensile Strength ($\times 10^6$ psi)	Young's Modulus ($\times 10^6$ psi)	Density (g/cc)	Specific Strength ($\times 10^6$ psi cc/g)	Specific Modulus ($\times 10^6$ psi cc/g)
Metals:					
High tensile steel	0.19	30	7.9	0.024	3.8
Molybdenum	0.20	43	10.2	0.020	4.2
Titanium	0.28	16.7	4.7	0.060	3.6
Aluminium	0.09	10.6	2.7	0.033	3.9
Magnesium	0.03	6.1	1.75	0.005	3.5
Beryllium	0.25	44	1.85	0.135	24
Fibrous, Polycrystalline or Amorphous:					
Wood (spruce parallel to grain)	—	—	—	—	3.8
Asbestos (crocidolite)	0.85	27	2.5	0.34	10.8
Boron	0.35	55	2.3	0.15	24
Carbon (UC Thornel)	0.20	25	2.0	0.10	12.5
Carbon (RAE I)	0.30	60	2.0	0.15	30
Carbon (RAE II)	0.43	33	1.74	0.24	19
Silica	0.51	11	2.2	0.23	5.0
E-Glass	0.25	10	2.54	0.098	3.9
High tensile glass	0.38	12	2.54	0.15	4.7
Whiskers					
Graphite	2.8	100	2.2	1.27	46
Aluminium oxide	2.2	76	4.0	0.55	19
Silicon nitride	1	55	3.1	0.32	18
Silicon carbide	3	100	3.2	0.94	31
Composites					
50 $^V/_O$ parallel silicon nitride in resin	—	27.8	2.2	—	12.6
30 $^V/_O$ random silicon nitride in resin	0.004	3.0	1.8	0.002	1.36
65 $^V/_O$ graphite whiskers in epoxy resin	0.160	20	1.87	0.086	10.7
75 $^V/_O$ boron fibre in epoxy resin	0.32	36	2.05	0.156	17.5
Random glass fibre 30 $^V/_O$ in Nylon-6	0.017	1.0	1.39	0.012	0.72
Parallel 40 $^V/_O$ glass fibre in resin	0.04	4.0	1.67	0.024	2.4
Parallel 50 $^V/_O$ glass fibre in resin	0.11	5.0	1.85	0.060	2.7
Parallel 40 $^V/_O$ carbon fibre in resin	0.10	22	1.54	0.065	14
Asbestos felt 37$^V/_O$ in resin	0.05	5.0	1.65	0.030	3.0
Beryllium 65 $^V/_O$ in resin	0.097	28.0	1.61	0.060	17
20 $^V/_O$ Mo wire in Ti alloy	0.14	21.5	5.82	0.024	3.7

Table 4.2 UK polyester consumption for reinforced plastic

Application	1963 (%)	1963 (tons)	1963 (%)	1963 (tons)	1964 (%)	1964 (tons)	1965 (%)	1965 (tons)	1966 (%)	1966 (tons)
Road, rail and air	30	3700	19	2600	18	3400	19	4800	20	5600
Translucent panels	25	3100	21	2800	19	3500	17	4300	17.5	4900
Other buildings	2	250	2	270	3	600	3	700	4	1100
Marine	16	2000	18	2400	17	3200	18	4600	17	4700
Electrical	5	610	4	540	4	700	3	700	2.5	700
Pipe and chemical plant	5	610	4	540	6	1100	8	2000	8.5	2400
Miscellaneous	–	–	12	1600	9	1700	9.5	2400	8	2200

The percentages related to total polyester production of which about 80 per cent is used for reinforced end-products. Both imports and exports of polyester resin have run at about 1,000 tons per annum since 1963 with slightly more imported; the import excess amounted to 500 tons for 1966, which is 1.8 per cent of total consumption.

Figures are based on Board of Trade data as quoted in annual January Market Survey Issues of British Plastics 1963 to 67

Table 4.3 Glass-fibre reinforced plastic usage in the UK

Use	Years 1962 (%)	1963 (%)
Road and rail transport	31	20
Air and missiles		6
Translucent panels	28	28
Boats	20	18
Electrical	10	10
Consumer	–	12
Pipes and chemical plant	5	–
Miscellaneous	6	6
Total weights grp (tons)	15,000	17,000

Courtesy British Plastics Annual Review, January 1964

This estimate tied in with information from other sources concerning non-structural weight.

All of the aerospace markets looked as though they could be significantly penetrated, provided that the price of carbon fibre was reduced sufficiently, and the users could be satisfied that it fully met their requirements.

Another general area of interest is shipbuilding, where weight savings are of very much lower value than in the aerospace field, since the ratio of structural weight to cargo is very much lower. In this area similar considerations to those described above led to the conclusion

that carbon fibre would need to reach prices in the order of 50 pence to 60 pence per lb before it could become competitive. Hovercraft could be of more interest as they lie between the marine and aviation fields and have specific problems, such as salt-water corrosion where carbon fibre composites would offer an advantage.

Some 100,000 tons of grp were used for road and rail application in 1966 with a growing market. In this area new materials must often compete with, for example, sheet steel, and grp has suffered from slow production rates due to the comparatively lengthy curing times of resins. However, significant weight savings can be achieved, for example, on road tankers. In one instance a saving of 19.5 cwt was obtained by replacing a steel tank with grp which increased mileage by 8.6 per gallon, saving the user £90 per year. Another manufacturer claimed that it was economic to save 1.5 tons weight at a premium of £300. These factors suggest that weight savings may be valued at 10 pence to 25 pence per lb for commercial operators. However, carbon fibre could not compete with grp in this type of application until its price had fallen significantly below £1 per lb unless other specific advantages could be identified. A large number of other potential markets, including containers, building, civil engineering, chemical plant and electric power transmission were explored in a similar way. In each case the question being asked was how much would a potential customer be prepared to pay for the advantages that he might derive from the use of carbon fibre composites.

The data was then assembled to give potential market sizes at different carbon fibre prices at a series of future dates. The price demand curves were not smooth continuous curves of the classic type, but showed a sharp discontinuity, due to the fact that the market is divided into three readily identifiable categories. Aerospace is prepared to pay a fairly high premium for weight-saving. In specialized applications or for reinforcement in local areas a fairly high premium might be paid, but lower than that for the aerospace industry, whilst for general purpose usage as a replacement for conventional materials the price would have to fall to the region of a few pence per lb. (Figure 4.2).

The next factor to be resolved is the price at which the product can be made. In the first instance a rough calculation was done on the basis of the known cost of the raw materials and the estimated costs of the pilot plant. This was then scaled up to commercial sizes.

Overseas markets were looked at briefly, but the possible effects of overseas production of a competing product were considered in greater depth. The implications of large-scale production in the US for example on the prices at which they could supply fibre, bearing in mind the lead time held by the UK, gave an indication that a British producer should be viable in the face of competition.

In this instance the potential markets were more than adequate to justify investment in R & D as the value of the product to the aircraft manufacturer and its expected cost of production would have been sufficient to give a fairly rapid pay-back on the development expenditure and plant costs. As information about the product became more widely known and potential users more able to assess its potential value to them, it would obviously be necessary to undertake periodic reappraisals as a result of which one's views of the market would be modified with regard to outlets, like penetration and time scale.

In addition to the simple comparative economic approach described above there is a need to evaluate carbon fibre against potentially competing materials such as ceramic filaments and whiskers. This is necessary to determine if the material we are developing is the best product or whether someone else could produce an alternative and cheaper product which would affect our potential markets.

The carbon fibre survey is a fairly typical example of the comparative economic approach to assessing new product markets at the earlier stages of their development. Essentially one is asking oneself what are the advantages of our new product, how much would people be prepared to pay for it, how much would it cost us to make, and hence does it appear worthwhile, bearing in mind potential competition from other products and companies? To assess the latter a fairly wide general knowledge of technology and of the ability of competitors is clearly very necessary.

Case-study 3 – The Market for a New Tool

A somewhat similar approach to that in case-study 2 has been applied in evaluating the market for hydrostatic extrusion equipment. Hydrostatic extrusion is a process whereby a metal is extruded through a die by means of fluid pressure. The process has certain advantages over conventional extrusion as lower forces are required to achieve the desired effect. There are a number of variants of the process involving augmentation of the extrusion force by the use of a mechanical ram, or by drawing on a length of the extruded product, and a rotary extrusion method known as hydrospin. The use of one form or another of augmentation assists in controlling extrusion and overcomes a number of difficulties associated with the purely hydrostatic process. Each variant has its own process economics and its own particular advantages.

Having first ascertained what the process involves and what its potential advantages over other processes might be the potential areas of application can be defined.

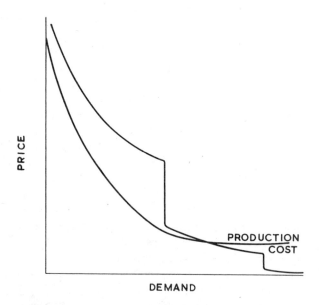

Figure 4.2 Price/demand curves (idealized).

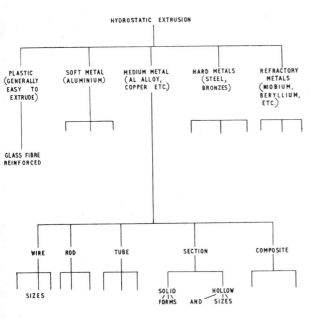

Figure 4.3 Hydrostatic extrusion.

A = Allotted annual component of capital cost plus interest where appropriate.

L = Annual labour costs including maintenance and managerial services.

W = Billet weight.

R_T = Annual output rate in terms of billets.

D_n = Cost of dies.

N_n = Die life in billets per die.

R_n = Annual output of billets for nth die.

P = Pressure vessel or replaceable liner cost.

F = Cycle life of vessel or liner.

M = Annual running cost of machine (power, lubricant, etc.).

Y = Cost per ton of raw material.

f = Fraction of material converted to saleable product.

x = Scrap value of material as fraction of Y.

Q = Cost per ton of shaping and preparing billets for extrusion.

These can be conveniently set out as shown in Figure 4.3 and the very act of setting them down in this way forces one to consider the full range of possible outlets and reduces the risks of prematurely dismissing any one area without due consideration. In principle a very wide range of materials can be extruded, from plastics to refractory alloys, and these can be converted to a wide range of forms.

The first stage of market appraisal involved finding the potential costs of the products produced by the hydrostatic extrusion process. This was done by devising a simple equation which set out the cost of the product in terms of capital, labour, maintenance, die life, pressure vessels, fatigue life, wastage, and throughput rates. All of the parameters are uncertain at the earlier stages of development but it is possible to set them down in such a way that the relationships are explained (see below). The likely range in which these factors can fall can be set by discussion with internal specialists who have experience in this field. Upper and lower limits of the costs can then be calculated for different throughput rates and the comparative sensitivity of product cost to the various input costs can be assessed.

The cost per ton of product will be given by C where

$$C = \frac{1}{f}\left(\frac{A+L+M}{WR} + \left\{\frac{D_1 R_1}{N_1} + \frac{D_2 R_2}{N_2} + \ldots\right\}\frac{1}{WR} + \frac{P}{FW} + Y + Q\right)$$

$$-xY\frac{(1-f)}{f}$$

This having been done an approach can be made to the firms who produce products for which hydrostatic extrusion is expected to be a technically acceptable substitute for current practice. The processes with which hydrostatic extrusion will be competing are shown in Table 4.4 and the cost of each competing process has to be determined in order to compare it with the cost of our new process. Very often this cannot be done with any degree of certainty as this sort of information is not readily made available. Though a crude approximation can be made from the market prices this sort of approach is usually so unreliable as to be useless. Usually it is a case of again applying upper and lower limiting values to the cost factors in a similar way to that done for the hydrostatic extrusion process. An added complication is that in reality one wishes to compare the costs of the competing processes as they will be in several years' time when presses have been developed and can be supplied. Likely improvements in the existing processes must, therefore, be taken into account. In this instance the forecasts of cost changes were based upon judgement of the potential for development bearing in mind the time for which the existing process has already been in use.

Once this comparative costing exercise has been carried out it should be apparent which types of product are likely to offer markets for the new process. The next stage is to determine more accurately what the potential market for the actual presses will be. A number of features assume importance. In the first place the price per unit product is highly sensitive to the throughput

Table 4.4 Competing processes

	Principle	**Other**
Wire	Drawing	Hot extrusion Propertzi process GE Dip process
Rod	Rolling mills	Hot extrusion
Tube	Rolling mills Drawing	Rolling and welding
Sections	Rolling Drawing Machining	Precision casting Powder metallurgy
Composite products	Cladding and rollings	

rate, and since the size of the press is determined by the size of the feedstock there is an effective minimum throughput rate at which the new process can substitute for the old. Therefore, it is necessary to examine the structure of the semi-finished metal product industry to ascertain which firms have sufficiently large throughputs to enable them to make use of the new process. This required minimum throughput can range from a very high level for things like copper rod and large sections, down to quite small throughputs for fine wire.

Having identified those firms which can be regarded as potential customers it then becomes necessary to examine the state of their markets. Unless these markets are growing it is highly unlikely that they will be eager to invest in new equipment. We must also consider the age, state, and degree of utilization of existing equipment in the industry, because if there is much spare capacity then there will be little incentive to install new equipment. The potential customer will have to compare the cost of installing the new process with the marginal cost of continuing to operate his existing process and this is a very tough obstacle to overcome, unless the existing process is proving excessively expensive or inefficient, or if demand is growing so rapidly that new plant has to be installed anyway. Basically, one is trying to estimate when the individual customer is likely to make his purchase. There is little point in asking the customer himself, since unless he is already actively considering installing new plant he will be perfectly content to wait and see what your development produces before giving any opinion. One has, therefore, to try to anticipate his actions and make a forecast of the likely rate of introduction of the new process into the industry.

In general it is preferable to make two forecasts. One

a pessimistic one based upon slow development allied with high costs and low incentive, the other an optimistic one based upon rapid development and a more rapid penetration of the market. This will then enable management to assess the risks against the potential returns.

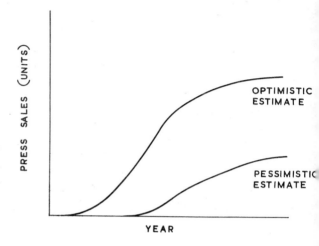

Figure 4.4 Market estimates.

Ideally one would hope to be able to attach probability distributions to the uncertain elements, or alternatively separate probabilities may be attached to a range of outcomes. This can be done in the hydrostatic extrusion case by setting distributions to the possible elements of cost in cost equation given above and producing a new mean and distribution for the unit cost of the product. Estimates can then be made on the probable market penetration associated with each cost and a distribution of probability of attaining different market penetrations built up. This distribution will give the management a better appreciation of the risks and prospects than the extreme range picture, although the latter may be perfectly satisfactory for the large majority of cases where the extremes are such that the decision is clear regardless of which part of the range the market lies in.

If one reverts to the original product relevance tree, Figure 4.3, the sales of presses of different types and capacities can be deduced based upon the likely demand for wire machines, tube machines, etc., and on the types of metal which have to be extruded and the extrusion ratios necessary. This information indicates the likely best individual markets, and the best types of equipment to develop and will assist in concentrating effort in the most potentially profitable areas.

This particular case-study serves to illustrate a number of important points about the assessment of new product demand. First, it is essential that the properties of the product or process are understood. Second, the attractiveness of the innovation must be viewed from the point of view of a potential customer, and this demands a fairly thorough knowledge of his business. Third, there is a considerable element of uncertainty in all estimates, particularly in the early stages of development so that the market cannot be described as a single figure outcome, but must be described in the form of a possible range, or better as a probability distribution. The whole purpose of R & D assisted by market research is to reduce the margins of uncertainty and to give greater confidence in forecasts so that their precision can be increased progressively as one approaches the production stages and the rate of expenditure increases. If proper decisions are to be made by management the true uncertainty in the market and the factors contributing to this need to be examined and expressed very clearly.

In this particular study, as in most, a 100 per cent sample of all producers of semi-finished products was clearly out of the question. A preliminary screening was undertaken to identify the major companies in the area, and a sample was drawn from these in order to ensure that well in excess of 50 per cent of total UK output was covered in the immediately important fields. Not a great deal of attention was given to the steel sector because the pressures required were well in excess of those that could be obtained in the short-term, though the benefits of attaining them looked potentially large.

Markets and Sales

Both the carbon fibre and hydrostatic extrusion examples were initially aimed at determining the potential markets for the products and the relevant time scales. However, the markets and sales do not necessarily mean the same thing. The potential market for a new product or process will never be realized unless confidence in the product has been established. Very few firms will be willing to disturb their production lines to introduce new untried products or processes unless they can be assured of an improvement in profitability. Thus, any innovation starts out in life with a 'credibility gap' and the means by which this is to be overcome needs to be studied from the earliest stages to ensure that the markets are ripe when the product finally emerges. The problem of generating confidence in a new large machine such as a hydrostatic extrusion press is no simple matter, since confidence can only be gained by the practical use of the equipment on a production scale for a reasonable period of time. This factor becomes increasingly important as development nears completion, but if the problem of creating confidence looks insurmountable to the sales team there would scarcely be any point in beginning the development in the first place.

Summary and Conclusions

This article has sought to illustrate some aspects of forecasting in the new product field by reference to real case-studies. The approaches described are not the only ones available, and a fuller treatment of other methods is given in a publication by IMRA.

The first example was aimed at indicating how one could set about the methodical appraisal of a customer's needs and use them as a guide to potentially profitable areas of research and development. At this stage the uncertainty in the forecast may be very high and its sole intention is to orientate resource allocation in the most rewarding directions. The outcome of this will then lead on to further market research in greater depth similar to that described in the second and third case-studies.

The other studies represent the second stage of depth of analysis in which one is attempting by comparative economic methods to set some limits on the potential market. These markets will be far better defined than the ones identified by the first study, but will still contain a high element of uncertainty because, at an early stage of development, costs, market acceptability, competition, and alternative developments can only be taken into consideration in a fairly general manner. Market surveys of this kind are useful as a more detailed guide to the allocation of resources to research and development activity, and for weighting the importance of different versions of the development.

The developments which follow the second stage market survey will yield more precise information on properties, and will yield a prototype product which can be used for test marketing so that the reliability of future market estimates can be increased still further.

In the new product field the market research, R & D, and marketing groups within the firm have to maintain close liaison and act in concert. All are dependent on each other for information which will make their own jobs easier and improve the quality and profitability of their output. There is no short-cut to market research in the new product field, a first essential is knowledge;

knowledge of the product, knowledge of the technological and economic environment, and knowledge of one's customers and their business. This knowledge must be allied with judgement in producing reasoned marke[t] appraisals. Neither is sufficient on its own, and both ca[n] only be gained with experience.

Exercises & Study Questions

Product Strategy

What are the stages of the product life-cycle? What are the differences between each stage in the product itself and in the market?

2 'Product strategy is a top management responsibility'. Comment on this statement.

3 Describe, in outline, a product strategy for each of the following organizations: a manufacturer of branded foods, a chemical company, the National Health Service.

4 What is the difference between corporate strategy and product strategy?

5 What businesses are the following organizations in: Shell Transport & Trading Co., Ltd, United Kingdom Atomic Energy Authority, Marks & Spencer Ltd, George Wimpey & Co., Ltd? What is their current product range and how might it be extended?

6 What are the essential stages in the product planning process? Who should be responsible for each stage?

7 Compare the contrast the following product strategies: 'First to market', 'Follow the leader', 'Me-too'.

8 'Much accent has been placed in recent years on the role of formal planning systems in the development and control of business activity.' What systems have been proposed for product planning? What are their strengths and weaknesses?

9 Describe the various techniques of technological forecasting. Suggest a possible application for each technique.

10 Your research department have come up with an idea for a powerful cutting device based on lasers. Outline a programme of market research to help determine whether you should proceed with the development of this idea.

Part II
Product Development

Introduction

The control of an organization's R & D activity is not easy. It is hard enough to decide on the size of the total budget, let alone how it should be allocated between the various competing projects. Little is known at the outset about the cost of taking an idea through to a marketable product, and about all that can be said is that the final cost will usually be considerably higher than the first estimate. A project's proponents are, understandably, enthusiastic about it and may shade the cost estimates to make it appear more attractive. Once it is under way and a fair amount of money has been spent it is difficult for management to cut their losses and abandon the idea. Sunk R & D costs are usually sunk without trace, and the claim goes that it will only need a couple of thousand pounds more. . . .

It is also difficult to judge whether the product will sell, and if it does, what the connection is between price and volume. Product research and market research must go hand in hand. The whole process is an uncertain one and managers must think clearly and plan carefully. Duckworth proposes three methods for estimating the total R & D budget. The analytical approach is based on the assumption that, if a company ceases to innovate, its profits will fall to zero over a number of years. By discounting back the difference between present profits and those in the future if no R & D were done it is possible to estimate what investment in R & D is needed. Alternatively, firms can match their expenditure to that of similar industries for which global figures are available, or build up a budget from the three categories of defensive, offensive and fundamental research. Read suggests a number of ways of allocating the budget. He proposes a linear programming technique, to enable best use to be made of the men, materials and money at the research manager's disposal. The trouble with this is that costs and benefits are seldom known with any degree of accuracy and this can invalidate the LP approach. The use of simulation is a partial answer to this problem.

In the next article of this section Andrews describes a method of reducing the uncertainty inherent in project cost estimation and of defining the upper limit of the financial risk involved. Two cost estimates are made: one is for the minimum programme that will be carried out in any case, even if everything goes perfectly, and the other is for the programme which will be required if everything goes wrong. The actual cost must be somewhere between these two, and the degree of certainty attached to that cost depends on how different the two estimates are. His method shows what needs to be done to bring them closer together.

Thomas, in the final article, presents some empirical evidence of forecasting accuracy in an R & D department. He found that forecasts varied widely and unpredictably as projects proceeded, and that initial estimates were often sufficiently inaccurate to render any formal selection procedure worthless. He stresses the need for documentation so that an organization can learn from past mistakes.

5.

The Determination of Total Research Effort
by W.E. Duckworth B.I.S.R.A.

Reprinted from the Operational Research Quarterly, Vol. 18 (4), December 1967 with permission.

Why Do Research?

The first fundamental question to ask in any survey of the factors affecting decisions about research in an industrial organization is, 'Why do any research at all?' This may seem a somewhat trivial query in present-day circumstances, but it is well to bear in mind that organized industrial research is a phenomenon of the twentieth century and nearer the middle than the beginning of the century at that.[1]

To put it at its crudest the strongest motivation behind industrial research and development is survival. It is not the only factor affecting a firm's survival (although some organizations in their euphoria and overenthusiasm – often in exculpation for neglect over past years – act as if it were), but it is one of the most important. An analysis of the fundamental operations essential to the survival of a company[2] shows that there are really three: innovation, manufacture and sale. The firm that does not sell its product, whether this be a manufactured article or a service, will clearly fail. Equally, the company which does not make or produce a saleable product or service will go bankrupt. What is often a little harder to appreciate is that the firm which is not prepared to innovate, to change its techniques and methods and occasionally its product, will also go out of business. This applies even at the lowest level of entrepreneurial activity. The one-man shopkeeper who does not take in new lines of goods, does not change his display, does not improve his service, will in the end drive his customers into the arms of those more enterprising than himself.

Why Evaluate Investment in Research?

Since innovation is one of the essential ingredients of survival it behoves a company to organize it on the same lines and with the same status as the other two requirements – manufacture and sale. It should have equal consideration for investment funds and not be treated as something on which money could be spent if available – a charity to be supported out of surplus profits. If this is done too long there will eventually be no surplus profits out of which to support the 'charity'.

It is therefore necessary to treat investment in innovation with, as far as possible, the same hard-headed calculation which attends investment in manufacturing equipment and sales promotion campaigns. Since, in most manufacturing industries a major source of innovation is R & D the two will be considered synonymous from now on.[1] The R & D need not necessarily be that promoted within an individual organization; the definition will include licences, patents and know-how purchased when required from outside sources. To avoid repetition all this will be classed as 'research'.

The difficulties of treating research investment in the same way as manufacturing investment are clear, but this is no valid reason for baulking the issue and running away from the problem. It is not yet possible to calculate the rate of return from a given investment in research because the very nature of innovation is the emergence of something new which cannot be predicted. Indeed, as Sir Solly Zuckerman[3] has pointed out, attempts to plan and predict research progress can stifle its creativity. All this is, however, to state the problem. It does not excuse us from attempting its solution. One of the functions of operational research is, after all, to solve problems of organizations which have so far defied resolution.

The determination of sales and advertising expenditure bears some relation to the problem of determination of research effort since the outcome is uncertain at the time the investment is made. This has not prevented operational research workers from making fairly sturdy attempts at sensible evaluation criteria,[4],[5] and a similar empirical approach to assessment of research effort will be suggested later in this paper.

The problem is rather more important in the case of research expenditure than with sales expenditure because the time scale for assessment of the response to a sales campaign is fairly short, usually weeks or months, sometimes days. Research often takes years to mature. The time lag between a really fundamental discovery in science and its widespread application is rarely less than 20 years. Hence, a company which invests too little in research can fall years behind and whole industries can decay until drastic action is taken. Some remedy is available in the purchase of know-how and the placing of sponsored research contracts, but a company which purchases too much of its knowledge from outside finds itself always behind in the race.

As will be shown later, there is a strong correlation between research expenditure and rate of growth. A company which desires to expand at a certain rate needs to determine the appropriate expenditure for this growth rate for, if it spends too little, it may lack the internal stimulus creating the new products and processes it needs. If it spends too much it may find itself wasting ideas and resources. It is vital, too, for the nation itself to have a realistic estimate of what it should spend on research. Lately, what was once regarded as a charity is in danger of being considered a monster. Government expenditure on civil research doubled in the years 1960 to 1966 from £110 million to £220 million per annum. In 1939 to 1940 it was only £4 million. Voices are now being raised against such a rapidly rising rate of expenditure. Before too much action is taken to check the growth of R & D it is necessary to assess whether there is a need to check it and, if so, at what level.

How To Evaluate Research Expenditure

There are two main approaches which can be considered. One is a broad approach of examining possible relationships between company or industry performance and total R & D expenditure irrespective of its composition. The other is a synthetic approach of attempting to build up an estimate of total research effort from the possible component parts – (a) fundamental research, (b) defensive research aimed at preserving the competitive position of existing products and processes and (c) offensive research aimed at developing new products and processes.

The broad approach will be considered first because it is in this field that most information is available, although of a meagre kind, and this enables some lessons at least to be observed. This approach itself falls into two categories, the analytical and the comparative.

A striking attempt has been made at the analytical approach by Hart.[6] He takes as his thesis the necessity for a company to carry out R & D in order to survive and calculates the maximum amount it is worth a company spending for this purpose. He assumes, with considerable justification, that if a company ceases to

innovate, its profits will fall to zero over a number of years, the time taken depending upon the 'obsolescence rate' of its products. Typical curves of this decline in profitability are shown in Figure 5.1 taken from Hart's article in which curves B to F represent the likely profit history of companies which cease to invest in research and in which the obsolescence rate is declining from B to F. Line A on the graph represents the target profit history if R & D is continued, i.e., the *status quo*. The area between line A and the appropriate curve in the family B to F gives a measure of the total investment it is worth the company making in R & D in order to survive at its current level.

Hart makes use of discounted cash flow techniques to determine the time scale of Figure 5.1 and, hence, it represents the realistic situation facing a company. If it is not prepared to invest in R & D in order to maintain its profitability at line A, it might just as well dispose of its assets and invest in someone else's enterprise. This is equally true if it has to spend more on innovation than indicated by the diagram in order to survive. Hart's analysis therefore predicts the *maximum* amount it is worth a firm investing in this one aspect of its activities.

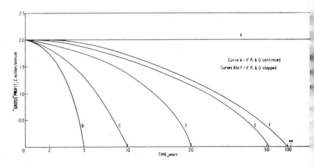

Figure 5.1 The relationship between gross profit and product obsolescence rate.

Hart's thesis has a strong intuitive appeal. It predicts that a company making a product which is rapidly obsolescent will have to spend relatively more on innovation than a company which is in a more stable market. This is logical and is also in accord with experience. Electronic equipment has a very high rate of obsolescence and the electronics industry spends a lot on research.[7] Buildings, on the other hand, are not replaced with the same frequency as transistor radios and the building industry has traditionally been resistant to innovation.

Hart has, in fact, calculated how the expenditure on

research should vary with obsolescence rate for a company with an employed capital and annual turnover both equal to £12 million and an annual net profit before tax of 15 per cent of turnover. The relationship is shown in Figure 4.2, again taken from his article, and this shows that for a very low expected product life the maximum proportion worth spending on R & D rises to about 15 per cent whereas for very stable products it falls to about 3 per cent.

It must be borne in mind that those are estimates of *maximum* expenditure and also only relate, strictly, to the hypothetical company postulated above. Nevertheless, the curve is an interesting guideline from which some interesting conclusions can be drawn, as will be shown later.

One of the first observations is that Figure 5.2 relates only to survival at the existing level of activity, discounted of course into the future value of money. Most companies aim at growth and this can be provided for in the Hart analysis by increasing the slope of line A. If, for example, one were to postulate a quite moderate growth of profits of 2 per cent linear per annum then after 50 years the annual gross profit on Figure 5.1 would be £4 million per annum. To achieve this it would be worth spending at an additional maximum annual rate of £800,000 per annum, i.e., 7 per cent of turnover. Thus a curve parallel to that in Figure 5.2 but 7 per cent higher up the ordinate scale gives the requirement for a 2 per cent linear growth-rate. Correspondingly higher curves would be required for higher growth-rates.

To achieve really fast rates of growth it could be worth spending quite phenomenal amounts on R & D. There is, of course, the danger that excessive expenditure on research could cause premature obsolescence, as seems to have occurred in pharmaceuticals. This is all the

more reason for endeavouring to estimate an appropriate level of R & D expense.

The Comparative Approach

The above figures represent the maximum it is worth spending. Just how far is it necessary to spend these amounts? Some data are now available, from UK and US sources, on the relative amounts spent on R & D by various industries and the respective rates of growth of these industries.

Table 5.1 below shows the percentage of net output spent by various UK industries on R & D[8] and the obsolescence period anticipated for this expenditure according to Figure 5.2:[2]

Table 5.1

Industry	Percentage of net output on R & D	Anticipated life (years)
Aircraft	35.7	0.5
Electronic	11.9	16
Instruments	11.0	18
Electrical	9.8	19
Chemicals	6.0	61
Non-ferrous	2.1	>100
Ceramics, glass, cement, etc.	1.1	>100
Steel	0.9	>100
Food, drink, tobacco	0.6	>100
Wood, paper, printing	0.25	>100

Although the anticipated life of the firms in the various types of industry cannot be estimated with any

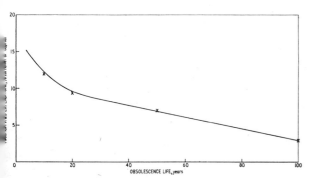

Figure 5.2 Maximum R & D expenditure as a function of obsolescence life.

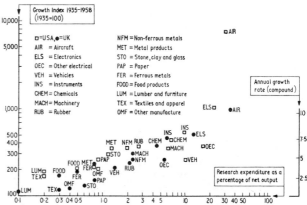

Figure 5.3 Research expenditure as a percentage of net output in 1958, and growth of industries 1935 to 1958.

certainty it seems likely that, with the possible exception of the aircraft industry, any firm which stopped development would disappear in a shorter time than that indicated by the above table.

Indeed, US and UK results[7] indicate that, on the above scale of expenditure, quite healthy growth-rates of up to 7.5 per cent have been possible with expenditure on research only up to 6 per cent of net output (Figure 5.3).

It is clear, therefore, that there is quite a substantial difference between what has been found in the past to be necessary to spend on R & D to achieve both survival and growth and what may be considered to be the maximum amount worth spending.

Should we then just accept this situation, be thankful that R & D is not costing as much as it might do, abandon the analytical approach and either rely upon the comparative approach, or try some other tack?

The indications are that life is not quite so comfortable as that; that although we may have got by so far without incurring expenditures comparable with those predicted by Hart the time may not be far off when we may be approaching these expenditures.

The reason is that research is becoming relatively more expensive, its productivity is declining. This is shown dramatically in Tables 5.2, 5.3 and 5.4 reproduced from an article by Croxton.[9]

Table 5.2 The relationship of US patent output to research expenditure.

Industrial research expenditure		US patents issued		
Year	$ million	Year	No.	No./$ million of research†
1953	3630	1956	46,800	12.9
1954	4070	1957	42,800	10.5
1955	4640	1958	48,400	10.4
1956	6590	1959	52,500	8.0
1957	7720	1960	47,200	6.1
1958	8350	1961	48,400	4.8
1959	9610	1962	55,700	5.8

† During third year preceding

These tables show how industrial research expenditure is related to the number of US patents issued, the number of scientific publications appearing, and plant and equipment investment.

It can be argued that these parameters, neither uniquely nor in combination, are a measure of research productivity. This may be so but they are certainly not unrelated to it. If a technologist does not, over the years, produce or contribute to the production of a patent, a paper or an idea worthy of capital investment he cannot be said to be very effective.

The disturbing feature of all three tables is that the return on research expenditure, as measured by all three criteria, has declined. Although these tables are specific to the US, and there are no similar tables available for the UK there is no reason to suppose that the findings are not general.

Table 5.3 The relationship of US scientific publications* to research expenditures

Industrial research expenditure		US scientific publications		
Year	$ million	Year	No.	No./$ million of research†
1953	3630	1956	22,000	6.1
1954	4070	1957	25,000	6.1
1955	4640	1958	28,000	6.0
1956	6590	1959	28,000	4.2
1957	7720	1960	28,000	3.7

* Abstracts of US articles appearing in *Chemical Abstracts*.
† During third year preceding.

Table 5.4 Relationship of plant and equipment investment to research expenditure – US conditions.

Industrial research expenditure		Plant and equipment investment		
Year	$ million	Year	$ million*	Ratio†
1953	3630	1956	47,300	13.1
1954	4070	1957	47,300	11.6
1955	4640	1958	39,400	8.5
1956	6590	1959	42,100	6.5
1957	7720	1960	45,300	5.9
1958	8350	1961	43,500	5.2
1959	9610	1962	46,100	4.8

* In constant 1957 dollars.
† To research expenditure three years before.

Falling research productivity is also emphasized by De Solla Price,[10] who shows that the cost per scientist has been doubling every ten years and rising as the fourth power of the number of *good* scientists. In the UK the percentage of GNP spent on R & D has risen as follows (Table 5.5):[6]

Table 5.5

Year	Percentage of GNP
1900	0.05
1938	0.25
1954	1.60
1963	2.70
1964	2.80

At its present rate of expansion this will equal the GNP by the year 2020.[11] The situation in the US is even more acute.[10]

It may be argued that a great deal of this expansion is due to the world military situation and is not bound to continue. Such statistics as there are available from purely industrial operations are not very comforting, however. The apparently satisfactory situation shown in Figure 4.3 may now be completely out of date since a survey by Ewell[12] has revealed that a growth rate of R & D expenditure of 10 per cent appears to be necessary to maintain a growth-rate of 3 per cent in the company's sales.

Clearly, a ceiling must be reached somewhere. The growth curve of R & D expenditure as a proportion of turnover or national income must be a logistic curve and not an exponential one. But how far up the curve are we? De Solla Price[10] suggests we are near the mid-point and that R & D expenditure may eventually settle at somewhere between 6 and 10 per cent of the GNP. However, before that happens there may be many fluctuations such as those shown in Figure 4.4 or new logistic curves may arise as in Figure 5.5. Curves of the latter type may arise in response to the future scientific challenge of developing countries which have hardly yet begun to tap their resources of scientific talent. As the pace of development quickens we may have to run faster still to stay in the same place. Toulmin[13] has discussed these curves further and pointed out that there may indeed be no clear upper bound to R & D expenditure, but that it may begin to lack definition as more and more of a company's activities became associated with innovation. When, for example, all factory processes are operated according to the techniques of evolutionary operation, who can then separate R & D costs from manufacturing costs? Figure 5.2 indicates how research expenditure rises with increasing obsolescence, particularly if some kind of economic growth is required. The more research, the more the development, the faster the obsolescence, and so the spiral rises. Standford Research Studies[14] of the life-cycles of products as technically

unsophisticated as home appliances have shown that the period from the time they were introduced until they reached their peak sales and began to decline dropped from 34 years for products introduced before 1920 to an average of 8 years for those introduced in the post-war period. In the aerospace industries products may be obsolete once the techniques of producing them have been learned.[15]

All this really sharpens the need for realistic determination of the amount of R & D effort it is worth mounting at any given time, especially for a country like Britain lacking both natural and financial resources and

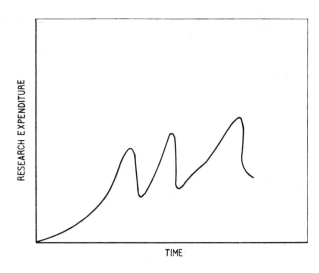

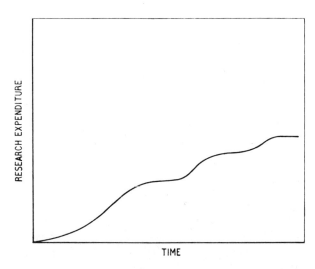

Figures 5.4 and Figure 5.5 Possible variations of R & D expenditure with time.

being forced more and more to live on its wits. If we lack the courage and conviction to spend enough then we shall rapidly lower our place in both the scientific and manufacturing worlds. If we spend too much we shall waste resources which should have been used elsewhere. There are already indications that we may have spent too much on the aircraft and atomic energy industries and not sufficient in shipbuilding and the constructional industries.

Since both the Hart type of analytical approach and the comparative approach both leave us with a great deal of uncertainty as to what the appropriate expenditure is, it may be useful to turn to a third techniue which can be called the synthetic approach.

The Synthetic Approach

This comprises building-up the required research expenditure from the three categories of defensive, offensive and fundamental research and is, broadly speaking, the method used currently by most companies for determining their research expenditure.

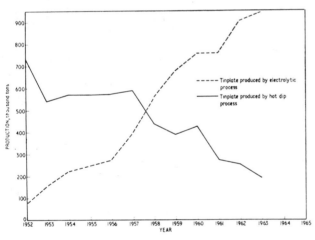

Figure 5.6 Tinplate production in the UK 1952 to 1963.

Defensive research is that needed to maintain the competitive position of existing products and processes and is generally devoted to cost saving and product improvements. Fairly realistic calculations can usually be made about the research expenditure which is worthwhile based upon the anticipated savings from successful projects.[16] The expenditure will clearly depend upon the number of processes and products in a company, the scope for cost reductions, etc., and the emergence of competitive products. The last point is illustrated for

tinplate in Figure 5.6. After 1957 it became clear that the electrolytic process was certain to replace the hot-dip technique and, hence, that further defensive expenditure on the latter would probably be wasted. This replacement of one product by another, e.g., thermionic valves by transistors, is one factor which must be borne in mind when applying Hart's technique to a particular situation.

The value of offensive research aimed at new products and processes is conditioned by the scope for innovation and availability of capital for exploitation of the research. Strongly allied with the latter is the need for the new products which would justify appropriate capital expenditure. It is possible that the British research effort in aircraft and atomic energy has been out of balance because there was neither the capital available nor the need to produce aircraft and power stations in the quantity which would justify the research.

It has been estimated that in the chemical industry from 5 to 15 dollars of new capital is required to exploit a dollar's worth of new product research.[17] This ratio appears to be particular to the money spent on research work directly related to the new product. An interesting study of ten chemical companies over a 13-year period[18] showed that, overall, capital expenditure needed to be three times research expenditure and that this total investment in research and capital expenditure yielded as good a return as the purchase of successful companies — a real alternative to investing in one's own company.

One method of determining the amount of spend on offensive research is therefore to relate it to the capital available to the company for exploitation. This is broadly the method used by the Rio Tinto Zinc Corporation in deciding its annual expenditure on trial boreholes in new mining areas, a situation analogous to new product research. Their ratio is in the region of 10 or 15:1.

It therefore seems that an important controlling factor in deciding the amount to spend on offensive research is the availability of capital to exploit the research, if successful. For an individual successful project something like ten to 15 times as much as the research costs will be needed for exploitation and clearly this must give every expectation of at least 15 per cent return to be worthwhile. For a company's overall research programme which will include defensive and fundamental research as well as some successful projects something between three and five times as much as will be needed in annual capital expenditure if the research effort is to be in balance. Table 5.4 shows how US industry is levelling-off at about this ratio.

It is interesting to compare the UK effort on aircraft and atomic energy research by this criterion. Aircraft cancellations have demonstrated only too clearly that the capital necessary to exploit aviation research has not been available in this country and, hence, the overall research expenditure was too high. Until the fairly recent escalation in the power station capital expenditure programme the level of atomic energy research seemed too high since, at £50 million per annum,[19] it needed a capital expenditure of £150 million per annum to justify it. This figure is fast being approached, however,[20] and therefore it can be argued with some justification that atomic energy research is now at an appropriate level. The *Financial Times* recently estimated that total capital expenditure in nuclear energy in Europe will have reached £12,000 million by 1990. The total research expenditure needed to justify this capital programme will then be between £2,500 and £4,000 million, or £60 to 100 million per annum. Therefore, the British nuclear research effort does not appear too large for future requirements *if* UK industry is to gain at least 50 per cent of the power-station contracts in Europe.

Finally, the proportion to be spent on fundamental research needs to be assessed. This is research aimed at finding out why and how phenomena occur. Applied research is the exploitation of these phenomena. Irrespective of whether a company carries out its own basic research or finances it from outside there are clear indications[17] that the more a company spends on research the greater must be its proportion spent on fundamental research, lest it misses whole new fields of discovery which could vitiate a large part of its applied research expenditure. In 1958 some large concerns in the US were spending 20 per cent of their research expenditure on basic research.[21] This has since probably been reduced, however.

Discussion

There are thus three techniques available by which a company may determine its appropriate research expenditure: the analytical method of Hart, the comparative approach and the synthetic one. More studies are clearly needed as to the relative value of these three solutions and, in particular, comparisons of the results of applying these three methods in particular circumstances. These studies will be far from easy because technical advance in any industry is not determined solely by its own research expenditure. A very striking illustration of this is provided by the comparison of the gas[22] and electricity[20] supply industries shown in Table 5.6. The research effort of the gas industry in relation to its sales has been consistently higher than that of the electricity industry and yet the rate of growth of the latter has been many times the former. Clearly, the electricity industry owes much to the research expenditure of manufacturing firms and to general technological

Table 5.6 Expenditure on R & D by the nationalized gas and electricity industries compared with sales of gas and electricity

	Gas			Electricity		
	1 R & D expenditure (£ million)	2 Sales of gas (£ million)	3 Sales therms x 10^9	4 R & D expenditure (£ million)	5 Sales of electricity (£ million)	6 Sales kWh x 10^9
1954-5	0.85	173.0	2.57	0.59	365.3	62.4
1955-6	1.00	185.1	2.59	0.67	369.9	63.3
1956-7	1.15	203.9	2.55	0.89	413.2	67.5
1957-8	1.22	210.2	2.59	1.10	464.3	72.7
1958-9	1.49	222.9	2.55	1.30	505.8	78.1
1959-60	1.37	222.3	2.54	2.20	537.8	85.7
1960-1	2.26	234.1	2.61	4.89	592.4	96.1
1961-2	3.24	248.8	2.68	6.07	669.9	103.7
1962-3	2.65	270.8	2.87	5.88	753.5	115.5
1963-4	3.10	277.8	2.92	5.76	821.5	121.5

advances which favoured the use of electricity rather than gas prior to the North Sea explorations.

Fairly urgent action is required, however, for the reasons stated earlier. Research expenditure is rising rapidly in many directions and there will continue to be many stimuli provoking still further rises in future. Productivity in research has declined and will decline still more. If resources are not to be wasted on a nationally disastrous scale then more realistic estimates must be made of the right proportion of research effort. In addition, the research carried out must be more efficiently planned.

Some people take the comfortable view that the growth of research will reach a natural limit at a country's capacity to produce scientists. Both De Solla Price[10] and Jewkes[23] show that we are still far below the expenditure level at which the supply of scientists becomes a real limitation. The choice is therefore ours — to learn how to estimate research expenditure on some national basis or to risk a profligate waste of skilled and expensive resources.

Conclusions

The Hart analysis shows that, in economic terms only, it is worthwhile to spend far more on R & D than we do at present. A study by Adams and Dirlan[24] showed that the American steel industry would not have needed the price increases it tried to win from President Kennedy in 1961 if it had spent much more on innovation in the previous decade. Research expenditure cannot, however, escalate too fast without being wasteful. It needs to be guided to an appropriate level. The studies discussed in this article suggest that an individual company should be spending about one-fifth of its future capital commitments on R & D if it is not to risk having to rely heavily on outside sources for its innovation or, even worse, to spend its money on equipment which will soon be outdated. The more advanced the technology the higher the ratio of R & D to capital expenditure. Hence, overall, this ratio is bound to rise since, if nothing else, the R & D should be effective in reducing the capital required to meet given production objectives.

Since the UK spends about 20 per cent of the GNP on capital goods its R & D expenditure should be at least 4 per cent of the GNP, not 2.6 per cent as at present. We must expect this percentage to rise to 7.5 per cent if we are to endeavour to be in the forefront of technological progress. When we reach this position, our balance of payments will be greatly improved because we should no longer need to import £400 million of capital goods annually, nor pay the US five times as much in license fees, etc., as we receive.

References

1 Barnes, C.E. (1964) Industrial research – Is it out-moded? *Business Horizons* 7, 85-92.
2 Brown, W.B.D. (1967) *Exploration in Management.* Heinemann, London.
3 Zuckerman, Sir S. (1964) *Opl Res. Q* 15, 287.
4 Benjamin, B. and Maitland, J. (1958) *Opl Res. Q.* 9, 207-217.
5 Ackoff, R. (1965) Allocation of sales effort, Proc. Conf. O.R. in Industry, Case Institute.
6 Hart, A. (1963) *Symposium on Productivity in Research*, pp. 27-32. Institution of Chemical Engineers, London.
7 National Institute (1962) *Economic Review* 20, 31.
8 *Industrial Research and Development Expenditure 1958* (1960) H.M.S.O., London.
9 Croxton, F.C. (1963) *Symposium on Productivity in Research*, pp. 8-15. Institution of Chemical Engineers, London.
10 De Solla Price, D.J. (1963) *Little Science, Big Science.* Columbia University Press, New York.
11 Blakeley, T.H. (1963) *Symposium on Productivity in Research*, p. 37. Institution of Chemical Engineers, London.
12 Ewell, R. (1955) *Chem. Engng News* 33, 2980.
13 Toulin, *Science Journal*, (August, 1966).
14 Stanford Research Institute (1962) *Planning, Action, Profits.*
15 Collier, D.W. (1963) in an Address to the National Security Industry Association, Washington, D.C., 14 March.
16 Mansfield, E. (1964) *J. Polit. Econ.* 72, No. 4, 319.
17 Vaughan, E. (1955) *Chem. Engng News* 31, 2277.
18 Yardstick for management. *Chem. Engng News* (1955) 33, 3606.
19 *Financial Times* (1965)1 April.
20 *Central Electricity Generating Board. Annual Reports.*
21 Little, A.D. (1958) *US Navy Report, No. P.B.* 151925.
22 *Gas Council, Annual Reports.*
23 Jewkes, J. (1960) *The Economic Journal* 70, 1.
24 Adams, Dirlan *Quaterly Journal Economics*, (May, 1966).

Notes

[1] This is really because no figures are available from any source about the total amount spent by firms on innovation, which would include innovations in administrative practice, etc. To treat this subject properly the whole expenditure on innovation should be considered.

[2] Figure 5.2 is not strictly apposite because net output and turnover are not equivalent. They are nearly so for the first few industries on Table 4.1, however, and the other industries have such a low obsolescence that the difference is immaterial.

6.

Approaches to R & D Project Selection
by Dr. A.W. Read

Reprinted from the IMRA Journal, Vol. 7 (3), August, 1971 with permission.

I am a member of a research department in the CEGB. I'd better make it clear before I start that I am basically still concerned with technical research. Research planning has been a part-time interest of mine for the last three years, but it's not my full-time activity and I don't claim to be a theoretical specialist. I'm a practitioner trying to apply to the real problems of a research department ideas which other people have put forward.

In addition to that I should also point out that I have been associated for the last two years with an R & D working party, at the Manchester Business School, and some of the ideas I shall mention have been developed here, so don't give me all of the credit or all of the blame for some of the ideas. I'll try and indicate, if necessary, where other people have contributed.

The main equation that governs research is research equals uncertainty. It's at the core of research; you can't escape it — without uncertainty there wouldn't be a research department. In this context I speak of technical research, but obviously the same thing applies where the word research is mentioned. This is at the absolute centre of what is being done.

The main problem in research departments is what research to do; what areas to investigate, what jobs to investigate in those areas, when to start, and when to stop. Now the broad areas of research are usually settled by the interests of the firm or the organization. The exceptions are either the 'way out' scientist in an industrial environment, who is so brilliant that you must hold on to him, but he's so unco-ordinated that you've got to let him do more or less what he wants, or university research, where the individual controls what he's going to do, within certain interests of the department. In general, however, the main research areas are settled by the interests of the firm. For example, in my own industry it would be extremely unlikely that we would spend most of our money on biology (although curiously enough we spend quite a bit of money in this area) but obviously as an engineering-based industry, most of our research money is spent on mechanical and electrical engineering types of problems. I'm a chemist, so the rule isn't proved, but it's basically correct.

Having settled the areas of interest and the rough size of the research department which in itself is an area that requires a great deal more attention, then what projects should be undertaken within these research areas? Now up till quite recently this has been very much a 'seat of the pants' decision, and as soon as you hear that you wonder if there isn't a better way of doing things. If there were a more ordered decision process, might it not produce a more ordered situation?

I think we've got to bring in my personal opinion here; that mathematical models of formal methods of research project selection and research resource allocation, are unlikely to be applicable in the immediate or even the distant future to what can be called fundamental research.

To choose an example from my own industry; super-conductivity. If this comes off, it's obviously going to be vital to the CEGB that we take full advantage of the new technology. But nobody can sit down at this moment of time and write an ordered list of projects to develop super-conductivity for transmission lines or for turbo-alternators or for electrical machines in general. So I would suggest that in areas such as this, that the organization has got to set aside a certain sum of money for pure gambling — to keep an interest in a particular problem area a certain amount of money must be spent, but the organization must not be too worried if the return doesn't appear for many years. The best analogy that I've heard for this is that of a sweepstake: a research sweepstake. If you don't buy a ticket, then you'll never get a prize. In the fundamental area, I think this is quite a good analogy. You've got to buy the tickets to get among the prizes, but you can't guarantee that you will ever get a prize.

So having got that out of the way, where can quantitative methods be useful? In the area, I would suggest, of development work and problem-solving; problem-solving in the longish term, the project taking one or two years rather than problem-solving in a very immediate sense.

A research manager often finds himself faced with a sea of men, and an array of research problems on which these men can be deployed. He therefore has two management problems, (a) to select the correct projects, and (b) to deploy his resources in the most efficient manner. This is what models are aimed at, this is the area in which they're trying to give the manager more information.

All models, however simple or complicated, need certain pieces of information. The problems that might be undertaken must be defined together with the resources required to to carry a project through to a point selected by the manager. A convenient point might be the end of the research stage of the work, but if required, development and plant costs can be added in. A measure of the benefits to the organization from a successful project must also be defined and then modified in some way by the chances of success for the project. The benefits have got to be on a common scale, otherwise it's impossible to compare one project with another. The most usual common scale is money, but the objectives of the research department might be to secure a maximum number of patents or to recruit a certain number of highly qualified recruits for the firm. Any objective is possible but all projects must have a benefit expressed in terms of this objective.

We have worked on a money scale and this is the scale that I shall talk about. The basic objective is that we are trying to maximize the money benefit from our list of projects.

First of all, although I said that uncertainty is right at the centre of things, let's assume deterministic values for the costs of projects and the benefits of projects, develop the model and then see how the uncertainty can be slotted in. The simplest model which can be used is the benefit/cost ratio model.

Table 6.1 refers to a four project example. Project numbers 1, 2, 3, 4 are along the top line and arbitrary units along the second line. Each project has a benefit and the benefit/cost ratio is on the bottom line. Now, if we assume that the total available budget is 68 units, then the benefit/cost ratio model is used by reading down the list of projects in decreasing benefit/cost ratio, until the money is exhausted. In this case projects 3, 4 and 2 are selected with a total benefit of 118, and project 1 rejected. This is a very simple model but in fact it's productive in certain situations.

It's satisfactory if all the costs are on one scale. You'll see that we've only got one cost in Table 6.1. Looked at from a global point of view at board level, research costs are all money. A man costs £X'000, a piece of equipment costs £Y'000 and all costs are the

Table 6.1 Projects incurring costs under one budget

(In this and subsequent tables the units of costs and benefit are arbitrary)

Project No.	1	2	3	4
Cost	28	40	12	16
Benefit	35	60	30	28
Benefit/cost ratio	1.25	1.5	2.5	1.75

Available budget = 68
Selection of projects 3, 4, 2
Total benefit = 118

same. Looked at from the local manager's point of view, a man is not equivalent to a machine. A mathematician is not equivalent to an engineer. You might be able to get rid of an engineer and get another mathematician but it will take time (it will take a year perhaps before the new man is contributing) and the year ahead is the thing that we're most interested in. So for the year ahead we're usually stuck with the budgets and men that are currently available, and the situation becomes more complicated to analyse. The next table (Table 6.2) shows the same basic information as in Table 6.1 but expressed in a slightly different form.

Here we've got the same projects with the same four benefits and same four total costs. But the cost has now been split-up under two budget heads, wages and capital. The total wages and capital cost comes to the total shown in Table 6.1. If you now read down the list using the benefit/cost ratio model, you would pick projects 3 and 4 and then the capital budget is used up. These have the highest benefit/cost ratios and give a total benefit of 58 units. Now this is a trivial example and you can rapidly see that projects 1 and 2 have in fact a total benefit of 95. Projects 1 and 2 which can be selected without overspending the budgets therefore are a better selection than projects 3 and 4. (Assuming only these four projects are available.)

Table 6.2 Projects incurring costs under two separate budgets

Project No.	1	2	3	4
Salaries cost	24	30	10	4
Equipment cost	4	10	2	12
Benefit	35	60	30	28
Benefit/cost ratio	1.25	1.5	2.5	1.75

Wages budget = 54
Capital budget = 14
Total budget = 68

This is just a toy example but it shows that the benefit/cost model leads to difficulties with more than one budget head.

The problem shown in Table 6.2 can be formulated as a linear programming model and an optimum solution obtained (Table 6.3).

Table 6.3 Linear programming formulation

Project	1	2	3	4	
Variable	x_1	x_2	x_3	x_4	
Project constraints	x_1				$\leqslant 1$
		x_2			$\leqslant 1$
			x_3		$\leqslant 1$
				x_4	$\leqslant 1$
Salary constraint	$24x_1 +$	$30x_2 +$	$10x_3 +$	$4x_4$	$\leqslant 54$
Eqpt. constraint	$4x_1 +$	$10x_2 +$	$2x_3 +$	$12x_4$	$\leqslant 14$
Benefit (known as the objective function)	$35x_1 +$	$60x_2 +$	$30x_3 +$	$28x_4$	

We have the same four projects but in this case, there's a positive x variable associated with each project x_1, x_2, x_3, x_4. Each of these variables represents the extent to which the associated project is chosen, in other words x = zero means rejection x = 1 means selection. This representation allows partial projects to be selected, in other words x can take a value between 0 and 1 which is a point I will return to.

The block in the figure, called project constraints, ensures that projects are not selected more than once, i.e., x_1 must be less than or equal to 1. If you didn't have that constraint in, the mathematical procedure would merely pick your best project time and time again.

The next blocks sets out the wages constraints and the capital constraints: we're saying that project 1 needs 24 units of wages, project 2 needs 30, etc., so that $24x_1 + 30x_2 + 10x_3 + 4x_4$ would be the total expenditure on wages if you did all the projects. But you set a limit on this, therefore the total budget must be less than or equal to 54. Similarly for the capital in the next row — it must be less than or equal to 14.

For the benefit row (objective function) if you do project 1 you get 35 units of benefit, if you do 2 you get 60, etc.

This is the four-project example set up as a linear programming formulation and all we need to say at this meeting is that it can be solved by a well-known technique suitable for a computer. You can solve the problem so that you get the best selection of projects which gives

the maximum benefit and it is mathematically certain that you've got the maximum benefit within the constraints. This is the basis of the model that has been used for the last two years.

The basic model can be enlarged very easily to take account of different types of staff. Instead of wages, we could put total number of chemists, total number of mathematicians, etc. Each of those total numbers would have a line, each project would have a certain requirement for chemists, or no requirement at all. You'd write down the row and there would be a limit on the number of chemists available. Similarly for engineers, mathematicians, etc. You can have as many budgets as you want. Our model has two, revenue and capital.

Now two extensions to this. So far we have considered one time period, say one year ahead and we've only looked at one version of a project. Now, this is where we can start to see how the uncertainties can be slotted into this model. There are often a number of ways of carrying out a given project. You can cram on all speed, get all the men to stand round the rig or the piece of plant or the burette or whatever and have them working night-shifts. Or you can take it very slowly, one man just pottering along for two or three years. You can perhaps have a completely different technical approach. Instead of having a man doing manual analysis of results, you could employ the computer for analysis of results. There are obviously, right at the beginning of a project, a number of ways in which it could be tackled. This has been introduced into this model by using the concept of project version and this has been quite a fruitful line of development.

Table 6.4 shows a two project example with project versions. The dots indicate that the problem goes on as far as required. There are two projects with three versions of the first project and two versions of the second project. With each of those versions there is a variable. x_{11} is version 1 of project 1; x_{12} version 2 of project 1; x_{13} version 3 of project 1 and so on.

The project constraint now is slightly different. We're saying that the total of $x_{11} + x_{12} + x_{13}$ must be less than equal to one. We're not telling the model which one it must select; we're just saying it mustn't select a total that's more than 1, it mustn't do the whole thing more than once. For each project version, x_{11} for example, we have 24 units of wages required and 4 units of capital. For x_{12} we have 28 units of wages and 4 units of capital and so on for the other project versions.

Again the benefit row is at the bottom of the figure. In this case each version will have a different benefit.

Table 6.4 Project versions

Project	1			2		
Version No.	1	2	3	1	2	....
Variable	x_{11}	x_{12}	x_{13}	x_{21}	x_{22}	....
Project constraints	x_{11} +	x_{12} +	x_{13}			$\leqslant 1$
				x_{21} +	x_{22}	$\leqslant 1$
Salary constraint	$24x_{11}$ +	$28x_{12}$ +	$30x_{13}$ +	$30x_{21}$ +	$30x_{22}$ + ...	$\leqslant 54$
Equipment constraint	$4x_{11}$ +	$4x_{12}$ +	$4x_{13}$ +	$10x_{21}$ +	$12x_{22}$ + ...	$\leqslant 14$
Benefit/cost ratio	$35x_{11}$ +	$45x_{12}$ +	$50x_{13}$ +	$60x_{21}$ +	$70x_{22}$ + ...	

The reason for this is if you're cramming on all speed you're presumably getting your results earlier and therefore perhaps you're picking up a sales opportunity or you're getting better market penetration. In my industry we may be avoiding a machine outage that otherwise would occur. Once a project version has been defined it must be followed right through and the benefit calculated.

We now start to introduce the uncertainty that people can do things in different ways; they can see they can do things in different ways and here the model is being allowed to choose its way amongst the versions that have been presented to it.

The final extension that we need to consider in the basic model for the purposes of this discussion is that of time periods (see Table 6.5).

Table 6.5 Multi-period budgets

Project No.	1	2	
Variable	x_1	x_2	
Project constraints	x_1		$\leqslant 1$
		x_2	$\leqslant 1$
Salary constraints:			
period 1	$24x_1$ +	$30x_2$ +	$\leqslant 54$
period 2	$20x_1$ +	$50x_2$ +	$\leqslant 50$
Equipment constraints:			
period 1	$4x_1$ +	$10x_2$ +	$\leqslant 14$
period 2	$2x_1$ +	$14x_2$ +	$\leqslant 16$
Benefit/cost ratio	$35x_1$ +	$60x_2$ +	

Here we have no project versions, just single versions, going on for different time periods. We must take account of the fact that a project starting this year with two men might need ten men next year and might need 20 the year after that. It's no use selecting this project on the basis of it needing two men if next year ten men

are not available. We can take account of this by noting that the project can go on into next year, determining the resource requirements for each year and organizing the matrix accordingly. I don't think I need go too deeply into this aspect except to say that multiple time periods can be taken into account quite easily.

In the practical model that we've used, we've also taken account of quite complex staffing arrangements; types of staff, also grades of staff – high-grade research officers through to laboratory assistants and mechanical fitters. Staff flexibility and recruiting can also be taken into account.

The model can be set up to recruit extra staff and it will identify where the extra men are going to be most useful. Project versions have been quite extensively used and a three-year model. The object has been to construct the model so that it represented the department as closely as possible.

The types of answers we get out of this are: the list of projects we should be doing, the resource utilization for this list of projects, how the staff needs to be deployed, etc. It also reveals what constraints are preventing us getting more for your money, e.g., shortage of testing facilities or a particular level of research officer.

So far, deterministic information has been used but, even so, the output of the programme gives some idea about the stability of the solution. It tells us for example, immediately how much the benefit of a projection be changed before it disappears from the solution. If the benefit of a project is £100,000 and the programme tells us that the benefit could drop to £1,000 before it disappears from the solution, then this is a very stable project, and is relatively insensitive to errors in benefit estimation.

With a linear programme formulation, the x variable can take any value between 0 and 1. We are up against a problem here in that the model could select doing half a project or 0.63 of a project or any fraction between 0 and 1. Ideally, you'd think that you want a model which only allows x to be 0 or 1, reject or select. This is a so-called integer model and it can be set-up in an analogous manner, but instead of x being less than or equal to 1, x is 0 or 1. In fact, this is not as attractive as it seems. There are a number of quite complex reasons for this but I'll only mention two here.

First, in practice we find that the linear programming model does not give very many partial projects and this has been shown in a number of applications. In a list of 30 projects, 60 project versions, possibly 5 per cent of fractional projects appear. They are a difficulty, but at least attention can be focussed on this 5 per cent. They can be reformulated if you like, so they become more nearly integer in the next run of the programme. The other major difficulty with integer programming is that it's very slow computationally. It has been shown a number of times that, with the present state of the art in integer programming, the sort of linear model programme that is solved in less than a minute on a large IBM machine will run on for 15 to 20 minutes when using integer programming. So that is a considerable difficulty and it's a considerable expense. You're talking about £100 for an integer programme run and £1 to £10 for an LP run.

So far I have set out the model and its deterministic. Uncertainty is right at the core of things, so how are we going to take some account of this? There is no magic answer to this problem as far as I have been able to see. Of course, the benefits are very uncertain. But if one looks at the historical picture of how much people said their projects would cost and how much they actually cost, this again is very uncertain. So, we don't know what the benefit is; we don't know what the cost is. We don't know how long we're going to go on. So how can we begin to tackle all this?

A three-stage process seems to me to be sensible. The first stage is to put in deterministic information as we have done above and then to range with the constraints. This can be done very simply since although a single run might take one minute, ten extra runs might take only another two minutes changing say, the wage constraint by a series of steps. This might be useful when a squeeze on research costs is on the horizon, or when a period of rapid expansion is imminent. When you begin to play with the constraints, to tighten them, to relax them, you begin to get a 'feel' for the stability of the solution. In practice, it usually shows up a few projects or a small number of constraints which are rather sensitive. The

mass of the selected projects will remain selected almost regardless of what you do, as long as you don't go to extremes and reduce everything down to a tenth of the size it is. The rejected projects will tend to stay rejected, even when the budgets are raised slightly. A few projects tend to shade in and shade out of a solution and these are obviously sensitive in some way. Their benefit is not big enough, they're trying to pull in too many resources of a particular type and so – at least at the first stage, you can concentrate the attention of estimating on to these sensitive projects, and we have been able to do this in particular instances. Projects that people were very happy should be in the programme have turned out to be very sensitive, and we've had to go back and look at these very carefully to see why they were dropping out of the programme and whether the assumptions that people were making when they were doing the estimates were correct or incorrect. We're trying to discover what's making these projects sensitive so that the manager is in a better position to make a decision about them.

I can show you two formal exercises that have been carried out by the R & D working party at the Manchester Business School. In the evaluation of benefits we used a basic discount rate of 8 per cent, which at that time was the recognized rate for this type of project in the CEGB and the Gas Council. The computer was used to try the effect of varying discount rates, between 4 and 16 per cent (Table 6.6).

Table 6.6 Effect on solution of variations in discount rate (benefit horizon = 20 years)

Project	$R = 4\%$	$R = 8\%$	$R = 16\%$
8	0.75 M	Rejected	Rejected
10	M	F	M
11	F	F	F
19	M	M	M
21	M/F	M/F	F
24	0.5 M	Rejected	S/M

Of the approximate 30 projects only six were affected by changes in the discount rate. The basic case is an 8 per cent rate and in that case project 8 was rejected, project 10 went fast speed (that's the meaning of the F's and M's); project 11 at fast speed; project 19 medium; project 21 part medium, past fast; project 24 was rejected. As the discount rate is varied, you can see the way things change. When the discount rate is increased for example, project 21 becomes more attractive and project 10 becomes less attractive. Project

24 is an interesting one. It is rejected in the basic case and picked-up in the other two cases. In this way a group of projects has been isolated that are sensitive to uncertainty and which therefore will repay more careful study.

The same thing here has been done with the benefit horizon since we can't just go on adding the benefits up for ever. Obviously, the discount factor will take account of this after some years, but you can't often look into the future with any certainty for more than about ten years. So we've tried the effect of varying the benefit horizon (see Table 6.7).

Table 6.7 Effect on solution of variations in benefit horizon (discount rate = 8 per cent)

Project	$y = 8$ years	$y = 10$ years	$y = 15$ years
8	M	Rejected	M
10	F	F	M
11	M	F	F
14	0.3 M	Rejected	Rejected
16	F	M	M
19	F	M	M
21	S/M	M/F	M/F

There are now seven projects being affected (the same model as Table 6.6). As you vary the benefit horizon, some things will get more attractive, some things will get less attractive. These are the type of games that can be played with the basic deterministic model. Already some feeling is emerging for the sensitivity and stability of the solution.

Now, stage two — which is to take some account of the uncertainty in achieving the benefits. Quite recently, we put up a proposal to carry out a piece of work at one power station, with the aim of helping another power station which has a particular problem. The work was to try and decide whether or not a change in the plant would be beneficial in solving the problem.

We set up a probabilistic network for the benefit evaluation (Figure 6.1). First of all we do the research and at the end of that two things happen. Either we'll have found that the change we're going to make has a beneficial effect, or it's got no benefits and it's therefore no use in solving the problem. This is the first either/or box and we had to guess the probabilities of the two legs; with a little bit of evidence from other places, we said it's roughly half and half.

If we find that the work *has* a benefit then again we've got another two branches opening up. The

modification could have quite a high benefit . . . in other words it could be a very good change to make, or it could have a lower benefit.

The probabilities we put on here were 0.4 and 0.6 — again judging from the little evidence we had already, we reckoned it was more likely that if it had a benefit it would be fairly low rather than fairly high. But if the modification has a high benefit, a number of things can happen. We can not only change the plant that's got the original problem (which has a certain benefit), we may not only solve *this* problem, we might be able to solve problems on other boilers at the same power station. In addition, we might even, if things really went very well indeed, be able to apply this change more generally, to other power stations around the board. The probabilities that we put on these were 0.6, 0.3 and 0.1.

On the other hand, if the benefit from making the change proves to be fairly low, then it's likely that we'd still change the plant with the original problem, because anything we can do here is beneficial. However, the most likely event with a probability of 0.8 is that we'll lose our research costs.

If there is no benefit from the plant change we're investigating, again the most obvious thing is that we lose the research cost — and that we reckon to have a probability of 0.8. But there is a slight pay-off even in finding no benefit because people around the board have been talking of making this change, and we reckon that there is a 0.2 per cent chance of saving the costs of other people making the change if we can prove conclusively there isn't any benefit. If we do nothing, somebody somewhere is liable to have a go.

This is the benefit network that we derived. Each of the final events in Figure 6.1 has a discounted benefit and an overall estimated probability of the event occurring in practice. What we therefore have obtained is a benefit/probability histogram or, if the points are smoothed, a benefit/probability curve.

What I've discussed up to now for the model has been the expected value of the benefit. We now seek some method of taking more account of the spread of possible benefits. Obviously, a project with a wide spread of benefits may be less attractive to research managers than a project with the same expected E value but a rather narrower spread of benefits. We can characterize a distribution of this type by the value of E and the standard deviation. We now require some method of taking account of this in the model.

A number of methods have been used to achieve this.

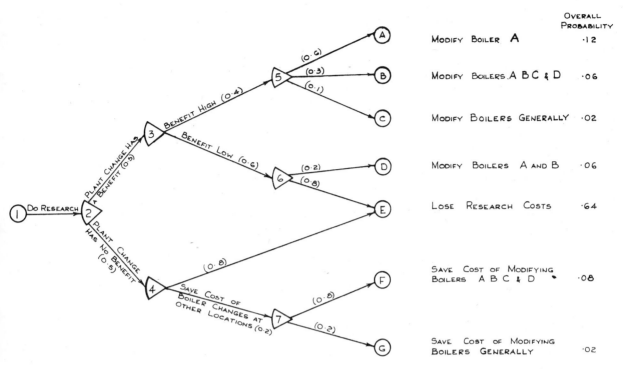

Figure 6.1 Probabilistic network for benefit evaluation.

One is to insert a constraint row into the model which sets a limit on the total variance of the portfolio. There are individual variances for each project and a limit can be set to the total variance. This limit can be varied to show what projects drop out and what come in at different levels – the usual sort of sensitivity analysis. This is mathematically slightly incorrect. Since it does not account for the partial projects but it has been a useful starter.

The other method is to roll the expected value and the standard deviation into one – to use a utility function. Instead of just using E, we use some expression of the form: $U = E - KJ^2\sigma$. K is a constant the derivation of which is a very subjective matter. A value of K can be derived by asking the decision-maker (the research manager in our case) certain carefully-loaded questions about his attitude to gamble. We have found it more profitable to take a series of values of K and to run the programme through with each value of K in turn to see what happens to the answers. Even the expression itself is not necessarily valid – it's just a semi-theoretical relationship. In practice, at the Manchester Business School, when we tried to ask people their attitude to risk, we found something like: $v = E - K\sigma$ which seemed to fit the experimental answers better.

That's stage two, taking some account of the

uncertainty of the benefit information. But we still, up to now, have the assumption that our costs for each project are deterministic. So we must try and take some account of the likely variations in research costs.

We can do it by utilizing the fact that the computer can produce very many linear programme solutions very quickly. It produces one solution in, let's say, a minute, it produces ten in two minutes and a 100 in five minutes.

If we have, for each project, a benefit/probability curve then we can arrange that the computer, before it solves the linear programme, selects a benefit value randomly from each curve. The value selected will be determined by the shape of the probability curve. A solution is then produced with this randomly selected set of benefits and the process is repeated many times – 100 or 200 is a convenient number. We have found that, for our data, there is quite a degree of stability about the solutions but certain interesting things do happen.

Some projects are fully selected half the time and partly selected half the time. We are once again beginning to pick-out now the projects which are fairly sensitive. Something which is selected a 100 times is obviously a pretty stable project and wherever the benefit happens to fall out it will be selected.

A further development of this type of simulation approach is to take account of the variation in costs. We've utilized the critical path networks that we employ to control our projects.

Quite recently we started a procedure of networking our projects for control purposes. We've gone to project leaders and said: 'This is your network, this is how you ideally see the project going but what would happen if you were delayed at a particular point? Would it take you longer, would you have to use more men?' We have generalized this procedure to cover the whole network for a project and have thus derived probabilistic resource network in the same way that the computer can be programmed to sample the benefits, the cost networks are sampled and a large number of solutions produced to indicate the stability to cost variations and the sensitive projects.

We haven't yet done the ultimate simulation which is to sample from the cost side and the benefit side together — we're still plucking-up courage to have a go. In all this, the difficulty is to know whether you're doing anything that's theoretically reasonable or whether the answers are only applicable to the particular data that you're playing with.

We have always used data from the real situation and for this data we've found certain things. We've found that the solutions are rather insensitive to the *spread* of benefits in the projects. We've found that with the rather smaller set of data that we chose the solutions were insensitive to variations in the cost. We found the answers very sensitive to variations in our total revenue budget. We don't know whether these are genuine events in the sense that they'll apply everywhere — we suspect not of course but you can only get answers to this by testing quite a number of practical situations. We've got to try and get other people playing with — not necessarily this model or even this type of model but this sort of approach to see what the problems are. It has been tested in a number of other industries but not very many yet.

These are the developments for the future: to think about applying this type of technique elsewhere, to hope that in the not too distant future integer programmes can be run as efficiently as the linear programmes and give the same information and to investigate the linear programmes approach in more depth.

Appendix

Comments by Dr P.M.S. Jones,
Programmes Analysis Unit, Chilton, Didcot

Market research is used by a number of technologically oriented companies and by government departments to aid in decisions about the relevance of R & D programmes. Simple tree situations arise from the idealized situation of sequential research, development, production and marketing, each with its own costs and probabilities of success but with the benefits dependent arising largely from the final marketing operation. We at PAU have progressed from single value probabilities of success through range values and now attempt to derive probability distribution functions for overall benefit which can then be used in the standard Bayesian manner to aid logical decision-making. Where succeed/fail alternatives occur in an exploitation chain the final benefit v. probability plot becomes a complex function.[1] Furthermore the expected benefit (= probability x benefit) does not correspond to a possible outcome of the project in hand but represents the statistical outcome for that project considered as part of a larger portfolio. The possibility of using game theory methods in such go/no-go situations is attractive and has been extensively explored in the defence field. James Hetrick[2] of A.D. Little has advocated its application in the business environment. Its possible use in simple competitive development situations with success/fail outcomes appears straightforward.

I would also like to say something about credibility. When I first heard Dr Allen speak on credibility I was fired with enthusiasm for an approach which seemed to offer an answer to many of the difficulties inherent in probabilistic methods, especially since the method was claimed to be of greatest value in highly uncertain situations. On trying the method in real-life situations of high uncertainty, however, I was disappointed on three counts. The credibility combination rules dictate that the lower credibility limit for addition is obtained by combining all the lowest credibility limits of the components and vice versa for the upper limit of complete credibility. Such an outcome seems incredible, and is far less attractive than using probability distributions whose combination give due recognition to the fact that it is highly improbable for all values in a composite function to lie at the same extreme end of their range. Second, for most R & D projects and marketing operations it is completely credible that the outcome will be failure although the probability of such an outcome may be very low. This results in highly uncertain situations in a very wide spread for the range of complete credibility within which these may be fresh grounds for arguing for a much narrower probability band of predictable form. The method, therefore, does not make use of all the available information. Where options are being considered the credibility approach may rank several as fully credible and offers no assistance to the decision-maker. Properly used, probability allows the relative chances of success of options to be spelled out explicitly.

As a matter of personal experience credibility has not proved helpful in highly uncertain situations but in well-defined areas the technique would be applicable. In these situations, however, probability functions are also more readily definable so that the need for the credibility approach vanished. Having said this I would add that attempts to develop alternative treatments are very valuable and worthwhile and I hope that Dr Allen will continue to explore this general field.

The Programmes Analysis Unit has also been keenly interested in the possible application of mathematical programming methods to portfolio selection problems and has sponsored studies by the Manchester Business School in this area. The linear, integer and dynamic programming methods permit optimization of a chosen parameter with a variety of constraints applied to resources. One of the most valuable uses of such methods can be in permitting one to examine the value of additional units of resource at the margin or even set an overall limit to the size of a portfolio by examining the margin or even set an overall limit to the size of a portfolio by examining the marginal return per unit of resource for a sample of hypothetical gross levels and selecting the gross value at which the marginal resource value equalled its opportunity cost, always provided the latter is known.

In practice difficulties can arise from several factors.[1] The benefit function which one attempts to maximize may be highly uncertain in individual projects so that the optimization procedure may be far more precise than the feed data warrant. This aspect is now under study at the MBS by Pearson and Gear. Second, benefits from individual projects may interact so that single unique values cannot be ascribed. Third, the individual project proposals will tend to reflect the experience and desire for additional work of the existing staff and the balance will be self-perpetuating rather than optimal. There are additional reasons for not using the method in setting overall programme levels in the cases I have studied.[1] Clearly, Dr Read has found the technique valuable in his own laboratory and I would hope that the improved version now being developed will be of use to a wider clientele including PAU but the programming methods as currently available are time-consuming and cumbersome to employ and, in my view, unlikely to find widespread application.

Reference

1 Jones, P.M.S. and Hunt, H. (1969) 'An Outline of Evaluation as practised by the Programmes Analysis Unit with Three Case-Studies', PAU Memo M12, HMSO.
2 Hetrick, J.C. 'Assessment of Opportunity and Risk', Long Range Planning, June 1969, 54.

7.

Reduction of Development Cost Uncertainty
by David Andrews

This article is a revised version of the original which appeared in Management Accounting, Journal of the Institute of Cost and Management Accountants in three parts from September 1971 to November 1971 and is reprinted with permission.

Introduction

When a decision has to be taken whether to start some new engineering development, it is increasingly important to know, with complete conviction, not only the probable cost, but also the upper limit of the financial risk involved.

The uncertainty of this risk is due partly to the cost of delays resulting from complexity — which can be dealt with by networking techniques — partly to the essential recycling of development programmes in consequence of accidents and discoveries, and partly to unpredictable costs resulting from innovation.

It is shown from historical data that initial cost estimates for engineering design and development have been about 1.2 to 1.8 standard deviations less than the mean of the dispersion of the costs actually recorded. The ratio of the modal cost outcome to the initial cost estimate has varied with the novelty of the project from about 1.2 to 4.9, so that, even if cost estimation techniques can be improved to permit modal costs to be estimated accurately, there is little benefit unless the dispersion can be reduced also.

The requirements for a new planning technique are derived. The method must be objective and realistic, dealing impartially with both predictable and unpredictable possibilities. As well as showing the dispersion of the probable cost outcome, it must also indicate the steps that can be taken to make the distribution more deterministic. Furthermore, all estimates must remain visible, and must be related to the work content of the actual programme outcome (whether predictable or not) so that they can be used for project management purposes later.

The ECA method — introduced here — has been devised to meet these requirements by assessing the costs of two programmes. One is of the minimum programme that will be carried out in any case, even if everything goes perfectly. The other is of the programme that will have to be carried out if everything goes wrong. The actual cost outcome must fall between these limits, and the degree of certainty about the outcome depends on how different these estimates are. The method shows what needs to be done to bring them closer together. The operation of the proposed method is discussed.

Competitive Pressures

There is no good reason for supposing that the financial control of prime and major contracts for engineering development will become any easier. Largely in consequence of military developments, engineering capability has been improved rapidly in the last few decades, and contractual demands have risen in step.

High interest rates and rising costs now tend to inhibit development unless a new field can be exploited, a major technical advance made or some economy of scale realized. The amount of work required to fulfil individual contracts, therefore, tends to rise and the number of contracts to fall.

In this situation, unsuccessful bidders may not long remain competitive in technology and may not be able to retain their position. The incentive to underbid is strong.

The only deterrent to underbidding is concern about the financial risk, and, in particular, about the allowances that ought to be made for cost escalation. The larger the contract and the more significant the advance to be made, the more important it is that the initial assessment of the risk should be convincingly dependable. The more important it is, too, that the means used subsequently for control of the work and expenditure should be effective.

In some areas, unfortunately, the less likely it is that either will be, because as soon as there *is* any useful advance in management science, competitive requirements become correspondingly more exacting. The financial problems of Lockheed and Rolls-Royce provide dramatic evidence of this, but there have been reports of difficulty from several companies including those concerned with chemical and process plants, ocean liners and nuclear power stations. We should expect similar trends in many more industries for the same reason. This is a fundamental problem affecting the control of all projects.

Problem Definition

The problem has three aspects. That which causes most general concern at the moment is the unexpected increase in the rate of growth of wage and salary levels. The second aspect is straightforward miscalculation of the cost of the programme as planned. It is not proposed here to discuss either of these aspects in detail.

Attention will be concentrated on the third aspect — the omission from the costed plan of much of the work that is done to achieve the object, which may account for the major part of the cost in some cases.

Contractual Constraints

The requirements written into contracts for the development of new products are of four general types, and for each of these at that time, and in that contractor's organization, there is a boundary separating the possible from the impossible.

The four types are price, date, technical performance and what may loosely be called 'behaviour in service'. Normally, only three of these types are fully defined, leaving the contractor some room to manoeuvre with the fourth if he gets into difficulties. If all four types are fully defined by the contract, the contractor may not be able to overcome his difficulties if his initial estimates are wrong.

A complete specification for — the fourth of these types — 'behaviour in service' would have two parts. The first would concern the reliability, or effectiveness, of functional things — safety, reproducibility of performance, compatibility with adverse environments, ease of maintenance, etc. If any factors for behaviour in service are to be specified, it is most likely that they will be among these. Apart from being easier to demonstrate, they are more general.

Endurance, time between overhauls, and other duty-dependent aspects may be peculiar to the particular application being considered. Development to achieve the requirement, and then to demonstrate the achievement, can be very costly and uncertain for requirements of this type. In any case, it is the service environment which provides ideal conditions for development and test.

As, in many respects, designs for straightforward

tasks may be satisfactory, customers have been able frequently to minimize overall capital investment by accepting some of the risks themselves. The required behaviour in service, therefore, often has been left ill-defined in the contract.

This situation is changing, however. The introduction of integrated systems, increased scale of operation for single units, and high interest rates, all combine to increase already high costs of unserviceability.

Unfortunately, the increase in the size of single units and the more advanced technology underlying their design have tended to increase also the time for repair or overhaul. There has been a greater trend for customers to demand assurances on all the factors which influence plant availability. Undoubtedly, this trend will grow.

For many products — particularly those sold direct to the public, which is influenced in its judgement by advertising, fashion and status symbolism — technical performance is not a major criterion but reliability is. In such cases, a manufacturer who meets difficulties may be able to concentrate on adequate reliability at some expense to his original technical objective. In this way he may, in fact, maximize cost effectiveness for his customers.

Cutting the Time

The third type of constraint mentioned is the time scale available. The contractor is rarely left without at least a target, and delivery dates are frequently emphasized by penalty clauses.

In any given circumstances, there is an optimum time for a given task carried out on proper sequence and without undue overlap or delay. In practice, there may be a fairly wide tolerance on this optimum time scale, because not all simultaneous activities can be optimized simultaneously.

To reduce time costs money — not too much for modest savings because organizations respond well to the excitement offered by a challenge. As the time scale is reduced, however, multiplication of effort is necessary to provide parallel solutions to problems until a point is reached at which even an infinite expenditure could not effect further saving.

Cost Plus Contracts

In the defence field, the reduction of the time to achieve exacting performance specifications without risk of unsatisfactory behaviour in service is frequently the principal objective. The contractor must then be free to adopt commercially uneconomic practices if needed to save time.

For this type of work, the practice therefore grew up of awarding cost-plus contracts. However, as the cost of development rose it became necessary to impose limits on the rate of spend so negating the advantages.

The evils of cost-plus contracts have been widely discussed. It is not frequently recognized, though, that the engineering (i.e., research, design and development) departments of private industry have a precisely similar relationship with their own directors. The annual rate of expenditure is controlled, but technical progress is not so easily determined.

Escalation probable

Estimation for, and control of, advanced technology is not easy and gross escalations in defence contracts have caused great concern. The report of the MinTech steering group, chaired by W.G. Downey[1] recalls that, in 1958, W.M. Hill found the average ratio of actual to forecast costs to be 2.8 for a sample of 100 British projects, individual cases having ratios of up to 5.0.

From comments made by Tischler[2] (Director, Shuttle Technologies, OART, NASA) it seems that a Rand report[3] in 1959 reached similar conclusions about American experience.

Methods of control instituted since then have effected some improvement, but the uncertainty of some projects has increased. In 1969, Tischler reported: 'Even after cost of living adjustments, actual design and development costs of aerospace equipment usually exceed early estimates by *several hundred per cent* . . . I conclude that these escalation factors can be projected into the estimates of new systems now being proposed.'

This confirmed the conclusion of the Downey steering group[4] the previous year: 'We do not see any lessening of the difficulties which now surround, particularly in the early stages, the preparation of programmes and cost estimates for advanced development work in the defence field.'

Dangers of reviews

Among practices evolved to deal with the problem of controlling the national spend rate are some that give earlier indication of the escalation trend, coupled with quarterly reviews of all projects at which decisions are taken on whether to continue, to slow down or to cancel the projects in hand.

The political and economic consequences of these uncertainties are considerable. Blackwell[5] points out that reference back to the government for more money, more time, or a downgrading of the technical objective re-opens the policy debate each time and gives fresh opportunity to the opponents of that policy to undermine it and secure its cancellation. This can be seen in the difference between the debates on Concorde and Apollo, the costs of the latter being broadly in line with the original global estimates.[6]

Cancellation of a major project, even at an early stage, can mean a loss of several million pounds. This should be seen, not merely as the loss of the resources employed, but as the loss of a non-recurring opportunity to work on a project that could have been successful.

To cancel a major project at an advanced stage in its development – like the TSR 2, for instance – is equivalent to destruction of the life's work of several hundred skilled men.

Unplanned Protraction

Undue protraction of programmes may cause total costs to rise. Momentum is lost; inefficiencies creep in; specialist manpower and facilities are not fully utilized; some activities, such as setting-up, are repeated unnecessarily; work is lost or neglected, and the output per manhour drops for psychological reasons. It will be seen later that – in the absence of a firm discipline to demonstrate the need for them – there is a danger that economy will be made on the features that would enable the planned programme to be maintained, making further, unplanned protraction a possibility.

Need for certainty

The known uncertainty of development cost estimation is a real obstacle to the development of desirable innovations when their adoption is dependent on the result of DCF and cost effectiveness calculations. The more realistic, and therefore higher, the cost estimate is, the lower is the calculated return. But then, because there is no firm discipline that permits the true degree of uncertainty of the estimate to be assessed, the high estimate is treated as if it were no more realistic than a low estimate. The dangers are that a project may be rejected when greater certainty would have justified another decision, or that the wrong choice may be made between alternative proposals.

The same uncertainty bedevils a contractor bidding

for a fixed-price contract. Normally, he would hope for a profit (though occasionally he might be prepared to share the risk of some advanced development with a customer if he believed that the resulting extension of his own capability would justify this). However, he may be inhibited from quoting keenly because he cannot be certain of the upper limit of the risk. This problem exists, too, when the value of the development content of an individual contract is a large fraction of his annual turnover.

So in every case, there is the need for some means to define convincingly the upper limit of the probable risk involved.

Subjective Assessments

In the early post-war years, contractors' main efforts were to solve the difficult technical problems involved in defence contracts. The idea of attempting to plan the developments in advance must have seemed insurmountable and no very strenuous attempt was made to tackle the problem.

As late as 1968, management consultants advising the Downey steering group on, *inter alia*, the methods used by some of the major contractors to the then Ministry of Aviation reported that estimates were based almost universally on subjective assessments at some critical point in their preparation.[7] In the absence of any firm method of assessing the risks this might have led to the best results, though by this time, sufficient experience had been gained to warrant a more analytical approach as Blackwell and Reed[8] showed.

Reasons for Underestimation

The Downey steering group alleged:[9] 'In the formative stages of a number of projects, firms have adopted what seems to have been a deliberately over-optimistic attitude and to have submitted estimates which made wholly inadequate allowances . . .' Three possible explanations were discussed.

The first was: 'It appears to be widely believed in industry that estimates which start at a low figure and rise gradually over the years as development proceeds have a greater chance of acceptance than those which are realistic from the start.' One reason why this should have been so has been noted already, though Haviland[10] alleges intent to deceive in some cases.

The report recognizes that officials have frequently been reluctant to accept pessimistic estimates, believing them to be conducive to high costs. This confirms the belief that industry is said to hold. I know that the same view was held by officials, too.

In the absence of any objective means of making allowances for possible escalation, cost estimates were frequently based on the minimum programme. Simonis[11] remarked: 'It was not for the supplier, if he wished to secure the contract, to suggest that he could not do the job in one go . . . price and date targets for any new project were put forward *and accepted* on the basis of 'nothing going wrong', i.e., a smooth run through the cycle of design, proto-build, rig test, flight evaluation, production release and certification.'

Simonis deprecates this but, as long as the basis is accepted, the approach cannot be criticized on moral grounds, even if it does give the right answer.

This situation is not unique to the aerospace industry. Trapnell[12] describes a case in the computer industry in which a management demanded revisions of a project until the estimate was acceptably low (about one-third of the original estimate). 'Three years later, when the project was complete and the actual cost became historical fact, it worked out at slightly over the original estimate.'

The third explanation, considered by the Downey steering group was that: 'The tendency for firms to underestimate has been encouraged in some cases by the Ministry of Aviation's practice of inviting a number of firms to submit competitive design proposals.' Actually there is merit in the design competition, but not in soliciting competitive quotations for cost-plus contracts. Pearson[13] defined what he called 'Fitzgerald's Law': 'That any brochure competition carried out sufficiently long would result in all parties being equal at a figure rather beyond what was reasonable.'

There are many people, in and out of government offices, who believe that many essential projects would never have been started had the true costs been known at the inception. Under-estimation in a large proportion of these cases arose because at the inception no one really knew what the final product would be like.

Improvements in Methods

As a result of the advice of the Zuckerman committee[14] much greater attention was given to early definition of the requirements, and led to a great improvement in practice. Bonser[15] summarizing the reasons for the success of the Nimrod programme is reported to have said: 'We took a lot of time writing not just a specification but an engineering specification. We finished up with a pile of books. These books have been rigorously followed ... I make it so difficult for anyone to change (the specification) that they have now reached the point where they do not even suggest it.'

Similar efforts were made in industry. Dollimore,[16] summarizing the reasons for the success of Hunting Engineering on another project made particular reference to the 'exceptional attention to detail in the early design study'.

Similar problems in the US led to the development by Walker and Sayer[17], of Du Pont, of the Critical Path Method and by Malcolm *et al.,*[18], of the US Navy Special Projects Office, of Programme Evaluation and Review Technique (PERT). Both methods are said to have been based on ideas put forward by C.D. Flagle in 1956.[19]

The reputation of PERT, understandably, was established by the dramatic effect that its use had on the time to complete the Polaris FBM programme. This did much to establish networking techniques in many industries.

It is recognized generally that one of the main virtues of these methods is the discipline they impose for early definition of the development plan and of the resources needed to carry it out. They are effective tools for preventing unnecessary delays in complex programmes.

Downey Proposals

This approach was formalized by the Downey steering group[20] in its proposals – after Zuckerman – that a comprehensive development cost plan (DCP)* be prepared for each project defining the time sequence of expenditure and technical progress, and that it be kept up to date by the contractor and used for work authorization at all stages.

The group recommended that, initially, work should be authorized in three limited phases, with full review at the end of each:

1 Feasibility study, six months duration, 0.5 per cent of cost.

2 Project definition, phase 1 nine months duration, 5 per cent of cost.

3 Project definition, phase 2, 12 to 15 months duration, 10 per cent of cost.

4 Full development, quarterly reviews, remainder.

---

* In American usage, DCP is a development concept paper which is rather different.

Harland[21] describes how the escalation trend rates are monitored in the quarterly reviews to anticipate the most probable outcome.

Undesirable Consequences

The British Government has taken a more reasonable attitude to the consequences of uncertainty than has the US Department of Defense, which became convinced that all that was needed to curb cost inflation was to impose strict financial restraints.

No doubt DOD was influenced by the high hopes placed in PERT, even by contractors. Lockheed, for example, who had been systems manager for the Polaris FBM programme advertised in 1962: 'Lockheed project planners can accurately predict the cost of future weapons and space systems, in dollars and in elapsed time, by applying these new management techniques.'

Between 1960 and 1966, the percentage of DOD expenditure covered by fixed price arrangements was raised from 57.4 per cent to 79.2 per cent[6]. This began to create great difficulties for DOD contractors.

Ironically, the company which seems to have suffered most is Lockheed. 'Lockheed's problems', said Simmons[22] 'are the result of heavy cost over-runs and ensuing cut-back in the C-5A programme. The cut-back of the C-5A from 115 to 81 threatens Lockheed with a loss of $500 million, while (other) government claims still to be adjudicated by the Board of Contract Appeals, add another $440 million.'

Ironically, too, the contract which Lockheed negotiated with Rolls Royce for the development of the RB 211 engine for the TriStar seems to have been very similar to those which created its own difficulties.

These facts provide an interesting gloss on the review of American practice in the report of the Downey steering group (pp 46-55).

The groundswell of concern caused the American Aerospace Industries Association to undertake a major survey of the problem through 1968. According to Drake[6], their primary finding was that 'existing DOD contracting policies are not compatible with the inherent technical uncertainty in the weapon system development process because "they do not give adequate or appropriate recognition to the unanticipated technical unknowns".'

PERT is not enough

There seems little doubt, therefore, that the use of PERT-based management techniques is not enough to give the degree of certainty expected.

Although PERT was specially devised for the Polaris programme, it was not intended, nor used, for cost control at all. Time had been the problem and it was on this aspect that the PERT research team had concentrated. The first document on the use of PERT/Cost for cost control was published in June, 1962[23] about the same time as the Lockheed advertisement referred to.

Strictly speaking, PERT is a system of probability, employing three values for estimating each activity — optimistic, most likely and pessimistic — but there has been a swing away from this in favour of 'simpler systems based on single time estimates (most likely)'.[24] Here, and in the US, multiple estimates have been found unsatisfactory, partly because of inconsistency between estimators and also because of the inherent difficulty of assessing relative values.

Important Distinctions

Before the Downey steering group was appointed, Blackwell and Reed[8] had launched a vigorous attack on the concept of the Zuckerman recommendations.[14] They considered the approach inflexible, that it inhibited the initiation of development work at a sufficiently early stage and that applying it to control costs would lead to the formulation of development plans that lacked novelty. 'No such assurance' (as that the objective will be achieved for the original estimates) 'can be given — nor should be sought — about any enterprise that has a high degree of novelty.'

Complexity

It is vital to an understanding of this problem to recognize that Blackwell and Reed were talking about something quite different from Bonser, Dollimore and others. The latter were concerned with large, very complex design problems the solution to which lay in the stabilization of the objectives and the organization of activities so that everything came together at the right time.

Bonser, in a personal letter has said: 'The development of a new aircraft is a very complex task (in which the risk) 'should be reduced by having a minimum number of risk areas. In my opinion, there should not be more than two major ones. . . . It is optimistic to think

that several major developments can be carried out simultaneously and brought to a successful and timely conclusion so as to allow the main development programme to continue without let or hindrance.'

Similarly, Harvey,[25] also an airframe man, distinguishes between the research element in R and D, the input-output relationships of which 'are subject to variability', and the development element 'which may account for 90 per cent of the R and D expenditure. . . . Development is a largely deterministic process exhibiting only incidental variability in some aspects. Any research content of development is usually unwanted as its presence indicates an irregularity in an otherwise smooth development process.'

Interaction

Blackwell and Reed, on the other hand, were concerned with the situation in which 'the buyer is fundamentally unable to define what he wants at the outset because what he wants is in some measure determined by what he can have. This, in turn, is not known until the project is in an advanced stage of development.'

In another part of the same article[8] they said: 'The approach is identical with that used in the study of learning processes in cybernetic theory and the various iterative mathematical techniques for solving difficult equations. A crude, but well defined solution is postulated and then, by a continuous testing of this solution against the fact of the situation (as they become available) the solution is intelligently refined.'

The problem as defined by these authors is that of aero gas turbine development. Because the compressor absorbs such a large part of the power available, improvements in the performance of many components have an enhanced effect. Similarly, the payload of an aircraft on long routes is considerably less than the total disposable load (which includes fuel) and that is considerably less than the all-up weight. A small reduction in fuel consumption, therefore, has a disproportionately large effect on airline operating economics or military aircraft performance.

The incentive to continue development right up to the point of entry into service and beyond is very strong and it is not at all unusual for an aircraft design to be committed on the supposition that some as yet unsolved engine problem will be solved in time. The innovation content of an engine development programme is, therefore, high.

Effect of Innovation

Tischler[2] has shown a strong correlation between observed mean cost escalation and the degree of novelty involved in any development. 'Design and development cost escalations, one must conclude, reflect degree of technological advancement being undertaken. *Innovations* in design and technology *during development* show the greatest escalation; a typical factor may be five, but escalations by a factor of 15 have occurred' (my italics).

One has to ask why networking techniques work well for aircraft but not for engines and why innovation *during* development incurs greater escalation than innovation *away from* development. Here, it is necessary to go back to the discussion on the problem of achieving and demonstrating the achievement of an adequate standard of behaviour in service. Harvey says that development to this end is a smooth and continuous process. As soon as something that has already been proved is altered, however, the work has to be done again.

Bonser recommended independent development, and retrospective fitment, of novel devices, to avoid disrupting the orderly development task. That is possible because the function of one item of equipment on an aircraft does not normally affect any other item significantly, with the notable exception of the effect of the engine on the aircraft as a whole.

In an aero gas-turbine, however, each component affects the operating environment of many other components. The introduction of some novel feature must be followed by extensive redevelopment. There is also the problem of creating the right environment in which to develop the innovation while the main development of many other components is continued.

Influence of Re-cycling

It would be inappropriate to discuss development technology here. Enough has been said to show that the real reason for the wide differences in the accuracy of estimates for the development of different types of equipment is the extent to which re-cycling of the development plan is inevitable when changes are made.

As an analogy, if aircraft development is like a game of halma, in which 19 men have to be taken progressively across the board from one corner to the other without turning back, gas turbine development is more like a game of snakes and ladders in which a single man moves nearly as often backwards as forwards.

It is not only innovation that causes re-cycling. In many development programmes there are long, integral chains of events which can be upset by common misadventures. In the case of an aircraft development, accidental loss of a prototype aircraft would be a striking example of this.

Although this discussion has centred on aircraft and engines, this is only because these illustrate the problem and because relevant data have been collected and analysed. The problems exist whenever the component requirements are defined by system analysis rather than by modification of an existing product.

Generally, therefore, a method is required which convincingly defines the upper limit of risk inherent in any programme and which derives this by examining the extent of re-cycling that could be needed.

Influence of Innovation

Figure 7.1 has been redrawn from the 1969 article[2] by Tischler, of the NASA Office of Advanced Research and Technology, in which he demonstrated a strong cor-

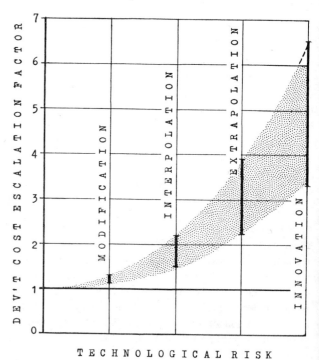

Figure 7.1 Diagram published by Tischler[2] showing the band (the shaded area) in which lie the actual cost escalation factors for half of the projects examined. The heavy lines on the ordinates have been super-imposed to show the values taken for the preparation of Figure 7.2.

relation between the observed escalation of cost and the degree of novelty involved in any development.

In a personal letter, he wrote 'The figure was originally derived by RAND[3] from historical cost data on aircraft and missile projects. To extend the data to more difficult project activities, I super-imposed and added unpublished cost escalation data from several later missile and space projects.'

In the article, he pointed out that the RAND report was 'written *before the space programme unfolded any data.* Nevertheless not one conclusion of that report can be disputed when placed against the back-drop of the space programme; even the quantitative relationships are borne out with astonishing fidelity.'

Figure 7.1 had been modified by Tischler, as his letter indicated: 'The RAND data, from my recollection, had used a numerical "degree of difficulty" as the abscissa. Because of the variety of project activities I felt that I could not rationally employ a numerical abscissa value. I, therefore, substituted semi-qualitative descriptors such as "modification", "extrapolation", etc.'

Tischler has provided no special definition of these terms, so the normal meanings must be assumed. Before analysing the figure, therefore, it would be as well to consider to what extent these classifications permit the various projects to be differentiated for this purpose.

Modification

The starting point for any modifcation is an existing product or process that is known to work, if only indifferently well. The change may be made to improve the design for its existing purpose (refinement), or to enable it to serve some different purpose not originally intended (adaptation).

The assumption is made that a great deal is already known about the product and that the changes made involve little risk. New designs using entirely conventional solutions to the problems raised probably fall into this classification, too, since their application is fully amenable to calculation.

Interpolation

This is the estimation of values for points in a series where these points lie between other points for which values are known. The values cannot be calculated[1] since the law is not known; they are inferred from observed empirical relationships. In some cases, the law may be very different from what is supposed. This class, therefore, includes new designs with features that are uncertain but which appear to lie within the range of what has been done before.

Extrapolation

By contrast, extrapolation is the estimation of values for points beyond the limits of previous experience, where it seems that those points are, nevertheless, part of the same series as those for which values are known. The degree of risk involved depends on how well the laws governing the known facts are understood.

Innovation

Obviously, when doing something completely new there is no previous experience to guide decisions and it is extremely difficult to assess the risk.

Causes of Dispersion

The headings of these classifications are readily capable of differentiation. The rating of individual projects is not so easy, because projects are not homogenous in difficulty. Even the most breath-taking innovation is associated with much that is interpolation or less, while many mere modifications incorporate some element of extrapolation.

Identification of the technological risk cannot be considered to be precise for particular projects, so there are bound to be errors of position along the abscissa, increasing the dispersion (scatter) of the results.

The ordinates, too, of the results are probably dispersed more than they would be for the effect of technological risk alone. At the time when initial estimates were made for most of the projects considered — and certainly for all of those considered by RAND — available estimating and management techniques were comparatively crude.

Cost escalations must have been enlarged through incorrect allowances for the rate of inflation, miscalculation of the actual work required to carry out the activities on the plan, unanticipated cost of delays resulting from poor programme control, and misadventure.

Dispersion would result, too, from the mixture of projects having complex but straightforward tasks and those having tasks with considerable 'circularity' in which parts of the programme have to be re-cycled when changes are made. Probably, more recent and current projects will show less dispersion and, perhaps, less escalation because of better cost estimation methods.

There is, however, no reason to suppose that escalation and dispersion will be eliminated in this way. Tischler's correlation shows convincingly that there is strong correlation between uncertainty and increasing innovation and (by implication) 'circularity', and none of the methods at present available attacks this.

Parametric Estimates

Figure 7.1 confirms from American experience, the same tendency, for estimators and officials to adopt initial estimates that fail to make adequate allowances for uncertainty. Evidently it is a human frailty to discount the possibility of any event that does not appear on the initial programme.

Evidently, also, governments must have required better indications for budgeting purposes. Hence, it has become the practice to make, in parallel, so-called 'parametric' estimates. Drake,[6] in 1970, claimed; 'Total programme cost estimates *can* be estimated quite accurately by applying past experience to existing programme parameters.

'Such past experience tends to eliminate the effect of most of the factors which lead to low initial estimates. For example: In 1961, using methods such as these, NASA estimated that the Apollo moonlanding programme would cost about $20 billion. This estimate, corrected for unanticipated inflation, has proved to be accurate within 3 per cent nearly nine years later. This "top-down" estimate has kept the moonlanding programme from public and congressional criticism for cost "over-runs", despite the fact that initial prices estimated from NASA in-house work plans totalled very much less.'

It would be dangerous to generalize from this isolated experience. One could well argue that NASA had taken full advantage of US national sentiment at the time when it submitted its budget; by all accounts the budget had not been arrived at quite as scientifically as Drake would lead one to suppose; and for all the money involved, there was but one technical objective – putting a man on Moon by 1970 – leaving plenty of scope for changes along the way. This does not depreciate the achievement, but it does raise doubts whether parametric estimates are vindicated thereby.

In 1965, Blackwell and Reed[4] published several graphs enabling an aero gas-turbine development estimate to be built up parametrically. One curve, for instance, showed the ratio

$$\frac{cumulative\ development\ cost}{unit\ production\ engine\ cost}$$

plotted against the ratio

$$\frac{elapsed\ time\ production}{engine\ lead\ time}$$

It is evident that both these ratios are critically dependent on the underlying assumptions and on historical influences and would be altered by changes in workshop organization and in development practice.

Equations for parametric estimation were recommended by the consultants advising the Downey Steering Group.[5] The form of the equation proposed for estimating the engineering man-hours for liquid propellent rocket engines is an excellent example of the dangers inherent in the parametric approach.

The form of the equation may well have fitted the data available when the analysis was made but it has entirely the wrong dimensions. It does not take account of whether the engine is pressure-fed or pump-fed, if the propellents are stable or cryogenic and whether the propellents ignite spontaneously or require energy for ignition. Also, it does not take account of the development background available for the propellent combination proposed, all of which are of great importance. It will be noted, however, that none of these is readily quantifiable, which is perhaps why the consultants proposed to use only thrust and mass flow, which are.

The most serious objection to parametric estimates, however, is that they are useless for any other purpose. In their conclusions, the Downey Steering Group[27] drew attention to the need for estimates to be 'based objectively on the work to be done' and for that work 'to be broken down and phased into discrete tasks which can be used to check achievement' so that the estimates can be used 'as an instrument of detailed budgetary control'.

On the other hand, parametric techniques could perhaps be devised to indicate the uncertainty inherent in any estimate, whereas the recommendations of the Downey Steering Group seem to presuppose that there is a unique, most probable estimate for any project.

Decision Tree Technique

Probability theory has been considered by Harvey[25] as a means of assessing the most appropriate level of research to achieve a guaranteed aircraft performance. He shows how an improvement in the precision of performance estimates leads to a reduction in the margin by which the 'target mean performance' has to be set above the guarantee.

He goes on to discuss the use of the 'decision tree' to estimate the relative probabilities of the success of alternative R and D paths, basing decisions on the 'expected monetary values' of those alternatives.

The decision tree method analyses each of the decisions and chance events in sequences which lead to a limited number of possible end-values. This type of analysis normally shows two or three possible consequences of a decision or chance event and probabilities are assigned subjectively to each. The probabilities of the alternative consequences of each single decision or event must add up to unity. so the probability of any one path is the product of the probabilities of all the decisions and events along it.

The problem we have here, however, is rather different. The end value of the successful development is the same for all paths but the cost of arriving at it depends on the path followed. To satisfy the requirements of the Downey Steering Group it is necessary to find the most probable path, not necessarily the cheapest.

Since the total uncertainty in this situation is compounded of anticipated and unanticipated events and decisions taken in consequence of them it ought to be possible, in theory, to consider sequentially every decision point and potential event point and so construct a similar tree. By assigning probabilities to each branch, the probabilities of all possible paths might be estimated and the cost of the most probable path determined.

There are several reasons why this is not practicable. It is impossible to assess the probability of unanticipated events, even if it is possible to recognize where they might occur. Even for anticipated events, the probability assessments are subjective and liable to bias for political ends.

The most important objection, perhaps, is the number of possible paths opened up by each event. For example, consider the alternative courses open, depending on the circumstances, in consequence of one isolated event, namely the failure on test of a single component.

Any one of the following might be decided on:

1 Delete the test.
2 Ignore the failure and complete the test with the same component.

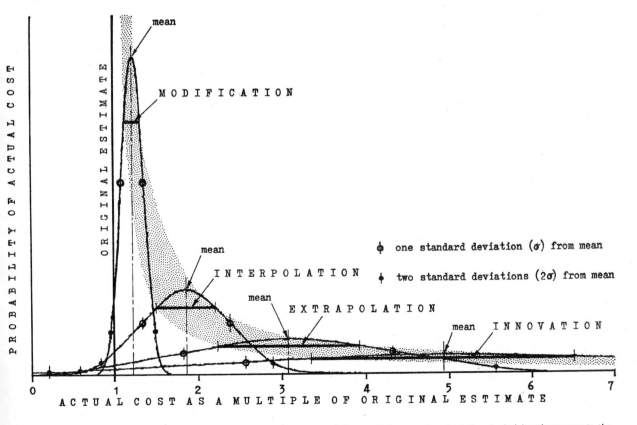

Figure 7.2 Interpretation of the data for the four main categories of Figure 7.1, assuming that the shaded band represents the inter-quartile range of a normal probability density distribution (see Table 7.1).

3 Repair the component and complete the test.

4 Repeat the test with the same component.

5 Repeat the test with a different component.

6 Modify the design of the component and repeat the test.

7 Take another design of component and repeat the test.

8 Research to find the cause of failure.

There are other possibilities. After an impossible amount of labour, the result would be almost an infinity of paths, all of negligible probability. This is very near to a true description of the real-life situation.

Probability Distributions

Referring to Figure 7.1, Tischler[2] stated that the shaded band included half the results plotted. If we assume that the results have a 'normal' probability density distribution, the upper edge of the band is the upper 'quartile' and the lower edge is the lower 'quartile', the band being the 'inter-quartile range'. In a normal distribution, the mode, or most likely value, lies in the middle of this range and is coincident with the mean and the median of the distribution.

Figure 7.2 shows the effect when this assumption is made; the four probability density distribution diagrams are drawn for the four identified ordinates that we discussed earlier. The characteristic dimension of this distribution is known as the standard deviation (sigma), which is the square root of the average of all the squares of the displacements of values from the mean. Sometimes called the root mean square or rms value, it is the distance from the mean to the points of inflection of the curve.

The ordinate values of this curve have little meaning in themselves. What is significant is the area contained between any two ordinates, in proportion to the total area underneath the curve. For instance, if we call the mean zero, the upper and lower quartiles occur at plus and minus 0.674 sigma respectively and contain half the outcomes. Plus sigma to minus sigma contains 68 per cent of all outcomes; twice that range contains 94 per cent of all outcomes while more than 99.7 per cent fall within the range of plus 3 sigma to minus 3 sigma. (See Figure 7.3.)

Criteria of Acceptability

In Figure 7.2, the areas under the four curves are the same, so that the relative heights of those curves indicate

the relative probabilities of their modes being realized. This is not a satisfactory view to take, though, because the acceptable tolerance on the cost is a constant percentage of the absolute value, which is greater for the flatter curves.

This is illustrated in Figure 7.3, drawn for the 'Modification' case and representing normal commercial risks. In this example the contract is assumed to give 19 per cent profit on the modal outcome (equivalent to 46.5 per cent on the initial estimate) and sigma is about 11 per cent. Twenty out of every 21 such contracts should make some profit.

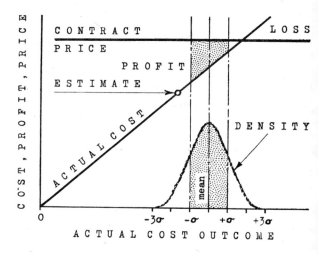

Figure 7.3 Diagram showing the influence of the dispersion of the probable cost outcome of any contract on the probability of making a profit. This is drawn for the same coefficient of variation as the modification case of Figure 7.2.

The situation is very different for the Innovation case shown in Figure 7.4, in which sigma is 48 per cent of the modal value. The probability that the actual cost will come out to be within plus or minus 11 per cent of the mode is now only 18 per cent – there are only two chances in 11 that the outcome will fall within this range. There is an equal probability that the cost will come out to be more than 143 per cent of the modal value, resulting in a very considerable loss.

The probability of making a loss is even greater if the probability density distribution is not normal but skewed, with the mode at a lower value than the mean. There are two reasons for thinking that this form of distribution may be more likely. With a normal distribution in the Innovation case there is a finite probability that the cost outcome may be zero or negative, which is obviously ridiculous. Also, *a priori*, while it is very difficult to reduce costs, it is comparatively easy to increase them — even without apparently wasting resources.

Figure 7.5 shows the effect of assuming, for the Innovation case, a beta distribution (Karl Pearson, type 6) having the same range for the modal half of all outcomes and the same coefficient of variation (i.e., sigma ÷ mean) but on a mean value that is now 6.35. Although the modal value has hardly altered, the

interquartile range has moved to the right and no longer includes the modal half of all outcomes; in fact, 68 per cent of all outcomes now lie to the right of the mode.

Table 7.1 shows comparable data for all four cases. It is evident that only the modification case would be tolerable commercially for fixed-price contracts. Even for budgeting for cost-plus contracts, modal estimates for Extrapolation and Innovation could be very misleading.

Table **7.1** Data used in constructing Figures 7.2 to 7.4 inclusive. The value P is the probability that the actual cost will fall within the band ± 11 per cent of the mode of the density distribution.

Technology	Mode	Sigma	P (%)
Modification	1.23	0.14	67
Interpolation	1.86	0.52	31
Extrapolation	3.08	1.25	21
Innovation	4.93	2.36	18

In other words, the conclusion arrived at by decision analysis is confirmed by the historical evidence; the probability that the cost outcome will be identical with any single estimate is negligible.

Moreover, no single estimate can adequately describe the difference in quality between a modal estimate for a Modification and a modal estimate for an Innovation. For reliable decisions, therefore, some indication of the dispersion of the probability density distribution must be provided. At least two estimates having a defined relationship to the implied probability density distribution are needed for this.

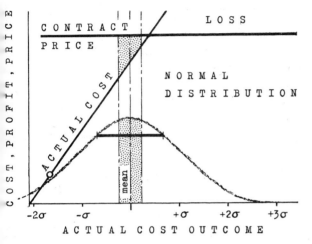

Figure 7.4 Diagram, similar to Figure 7.3, but with a coefficient of variation similar to that of the innovation case of Figure 7.2. The shaded area in this figure represents ± 11 per cent of the mean value, as in Figure 7.3.

Use of Multiple Estimates

In planning to use multiple estimates, a repetition of what happened to PERT must be avoided. As originally devised, PERT had required the assessment for each task of three estimates (optimistic, most likely and pessimistic) but, within a few years of its introduction, the use of a single estimate had become almost universal.

The underlying reason, probably, was that all three estimates were for the same nominated task; and while it is true that the same amount of work does not cost the same in all companies, or in all circumstances in the same company (which is why project managers have been able to achieve notable improvements where they have been appointed), the variation observed is not readily associated with the task itself.

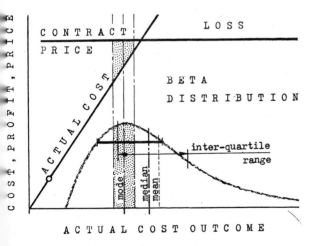

Figure 7.5 Diagram similar to Figure 7.4 but with a beta distribution assumed instead of a normal probability density distribution.

This difficulty can be avoided by identifying those differences in work content that are responsible for the different estimates used to describe the dispersion of the probable cost outcome. Those differences must reflect realistically the degree of innovation in the project and of circularity in the programme, and be derived by completely objective means.

Objectivity

'Objective' has become an emotionally-toned word; the fact that an estimate is objective does not make it 'true'. It means only that it has been arrived at directly from the facts by agreed or ascertainable rules. Any number of estimators, given the same facts, would produce the same estimate, but it could still be misleading.

Minimum Possible Cost

A good example of an objective estimate is one that allows only for the activities on the planned programme. In fact, it is because it is objective that this type of estimate has been so acceptable in the past. Probably, most of the initial estimates relied on for the preparation of Figure 7.1 were of this type.

It is very interesting – and, for our purposes, important – that the figure reveals a consistency amounting almost to a rule: 'Initial estimates made of the costs of new projects are characteristically 5/3 sigma less than the mode of the probability density distribution of what those costs will come out to be.' Within the limits of accuracy of the data, this seems to be true equally for Modification, Interpolation, Extrapolation and Innovation. (If the distribution is skewed, the displacement may be as high as 7/4.)

If the supposition is correct that these initial estimates were based on the assumption of everything in the programme going to plan, it would be reasonable to expect them to be the 'minimum possible' and at the 'left tail' of the probability dispersion, where they are found.

Maximum Probable Cost

Only one more estimate is needed to indicate the dispersion. The 'most probable' estimate is not acceptable, because probability assessments cannot be made objectively. The remaining possibility is to attempt to define a point near the 'right tail'.

It would be every bit as objective to assume that nothing goes according to plan, and to evaluate the consequences of that as to assume that everything does go right first time, provided that there can be certainty that all potentially untoward events are identifiable. The attractive feature of such an approach is that inevitably it would have to take account of both the uncertainty of the technology and the circularity of the programme.

Project Management

Identification of potentially untoward events in this way, while the programme is being planned, provides opportunity for the programme or its objectives to be adjusted to mitigate the 'criticality' of consequential situations. This would cause the dispersion of the probability distribution to be reduced, creating conditions in which the single most probable estimate so desired by administrators could be made more deterministic.

To be really effective for project management purposes, as the Downey Steering Group required,[6] the method should do more than indicate what happens when something is done; it should guide decisions about what ought to be done.

Thus, it should be possible to define, at the earliest possible moment, the research and further study that, when completed, will reduce the uncertainty of the cost outcome. At the same time, normal networking techniques will indicate the latest date for completing that work if it is to reduce technological uncertainty before irrevocable actions are taken.

Resource Planning

The method should help, too, with resource planning; in particular, in determining the amount of work that should be done by each department.

It was probably this difficulty of determining the level of activity appropriate to any task that, more than anything else, made officials reluctant to accept estimates containing allowances, put in to cater for unanticipated unknowns, but so easily dissipated in unnecessary work.

As the Downey Steering Group[8] remarked, 'efforts to keep estimates down may be a necessary element in cost control'. In resolving the resulting conflict of interests 'neither technical branches nor finance branches are in a strong position. Lacking authoritative guidance based on proper records of past programmes and costs, and an adequate organization to collate and analyse them, technical branches are uneasily aware that any assessment of project costs depends very much on personal judgement and the interpretation put on past experience by whoever is making the assessment and that they are not well placed to sustain convincing arguments in favour of a particular level of expenditure.'

It may therefore be considered a requirement of the new method that it should place reliance on historical records only for estimation of the cost of carrying out defined work and not for deciding what work should be done.

Additional work to reduce dispersion should be clearly differentiable from the task to be done if all goes well. In the case of cost-plus contracts, those who authorize expenditure should be able to recognize the identified consequences of untoward events and to participate in decisions concerning the extent of insurances or contingency funding that should be provided. It does not follow necessarily that every possible contingency would be offset.

As a project proceeds through its development, the degree of certainty of what the cost outcome is likely to be should increase. It is very desirable that the particular milestones which remove uncertainty should be separately identified and associated with provisions made. The passing of a milestone like this frequently releases resources which can be used for other purposes.

Excess Cost Avoidance

The identification of potentially untoward events and the reconstruction of the programme to mitigate their consequences and so reduce the dispersion are the objectives of the ECA (excess cost avoidance) method, which therefore extends the capability of network techniques to deal with these aspects.

The novel and critical feature of the ECA method is the estimate made for the probable limit of financial risk at the right tail. For the ECA method to be valid, this assessment must satisfy three conditions absolutely:

1 It must comprehend the worst concatenations that can occur, regardless of their probabilities.

2 The determination of potential, untoward discoveries and events must be objective and based on information available at the time of assessment.

3 Compilation of the estimate must be as systematic and dependable as double-entry book-keeping.

Each condition is discussed in detail below. First, the technical significance of this estimate must be noted. It is correctly described as the 'maximum probable' and not the 'maximum possible' estimate because, with a skewed probability distribution, there is no absolute maximum.

If the ECA is used correctly, the most probable cost outcome will lie between the minimum possible and the maximum probable estimates, and the probability that it will reach the latter is very small, indeed. However, unless this upper estimate is so large as to be meaningless for decision purposes, there must remain some possibility that it can be exceeded.

Instead of invalidating ECA, this makes it a strong tool for project management. The maximum probable estimate is prepared on the assumption that all contingencies are met with normal efficiency. When need arises, therefore, sub-networks and cost estimates are available for planning and monitoring the work. Unfortunately, it will be possible always to increase this expenditure by inefficiency or waste.

Although ECA was not devised as a solution to the problems of estimating for inflation and miscalculation, industrial action and other non-engineering hazards, it would be prudent to make appropriate allowances for these in the maximum probable estimate. On the other hand, it must remain a matter of judgement whether to allow for contingencies already covered in other ways — for instance by insurance, government guarantee, or by the ability to vary income in proportion to inflation.

The Worst Concatenation

The ECA method explores what happens to the programme when every assumption is found to be invalid, every deduction wrong and every planned event frustrated or late. In this investigation, rigorous use is made of the so-called law known variously as the law of maximum inconvenience, 'Gumperson's law' or by less polite names.

This 'law' states: 'If something untoward is going to happen, it will do so when it can cause the most inconvenience.' It is to our advantage that this is only a waggish and pessimistic comment on life; the situation we are trying to describe is seldom realized.

Allowance is made in this upper estimate, not only for what happens when everything has gone wrong when it could do most damage, but for those repetitions of events that may be planned in order to determine the causes of difficulty, or that are the fortuitous consequences of several alternative, but unrelated, causes. It is not evident that any useful purpose would be served by taking account of further possible misfortunes.

Determination of the Untoward

The root of the ECA method is an analysis of the programme network. Depending on the convention adopted, each arrow or node on this represents an activity which, it is expected, will be completed in a certain time. In effect, it is a statement of the events that should occur in sequence, and of the dates by which they should have occurred. Circumstances can alter this in one of four ways:

1 Something does not happen that should.
2 Something does not happen when it should.
3 Something happens that should not.
4 Something happens when it should not.

The last two cannot be predicted. This would require invention and, if this were necessary, ECA would be impossible. Fortunately, they may be disregarded immediately because unless they obstruct the programme they do not matter; if they do obstruct, their effect immediately appears under one or other of the first two headings.

It may be necessary sometimes to analyse the potentially untoward situation very carefully to ascertain the particular combination of circumstances that could cause it.

The consequences of delay in completing any activity are readily deduced from the network itself, so determination of the most serious consequence presents no difficulty. It will be noted that this implies a particular case of something happening when it should not.

The result of the frustration of any essential activity, however, is not so readily determined. Only in very exceptional circumstances would the frustration be absolute, for this would imply the failure of the whole project. The normal consequence would be the re-cycling of some part of the programme, based on the additional experience gained.

Re-cycling could vary from a single modification, followed by the repetition of a single test, to the redesign and replacement of a prototype, followed by repetition of a major part of the test programme.

Step by Step Analysis

In most cases, therefore, special knowledge of an activity is needed before the most serious consequence of any untoward event can be defined. This knowledge is built up systematically in a step by step analysis begun during the project definition study and continued throughout the design phase as each design solution is prepared.

These individual analyses are collected and organized during the preparation of the planning network on which the minimum possible estimate is based; the consequences found to be most serious form the maximum probable estimate.

The analysis of potentially untoward discoveries and events, that leads directly to the maximum probable estimate, devolves from the planning network on which the minimum possible estimate is based. It follows that the absence of any record of a completed analysis for any particular event number automatically warns that the upper estimate is incomplete.

Considered in isolation, this correlation of potential consequences with event numbers is not enough for conviction. The danger remains that for any activity there may be more than one serious consequence.

These alternatives are revealed by the step by step analyses referred to above. By identifying each of these with the event numbers on the planning network, a complete contingency analysis is provided. Moreover analysis of the programme network and the step by step analyses should cross check. Since both are objective this check may be repeated at any time and should give reproducible results.

There is a danger, when the estimated value is the final product of any analysis, that an error may lie undetected for many months, solely because the analysis is never re-examined. With the use of the ECA method for planning and monitoring, this is unlikely to happen.

Estimates remain subject to day to day scrutiny and it is almost inconceivable that any major error would not soon be discovered. This may become more self-evident in the discussion on this aspect of the ECA method later.

Technically and in human terms, therefore, the methods proposed for finding the maximum probable cost appear to be credible and to afford the degree of conviction required for financial judgements.

Limitation of Effort

An inordinate amount of work would be needed to carry out a full ECA analysis of every opportunity for misfortune in a development programme even if it were possible to find the team to do it. Fortunately, experience suggests that these events may have something like a modified Pareto distribution with a few of the potential untoward occurrences accounting for most of the risk.

The majority of the potential misfortunes are, probably, of small significance and easily covered by the usual allowances for the minor upsets of a normal development programme. The full rigour of ECA should, therefore, be reserved for that small fraction – say, one-fifth or one-tenth of the total – which is important.

An absolute criterion is needed here to sort out the important from the unimportant while the analysis is still in hand; obviously, it should not be necessary to do all the work before deciding which results to reject. The most convenient filter appears to be the duration of the delay which will be caused by the potential untoward discovery or event.

Delays incur cost not only because staff are left without essential activity but also because they find themselves some less essential tasks, which also require manufacture and test, or technical or computer time.

Delays in completing one part of the programme may limit the time available for another part of the programme which, in some cases, may limit freedom of action in overcoming a technical or production difficulty. The probability then is that the solution that must be adopted may be less than ideal, bringing other problems in its train.

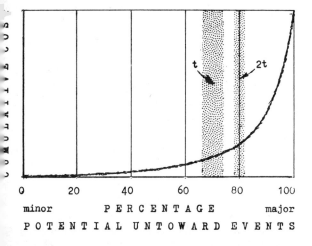

Figure 7.6 Sketch shows suggested use of two threshold indicators for defining the important region in a possible distribution of financial risk over the range of potential misfortunes.

Thus, some delay time 't' days can be accepted as a threshold value and any consequence ignored which appears, on initial inspection, to incur a delay of less than this. If it appears that some consequence may cause a greater delay, more detailed consideration can be given but only if it appears that the delay will be greater than another threshold value – say, $2t$ days – should a full cost analysis be included in the estimate.

The value chosen for 't' is a matter for judgement, dependent on the duration of that part of the development programme devoted to experiment and test. It may be no more than a day or two.

Figure 7.6 shows, on a hypothetical distribution, the effect of using the two threshold indicators suggested, the zone of one having twice the slope of the other. There is no information available to suggest the shape of the distribution and it may not be the same for all types of development. So it would be advisable to ascertain this first by investigating every adverse consequence in a small, but representative, sample.

Multiple Consequences

The possibility of multiple occurrences of a particular untoward event raises a problem of special difficulty. There are three possible cases to consider.

One is an untoward event caused by a technical fault when there cannot be a guarantee that the data made available during the testing which preceded the discovery of the fault will be adequate to ensure full diagnosis and cure. The procedure is to design the test programme that would provide the solution and to include the full cost of this.

If the possibility of the untoward event is identified by its consequences, without a specific potential cause having been noted, some convention must be used. If one could guarantee that the event would identify the cause, there would be no difficulty in putting it right.

If the cause remains obscure after the event – as has happened – identification depends very largely on the skill, experience and knowledge of the development engineer. Such cases are comparatively rare and the most appropriate procedure is to suppose a cause which needs full investigation and to treat accordingly.

A third case is that in which a given untoward event could result from several alternative causes. These must be scrutinised to see if the occurrence of the event eliminates more than one cause. If each is found to be independent of the others, and could cause difficulty at any time, its consequences should be included in the maximum probable cost estimate.

Development Planning

The ECA method was not devised merely to show the probable upper limit of financial risk inherent in any development programme, useful though that is. Its main purpose is to inform the planning of the development programme to avoid unnecessary expenditure, incurred by untoward discoveries or events for which adequate pre-provision has not been made.

The method is used to identify the principal elements that could escalate cost, and so to alter the circumstances of each so that it is eliminated as a potential cause or substantially reduced in effect.

There are four ways only in which this excess cost can be reduced. The most attractive is to rearrange the programme to resolve all uncertainties, which could be potentially serious, before any major commitment is made. Proof of the effectiveness of this solution is seen in the 'Modification' case discussed earlier.

Nominally, this is normal commercial practice: however, competitive pressures frequently compel departure from this ideal and the importance of timing sometimes is overlooked. One of the main conclusions of the Downey Steering Group[27] was that decisions to go ahead 'must be postponed until it is possible to resolve the major uncertainties of the project' (it must be noted that 'uncertainties' in this context may not have exactly the same meaning as in the ECA method).

Avoidance of Novelty

There is now a marked tendency to eschew projects with major uncertainties. Foster,[5] for instance, talks about DOD policy on materials as an example of new DOD policies on R and D. 'We must eliminate', he says, 'three syndromes which have developed over past years: overestimating the true value and underestimating the real cost; getting glued to 'fads' at the expense of new or modified conventional materials; and being entranced by sophistication and forgetting the more straightforward approaches.'

Novelty cannot be avoided always, however. Blackwell and Reed[8] point out that engine development time exceeds that for airframe development so that, ideally, engines should be started in advance of requirements.

They suggest that this difficulty may be overcome by developing 'building bricks' — elements of engine technology — for use later. As they emphasize, there is a difference between what they advocate and conventional applied research because the latter does not lead to any significant reduction in the degree of innovation in the project concerned.

Alternative Solutions

In a personal letter S.H. Bonser[15] has suggested that wherever possible innovations should be developed in parallel with the main project, leaving no more than a couple of major innovations in the main development programme. This is practicable if the innovation does not have repercusions on other parts of the project and if conventional solutions are adequate for the duties required during the main development programme.

This is not always the case and the success of the project may then depend on the solution to some particular problem. In these circumstances, it is usual — though apparently not invariable — for two or more designs to be developed in parallel.

From the argument of the ECA method, each alternative must provide a complete, fully acceptable solution which meets every requirement of the design specification and is developed within the same time scale. The alternative designs must incorporate alternatives to all the important assumptions and the estimate must contemplate the possibility of the need for further development of a design that embodies a different combination of these assumptions.

In some cases, it may not be possible to devise more than one possible solution to a problem. The cost dispersion implied by the maximum probable cost is then open-ended. It can be closed only by experimental proof.

Conditions of use have an influence on every design and until that design has been fully tested in a representative environment it cannot be accepted as a valid solution. Unless the validity of every assumption in combination with all other assumptions can be proved beyond doubt, no fixed price contract or performance guarantee should be entered into. Additional, early experiment is therefore the third way to reduce development cost uncertainty.

Insurance action

Finally, if all preventive means fail, steps can be taken to mitigate the consequences of the untoward event, should it occur. Insurance action may take one of several forms: additional long-dated material may be ordered from an alternative source, the manufacture of some critical component may be advanced to allow time for re-make if defective, spares may be provided, or a pre-production batch may be made to provide spares if these are needed in a hurry, a duplicate test rig may be set up in case one is damaged, and so on.

Most frequently, this analysis will show the marked reduction in the dispersion of the probable cost outcome resulting from reduced lead-time and from quick reaction-time when modifications or replacements have to be made. One possibility to be evaluated, therefore, is the provision of surplus manufacturing capacity to reduce the length of the queue.

Controlling the Cost

Most of these solutions involve some extra cost by comparison with a minimum programme. The resulting 'minor estimate' will then be greater than the minimum possible estimate, but it will still be at the left tail of the new distribution and will be more deterministic.

The aim is to adjust the programme so that planned cost is close to actual. The actual cost then should be minimal because experience shows that, in general, properly planned corrective actions cost less than stop-gap measures devised when the situation is already out of control.

Permission to include these additional contingent expenditures in the minimum possible estimate should properly be obtained from the person or body authorized to release the funds. Because a potential untoward discovery or event has been recognized, it does not mean that the programme must automatically be modified to reduce financial risk.

The probability of that particular misfortune may be very small and the financial authority is entirely within its rights to exercise a subjective judgement on whether the probability of the risk and the seriousness of the contingent consequences justify the additional – and certain – cost.

These estimates should be kept under continual review as certainty replaces hypothesis in relation to each assumption or activity. In some instances this may show that resources held against a particular contingency can be released; in other cases, it may show the wisdom of additional provision for some future potential untoward event.

The financial authority must take full account of the maximum probable cost estimate and must accept that, if no step is taken to avoid the consequences of some untoward event, the estimate cannot be changed. On the other hand, this does not imply that the expenditure authorized should much exceed the 'minor estimate'. Funds to cover overspend up to the limit of the corresponding 'major estimate' should be kept available at appropriately short notice.

Documentation

The information required for the ECA method is derived from many sources over a relatively long period. It must be organized for the preparation of credible estimates and control documents and be revised periodically as work proceeds. Without systematic and well indexed documents, there can be little hope of achieving the objectives.

The present proposals envisage that documents should be prepared in parallel with other technical information, from the product specification onwards, achieving a complete schedule in time to prepare the planning network.

Carefully-worded product specifications have always been essential for fixed price contracts. For cost-plus contracts and private-venture work this used to be less common, mainly because of a desire to take full advantage of every technical opportunity that arose. Even here the technical and commercial advantages of a comprehensive specification are much more widely recognized now, with benefit to product quality and development economy.

The systematic use of these documents for technical purposes other than design is comparatively recent. Botfeld and Earle[30] in a paper presented to a 1971 conference described proposals for documentation establishing validation procedures for the proposed NASA space shuttle on the basis of a step by step analysis of the mission phase. The procedure suggested for ECA has much in common with this.

Great benefit is derived from statements of design requirements and assumptions underlying individual design schemes. These are helpful in defining the interface conditions between related schemes, especially when these are prepared by different people at different times. They, or the information they contain, are essential for planning environmental test and development programmes.

They serve also as valuable historical records, particularly when associated with relevant test results, and can be referred to if similar designs have to be prepared later.

The ECA method needs these design statements for the assumptions they record and for the guide which they give to the probabilities of the potential risks. The usefulness of the ECA method depends on a comprehensive statement of assumptions, and the design statement facilitates the checking of this from the dimensions of the design problem. In this connection, it may be helpful to have standard check lists.

Design information is disseminated not only on drawings but also in planning and process instructions, standards and other documents. These, too, must be considered for assumptions.

The potential causes of untoward events which must be sought at this stage are five:

1 Defect in, or incompleteness of the theory, or absence of any valid theory on which a design solution is based.

2 Incorrect selection or misuse of theory, or inaccuracy in applying it.

3 Inability to produce to the required standard and in the manner proposed.

4 Defect in material or other temporary obstacle.

5 Accident to prototype, or product, when complete.

The potential consequences and possible means of avoiding them should be examined and recorded. The document for this could have the column headings shown in Table 7.2; this relates the information to the event number on the planning network.

Status

The uncertainty of the financial risks created for imaginative projects by unanticipated unknowns is a critical problem. Attempts to deal with it by allowing for selected particular unknowns which can be anticipated have not been successful.

The ECA method therefore proposes to comprehend all possible unknowns, leaving selection from among them to the events themselves and to use statistical probability distributions for decision purposes. This makes the method useful also in the planning and management of projects.

Although this new proposal is sound in theory, and is consistent with practices successful in related fields, it may require still further development and adaptation to the needs of individual organizations. Even in its present form, however, because it ensures that attention is given at the start of a project, to minimize the potential consequences of uncertainty, it goes far towards satisfying Harland's precept[21]: 'The art of project management is to ensure that nothing is entirely

Table 7.2 Column headings proposed for ECA step by step analysis records.

Analysis number and date
Project number and description
Drawing or document number, issue number, date
Component or activity
Assumption or event investigated
Possible failure:
    Description
    Network affected: number, issue number, date
    Path (event) number
Consequences of failure:
    Additional work
    Estimated delay to programme
    Estimated cost of consequences
Prevention or amelioration:
    Avoidable consequences:
        Means of avoidance
        Cost of avoidance
    Unavoidable consequences:
        Cost of unavoidable consequences
Total cost element of distribution

unexpected. This may not be newsworthy but it should be economic.'

References

1 Report of the Steering Group on Development Cost Estimating, HMSO, London, 1968 (hereafter called 'the report'), 1, p 3.
2 Tischler, A.O. A Commentary on Low-cost Space Transportation, Astronautics and Aeronautics, 7, No 8, August, 1969, pp 55-60.
3 Marshall, A.W. and Meckling, W.H. Predictability of the Costs, Time and Success of Development, RAND Report P-1821, Dec 11, 1959 (quoted by Tischler in ref 2).
4 The Report, as (1), 1 p 56.
5 Blackwell, B.D. The Initiation of Projects, Journal Royal Aeronautical Society, 71 No. 677, May, 1967, pp. 331.
6 Drake, H.B. Major DOD Procurements at War with Reality. Harvard Business Review, Jan/Feb, 1970, pp 119-140.
7 The Report, as (1), 1, p 100.
8 Blackwell, B.D. and Reed, A.V.N. Development Management and Cost Control, Journal Royal Aeronautical Society, 69 No 660, Dec, 1965, pp 813-24.
9 The Report, as (1), 1, p 29.
10 Haviland, D.W.G.L. Relationships between Government and Aeronautics, Journal Royal Aeronautical Society, 70, No 663, March, 1966, pp 382-4.

11 Simonis, E.A. Written Contribution to Discussion, *Journal Royal Aeronautical Society*, 69, No 660, Dec, 1965, p 823.

12 Trapnell, F.M. How to Run R and D, Management Today, Oct, 1970, p 123 *et seq*.

13 Pearson, H. Discussion, *Journal Royal Aeronautical Society*, 69, No 660, Dec, 1965, p 822.

14 Report of the Committee on the Management and Control of Research and Development (Chairman: Sir Solly Zuckerman), HMSO, London, 1961.

15 Bonsor, S.H. (identified as 'Speaker No 3' in the Summary by B.D. Blackwell of the Discussion at a Symposium on Project Management), *Journal Royal Aeronautical Society*, 73, No 697, Jan, 1969, p 43.

16 Dollimore, G.P. Practical Applications of Planning Development Programmes and New Management Techniques, *Journal Royal Aeronautical Society*, 71, No 675, March, 1967, pp 193-201.

17 Walker, M.R. and Sayer, J.S. Project Planning and Scheduling, Report 6959, E.I. du Pont de Nemours and Company, Inc, Wilmington, Delaware, March, 1959.

18 Malcolm, D.G., Roseboom, J.H., Clark, C.E. and Fazar, W. Applications of a Technique for R and D Programme Evaluation, Operations Research, 7, No 5, 1959, pp 646-669.

19 Moder, J.J. and Phillips, C.R. Project Management with CPM and PERT, Reinhold, N.Y, 1964, p 2.

20 The Report, as (1), 2, pp 3-8.

21 Harland, R.E.W. Project Management at the Ministry of Technology, *Journal Royal Aeronautical Society*, 71, No 684, Dec, 1967, pp 821-6.

22 Simmons, H. Working Out the Lockheed Dilemma, Astronautics and Aeronautics, 8, No 7, July, 1970, pp 14-5.

23 DOD and NASA Guide, PERT/Cost Systems Design, US Government Printing Office, Washington, DC, June, 1962 (quoted in ref 19).

24 Davis, H. The Management of Cost-Reduction – Method or Myth? *Journal Royal Aeronautical Society*, 70, No 666, June, 1966, pp 639-48.

25 Harvey, R.A. A Probablistic Approach to Aeronautical Research and Development, *Journal Royal Aeronautical Society*, 74, No 713, May, 1970, pp 373-80.

26 The Report, as (1), 2, p 26.

27 The Report, as (1), 1, p 69.

28 The Report, as (1), 1, p 30.

29 Foster, J.D. Jr. New DOD Policies that Begin with Materials, Astronautics and Aeronautics, 8, No 7, July, 1970, pp 72-74.

30 Botfeld, B. and Earle, D.W. The Design of a Test Logic and Constraint Network for the Space Shuttle Programme, AIAA paper No 71-309 presented at the AIAA Space Shuttle Development Testing and Operations Conference, Phoenix Arizona, March, 15, 1971.

Note

[1] In mathematics, the term is sometimes used when the law is known but the accuracy required does not justify the labour of calculation.

8.

Some Evidence on the Accuracy of Forecasts in R&D Projects

by H. Thomas

Reprinted from R & D Management, Vol. 1 (2), February, 1971 with permission.

Introduction

In recent years many formal attempts, e.g., Baker & Pound, have been made to help R & D management assess the worth of R & D projects and select those most worthy of inclusion in the R & D programme. Most of these attempts are based on financial appraisals of a project's worth and require estimates of the costs and likely revenues that will result from the adoption of a given project. It is clear, therefore, that the validity of any measure of worth for a project is dependent upon the accuracy of the estimates of cost and revenue associated with that project. Unfortunately, the limited amount of evidence so far presented suggests, in particular, that cost estimates are extremely inaccurate.

In this article, therefore, I have tried to add some further evidence on forecast accuracy for a number of industrial R & D projects. We begin with a short review of the existing literature evidence and continue with an analysis of the past effectiveness of R & D work and, in particular, of forecast accuracy.

Literature Evidence

A useful distinction between the range of studies on forecast accuracy is achieved by evaluating the evidence on forecast accuracy in military R & D separate from evidence pertaining to industrial R & D.

Perhaps the pioneer analysis of estimate accuracy in R & D projects was carried out by the RAND Corporation economists, Marshall & Meckling[2]. They studied 22 military development projects and analysed the extent of forecast inaccuracy in the orginal initial cost estimate by dividing the latest possible cost estimate by the initial estimate. By doing this they showed that, on average, the most recent cost estimates exceeded the earliest available estimates by between two and three times and that forecasts were more inaccurate when the project's level of technical difficulty was greater. Marshall and Meckling also showed that there were inaccuracies in the forecasts of time necessary for completion of R & D work which, on average, indicated that projects took 50 per cent more R & D time than that specified by the earliest estimate.

Peck and Scherer[3] in their analysis of the weapons acquisition process in the US calculated estimate errors for aerospace developments and found that, on average, the latest cost figures were over three times the initial estimates and that actual times for R & D work were, on average, over one-third more than initial estimates.

It can be seen that both the previous studies are in close agreement about the extent of forecast inaccuracy in cost and time estimates. A very thorough study by Summers[4] of cost estimates on 68 military R & D projects confirms the evidence of the earlier studies about the existence of a 3-fold inflation in the initial cost estimate by the time development work has been completed.

The evidence in relation to military R & D, therefore, points to large inaccuracies in the estimates of cost and time factors and is consistent over a sizeable sample, approximately 100, of government-sponsored R & D projects.

Industrial R & D, on the other hand, is carried out mainly for commercial reasons and is, thus, often of a lower level of technical difficulty. *A priori*, therefore, we would expect that forecast errors would be of a lower level of magnitude.

Mansfield[5,6] has probably pioneered the detailed study of project selection mechanisms in industrial R & D. In a study of an equipment laboratory in the US he found for a sample of 45 R & D projects that initial cost estimates were very accurate and representative of the actual expenditures incurred on R & D. Time slippages in project completion were present in about one-half of the projects he studied and performance objectives were met in most cases.

Meadows[7] has collected evidence on forecast accuracy for 59 projects from two chemical laboratories. He found that only about one-half of the firms' R & D spending results in commercially-successful products. The ratios of actual to initial estimated costs gave values of between 1.25 and 4 (average 3) for projects that were either technical or commercial failures and values around 1 for commercially successful projects.

Allen and November[8] have collected information on the accuracy of forecasts and present seven case-histories of novel projects in the chemical industry. These findings showed that in five cases out of seven, forecasts were far too small in relation to actual final values, whereas in two cases initial forecasts of costs were larger than actual values. Their analysis also gave some evidence on forecasts of R & D completion time and benefits (price, sales volume, etc.), that would accrue from commercial adoption of the project. Predictably, Allen and November found that errors in the forecasts of benefit variables, i.e., price and sales volume, can affect the project's predicted financial outcome considerably, but that errors in various cost components, e.g., R & D, raw material, etc., can also have an important influence.

It is fair to say that the evidence from the three industrial studies[6,7,8] is not consistent. Mansfield's equipment laboratory is an example of a case in which the error in forecasts of costs is very small. Further, even though time slippage in R & D occurred, most of it could be explained in terms of the individual project's nature and staffing. Meadows's chemical laboratories exhibited greater inaccuracies in forecasts of cost for projects that were either technical or commercial failures than for commercially successful ones. Overall, however, actual cost values were between two and three times initial estimates of cost. Allen and November found optimistic biases in cost estimation and in the prediction of benefit variables such as price and sales volume.

A further study[9] examines estimates and outcomes for 84 projects in electricity generation research. The results for cost estimates are broadly similar to those obtained by Meadows and Allen, showing the same optimistic bias.

It is reasonable to conclude, therefore, that in government-sponsored R & D there tend to be consistent over-optimistic estimates of likely costs and times to project completion. In commercial R & D, errors in forecasts would seem to be a function of the type of industry, the product produced by the firm and the organization structure of the individual firm. Stronger conclusions will be obtained only through the accumulation of evidence from R & D case-histories in industry. In the next section a number of projects from firms A and B in the electronics industry are thoroughly analysed and presented.

Retrospective Analysis

Methodology

The approach adopted in analysing firms A and B was to establish a representative sample of past projects undertaken by the firms and then to try and piece together from formal records, accounting data and discussions with project engineering personnel, how these projects started and evolved through time. Given this reconstruction we can then carry out analyses of forecast error, of the resolution of uncertainty through the life of the project and of the reasons for changes in the technical and commercial objectives of a given project. Such a method of research requires painstaking evaluation of documents and records and constant checking of formal records against the informal opinions of project personnel. Often, formal information systems can have in-built biases because employees deliberately, but without fraudulent motives, misrepresent pieces of data in order to present a favourable case to higher management levels. The research method, therefore, has to be a variant of an anthropologist's technique of participant observation except that the evaluation of the project is pieced together in a retrospective manner with the researcher accepted, in as far as this is possible, as a member of the organization. In order that I was seen to be a member of the organization I was required to spend one day per week in each firm working the same hours as other employees. The primary aim before the research was undertaken was for me to gain the confidence of the engineers in the firms under study and to reassure them that the results of the study would not be used by management as a means to assess relative efficiencies and abilities. In this aim I consider that I was reasonably successful.

Data

In the following section we present a brief description of each of the projects evaluated in firms A and B. This description is necessarily limited by the desire to avoid identifying the firm or the exact nature of the project. The description is given primarily to provide an awareness of extraneous factors to be borne in mind in considering results of the later analysis.

Firm 'A'

Project 1A

One of a projected family of instruments for electronic

measurement. The objective of pursuing the concept of the family of instruments was a result of a company plan to produce a range of test instruments in an area not previously exploited by the company. Market potential was considered by the company to be considerable and the expertise within the R & D laboratory available to carry out the work.

Project 2A

A complementary instrument to 1A produced to extend the product line.

Project 3A

The final member of the first phase of the series 1A/2A set of instruments. This was produced to provide a complete measurement system for the customer and to provide training for existing engineers in the technical area before the launching of the second phase of this system of instruments. Again, market potential for the system was estimated to be considerable.

Project 4A

A measurement instrument sponsored and planned by the laboratory management to follow on and replace an existing instrument. The modifications were designed to improve the capability and performance of the device. The market potential was thought to be large.

Project 5A

A redesign of an existing instrument for a specific customer. The request for the research to be done emanated from the sales division who considered that the market offered was profitable to the company.

Project 6A

An instrument specifically planned by the laboratory management to place the firm in a new area of electronic measurement. Again, the market was considered to be very large and the measurement area one with great long-term potential. As a result the project was felt to be, to a small extent, a learning exercise as well as a profitable venture for the company and its technical staff.

Project 7A

To design an electronic measurement system to meet known existing demand. Again a family of instruments was planned and in this case it was considered reasonable to view them as one rather than three distinct projects. The idea for the project was generated within the laboratory.

Project 8A

An instrument designed and planned to be used as a complementary instrument to an existing successful product marketed by the firm. The market for the instrument was thus considered to be steady but not considerable.

Project 9A

An instrument designed as a result of technical 'fall-out' from the project 1A series. Considered to have a useful market potential and overall benefit for the firm.

Project 10A

An instrument designed specifically to a special contract from a customer. Sales department considers the development will be extremely profitable for the firm and the laboratory regards the development work as being a fairly simple task.

We now present four projects which were shelved by the firm. Owing to the fact that records for shelved or failed projects are very difficult to trace, the documentation or description in these cases is not up to the standard of the previous sample of ten.

Project 11A

An electrical measurement instrument to fill a gap in the firm's product line. Market potential uncertain and ultimate benefit to the firm not considered to be very great.

Project 12A

An extension of the project 6A range of instruments. Considered to have both good market potential and profitability prospects.

Project 13A

An instrument designed to a contract specification from an outside customer. Both market potential and benefit are calculated to be large and the involvement in a new measurement technique technically appealing.

Project 14A

A fall-out from the 1A series of instruments. Undertaken largely because of the spin-off, even though market potential and benefit were estimated to be barely satisfactory.

The above sample of projects is considered to be a representative sample of the work undertaken by firm A over the 5-year period 1963 to 1968 including the early months of 1969.

It should be noted that this firm has a formal evaluation and review system for R & D projects. Briefly, if the R & D manager decides that a project idea is worthy of further consideration a preliminary evaluation of specification, design, and project economies is carried out. If this proves positive the project engineer assigned to the investigation phase of the project must estimate certain economic factors: cost, eventual quantity sold, price and profit rate, and calculate a preliminary benefit/cost ratio for the project. Then, if the value of this ratio is greater than some minimum corporate target, a decision is generally made to recommend inclusion of the project in the R & D work of the firm, subject to the availability of resources. The nature of this project selection process should be borne in mind in reviewing the tabular analysis of retrospective data.

Firm 'B'

Project 1B

This project has been created from a large number of individual projects which on individual analysis might not appear profitable but when viewed as a system are attractive to the management of the firm. The system embraces a 'bread and butter' range of measuring instruments of high quality with the advantage of cheapness and reliability at the expense of extreme technical sophistication. The family of instruments has been continually developed and new additions, modifications, etc., are introduced to sale at the same time as development is proceeding.

Project 2B

This project has largely been sponsored by outside contract. It is an instrument in a new area for the firm and is intended to compete with a couple of existing products which do not have the performance and specification of the new instrument. The instrument is an attempt to build a bridge-head for the firm in the area, with a view to further long-term expansion. The attraction of the project is enhanced because a large proportion of risk capital is provided from sources external to the firm.

There are a number of other projects that could be presented but the level and quality of past records is not sufficient to maintain the same standard of analysis as with previous projects. The problem with firm B is that records of expenditure on R & D projects have only recently been started and market and cost evaluations of

projects are in most cases no more than 'ball-park' estimates. Analysis based on such data would obviously have only a spurious claim to validity.

Analysis of Data

In this section we shall try to assess:

1 The accuracy of forecasts of variables related to the projects.

2 The change in these forecasts through time and the resolution of uncertainty.

3 An identification of the sensitive variables in evaluating the prior success of a project.

4 The usefulness of the return factor index of firm A in giving a valid measure of worth of project and predicting the eventual financial outcome of a project.

1. Forecast Accuracy

Typically, the decision to include a project within a firm's R & D portfolio is dependent upon a preliminary process of evaluating the worth of the project to the firm. The methods by which firms evaluate projects vary from the fairly informal, rough appraisal of a firm like firm B to the more formal economic appraisal of factors such as likely cost and revenue cash flows and the calculation of a rate of return factor. An example of the latter type of approach is the procedure adopted by firm A.

If a firm calculates a return factor it requires estimates of economic factors as inputs to this calculation. It can be seen fairly easily that a return factor of the form revenue/cost can give misleading values if the forecast inputs are not accurate. If a decision to undertake a project is based solely on the figure of merit given by a return factor without allowing for inaccuracies in the forecasts of inputs the firm may commit heavy expenditures to a worthless project and reduce the value of its total research work. We shall not discuss here whether firms should use return factors to aid them in their project selection decisions. I take the view that whatever method they use to appraise a project, better decision will come on average from better forecasts of market and cost factors.

In Table 8.1 below ratios for firm A of the actual values that eventually occurred to the earliest available estimates of the relevant factors are presented, i.e., those on which decisions were based. Firm A evaluates how much the development will cost (and how long it will take), how many units of the end-product are likely to be sold over an estimated *life* for the product and what the market price for the product will be. It should be noticed that columns seven, eight and nine assess the degree of technical advance (small, medium or large) of the end-product, the final status of the project in terms of technical and commercial success and the source of the idea to develop the product (L = laboratory, C = customer). For almost all the projects it is too early yet to assess whether the engineers assessed the likely market life for the end-product correctly.

Some comments must be made at this point about some of the items presented in Table 8.1. First, column three is obtained by adjusting the ratios in column two for the influence of changes in price levels. The adjustment is thus the familiar one for the effects of inflation and it was carried out in the following manner. From previous accounting records of cost breakdowns for the R & D department the ratio of overhead costs, including occupancy costs, wages and salaries, to materials cost was approximately 1:1. With this 1:1 relationship established, official statistical publications were then consulted to find out the rate of increase of earnings and materials costs over the period of study. Tables in the *Monthly Digest of Statistics* for the average earnings of all employees in the engineering and electrical goods industry, and for the wholesale price of materials used in the engineering and electrical goods industry, were used to measure the rates of change of earnings and materials costs over the period of study. It was further assumed that overhead costs would reasonably be considered to be strongly correlated with

earnings costs and, therefore, could be adjusted by the measure for the rate of change of earnings. Then, for each project, an index was constructed giving equal weight to overheads and materials costs to allow for changes in price levels over the development period of that project.

It is important to remember at this point that the measurement of ratios of final to initial values of cost and other factors is complicated not only by the effects of inflation but also by changes in project objectives that become apparent during the development period. Where it has been considered necessary to adjust for such changes as this the adjustment has been carried out. However, the adjustment is subjective in two respects. First, the situations in which other factors have influenced costs or other factors are judged subjectively by the investigator, and second, the magnitude of the adjustment necessary to allow for the bias introduced can only be subjectively assessed. This is why Marshall and Meckling[2] found it necessary in their work to provide two sets of adjusted estimates, one constructed by Eugene Brussell and the other by Robert Summers. They commented that the tricky nature of the adjustment process and the element of subjective judgement necessary means that no two estimates will give the same weighting to the elements in the adjustment process.

It is considered worthwhile here to show the rough magnitude of the adjustment. However, it must be remembered that the adjustment is dependent upon this investigator's judgement of the assumptions and objectives on which initial estimates were made in firm A.

Table 8.1 Firm A – projects 1 to 10 – Unadjusted ratios of final values of factors to earliest estimates.

Project	Cost	Adjusted cost	Quantity sold	Time for development	Price	Degree of technical advance	Status of project	Idea source
1	2.76	2.37	1.43	1.15	1.22	M	TS, NCS	L
2	2.74	2.35	2.00	1.15	1.52	M	TS, CS	L
3	2.72	2.33	1.71	1.15	0.87	M	TS, CS	L
4	1.05	0.87	0.16	1.0	1.00	S	TS, NCS	L
5	0.7	0.33	0.66	1.4	0.83	S	TS, CS	C
6	3.66	3.42	1.18	1.0	3.42	L	TS, CS	L
7	1.11	1.04	0.13	1.4	1.92	S	TS, NCS	L
8	1.53	1.44	0.2	1.5	0.46	S	TS, NCS	L
9	2.54	2.54	0.5	1.0	0.57	S	TS, NCS	L
10	3.77	3.52	0.25	1.2	0.94	S	TS, CS	C

Note: TS denotes 'technical success'.
CS denotes 'commercial success'.
NCS denotes 'not commercial success'.

Any subsequent measurement of estimate error here must be viewed in the light of the difficulties of not knowing on exactly what criteria any of the estimates were made. The approach of this study is to treat cost estimates (as Marshall and Meekling do), however they are generated, as if they were estimates of the cost of achieving the expected levels of performance by a specified date. In this way, by measuring the change in the estimates over the development period, we obtain a measure of the uncertainty inherent in the R & D decision. Later in this article I will try to isolate and analyse the sources making up the component of uncertainty in a project.

We must return now to some other features of Table 8.1. The seventh column in the table, on the degree of technical advance of the projects, was obtained by asking the research and development manager and the project engineer for each project to come to an agreement about the technical nature of the project and assess it on a three-point scale; small, medium and large. The eighth column was obtained from the company accountant who assessed whether the final return factor for the project did or did not meet the corporate targets. The final column on the source of the project idea was obtained by the investigator by the process of interview and perusal of project records. It is to be noted that Table 8.1 does not include the data on the four technical failure projects of firm A. These are treated separately because of their unique characteristics. The relevance of the information in Table 8.1 is that it shows the inaccuracies that exist in early forecasts of various factors and enables us to assess their extent and influence on the revenue/cost ratios. In this way, it may be possible to suggest methods which make allowance for inaccuracies in forecast inputs in order to improve the effectiveness of return ratios as aids in new product development decisions.

Specifically, the fifth column indicates that the firm is well able to forecast with reasonable accuracy how long the research and development work will take. This result is explained in large part by the firm's policy of trying to meet deadlines wherever possible and its adoption of network analysis techniques for project planning. Trade-offs of extra resource inputs are frequently tolerated and accepted by the firm in order to fulfil time targets.

It is equally clear from the results in column two that in most cases the values of cost forecasts tend to be far less than actual final outcome values. A contributory factor is clearly the extra resources that are often injected into a project in order to ensure completion by a given date. Also, the influence of changes in price levels and expected output levels can have a significant effect. Nevertheless, the results indicate considerable weaknesses and over-optimism in the forecasting of costs. This result is consistent with the nature of over-optimistic biases found in the other studies and is of greater importance because the firm here has a well-organized information system and is efficiently run.

On the revenue side in most of the cases it is clear that early estimates of quantities sold tend to overstate the actual final position by a considerable amount. This highlights the fact that marketing a new R & D generated product (i.e., knowing its likely market) is difficult, and past data on sales are not likely to be helpful unless the firm is selling in a well-defined technical market. Unfortunately, well-defined markets exist in very few cases. Despite the difficulties in quantity estimation the extent of the error can be explained in part by biases which engineers admit are widespread when they are asked to evaluate the worth of a project by some form of return factor index. Because engineers often become very keen on the technical potential of a given project they feel quite justified in providing estimates as inputs to the return index which will tend to make the value of that index appear attractive in financial as well as technical terms. Engineers in firm A confess quite freely that they adjust estimates of costs and likely sales to make the return from the project look sufficiently attractive to the firm's managers. They justify this on two grounds. First, that estimates of costs, sales, etc., are in any case subject to great uncertainty and are thus useless for evaluating projects. Second, that it is unrealistic to use an index of worth as the sole criterion for project initiation and adoption. Some allowance must be made for technical worth in the construction of the index.

It is interesting to consider whether the extent of accuracy in the estimation of the various factors related to a project's worth varies with the degree of technical advance of those projects. Table 8.2 provides a break-down of estimation performance by the magnitude of technical advance of a project.

It is clear from this analysis that there are differences in forecast error between projects of limited and great technical difficulty. Because we have few cases of large technical advance it is more relevant to aggregate the cases of medium and large technical advance in the table. Actual costs tend to twice as much as initial estimates in the case of small technical advance and about three

Table 8.2 Firm A — mean and standard deviation of ratios analysed by degree of magnitude of technical advance (values in the table are mean or average ratios)

Economic factors	Small (six observations)		Medium and Large (four observations)	
	Mean F ratio	SD	Mean F ratio	SD
Cost	1.78	1.16	2.97	0.46
Adjusted cost	1.62	1.19	2.62	0.57
Quantity sold	0.31	0.21	1.58	0.36
Price	0.95	0.22	1.75	0.06
Time	1.25	0.52	1.11	1.14

times in the case of medium to large technical advance. Even if allowance were made for inflation over the development period the relative difference between the small and medium to large cases would be of approximately the same magnitude. This result suggests that cost forecasts are more accurate when the degree of technical uncertainty is small and vice versa. Such a conclusion is in agreement with the ratios of about three found by Peck and Scherer[3] for a number of government-sponsored R & D projects, since these projects tended in most cases to have a considerable area of technical uncertainty.

It is difficult to come to a firm conclusion about inaccuracies in sales (or quantity sold) forecasts. When the technical advance of a project is small, on average we find that final sales over the period are only about one-third of the initial estimate. On the other hand, medium to large technically advanced projects tend to produce sales greater than initial estimated values by a mean factor of about half. Certainly, technically advanced products will tend to define a market of their own and not often be subject to severe competition. Projects of a more limited degree of technical advance tend to be improvements to existing ranges or 'gap fillers' in the firm's product line and thus are subject to competition from a number of other firms already in the market. A simple explanation of the results produced in the table may merely reflect inability to estimate market size either in the case of a new technically advanced instrument, when other firms may be doing research designed to produce a similarly technically advanced instrument at roughly the same time, or in the case of small detailed improvements to an existing product when consumers may prefer a more limited specification or one of the range of instruments available from other firms. However, if we had more observations available we might have found that if firms can afford to do high risk, technologically advanced R & D and succeed in their development work, their eventual market might be much larger than if they concentrated on a low risk, diversified R & D portfolio. A conclusion of this nature would be a statement, if true, of the extent of research economies of scale.

Price forecasts seem to be very accurate in the case of small technical advance but underestimated initially in the case of medium to large levels of technical advance. Because medium/large levels have greater degrees of technical uncertainty we have seen already that development cost estimates tend to be severely underestimated relative to projects with much smaller levels of technical advance. Since firm A sets its prices by means of full total costs plus a mark-up it is not surprising that final prices are greater than initial estimated prices in cases of high technical advance. In addition, where technical advance is larger, the market is less well-defined and this further complicates meaningful estimation of prices at an early stage in the development life of a project.

As we have noted already there is no real difference between projects of different levels of technical advance in their ability to fulfil time objectives. Nothing can be inferred from this fact other than it is a direct result of two factors, first the strict control system for R & D adopted by the firm and, second, the firm's policy of completing its R & D work on time even if extra money and resources have to be incurred.

A further analysis of the figures in Table 8.1 by extent of final commercial success provides an interesting picture. This is shown in Table 8.3.

It can be seen that commercially successful projects exhibit greater errors in forecast estimates than non-commercially successful projects except for forecasts of eventual market. This can be explained partly because three out of the five commercially successful projects represent significant degrees of technical advance compared with only one of the non-commercially successful projects. We have seen that high technical advance projects tend to define markets of their own, and no matter how much the escalation of costs these are regained by the firm via a full cost pricing policy. The evidence for this firm at least suggests again that to be commercially successful and useful, R & D strategy is to engage in an R & D programme with its objective as the development of technically advanced rather than 'bread and butter' projects. This strategy can be developed on a rational and formal basis if estimation procedures for cost and sales factors can be improved. This task is perfectly possible and the answer lies not in sophisti-

Table 8.3 Break-down of projects into those which were eventual commercial successes and failures. Analysis of forecast accuracy on economic factors between the two cases.

| | Commercial success | | | | | Commercial failure | | | | | |
| | Cost | Mean and SD of ratios for | | | Time | Cost | Mean and SD of ratios for | | | Time |
		Adjusted cost	Quantity	Price			Adjusted cost	Quantity	Price	
Mean	2.72	2.39	1.16	1.52	1.18	1.78	1.65	0.48	1.03	1.21
Standard deviation	(1.23)	(1.28)	(0.23)	(1.1)	(0.01)	(0.81)	(0.76)	(0.55)	(0.53)	(0.22)
		(based on five observations)					(based on five observations)			

cated OR models but with the individual engineer. He must be made more aware of economic and accounting factors and how they inter-relate with, and bear on, various engineering designs and configurations. Inaccuracy of estimation is not a function of poor engineers in the UK — they seem to produce similar forecast estimation behaviour to those in the US — but merely a function of poor engineering training with its narrow emphasis on purely technical considerations.

We could generate further tabulations to show the inter-relations between factors, such as the timing of a forecast or the degree of technological advance sought, which are sources of uncertainty in forecasts about R & D projects. On the evidence presented thus far we would expect that forecasts would tend towards the true value over the length of the development period but that the ratios at all points in the development would tend to be greater for more technically advanced projects if only on the dimension of development costs. To some extent we are overlapping and prejudging the results of the section on the resolution of uncertainty and so we will await the more detailed analysis of that section.

It has not been considered worthwhile to provide figures of the initial and final estimates of the various economic and time factors for the technically unsuccessful projects of firm A's portfolio. The reason is a simple one. These projects have been terminated for different reasons — poor initial feasibility, shortage of skilled labour resources, rapid cost escalation and so on. As such, comparison of 'final' estimates against initial ones is not meaningful because 'final' does not relate to a unique point in time (such as the end of the development period with technically successful projects) and thus comparison of results with other more successful projects is rendered worthless.

However, in Table 8.4, ratios of the latest available estimates of cost for each of the four projects before termination to the initial estimated total development cost and a short explanation of the reasons for termination of the project are presented.

Table 8.4 Cost ratios.

Project	Ratios	Reason given
11A	1.04	Uncertain market; low return factor.
12A	1.82	Rapid escalation of initial cost estimate.
13A	2.1	Political difficulties with contract.
14A	1.1	Instrument not viable in market.

Too much reliance should not be placed on the reasons given for project termination because observation has shown them to be convenient rationalizations and not statements of reality. In fact, project 11A has now just been reinstated in the laboratory largely because personality differences about the relevance of the project have been resolved. Further, project 12A is now again under active consideration because sufficiently skilled engineering resources have been available. It is my view that if project 12A had been undertaken at the time of its inception the company would have had a huge commercial success in the light of the market reaction to project 6A's final end-product. Thus, for comparative purposes we cannot say much about projects that were technical failures in this firm. It is surprising in view of the former argument that Meadows[7] in his study analyses ratios for a number of projects that turned out to be failures or were terminated. Obviously, since reasons for failure or termination are never the same in each case and are not necessarily meaningful in technical terms, it is misleading to give information on forecast ratios in these cases.

The evidence available from firm B on forecast accuracy is far less detailed and comprehensive. It is useful to remember that records for firm B on R & D projects have until recently been kept only in those cases where outside risk capital is a major source of finance. If we take note also that appraisal of projects is very informal and economic estimates related to R & D projects are no better than 'guesstimates', then it is clear that an analysis as detailed and thorough as that for firm A is not possible in this case. However, we can only say here that project 2B does provide us with some estimates of cost, price and sales per annum because the sponsoring agency required information of this nature when it gave the risk capital and subsequently when it reviewed the progress of the project. The estimates made for this project should be considered as being an example of the best possible estimating behaviour — 'bread and butter' R & D projects are approved on the basis of highly informal and speedy subjective evaluations. The information available from project 2B is given in Table 8.5 below.

Table 8.5 Firm B — unadjusted cost, price and sales ratios of final to earliest estimates — project 2B.

Factor	Ratio
Cost	2.25
Price	1.4
Sales	0.2

Note: The sales ratio is based upon the first year's actual sales for the instrument and the initial estimated value for sales per year.

This project can fairly be regarded as being technically advanced in nature so that the inaccuracy of cost estimation is understandable and perhaps a little bit smaller than with firm A and the ratio obtained in other R & D studies. The price estimate inaccuracy is again of the same order as for a technically advanced project in firm A and consistent with the level of cost escalation given the practice of full cost pricing in the firm. The short-fall of actual sales, however, differs from the case of firm A in which the opposite occurred for technically advanced projects. The difference might be explained by the marketing oriented approach in new product planning present in firm A. However, it is true to say that firm B has had the same short-fall experience with a couple of sponsored projects it undertook some years previously and which protect engineers raised when the poor sales performance of project 2B was discussed with them. Since we have concrete information on 2B only, we should perhaps emphasize that discussions with project engineers in firm B about previous projects yielded the general impression of a tremendous lack of awareness of the importance of economic factors such as

cost and sales of a project, and where 'guesstimates' of the values of cost and sales had been made they tended to be wildly inaccurate and almost random in comparison with the true value.

In our discussion of the available literature we found evidence of huge inaccuracies in estimation in government-sponsored R & D projects. The aim of this limited initial analysis was to provide similar case-study evidence for R & D carried out in private industry. The results of this study for the electronics industry show the presence of large inaccuracies in cost and sales estimates. The work of Meadows and Allen[10] showed the presence of similar inaccuracies in chemical laboratories, but Mansfield's equipment laboratory seems to have been very efficient in its estimation procedures. Mansfield's firm, of course, had a very efficient control system for R & D but so did firm A in this study. Maybe the type of control system in Mansfield's case was more suitable for the firm than firm A's control system. Nevertheless, despite this fact that some of the evidence does not point to large inaccuracies of estimation for R & D projects, we can state with a modest degree of certainty that inaccuracies of estimation are similar in both industrial and government R & D. Further, the correspondence is greater the higher the degree of technical advance of industrial projects.

It is clear that with the degree of inaccuracy at present found in project appraisals, measures of worth of projects based on these estimates may give an incorrect assessment of the value of each project to the firm. Until forecasts can be improved, adoption of selection techniques for R & D projects based on estimating likely financial rates of return must proceed with caution. In any case, a decision should never be made solely on the basis of the value of the rate of return factor and must be combined with technical and other relevant evaluations. In our analysis of uncertainty resolution we will try to isolate the sources of uncertainty and specify which estimates are always very inaccurate so that efforts can be made to improve forecasts through greater knowledge of the sources of inaccuracy.

2. Uncertainty Resolution

Thomas Marschak[11] in discussing the nature of the development process considers it to be a process of uncertainty reduction or learning. The learning process is achieved by applying some strategy to allocate and reallocate effort amongst uncertainty reducing possibilities as the process of development spans out. This idea of the nature of the development process is one which is supported by earlier evidence in this article. In fact, the RAND Corporation through a number of its research personnel such as Marschak[11], Klein & Meckling[12] and Nelson[13] can be regarded as being the originator of this view of the development process. We need here to provide evidence about the nature of uncertainty in industrial development and parallel it with the RAND view of the military development process. Such a comparison is essential in view of RAND's preoccupation with the parallel path strategy for R & D.

A parallel path strategy for an R & D manager is first to carry out a preliminary evaluation (by means of indices or informal methods) of a batch of projects. Then, a sub-set of this batch is selected for further consideration and research work is initiated on them. The *rationale* is that it will be apparent very quickly which projects of this batch are not valuable because the initial uncertainty surrounding them will be resolved quickly under experimental conditions. The engineer can only really know a project's feasibility if he carries out some R & D work on it. Such learning by doing is said to eliminate worthless projects efficiently and quickly and is the basis on which the formalized parallel path strategy builds.

The strategy is dependent upon one assumption, namely that uncertainty about projects is resolved quickly through time. This can be measured by observing the forecasting performance of engineers in estimating various factors related to R & D projects at different points in time through the development period and studying the extent to which forecasts improve with time (and hence how quickly uncertainty is reduced).

The only evidence available in this study about uncertainty resolution is from firm A. In certain cases with technically unsuccessful projects the basis for their decision to suspend work on a project for an indefinite period has been stated (see Table 8.4) to be because the latest available estimates of cost, sales, etc., present a clearer picture of the true worth of the project to the firm. Since the firm was never able to find out the true value of costs, sales, etc., (because they never completed the R & D work), the firm's decision implicitly assumed that latest available forecasts present a more useful decision tool than initial forecasts. We have to ask whether this has been true of forecasts on technically successful projects.

A detailed analysis of the forecast evidence is presented below. This analysis comprised graphs of the behaviour of the forecasts of cost, quantity sold, price

and the associated measure of worth, and the return factor at discrete points within the development period. It should be noted that the number of points evaluated varies with the length of the project, the technical obstacles that occur and the routine need for forecasts. In fact, forecasts are typically made every 4 to 6 months and also when a significant problem, economic or technical, occurs during the project's development. The

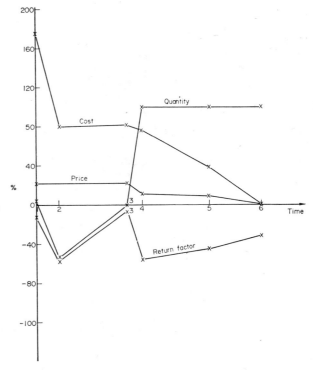

Figure 8.1 Project 1A – graph of *I* against time.

Table 8.6 Project 1A – values of *I* (percentages).

Times during development period	Development cost	Price	Quantity sold	Return factor
1	176.4	22.5	4.3	−12.5
2	80.0	22.5	−54.5	−57.3
3	81.4	22.5	0.0	−6.7
4	75.9	11.4	100.0	−55.7
5	36.2	9.1	100.0	−45.3
6	–	0.0	100.0	−31.4

Note: The last period is the end of the development period, uncertainty still remains about quantity sold and final return, but not about price and development cost. The periods are of variable length.

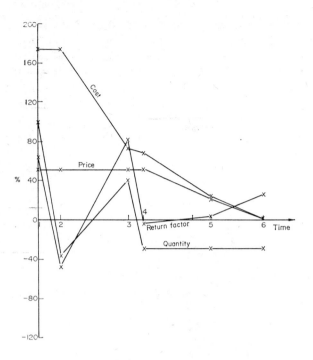

Figure 8.2 Project 2A – graph of *I* against time.

Table 8.7 Project 2A – values of *I* (percentages).

Times during development period	Cost	Price	Quantity sold	Return factor
1	173.9	51.1	100.0	64.3
2	173.9	51.1	−36.8	−47.7
3	72.4	51.1	40.0	81.6
4	67.7	51.1	−30.0	−6.8
5	23.9	21.4	−30.0	+3.0
6	0.0	0.0	−30.0	+25.4

Table 8.8 Project 3A – values of *I* (percentages).

Times during development period	Cost	Price	Quantity sold	Return factor
1	172.1	−13.3	71.4	0.0
2	172.1	−13.3	−45.4	−68.2
3	72.6	−13.3	20.0	10.5
4	72.6	−13.3	−40.0	−44.7
5	31.0	−13.3	−40.0	−27.6
6	0.0	0.0	−40.0	10.5

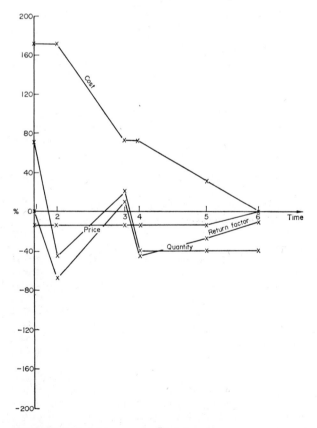

Figure 8.3 Project 3A – graph of *I* against time.

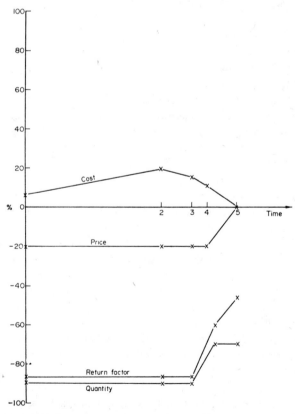

Figure 8.4 Project 4A – graph of *I* against time.

Table 8.9 Project 4A – values of I (percentages).

Time during development period	Cost	Price	Quantity sold	Return factor
1	6.2	−20.0	−90.0	−86.4
2	19.4	−20.0	−90.0	−86.9
3	15.4	−20.0	−90.0	−86.9
4	10.3	−20.0	−70.0	−60.0
5	0.0	0.0	−70.0	−46.0

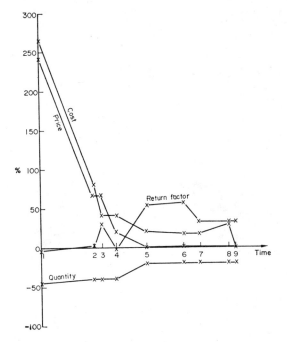

Figure 8.6 Project 6A – graph of I against time.

Table 8.11 Project 6A – values of I (percentages).

Times during development period	Cost	Price	Quantity sold	Return factor
1	265.9	242.9	−45.4	−4.0
2	81.7	66.7	−40.0	2.1
3	41.9	66.7	−40.0	29.7
4	41.9	20.0	−40.0	−2.0
5	19.9	0.0	−20.0	54.8
6	17.8	0.0	−20.0	57.4
7	17.8	0.0	−20.0	33.3
8	29.9	0.0	−20.0	33.3
9	0.0	0.0	−20.0	33.3

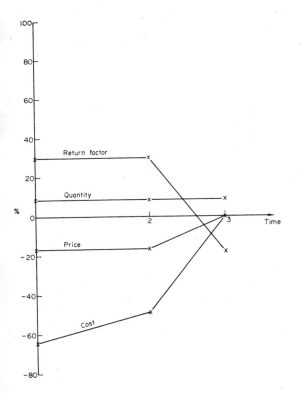

Figure 8.5 Project 5A – graph of I against time.

Table 8.10 Project 5A – values of I (percentages)

Time during development period	Cost	Price	Quantity sold	Return factor
1	−64.2	−16.7	8.3	+32.6
2	−48.8	−16.7	8.3	+32.6
3	0.0	0.0	8.3	−18.7

Table 8.12 Project 7A – values of I (percentages).

Times during development period	Cost	Price	Quantity sold	Return factor
1	15.8	56.7	−62.5	−47.6
2	15.0	56.7	−70.0	−54.2
3	10.3	56.7	−70.0	−50.0
4	−22.8	34.3	−70.0	−50.0
5	−29.5	34.3	−80.0	−71.1
6	0.0	34.3	−80.0	−71.1

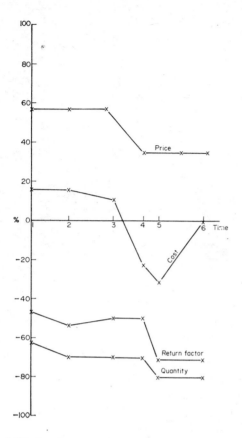

Figure 8.7 Project 7A — graph of *I* against time.

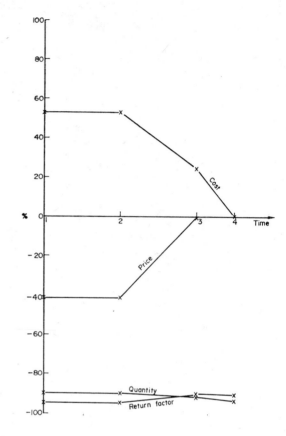

Figure 8.8 Project 8A — graph of *I* against time.

Table 8.13 Project 8A — values of I (percentages)

Times during development period	Cost	Price	Quantity sold	Return factor
1	53.1	−44.4	−90.0	−95.0
2	53.1	−44.4	−90.0	−95.0
3	27.3	0.0	−91.7	91.1
4	0.0	0.0	−93.8	−91.8

Table 8.14 Project 9A — values of I (percentages)

Times during development period	Cost	Price	Quantity sold	Return factor
1	153.7	−42.9	−68.8	−91.0
2	0.0	0.0	−37.5	−18.2

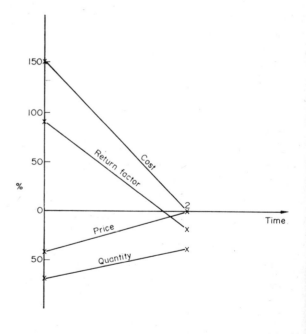

Figure 8.9 Project 9A — graph of *I* against time.

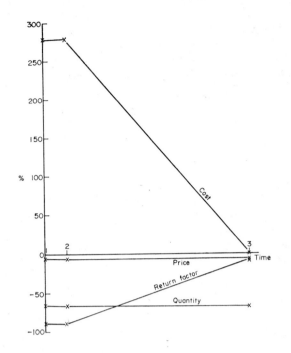

Figure 8.10 Project 10A — graph of I against time.

Table 8.15 Project 10A — values of I (percentages)

Times during development period	Cost	Price	Quantity sold	Return factor
1	276.7	−6.0	−66.7	−87.9
2	276.7	−6.0	−66.7	−87.9
3	0.0	−6.0	−66.7	− 7.0

variable plotted on the graphs presented below is the forecast inaccuracy where the degree of forecast inaccuracy is measured by the index:

$$I = \frac{\text{actual value} - \text{forecast value}}{\text{forecast value}}$$

expressed as a percentage. In the tables which accompany the graphs the values of I for each factor on the ten technically successful projects are presented.

The main conclusions that can be drawn from the preceding analysis of forecast behaviour are as follows. If we consider the general trend in forecasts of cost, sales, price and return factor we find that, first, cost forecasts or predictions certainly get closer to the true value over time, in fact they converge on the actual value through time. However, in most cases cost forecasts converge on the true value slowly and it requires about 50 per cent of

the development period (actual times for the projects are not given here for reasons of confidentiality but, although forecasts are not made at equal intervals of time during the development period, it is reasonable to consider the middle forecast as being made approximately half-way through a given project) before the bias in the forecast becomes sufficiently small for us to say the uncertainty in our cost estimate has been satisfactorily resolved. This slow convergence of cost estimates on the actual value was also found in the Allen and Norris study.[9] Second, estimates of final price are sufficiently close to the final value in nearly all cases, with the important exception of project 6A, for us to infer that uncertainty in price forecasting is generally small and that initial estimates provide satisfactory guidelines for the final values. It is significant that a large measure of uncertainty is apparent initially in project 6A which is technically very advanced. However, we can see that by period 4 in the case of project 6A the uncertainty in price was only 20 per cent, reflecting more than anything else the massive resolution of initial uncertainty in the cost forecasts since, as we have noted before, price tends to be proportional to costs of development and production in this firm.

Third, in most cases, estimates of sales tend to oscillate widely about the true value without a consistently convergent pattern on the final value. This finding reflects the great degree of uncertainty that is faced by engineers and marketing managers in estimating market conditions for a product generated as a by-product of the R & D output.

Fourth, if we analyse the behaviour of the return factor index, into which estimates of the above three factors are placed, we find, predictably, that uncertainty about the worth of the project is not resolved quickly through time because of the degrees of uncertainty inherent in cost and sales forecasts.

We have now looked in general terms at the behaviour of the individual forecasts and we must consider a number of general issues on which this study provides guidelines. We should note immediately that the evidence hear leads us to infer that uncertainty about project outcome, sales and cost remains until a significantly large proportion of the development period has elapsed. This is an important inference because it suggests that a parallel path strategy for a firm such as A, working an industrial, applied, product-orientated R & D network, is a costly proposition. The mere fact that uncertainty is only slowly resolved implies that 'learning by doing' on projects will be costly and produce high project wastage rates even allowing for any subsequent spin-off which may occur as a result of technical personnel doing parallel work in a number of technical areas.

Another equally important point is that the greatest degrees of uncertainty are evidenced in cost and sales forecasts. How can we improve these forecasts? A further article,[11] considers the extent to which we can use previous estimating experience to revise present or future experience, but it is important to state here that we should try to extract from past data, however rough they may be, lessons from which future estimating practice can be developed and improved. An additional source of improvement would be to educate the engineer and manager more about the characteristics and nature of the R & D process and, in particular, about the close interactions between economic and technical factors on a project.

Cost and sales, as we have seen, are the areas of great forecast uncertainty. However we should ask how much the area of uncertainty is clouded by the uncertain technical or design nature of the project. In particular, is there a correlation between changes in the objectives of projects and inaccurate forecasting behaviour? Unfortunately, in this study our sample of projects is so small that on only one project was there any significant change in project objectives. The project on which this occurred was project 6A and we noted already the huge improvement in the cost and price forecasts that occurred in the fourth period of the development stage of 6A. Basically, instrument 6A, which is a specialized testing instrument, had a change in performance and design specifications between the third and fourth period. The changes, though not major, were a function of a number of factors including greater technical awareness, the need for certain features to be added to the original design and the need for a greater measurement range for the instrument's performance in a number of areas of application. Discussions with project engineers brought out that such changes in objectives, if known initially, would have increased the initial estimate of cost by no more than 50 per cent which would have the effect of reducing the forecast inaccuracy for cost as a whole by no more than 15 per cent. Clearly, the engineers feel that the uncertainty about the project was such that lack of knowledge of the final design configuration is not sufficient on its own to explain the extent of forecast inaccuracy. They mentioned factors like technical uncertainty and the lack of appreciation of how long and how much it would cost to carry out the work as being much more important.

With project 6A the price estimate was made more realistic after the change in objectives, showing that cost forecast uncertainty has a great influence on price forecasts.

Sales forecasts on 6A, though consistently underestimating the final values, were moving and converging slowly towards the final value. This may mean that market estimation is easier for more technically advanced projects — a point that was brought out in our analysis of forecast ratios earlier.

I have not attempted here to break down the values of I by degree of technical advance or commercial success. There are two reasons for this: first, the analysis would tend to be repetitive given the earlier breakdown of F ratios, and second, the analysis can be carried out simply enough from observation of the graphs by the reader. The important point in this section is that we provide evidence on forecast behaviour which is not available elsewhere in great detail and enables us to conclude that uncertainty resolution on the R & D projects studied here is generally a slow process. As a result, a 'learning by doing' or a parallel path R & D strategy might prove to be much less useful in industrial R & D than military R & D contract work.

3. Sensitive Variables Related to Project Success
This means the sensitivity of the worth of a project to forecast inputs, e.g., cost. The reason for the inclusion of this short section is to assess the degree of accuracy necessary in forecasting factors such as cost related to R & D projects. It is clear from parts 1 and 2 of this section that, as far as the worth of a project is concerned, a high degree of accuracy in one forecast may be far less important than that same degree of accuracy in another forecast. We have seen that the satisfactory evaluation of the worth of a project is dependent upon accurate cost and sales forecasts and that the measure of worth is relatively very sensitive to inaccuracies in cost and sales forecasts but fairly insensitive to inaccuracies in price and time forecasts. Clearly, an error in a forecast is going to be the more relevant to the measure of worth if the variable being forecast has a large effect in financial terms on the outcome of a project. For example, a 10 per cent error in costs of £50,000 per year will be a larger absolute error than a 10 per cent error in sales estimated to be £10,000 per year. The simple point is that the larger components of financial outcome will have a relatively greater effect on that outcome than smaller components.

Further, some forecasts such as costs and sales have greater variability and bias than others and so tend by their very nature to have a greater influence on eventual financial outcome.

4. Validity of the Return Factor Index as a Measure of Project Worth

Firm A uses a formal selection index, basically a ratio of the form revenue/cost, to evaluate the worth of research projects. Ratios like firm A's index require estimates of cost of development, and sales and revenue variables which we have already seen to be very inaccurate in most cases. Such large inaccuracies in the estimates of cost and sales factors can make the measure of worth of a project relatively useless.

There is, of course, a further more important question to discuss when considering the validity of a measure of worth such as a return factor, namely, how sure are we that the revenue/cost ratio is an adequate measure for evaluating the worth of an investment project such as a R & D project? Should projects be evaluated solely in terms of financial criteria?

Table 8.16 F ratios of final return factor values to initial return factor estimates.

Project	F ratios	
1A	0.88	
2A	1.64	
3A	1.00	
4A	0.14	
5A	1.35	
6A	0.96	
7A	0.24	Mean F ratio for technically advanced
8A	0.01	projects = 1.12
9A	0.11	Mean F ratio for non-technically advanced
10A	0.12	projects = 0.33

In the analysis we shall first consider the inaccuracy in the initial return factor or prediction in terms of its closeness to the final return factor. We then consider what other financial criteria would be more useful in analysing the worth of research projects and, in particular, criteria based on the actuarial principle of discounting cash flows.

If we now consider Table 8.16 we find our usual analysis of F factors, i.e., final values/initial estimated values for the return factor indices. It would appear from the table that return factor predictions are better for technically advanced than for less technically advanced projects. This is more by accident than design

since if we refer back to the behaviour of sales and cost forecasts through time for the technically advanced projects we find that in most cases changes in cost forecasts are associated with compensating changes in sales forecasts either instantaneously or a number of periods later. The net effect of these changes on the project return factor index is to leave the value of the return factor at the end of the project's life approximately the same as it was initially. This difference also can be explained in a different way by referring back to Table 8.2. In that table we found that the mean F ratios for cost, quantity sold, and price for more and less technically advanced projects were 2.97, 1.58 and 1.75 and 1.78, 0.31 and 0.95 respectively. If we now remember that a return factor ratio is of the form revenue/cost, final ratios as compared with initial ratios for technically advanced projects will be about the same because the increase in the denominator cost is met by corresponding increases in the numerator, which is proportional to price times quantity sold. Similarly, for less technically advanced projects cost escalates (i.e., the denominator increases in size relative to the numerator which decreases because of the reduction in sales forecasts). The net effect is, therefore, to reduce the value of the return factor.

We can see, therefore, that return factor predictions are affected by the weaknesses inherent in the input forecast such as sales and cost. Because sales and cost forecast inaccuracies tend to cancel out in the case of technically advanced projects but not in the case of less advanced projects, the difference in the research team's ability to forecast return can be explained. It is clear, therefore, that the validity and usefulness of the return factor index is severely weakened by problems in the forecasts of sales and costs.

Any return index is thus dependent upon the accuracy and method of presentation of forecast variables. Its validity is also dependent upon the extent to which it represents the financial operations of the firm. There has been a great deal of adoption in recent years of techniques for financial appraisal which take full account of the time value of money. Such discounting techniques are based upon the inverse of the actuary's principle of compound interest. The attraction of the techniques for the manager of the firm is that they take full account of the distribution through time of the cash flows accruing to investment and earnings. They clearly differ from the type of return factor index of firm A which is a ratio of revenues/costs and where revenues are treated as being of the same worth to the firm even if they occur predominantly towards the end of a project's life. A discounting criterion would weight revenues and *costs*, if necessary, by the interest rate factor which reflects the time value of money.

In Table 8.17 below we present ratios of the net present values of projects 1 to 10 to their initial cost. The net present value (NPV) criterion has been obtained by discounting each project's gross cost and revenue cash flows by the appropriate cost of capital or discount rate for the firm and obtaining the NPV by treating discounted revenues as positive quantities and discounted costs as negative quantities. If the firm has only finite amounts of money available for investment in R & D projects, it is reasonable to consider NPV per unit of money employed, i.e., cost as a measure of worth of an individual research project.

Table 8.17 Ratios of net present value to initial cost for 10 projects in firm A.

Projects	Ratio (NPV) cost	Ranking of projects in terms of NPV/cost	Ranking of projects in terms of FRF	Ranking of projects in terms of IRF
1	1.48	6	6	9
2	2.78	1	1	7=
3	1.25	7	4	7=
4	2.15	3	7	2
5	2.45	2	2	6
6	1.60	5	3	5
7	0.06	8	9	10
8	−0.71	10	10	3
9	+0.03	9	8	4
10	+1.75	4	5	1

Columns three, four and five of this table show a ranking of each project in terms of its worth to the firm under the NPV/cost, final return factor (FRF) and (IRF) criteria respectively. No meaning should be read into this ranking about selection between projects because these projects occurred in the period 1963 to 1969 at random intervals. The ranking is merely undertaken to show that different criteria assess the worth of projects differentially and result in return factor or worth predictions that do not imply the same decisions to adopt or select a project by the firm concerned.

It is clearly argued here that predictions of final financial outcome of a project will improve with better forecasting of economic factors and adoption of financial discounting criteria of project worth. Financial outcome is not the sole criterion of worth of a project because of the need for the firm to develop its R & D

expertise in several technical areas. However, if the engineer/manager better appreciates the interaction between technical and financial factors then the efficiency of project selection decisions is likely to show a significant improvement.

Summary Statement on the Performance of the R & D Department in Firm A Over the Period Studied

In this very short section we consider the global performance of the R & D department in firm A over the period studied in order to put the cost/benefit analysis into perspective. Over the period of study 31.3 per cent of the resources available for R & D expenditure have been spent on projects that for one reason or another one-third of the 'wasted' R & D resources have value to the firm, then we can say approximately 80 per cent of the R & D work has contributed to commercially orientated products. This compares with an average percentage for the ten firms in electrical engineering industry in the Federation of British Industry[13] enquiry of 63.5 per cent. This would suggest that the efficiency and product orientation of this firm in R & D work is better than average and if the percentage distribution in the FBI survey is a criterion at a high level of efficiency relative to other firms in its industrial sector. Certainly when viewed in relation to manufacturing industry as a whole, on the basis of the 1959/60 FBI evidence, it has operated extremely efficiently in the R & D area.

Summary and Conclusions

The purpose of this analysis has been to look retrospectively at the results of the R & D work in two firms, A and B. We found initially that records were only adequate enough in A for a detailed analysis to be carried out and that firm B's performance could, from subjective observation, be considered to be less efficient than A's.

The *rationale* for the analysis is to learn more about the characteristics of the R & D process by piecing together the past performance and operations of the R & D department.

The main conclusion from the evidence presented here is that forecast inaccuracy is of the same order of magnitude in the two firms studied as in the chemical firms considered by Allen and Meadows.[10] Further, for projects with a high degree of technical advancement the inaccuracy of estimation is of the same order of magnitude as in the military R & D studies of Peck and Scherer[3], and Marshall and Meckling.[2] The behaviour of forecasts through time is found to be unpredictable and indicates clearly that the uncertainty present in the R & D projects is not resolved quickly during the development period. Estimators find it most difficult to forecast costs and likely sales and it is found that relatively small inaccuracies in the forecasts of both these variables can have much larger effects on the measure of worth or likely rate of return from a project.

It is not difficult, given the evidence evaluated here, to understand why formal models for the selection of R & D work are difficult to construct. Even firm A which had a formal selection index suffered from large inaccuracies in estimates of costs and sales factors which suggests that more attention must be given to organizational considerations before formulating project selection models for individual firms. In particular, the relation between estimated and actual project outcomes must be documented retrospectively by each organization. Inaccuracies in estimation can reflect organizational, social and technical factors present in the individual firm which must be understood in greater depth. In addition, relatively little is known of the nature of uncertainty in R & D projects and, more importantly when estimates become sufficiently reliable for a reasonable discrimination, between the worth of various R & D projects to be effected.

I must repeat again that inaccuracies in estimates are important because of the uses to which they are put. In the case of R & D these estimates are used as the basis on which firms decide to allocate financial and technical resources between various projects. It is clearly the function of such estimates to improve and stimulate better project decisions. Unfortunately, the evidence shows that estimates are very often unreliable and only become relatively more reliable much later in the development period. Consequently, resource allocation decisions involving the calculation of return factors and based on estimates which are so inaccurate can only be regarded as worthless.

References

1 Baker, N.R. & Pound, W.H. 'R & D project selection: where we stand', I.E.E.E. Transactions on Engineering Management, (1964) Vol. EM-11, No. 4 (Dec.).

2 Marshall, A.W. & Meckling, W.H. 'Predictability of costs, time and success of development', The Rate and Direction of Inventive Acitivity (ed. R.R. Nelson), (1962) Princeton Univ. Press.

3 Peck, M.J. & Scherer, F.M. 'The Weapons Acquisition Process', (1962) Harvard.

4 Summers, R. 'Cost estimates as predictors of actual costs: a statistical study of military developments', (1968) Strategy for R & D (eds T. Marschak, T.K. Clennan, and R. Summers), Berlin. Springer-Verlag.

5 Mansfield, E. & Brandenberg, R.G. 'The allocation, characteristics, and outcome of the firms R & D portfolio: a case study', Journal of Business (Oct.) (1966).

6 Mansfield, E. 'Econometric Studies of Industrial Research and Technological Innovation', (1968) New York, W.W. Norton.

7 Meadows, D. 'Estimate accuracy and project selection models in industrial research', Industrial Management Review, (1968) 8, No. 3 (Spring), pp. 105-121.

8 Allen, D.H. & November, P.J. 'A practical study of the accuracy of forecasts in novel projects', Tripartite Chemical Engineering Conference, Montreal (Sept.). Reprinted in Chemical Engineer, (1968) No. 229, (June, 1969), p. 252.

9 Allen, J.M. and Norris, K.P. 'Project estimates and outcomes in electricity generation research' Journal of Management Studies (Oct.), (1970).

10. Meadows, D. and Allen

11. Thomas

12. Klein, B.V. & Meckling, W.H. 'An application of operations research to development decisions', Operations Research, (1958) 6.

Klein, B.V. 'The Nature of Military R & D', Rand Corporation, (1960), p. 1818. Santa Monica, California.

13 Federation of British Industries 'Research and Development in Manufacturing Industry, 1959-60'. (1961.)

Nelson, R.R. ('Uncertainty, learning, and the economics of parallel research and development efforts', Review of Economics and Statistics (1961).

Exercises & Study Questions

Product Development

1. A recent study showed that for every 58 projects that are considered for development, only one will be a market success. Suggest reasons for this.
2. What steps would you take, as a manager in charge of product planning, to improve on the performance described above?
3. Comment critically on the following methods of setting next year's R & D budget: a proportion of this year's sales, a proportion of next year's budgeted sales, the same amount as other firms in the industry, NPV of lost profits if no R & D were done, what is left over after all other expenses and a reasonable profit margin have been allowed for, what is needed to do adequate offensive, defensive and fundamental research.
4. 'An organization must innovate or die.' Is this true?
5. There is evidence that the productivity of industrial research is declining. How would you alter this trend?
6. Your research budget for next year is £175,000. Which of the following projects would you under-take?

Project No.	1	2	3	4	5	6
Equipment cost (£'000)	50	17	34	41	15	30
Salaries cost (£'000)	16	10	5	20	13	11
NPV of expected profit (£'000)	80	70	50	80	40	60
Rig time (hours)	0	1000	4000	2000	500	500
Chemist time (hours)	1500	1000	0	2000	500	1000

If your equipment budget is £135,000 and your salary budget is £40,000, would this alter your choice? You have one test rig, which can be run for 5,000 hours per annum, and two graduate chemists who each work 2,000 hours per annum, which projects would you do? A new test rig costs £100,000. Capital and running costs are £5/hour. Should you buy one? You can hire chemist for a total cost of £5,000. Should you do so?

7. Using the definitions given in Andrews' article, Projects 1 and 5 are innovations, projects 2, 3 and 4 are modifications and project 6 is an interpolation. How would you plan and manage your R & D effort for the coming year?
8. It is very difficult to estimate the costs and revenues for R & D projects. How do inaccuracies in estimation affect project selection procedures, and what can management do about this?

Part III
New Products

Introduction

The final stages of development and the market launch are of crucial importance in the life of a product. It is at this time that the organization is exposed to the greatest risk. A considerable sum of money will have been spent on research, both on the product itself and on the marketing strategy which will be used. Advertising space will have been booked and in some cases paid for, 'selling-in' to the distribution channels will have started, and no revenue will yet have been earned. Even after it has been launched, no-one can be sure whether a product will be a success or not. In spite of the growing sophistication of marketing men in the planning of new product development, and in the collection and analysis of information, a high proportion of new products fail and are withdrawn from the market.

With everything happening at once it is important that the various activities are carefully scheduled and that there are no barriers to the rapid feedback of information from the market-place. The launch should not be held up because the bottle tops are not ready or because the salesmen have not received the new brochures. G. Pedraglio, in the first article in this section, says that elaborate scheduling devices, such as PERT networks, are not in themselves enough to eliminate confusion. The whole company has to be organized for new products, so that responsibilities are clearly defined and the various departments involved co-operate with rather than fight each other.

Charnes *et al.*, with DEMON, have designed a decision model whose principal feature is that new information is incorporated systematically as the project continues. A project moves through several stages, at the end of which a decision has to be made to drop the idea, gather more information or proceed to the next stage. Each decision is based on the information accumulated so far; in the early stages average values are used, but as marketing research is carried out so the parameters are changed. The criterion used is profit, and the model picks the decisions yielding the greatest profit. B.K. Chesterton's article is a case-study of a company which has to programme the relaunch of an existing product and at the same time decide on the future strategy for a new product which is in test market. He analyses the problem by means of a decision tree and highlights the problems associated with this type of analysis: constructing a tree which incorporates an adequate number of alternatives while at the same time remaining comprehensible and also obtaining sensible values for the subjective probabilities attached to the branches.

Product testing is an important research activity. Tests on existing brands can reveal customer preferences, weaknesses in formulation, and gaps in the product range. This information is of great value to those in charge of new-product planning. In the same way, tests on development products can show if changes are needed in the products or the way in which they will be marketed. Penny *et al.*, review the existing literature on product testing methods. They conclude that the market researcher must work back from the market, asking in turn: 'What is the problem?', 'How do customers see this problem?' and 'How do we measure their perceptions?'.

The last article in this section, by P.M. Doyle & C.B. Weinberg, is written from a different angle, that of the distributor. Supermarket buyers are offered a stream of new products, and they cannot accept all of them. Doyle & Weinberg outline a screening procedure based on rating new products along eight dimensions and comparing the resulting score with the scores of past products whose performance is known. Their procedure leads to one of three answers: accept, reject or test.

9.

Getting into Shape to Manage New Products
by Gerard Pedraglio

Reprinted from European Business, No. 30, Summer 1971 with permission.

Introduction

New-product management, the thriving offspring of modern business enterprises, is growing by leaps and bounds and basking in the prospects of what looks like a rosy future.

This doesn't mean that new products are accounting for the lion's share of economic activity. A 1966 McGraw-Hill survey showed that a mere 15 per cent of commodity sales in the US involved products under five years old, and this percentage was demonstrated to be even lower in all the other countries. Rather, new products are enjoying their stellar role in the dynamics of the economy and progress of enterprises.

Figure 9.1 shows the slice of the pie represented by the sales of products launched between 1957 and 1960 in the increased turnover noted in the US for a number of sectors during that three-year period — the effect of innovation on corporate growth is as plain as the proverbial nose on the face.

The effect is especially striking when it involves either a field in advanced technological industry, like that of computers, or a mass marketing sector whose products must be distinct from one another and must at the same time be tailored to suit customer requirements and fancies.

The new product thus looms simultaneously as a means of survival — in answer to the generalized and frequently speeded-up curtailing of the life-spans of existing products — and as an offensive weapon: the more dynamic firms are basing their strategies on planned innovation.

However, both the means and the weapon are costly and tricky to employ. For one thing, research and, to an even greater degree, development form a growing financial burden and are responsible for no small part of the continuous, relatively onerous increase in overhead in the large companies. For another, the risks inherent in developing and releasing an innovative product substantially swell this cost.

Product research: wealth, whimsy or waste?

Figure 9.2 depicts the mortality rate of new-product projects on the basis of a Booz, Allen & Hamilton survey of 51 American firms. The evolution of the new product has been broken down into five successive phases:

1 Exploratory studies leading to the formulation of the idea with a view to its industrial development, making it possible to ascertain whether the idea is sound and worth keeping on ice for fuller investigation.

2 Engineering studies, leading to the definition of a development programme and of the characteristics to be incorporated into the product, and also including an economic analysis of the product's anticipated contribution to the company's goals.

3 Actual development, whereby the idea is converted into a prototype or a marketable sample of a product.

4 The market test, either substantiating or ruining the hypotheses concerning the new product's market acceptance.

5 Final launching, with the company's reputation at stake along with its commercial and financial means.

The survey was inter-sectorial and the graph curve in Figure 9.2 characterizes a widespread phenomenon.

It is interesting to note that 58 ideas had to be considered in order for a single new product to successfully work its way up through the various stages. For the separate stages in the lifetime of the new product, Figure 9.3 shows the amount represented by expenses, leading to the project's either being crowned with success or shelved and cast into oblivion. However, these figures must be taken with a grain of salt — no piece of research is ever a total loss, and the improved state of knowledge it has yielded can subsequently prove valuable, and should be harnessed for other purposes. Still, 75 per cent of the money tied up in new-product research is spent with no direct profit, and two thirds of the sums 'squandered' are earmarked for the development phase.

Another Booz, Allen & Hamilton survey covering 54 American firms — leaders in their sectors — involved 366 recently-launched new products and showed that 57 per cent of the latter could be considered as shining successes, while 10 per cent had to be written-off as stark failures. These figures are rather more encouraging than not. Figure 9.4 provides an idea of the percentage of final successes, including market releases, among the new products sector by sector.

What the survey actually reveals is that, although these percentages of commercial successes display relatively little variation in terms of sectors, they do differ considerably among the firms in a given sector. The reason for this can be found in the discernible differences in the quality of management from one firm to the next as regards new products.

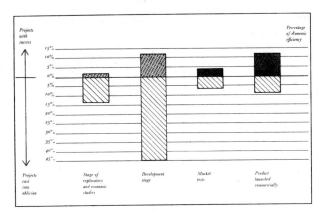

Figure 9.3 Economic efficiency of expenditures for new products in terms of development phases.

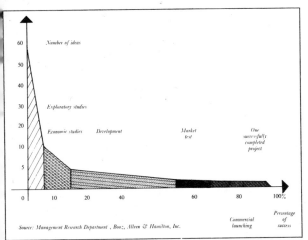

Figure 9.1 How new products increased sales in the US, 1957 to 60.

	Ideas for new products %	Projects in development %	New products launched %
In percentages of:			
Chemicals	2	18	59
Packaged foods	2	11	63
Electro-mechanical	1	13	63
Metallurgy	3	11	71
Engineering	2	21	59
Raw materials processing	5	14	59

Figure 9.4 Success of new products after market launching.

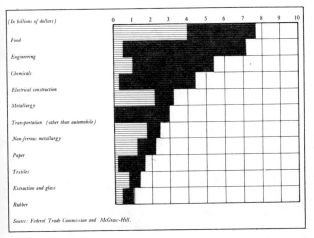

Figure 9.2 Mortality rate of new products by development phases.

The latter indeed pose problems of a highly particular kind to companies. Exactly what are these problems?

In this connection some 30 or so companies that had reaped fairly promising results with their new products were quizzed. The question we asked was, 'What is the nature of the problems that prevent you from achieving better results with new products?' The replies to this are analysed in Figure 9.5.

More than half the problems listed are related to organization. Over four out of five companies reported that they were experiencing problems of this kind.

The survey further delves into the kind of organizational problems experienced by companies that reported meeting up with them in this sphere of activity. Figure 9.6 illustrates the results of the answers to this query.

If the problems of organizational structure, which are frequently the most acute ones, are relegated to second place in this study, the reason is that most of the companies surveyed, all of which can boast of extensive new product experience, conceded the importance of the 'innovation' function and had already reached conclusions as to its consequences for structures. The co-ordination and integration of the firm's overall efforts are the problems they find to be toughest at this stage of the game, hence the stress on accurately defining individual responsibilities in resolving conflicts between targets through improved liaison and communications.

Organizing for innovation thus looms as one of the most urgent and delicate needs of companies that must keep on their competitive toes.

Electro-form thought it had all the problems licked

Electro-Form is one company that thought it had all its problems licked and was ready to tackle new-product management.

Electro-Form specializes in the manufacture of electric cables. It puts out a varied range of products, since the market sectors involved are extremely diverse – all the way from laboratory apparatus such as X-ray generators with telephone facilities up to outsized devices, mine detonators, etc. Its cables are put to an impressive range of uses, and they require continuous innovation.

The company was structured on the basis of main functions: under the director general, there was a production manager, business manager, research manager, financial manager, and personnel manager.

The business manager was in charge of sales, organized by areas, and of the marketing department, which was supervised by a marketing manager. The latter had nine department heads reporting to him:

1 Four product heads, each of them responsible for a product line.
2 One chief engineer, together with his product engineers.
3 Four heads of the sales-promotions departments: market surveys, advertising, follow-up, and prices.

The chief engineer and his product engineers were responsible for adapting products to market requirements and to improved customer follow-up service.

The research manager had a man in charge of defining products and their characteristics for manufacturing specifications under him.

Lines of procedure had been set up and were being applied in the development of new products:

1 The marketing manager kept the departments concerned posted regularly on details of plans and proposals for new products.
2 The research department issued periodic progress reports on the state of project developments.
3 Detailed instructions governed the semi-industrial market testing of new products.
4 A research committee staffed by members of top management kept all the departments regularly and fully abreast of the progress of the main projects.
5 The technical specifications for new products were worked out and issued by a particular section in the research department; these constituted the fountainhead of data for all the departments involved in the manufacture and sales of the future products.

All this notwithstanding, co-ordination had obviously fallen down on the job somewhere along the line. Shortcomings showed up in the form of delays in launching new products, of faulty integration of programmes into the firm's overall policy lines, of poor adaptation to market requirements, and of let-downs in team spirit among the personnel in the various departments.

No truly coherent programme for new products

The analysis more particularly points to the following weak spots:

1 Long-term commercial goals were not translated into specific requests for product renewals. There were no truly coherent, detailed programmes for new prod-

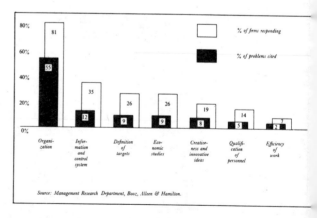

Figure 9.5 Nature of the specific problems raised by new products (according to firms with major innovation policies).

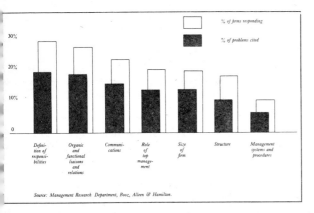

Figure 9.6 Organizational problems arising in the same firms.

ucts. As a result, since the ones that reached develop-ment failed to fulfil previously defined objectives, they loomed up more as a defensive than an aggressive means.

2 The responsibilities in connection with a new product were ill-defined and too scattered – they were spread out over the product heads concerned, who exerted their influence primarily in the project's starting and final phases; the product engineer in the business manager's department; and, in the research department, the men in charge of the development and technical specifications of new products. For the final develop-ment and defining of a product, each man considered that he had a responsibility. The research committee theoretically enjoyed final responsibility for new prod-ucts, but the fact was that it did not convene regularly, its deliberations were not up to snuff, and it failed by a long shot to fulfil its actual supervisory role. As a result, in most instances the research department simply dreamed up and decided on its own programmes.

But, since several departments in the marketing and research branches were jointly responsible for the technical definitions of products and for deciding jointly on specifications, frequent delays and compromise measures occurred, attesting to the difficulties hindering any attempt to reconcile points of view.

3 The serious lack of co-ordination between the branches participating in the development and launching of new products – the marketing, research, and prod-uction departments – was sorely detrimental to the efficiency of the corresponding programmes.

The various departments suffered from the short-comings of top management, which were due more especially to the inadequacies of the research committee; in fact, the persons in charge of research had gained a position of undue authority in the new-products policy, thereby fostering attitudes of mistrust, defence, and frustration on the part of the dealers.

4 The company failed to resort to the most important procedures in the development of its new products, specifically the following:

(a) A continuous programme for the identification and assessment of new ideas.
(b) A system of budgetary and financial control for individual projects.
(c) A set of selection criteria and a method of comparative assessment of the various projects.
(d) A method for calculating the probabilities of the success of a project.
(e) A simplified procedure for getting new-product specifications set down in black and white (for-merly, it had required six signatures!).
(f) A uniform system for codifying projects in the research and marketing departments.

In the face of the situation analysed above, the recommendations issued by Booz, Allen & Hamilton to increase the efficiency of the new-product programme were of three different kinds: organization of projects and planning on a long-term basis, structural reorganiza-tion, and setting up a set of procedures constituting a complete system for the management and control of new-product development.

First, projects were broken down into three cat-egories on the basis of the degree of innovation that they represented, so that optimum division of resources among these three categories could be achieved in terms of the requirements, and hence of the product renewal goals on the short-, medium-, and long-term bases, and also in terms of the risks involved.

In this light, the role of long-term commercial planning as the basic framework for the company's long-term planning was recognized: research and manu-facturing plans were to be issued as the outcome of commercial planning, not as a preliminary to it. The planning process was reassessed, specifically with regard to the determination of the goals of new products, to the communication of these goals to all the levels concerned, and to de-multiplying them into operational sub-goals for each of the several departments. These goals had to be as specific and fully quantified as possible, and had to include accurate indications concerning:

1 The anticipated sales and profits to be expected

Figure 9.7 How responsibilities at Electro-Form changed.

BEFORE

Marketing		Research	
Product manager	*Product engineer*	*Product development*	*Definition of products*
1. Responsibility for a product line, plus its engineering, development, and promotion.	1. Engineering and development of a product line.	1. Research, engineering, and development of new products.	1. Defining production specifications and getting them approved.
2. Responsibility for technical performance of products, their specification and profitability.	2. Responsibility for technical development and specification of products, production cost studies, and ways and means.	2. Interpreting the marketing department's estimates *vis-à-vis* customer requirements.	2. Defining requirements for raw materials for manufacturing new products; defining specifications of new products.
3. Contact with customers, technical assistance to salesmen for product promotion, negotiation of sales contracts, familiarity with special customer problems.	3. Technical assistance to salesmen for product promotion and study of customers' technical problems.		3. Solving inter-divisional problems of technical specifications.
4. Representing the firm at professional gatherings.	4. Writing the technical literature and representing the firm in professional technical relationships.		4. Carrying on closely-developed relationships with customers and suppliers.

AFTER

Marketing	Engineering department		Research	
Product manager	*Product engineer*	*Product specification*	*Product development*	*Standards Department*
1. *Changed:* Responsibility for the management and promotion of an accepted product line.	1. *Changed:* Responsibility for final development of products, for production cost studies and profit margin studies for accepted product lines.	1. *Changed:* Defining product specifications and getting them approved by business manager.	1. *Unchanged*	1. *Cancelled.*
2. *Cancelled.*	2. *Cancelled.*		2. *Cancelled.*	2. *Unchanged*
3. *Unchanged.*	3. *Add:* Visits to customers.		3. *Add:* Technical assistance to departments requesting it.	3. *Cancelled.*
4. *Unchanged.*	4. *Unchanged.*		4. *Add:* Participation in the firm's scientific reputation through publications.	4. *Unchanged*

⟶ *Arrows indicate fields of conflicting responsibilities between units.*

rom these new products, and what seemed to be the most likely prospects for success during their first few years of existence.

2 The nature of these products.

3 The specific markets at which they were aimed.

4 The performance levels of these products and the criteria for basing the decision to launch them.

With regard to structure, the following changes were suggested and put into effect:

1 The ailing research committee, which had been found sadly wanting, was replaced by a far more powerful development committee, headed by the director general, and composed of the business manager and the research and production managers, in addition to a secretary about whom more will be said later.

This committee was responsible for deciding on the progress of each project from one phase to the next, up to its final acceptance. Its work also included the issuing of instructions to the research department and supervision of the latter's activities – this being the job that should have been done by the original committee.

2 A new position was created, that of new-products manager, who automatically becomes the secretary of the development committee and co-ordinates all the activities and studies pertaining to new products. He is responsible to the business manager. His main duties include managing the budget, stimulating the continuous development and control of each individual project, activating all the studies carried on in the various offices concerned with new products, organizing brain-storming sessions, weighing suggestions for new projects in their initial phases, and preparing reports on the evaluation of projects.

Projects of average or only slight importance come directly under the responsibility of the line managers and, hence, under that of the marketing manager in the second degree.

The job of issuing product specifications was transferred from the research department to the office of the chief engineer of the marketing department. This office thus concerns itself with the engineering of new products and their technical definitions.

Organizing the life stages of new projects

Lastly, a new system was implemented for controlling and directing project lifetimes. This system is based on the need for organizing individually each of the successive stages in the lifetime of a project – exploration, preliminary research, economic evaluation, technical development, commercial development, and the final launching.

Figure 9.7 illustrates the sequence of these phases on the basis of project categories.

Among the various procedures developed, the following are noteworthy:

1 A programme designed to stimulate new ideas within the firm, including financial incentives.

2 A system for computing the amount of time and money spent weekly on each project, with an analytical break-down.

3 Cost studies and criteria for appraising projects in their various phases.

4 Framework and method for evaluating the prospects for the success of the projects at different levels of economic performance.

5 Reducing from six to two the number of signatures required for defining the specification of new products.

6 Uniform code for project reference, overall company planning.

7 Accurate definition of the responsibilities of each of the department heads in the three branches of management.

8 A simple and coherent system of progress reports for each project, integrated with the Management Information System, which sums up the results achieved vis-à-vis goals and with the budget control system.

The outcome of these changes was a many-facetted one.

First, top management enjoys greater authority over the orientation and control of the development department's activities. It acquired the means for assuming

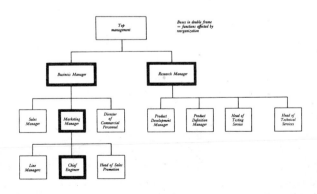

Figure 9.8(a) Structure before reorganization.

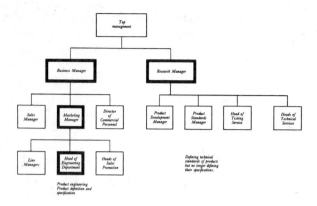

Figure 9.8(b) Structure after reorganization.

increased responsibility and having more of a say in the preparation of the company's future.

The marketing department has retrieved one of the essential means for its mission, i.e., the managing of new products, but it is obliged to concern itself to a wider extent with constraints and difficulties of a technical nature.

The Management Information System has been completed, specifically as regards project costing and means of control. From this, management has derived increased possibilities for issuing new market policies in full awareness of the situation.

Lastly, concern with economic performance has become the main-spring for releasing all the important decisions.

This reorganization was accompanied by an effort on the part of top management to improve team spirit as well as the relations between the members of the personnel in the various departments.

On the basis of this example, of the conclusions yielded by our surveys, and of our experience with these problems, let us now single out a few general ideas pertaining to the organization of a company that assigns suitable importance to an innovation policy.

Teamwork rather than goodwill

The two basic principles are the following:

1 The definition of an innovation policy and controlling its achievement is a responsibility that properly devolves upon top management. It therefore lies outside the province of either marketing or research.

In a complex, decentralized company the bulk of this responsibility will, of course, devolve upon the manage-

ment of a division assigned to a given product line. But even in this latter case, the top management of company or group will have to participate in specifying the development rate and possibly the fields for product innovation, and will also have to keep an eye on the share represented by the latter in the evolution of profits.

2 The genesis of the creation and launching of new products is the result of teamwork. It requires close co-operation between all the functional departments and top management. This co-operation cannot be merely left up to the goodwill of individuals. It has to be organized, nursed along, and bolstered up. This implies the defining of specific tasks and responsibilities that are updated in terms of the evolution of the various projects, and a sufficient delegation of authority for each partial task within a project. It further implies that top management is keeping structures flexible and adaptable so that they will not get bogged down in the exploitation of existing products.

The structure of the company is therefore at stake. New products can be handled by three kinds of structural elements – a new-product committee, inter functional teams for each project, or a particular department.

As a matter of fact, it is becoming increasingly frequent for innovative firms to set up new-product departments. In three Booz, Allen & Hamilton surveys performed in the US, covering the same large companies in 1956, 1960, and 1964, the percentages of those resorting to this structural solution were, respectively 22, 56 and 86.

This trend corresponds to a continuous evolution of organizations. In an initial phase, the new product is considered as a technical improvement or discovery developed by the company's R & D department which it would be advisable to introduce into the existing product line – the new product poses, successively, a technical, a marketing, and a management problem when it is being actively exploited. Actually, it is the research and development manager, a technician, who has the authority over new products. In industries in which innovation plays a determining role, he shares this authority with the director general.

When the firm further commits itself in the complex business of preparing for its future, it becomes more aware of the importance of the connections between the commercial, financial, human, and technical aspects of new-product policy. The governing committee, if there is one, is increasingly involved in the corresponding decisions and the inter-functional co-ordination that they require.

A new-product department is not enough

In general, an inter-functional committee specifically responsible for new products is created to ensure this co-ordination.

But this committee soon discovers that, lacking any direct control over any of the functional aspects of the projects, its co-ordination is more often than not ineffective, because it is carried on from too lofty a level and at too remote a distance. The ensuing phase often involves organizing inter-functional teams for each project and appointing persons to be in charge of all the aspects of a new product.

The normal process of development, then, is to group these teams under the orders of a new-product manager, thereby constituting a new-product department.

Nor does the evolution of the organizations stop here. The one shown in Figures 9.7 and 9.8, which does not recur as regularly as may be popularly believed, would seem to lead to the modern form of structure that consists of an exploitation department and a future department. The latter will include the new-product department — including products for the preparation of the company's future resources in men, know-how, equipment, and funds — and the instruments for devising medium- and long-term policies and strategies.

There is a prefiguration of this future department in the organization of existing new-product department.

The typical responsibility pattern of such a department is the following:

1 Jointly with top management, setting goals for product renewal and diversification.

2 Devising and adopting the corresponding policies and programmes.

3 Planning exploitation and research on new ideas based on existing products.

4 Agreeing or refusing to pursue work on a project at each phase in its lifetime, and deciding on the launching or abandoning of products.

5 Adopting the specifications for new products.

6 Recommending the eventual improvements to be added to new products.

7 Co-ordinating marketing tests and product launchings with the technical development of new products and the preparations for implementing their production.

8 Directing and supervising the inter-functional teams for products.

9 Ensuring the company sufficient creativeness and flexibility to enable the long-term new-product policy to be carried out to a successful issue in the future.

How company size effects new product development

A new-product department thus constituted can be attached only to an extremely high level in the hierarchy.

Our latest survey, covering 56 companies having such a department, yields the following:

Attached to the director general	33 per cent
Attached to the marketing manager at the highest level	34 per cent
Attached to the R & D manager	13 per cent

The increasing order of these percentages also corresponds to how the wind is blowing in the evolution of business firms, which strikes us as being both normal and desirable.

The size of a company naturally affects the organizational structure to be used for new products. In medium-sized companies, the management committee or, in its stead, the top management, acts as the function that concerns them. In larger companies, especially in those in a highly competitive situation, the trend is toward creating a new-product department. In multidepartmental, highly diversified companies, such a department can be found at different levels of the structure — at that of top management and those of the departmental managers.

Good communication means good innovation

The particular function of the conceiving, development, and final launching of products designed to provide for the firm's future must be recognized as a permanent function of top management and should constitute one of the latter's most fundamental responsibilities.

By its nature, moreover, this function clearly integrates all the others — the decisions concerning new products should be neither purely technical, nor purely commercial, nor purely financial. And the work itself leading up to these decisions should be inter-functional and tightly co-ordinated. As it happens, the resultant exchanges of viewpoints are also the best conditions for creativity: success in innovation is conditioned by the ease of communications and liaison within the firm. This

Table 9.9 How a new product moves through the organization.

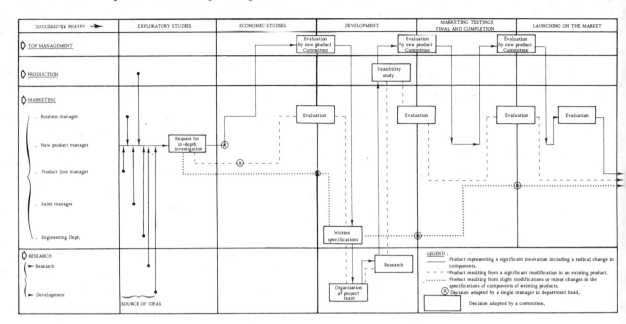

is embodied in the concept of inter-functional teams responsible for the complete development of a project and producing, for top management, integrated information concerning this project. In this case, the management's problem is much less one of co-ordinating efforts on projects and much more one of co-ordinating the firm's resources in terms of a short-, medium-, and long-term programme. The chances for the success of the innovation policy, and hence of the future results, are thereby improved, but the difficulties of the internal organization are also ncreased.

All of which goes to prove once again that the taut ship of rigorous management has no equal for plying the charted seas of modern business.

10.
DEMON: A Management Model for Marketing New Products

by A. Charnes, W.W. Cooper, J.K. Devoe and D.B. Learner

© 1968 by the Regents of the University of California.
Reprinted from California Management Review, Vol. XI (1) pp. 31-46 by permission of the Regents.

The function of new-product marketing has become of major importance and concern to business management in response to consumer demand and also in response to expanding R & D activities. Its importance was already evident by 1961, when, as an article in *Business Week*[1] reported, almost one out of every seven sales dollars was generated by products that did not even exist five years before. Some of the reasons for concern are illustrated in a recent survey[2] which shows a high failure rate for new products, even in well-managed companies. In fact, a 60 per cent failure rate was experienced among new products that had progressed all the way through test marketing.

These data apply to well-managed companies; hence, it seems safe to assume that this failure rate was sustained in the face of the best that modern management could supply in the form of systematic procedures for assembling, combining, and exploiting marketing information. (This failure rate does not include lost opportunities occasioned by an erroneous decision not to market a product.) Collecting such marketing information, usually in the form of elaborate, detailed manuals that are maintained along with checklists, formulae, electronic computer codes, checking, and verification procedures, can be expensive. These activities are often justified on the grounds that the results will aid in the important decision to 'market nationally' — where many millions of dollars may be expended — or the equally important decision to stop further efforts at commercialization and absorb the penalties.

The volume of marketing information can reach a point where full exploitation cannot reasonably be expected, even when electronic computing aids are available. Something more than volumes of data and high-speed computers are apparently required for analysing and exploiting such data.

Consider, for instance, a development sequence in which one marketing study may point only to the (apparently frustrating) need for further study. Under these circumstances, as might be expected, only the most recent study in such a sequence is considered —

generally to the neglect of previously collected data. That is, data from previous studies are ignored or considered at best in perfunctory and unsatisfactory ways difficult to relate to the marketing decisions at hand. This would seem to raise some question as to whether some or all of the previous studies involved substantial wastes of funds and time in order to assemble data that were not wholly relevant or, perhaps worse, whether relevant and valuable data were wasted because of inadequacies in the available tools of analysis.

Other problems can be cited, of course, besides those involving data assembly and treatment. Among these problems might be included the need for better ways of ascertaining how the proposed marketing endeavour might affect other (non-marketing) aspects of company policies and activities.

Marketing New Products

These problems and others will be noted or elaborated in this report on our nearly four years of research which have resulted in a management model called (DEMON) (Decision Mapping via Optimum Networks).[3] for marketing new products. This model is composed of two major components:

1 Detailed study and analysis of some 200 actual cases, plus interviews with experienced marketers, to establish the pertinent data requirements and relationships among marketing elements, with special reference to consumer packaged goods.

2 The other component addresses the need for developing new mathematics to exploit these data and relationships with the flexibility and power that are required for dealing in a more profitable manner with the ever-changing world of new-product marketing.

As a marketing management system, DEMON:

1 Focuses on a clear-cut consistent objective for marketing new products — maximum profits.

2 Integrates financial, marketing, and production considerations into a comprehensive, practical plan for action.

3 Develops marketing plans in a flexible, dynamic fashion, constantly responding to changing priorities that result from the way the world changes.

4 Considers the way all these factors interact in a simultaneous manner, thereby eliminating that old saw – 'all other things being equal' – when we know they never are.

Managerial Aspects

The DEMON network

We will discuss the managerial rather than the mathematical aspects[4] of DEMON. Figure 10.1 depicts the possibilities for marketing activities and decisions for a new product. There are, of course, many reasons motivating new product introduction, such as: profit potential, protecting the market position of established products, forestalling competition, utilizing excess capacity, or establishing an outlet for by-products that would otherwise go to waste.

These motivating considerations and the available marketing evidence are reviewed and evaluated at the stage labelled 'evaluation I' in Figure 10.1 and may be so compelling that a decision to 'go national' should be reached. This is the intended significance of the arrow, or line, pointing from evaluation I to the node labelled 'go'. 'Go' abbreviates the decision 'go national', i.e., commence marketing on a national scale – with all its attendant cost of implementation. Such costs, although not shown in Figure 10.1, form an integral part of the model and bear on the decisions made through its use.

Evidence may also, of course, be overpowering on the negative side. The label 'no' represents the alternative 'no-go' decision which then halts further programme development and expenditures.

As a third alternative, the evidence may not be sufficiently decisive to warrant a 'no' or 'go' decision, although continued development of a marketing programme is warranted. Note that such a continuation may be warranted even when already available information suggests that marketing of the product will be profitable. For instance, if merely minimum acceptable profit prospects are in view there may be development

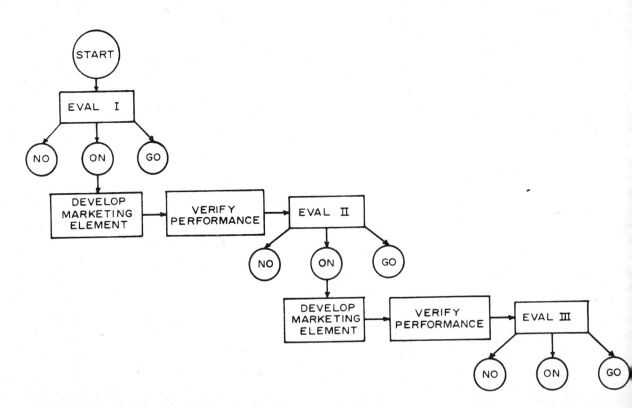

Figure 10.1 Possibilities for marketing activities and decisions for a new product.

opportunities for achieving greater profits. Such increased profit prospects will, in general, be attainable only by changing and improving the performance of some aspect of the marketing plan. Ascertainment of those aspects which should be changed in the marketing plan may require some collection of additional data, but this only raises a question of the best study sequence in the light of already assembled data as well as the still further study possibilities, and so on.

Suppose, for instance, that the profit possibilities are acceptable even at evaluation I. Taking this into account, DEMON might nevertheless signal movement to the on stage of evaluation I, rather than go national. This occurs because changing the performance of one or more elements of the marketing programme is likely to open new, better, and previously hidden profit possibilities. Such changes can be time-consuming. For example, profit possibilities might improve by changing the product formulation or by changing advertising effectiveness through a different copy. The development of products promotions and copy requires expending time – time during which the marketing world and various marketing elements may change. These changes are not ordinarily reflected in the marketing plan developed at evaluation I. Thus, the results of these changes on profit prospects must be determined if continued planning is to have real meaning.

The market-place performance of each changed marketing element can be verified by market research. If a product formulation is changed, the resulting change in consumer behaviour estimates is useful in adjusting other marketing plan elements to strive for maximum profits, thus capitalizing on the newly revised product performance.

This new perspective for market research underlines its role in providing market performance feedback for management planning. Subsequent evaluations using verified performance of other marketing elements can uncover marketing opportunities unforeseen when the initial plan was developed. So the DEMON network overcomes one of the major shortcomings of traditional new product planning – viz., the long time-lag between developing and implementing a new-product plan which often leads to obsolescence in the implemented plan. DEMON side-steps this problem through the use of continued verification of the likely performance accomplishment of each marketing element. These current performance accomplishments are then fed back to modify other plan components – always with maximum profit as the objective.

In short, via the 'on' alternative we move through the stage labelled 'develop marketing element' to the stage labelled 'verify performance' where DEMON selects the best from among the available market research study possibilities. This selection considers both the costs and quality of the data that are likely to be secured by each study alternative.

Figure 10.1, then, illustrates the sequential development and assembly of marketing programmes. In a flexible manner DEMON proceeds to consider all marketing programme possibilities and their profit/cost prospects in the context of accumulated study data. On this basis it contingently selects the marketing elements that should be improved and specifies market research required to verify that improvement.

It is important to emphasize that DEMON is not a static, one-time-only analysis. As each marketing element is developed and its performance verified, additional evaluations take place. In this manner, DEMON integrates the most recent market performance with accumulated data and evaluates the result in the context of changing market conditions. The process of developing the maximum profit marketing plan is one of continuous adaptation to the changing world, until a 'go' or 'no-go' decision can be reached with some reasonable degree of assurance of its success.

Elements of Programme

The marketing relations

The other major component of this system is the marketing relationships uncovered by studying 200 or so actual cases. Figure 10.2, also portrayed in the form of a network, indicates how relationships between advertising expenditures, advertising copy, product performance, distribution, etc., are employed. Thus, (advertising expenditures) give rise to media audiences (gross impressions) and so on, until triers (of the product) are converted to users and then, via a unit price, the actual quantity of consumer sales is derived. Here advertising expenditures are viewed as directed toward generation of product trial (or triers). Other routes to developing product trial are also possible. See, for instance, 'promotion' which also has a link with 'triers'.

Differing expenditures may be allocated to promotion and advertising and, in concert with other factors, such as distribution, audience composition, and copy content and execution, can affect trial and usage rates. Each of these factors is an important element of a marketing programme. Using the relationships between

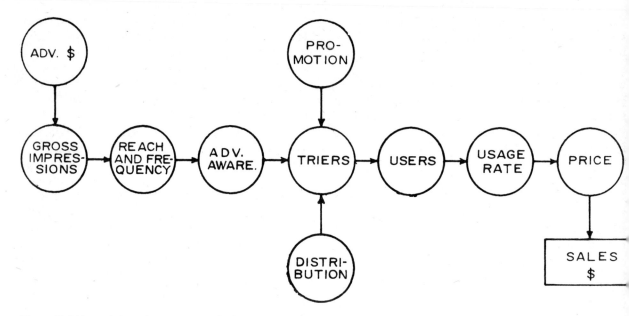

Figure 10.2 How relationships are employed.

these elements, as estimated from the case studies, DEMON determines, at each evaluation, the combination of values for each of these elements required to maximize profits. Note that this implies optimal expenditure levels for both advertising and promotion activities.

Changing any element of a marketing programme in response to an 'on' decision is intended to influence market behaviour. Thus, the verified performance results of some alteration may serve to open prospects of still further profit improvement in the marketing programme. DEMON and its associated mathematics are designed to consider such contingent prospects by systematically exploiting all accumulated marketing information to obtain improved profit possibilities; this is in contrast to traditional methods which simply react to the most recently available information. In this way the dynamics of a changing market are explicitly considered and evaluated to obtain an optimal marketing programme.

These marketing relations have both an evaluative and diagnostic planning value. In the evaluation I stage, the average relation (based on the case-studies) is used to forecast profit expectations. In subsequent evaluations, as marketing element performance is verified, these average relations are replaced by the current measurements provided by marketing research studies.

For example, the case-study relationships might indicate that 40 **per** cent of those aware of the advertising are likely to try the product. This 40 per cent advertising awareness to trial ratio would serve as the benchmark. An advertising test measuring actual purchase behaviour might show that 50 per cent of those aware of the advertising have tried the product. The average awareness to trial ratio (40 per cent) would be replaced by the actual ratio (50 per cent) describing the performance of the tested advertising. In this manner average performance expectations for each marketing element are replaced by performance ratios unique and specific to the marketing plan under development. In this manner the marketing relations serve to evaluate performance; they can also be useful in diagnosing why events occurred the way they have.

Let us suppose, for example, that test results show that 60 per cent of the target market can recall the advertising. This is a rather high awareness achieved. Similarly, let us suppose that 20 per cent of the target market try the product – a low trial rate. Diagnosis of these two results shows that execution of the advertising is sufficiently powerful to bring under the sales tent for this product almost two out of three persons in the target market. However, the content of the advertising – its motivating power – is feeble, since only two out of ten in the target group try the brand. Creative effort should thus be directed to improving the 'meaningfulness' of the sales message, without concern for improving the stopping power of the advertising. Reverse results of awareness and trial ratios would point out the need to get more consumers under the tent, perhaps by creative use of a black eye or a white tornado. Additional creative concern over the content of the sales message would then be unnecessary, since 60 per cent of those who display this awareness of the advertising find it sufficiently compelling to try the product.

Product performance can be diagnosed from the trial to usage performance ratio. High trial and low repeat (usage) are indicative of products that promise performance but do not deliver it. Low trial levels coupled with high repeat purchase describe highly successful product performance on a promise that is inadequately communicated to the target market.

In a similar fashion, the other performance ratios serve for evaluative and diagnostic uses: expenditures to promotion redemption, salesmen to distribution, and price to triers. These ratios tell how well the marketing plan may perform and the reason for such performance. The critical notion in DEMON's use of these data is the manner in which current information is used to replace obsolescent information that might lead to erroneous forecasts and decisions.

Corporate objectives, policies, and constraints
The market and its dynamics are important. So are corporate objectives, policies, and constraints. It has not always been easy to ensure that general management policies are adequately reflected in marketing pro- grammes which are evolved mainly in response to changes in market behaviour. Hence, as already noted, there is a problem of fitting the product's marketing strategy (and its consequences) to other aspects of corporate policy as well as vice versa. This does not mean, however, that these policies should be regarded as fixed and static in contrast to the dynamic marketing phenomena that are encountered. DEMON provides ample opportunities; indeed it requires systematic review and revaluation of existing new product policies and objectives as can be illustrated by reference to the often-used concept of a payback period.

Payback, or break-even analyses, are often used as criteria, along with requirements such as minimum profit potential to guide and evaluate the prospects for any product's potential. For example, marketing policy may require that no new product should be marketed unless the anticipated profits pay back the initial marketing outlays within a prescribed time period (except in extraordinary circumstances, e.g., if it became apparent that a competitor was on the verge of a new marketing

venture). Caution should be exercised in the use of such formulae, however, because they very likely represent oversimplifications resulting from an inability to deal effectively with all the pertinent corporate policies and objectives. Payback as a desirable control on investment risk should be carefully distinguished from payback as an objective. Cast in the latter role, payback has generally achieved priority over all other considerations, including maximum profit, insofar as the latter requires considering prospects and action which extend beyond the end of the payback period. Although the payback approach has become an almost universally accepted way to evaluate new-product marketing prospects, this should not be permitted to obscure the deficiencies that accompany its use as an over-riding criterion for planning.

Payback *v.* maximum profit is an issue of long standing in finance, capital budgeting, and related areas of study. Indeed, it is almost a classic exercise in finance textbooks and courses to show the many inadequacies of the former (payback) in contrast to the latter. The supposition, however, is that the choice of one of these as a marketing (or finance) objective necessarily pre- cludes any use whatsoever of the other.

But this is not the way in which the matter is treated by DEMON. The issue of payback *v.* maximum profit is resolved by DEMON in ways which allow both to come into focus for explicit consideration. Consider, for instance, the argument that planning via a payback approach inadequately deals with important factors in the introduction of a product and hence might better give way to some other objective, such as 'maximum profit'. On the other hand it must be admitted that the introduction of a new product is attended by significant marketing risks as well as data uncertainties arising from the studies that have been (or might be) conducted, and payback control may represent one way of dealing with these risks.

How then should the issue of payback and profit – especially maximum profit – be resolved? The DEMON model was designed so that both factors could be accounted for in decision-making. When this is done, many possibilities emerge for combining risk control, via payback, with profit opportunities. One such possibility is to establish profit as the objective and to assign payback the status of a constraint that screens out unacceptable investment risks. For instance, suppose a company is unwilling to accept greater than nine to one odds that payback will not be achieved within two years after a 'go' decision. Marketing programmes which have greater risks (longer payouts) are then screened out, irrespective of their profit potential. However, DEMON operates so that any significant profit prospects that may be uncovered are presented for management review, and policies may be revised if warranted.

Further attention should be given to the way in which this screening is accomplished. Supposing for example, that the stipulated payout period is set at two years. Evidently, this cannot be absolutely guaranteed with probability in most marketing contexts. Instead, such a context would appear to warrant an approach in which one specifies the acceptable odds that are implied by statements such as 'the probability of achieving a two-year payout is 0.9', while 'the probability of achieving payout in 2.5 years is 0.95', and so on.

The above ideas are accommodated via 'chance constraints' which extend ordinary linear programming so as to make the optimizations (under constraints) applicable, even in situations where the data are uncertain. Hence, it follows that in such cases the constraints of ordinary linear programming must give way to those of 'chance constrained programming'[5] which allow the constraints to be violated, but only with specified probabilities such as are indicated by the statement that 'a two-year payout period will be achieved with 0.9 probability', and so on.

Bearing this use of risk constraints in mind we next turn to the objective that should be pursued after the specified too risky alternatives have been eliminated. The meaning of the DEMON objective Maximum Expected Maximum Profit (MEMP) can be explained by reference to Figure 10.1. For every marketing programme that results in a 'go' decision because it exceeds some given profit level, DEMON adjusts the content of that programme, the marketing elements, to obtain maximum profits. Further, DEMON selects the best (or maximum) of these 'go' marketing plans for implementation. This, then, is what is meant by MEMP – a maximum profit plan is arranged for each 'go' possibility and the maximum of all such 'go' possibilities is selected. MEMP is to be secured within the context of corporate policies, such as the already indicated payback. Other corporate policies or constraints such as budgets should, of course, also be included in DEMON as required.

Any arbitrary constraint or management control device may inadvertently conceal profit possibilities that come into view as the controls are removed. This notion applies to budgetary limitations as well as payback constraints. At each consecutive stage of DEMON, the management constraints may be altered to explore

opportunities that otherwise might be lost from view. This means that DEMON can reveal the nature of the policy alterations that would be required to produce a 'go' or 'no' decision at the earliest opportunity. By comparing these new policies and results with the original policy constraints, management is supplied with a systematic basis for evaluating profit potentials and altering its policies and objectives accordingly.

An Example

A case-study

To make these notions more concrete, let us consider a corporation that desires to introduce a new brand into a drug product category. After receiving appropriate approvals for new drugs from the food and drug administration, management initiates development of its marketing programme via DEMON. Since DEMON is founded, in part, upon known relationships between various marketing elements (Figure 10.2), these relationships can be combined to produce an estimate of the most likely profit for a new brand in a product category. This maximum profit is then evaluated relative to corporate policies. Two kinds of information form the starting point for DEMON's initial benchmark evaluation:

1 Management policies that reflect the way the company is supposed to behave.

2 Marketing data that reflect the way the world is behaving.

During this initial study and development phase, DEMON develops a marketing plan for implementation during a later planning period. The planning period serves as the basic time frame of reference for all marketing programmes developed by the system. In this example, the manufacturer established five years (from the date of national introduction) as the planning period. Of course, the longer the planning period, the greater the uncertainty surrounding plan accomplishments. DEMON does specify the extent of this uncertainty to show how likely it is to affect management decisions.

The initial DEMON evaluation involves one assumption. The marketing plan that leads to the five-year accomplishment, noted in Figure 10.3, is based upon average performance of advertising, product, sales force etc. Average performance is assumed at this point simply because it is most likely to occur. The marketing

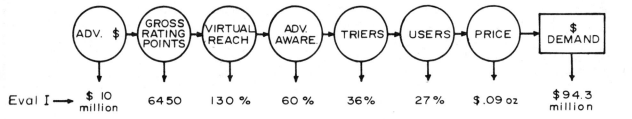

Figure 10.3 DEMON case-study based on average performance.

plan in Figure 10.3 requires no data that would not ordinarily be available at the time the product is available for marketing commercialization.

Figure 10.3 shows that, were the decision to 'go national' implemented (immediately), the likely sales accomplishment over the five-year planning period would be $94.3 million. These sales would be achieved with a price of 9 cents per ounce; average product performance leading to 27 per cent users, and average advertising content and execution achieving awareness of 60 per cent among the market target. The cumulative five-year advertising expenditures in consumer media necessary to achieve these performances amounts to $10 million. This case-study does not include consumer promotion expenditures and distribution costs nor does it indicate in detail the rate at which the advertising funds will be expended. Of course, all these factors play an integral role and are, indeed, considered in normal practice, although not present here.

The best advertising expenditure is determined by examining the range of expenditures to discover which level leads to the greatest profit at the end of the five-year planning period. The first benchmark evaluation asks: What advertising and promotion expenditure is required, over the planning period, so that the five-year profits will be as large as possible, considering average performance on the part of all the elements in the marketing plan? In this example, the answer is $10 million. It should be noted that other performance levels of the marketing elements will, of course, require a different advertising expenditure in order to maximize the five-year profit. If an above-average product formulation were coupled with average advertising content and below-average sales force performance, the advertising expenditures (and values in Figure 10.3), required to maximize profits would in all likelihood be quite different. Assuming different product, advertising, and sales force performance is equivalent to assuming a different marketing mix, it appears intuitively sound

that different expenditures would be required to maximize profits from different marketing plans. What we seek in developing a marketing plan is the maximum profit, considering all levels of expenditure and all combinations of marketing mix.

Table 10.1 shows the profit implications of the marketing plan in Figure 10.3. The first column illustrates likely plan accomplishments, and the second column shows managerial requirements. The maximum likely profit of $24.8 million far exceeds management's requirements of $6.4 million. If profitability were the only consideration, a 'go national' decision would be justified, the assumptions and quality of data notwithstanding.

Table 10.1 DEMON case-study: profit implications.

	Evaluation I	Results policies
Profit	$24.8 million	$6.4 million
Risk	±$62.0 million	—
Confidence of 'go' profit	43%	70%
Pay-out period	3.5 years	3.5 years
Confidence of pay-out period	36%	70%
	12 yrs. @ 70%	

In many similar circumstances, a basic question is that of the accuracy of information or 'How good are the data?' The figure in the second line of Table 10.1, labelled 'risk!', summarizes in one number just how good the data are. This data uncertainty arises from three different sources: errors in the sales forecast, errors in market research, or errors in the marketing relationships. Such unreliability has always existed, and it has indeed been difficult in the past to provide a realistic answer to the question of data quality. The notion of 'risk' does not eliminate this uncertainty, but it does answer the question directly, in terms related to maximum profit. Thus, while the maximum profit might be $24.8 million, the uncertainty or unreliability of that estimate is $62 million. Risk does not mean that we should infer that there will actually be a loss of over $37 million (62.0-24.8 = 37.2), since obviously the venture would never be permitted to continue long enough to incur such a loss. It does mean that the uncertainty of achieving the maximum profit is almost three times the amount of profit that can be achieved.

Additional insight concerning risk can be gained by referring to the confidence figure in the second column of Table 10.1. As indicated in the second column, management required odds somewhat better than two to three (70 per cent) to achieve at least $6.4 million before being willing to make a 'go' decision. These odds reflect the fact that very few things can be predicted with certainty. The odds say, in essence, 'If we want to be absolutely certain of achieving $6.4 million, we would probably do nothing, since in business we can be sure of nothing. As long as we are willing to gamble, with odds better than two to one in our favour, we'll 'go national'.

The odds in the first column (43 per cent) reflect the effect of the risk and the likelihood of achieving the 'go' profit of $6.4 million. Although the maximum profit may be $24.8 million, because of data uncertainty the odds of achieving even $6.4 million are little more than three to five. So the accumulated uncertainty has effectively lowered the odds of achieving the target profit. These risks and uncertainties have always existed, as reflected by management's general reluctance to take action based upon market research data. DEMON uncovers the effects of these uncertainties and relates them to the decision at hand, making the decision itself more straightforward.

Referring again to Table 10.1, management policy requires that new products pay-out, or break even, at 3.5 years. Clearly, this does not mean that pay-outs of 44 or 48 months are unacceptable. It does mean that management wants to break even at 42 months, with some reasonable chance of success. The required degree of assurance is indicated in the second column at 70 per cent. Once again, because of uncertainties surrounding the way in which profit will accumulate, the likelihood, or odds of achieving pay-out in 3.5 years are only slightly better than one in three (36 per cent). Upon seeing the odds of making a 42-month pay-out the marketing vice-president asked, 'If I demanded 70 per cent odds, how long a pay-out period would be required

to give me that confidence?' The answer in the last line of Table 10.1 prompted the reply, 'No wonder we've introduced so many products with 12-year payouts!'

The managerial implications of the marketing plan developed in Table 10.1 and Figure 10.3 show that the brand has great profit potential, although at this juncture, because of the uncertainties in the data and the implications of various management policies, the decision must be to continue 'on'. Such a decision affords the opportunity to examine the implications of alternative marketing actions that might be taken to improve profit potential. As a diagnostic aid it is possible, for example, to examine the expected relation of advertising expenditures with profit.

It is clear from Figure 10.4 that the greatest profit ($24.8 million) occurs at $10 million expenditure, and profit decreases as more or less funds are expended. The rates of drop in profits from over- or under-spending are not equal. For example, 50 per cent greater expenditure ($15 million) results in about $22.5 million profits, whereas 50 per cent less expenditure ($5 million) turns up only $17.5 million in profit. Thus, Figure 10.4 shows that it is more profitable to overspend than underspend on this new product's advertising. This is hardly a world-shaking conclusion, since the same rule of thumb has generally been followed by knowledgeable marketing managers. The point of significance is that the question of 'how much?' to over- or under-spend can now be answered with some degree of realism, by examining the managerial implications that may be associated with Figure 10.4.

Other examinations of leverage on profit by product performance, price, size of sales force, etc., can give the

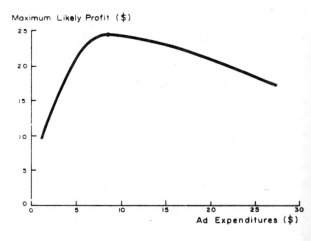

Figure 10.4 DEMON case-study: evaluation 1.

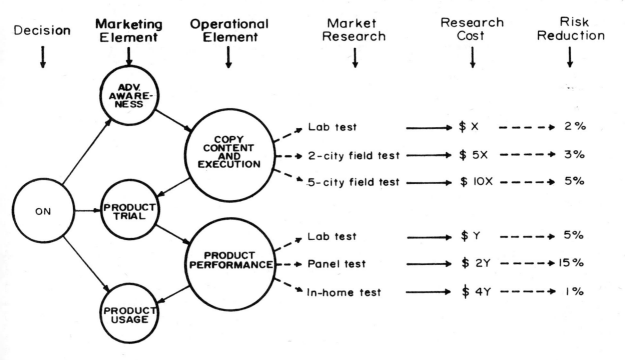

Decision	Marketing Element	Operational Element	Market Research	Research Cost	Risk Reduction
↓	↓	↓	↓	↓	↓

ADV. AWARE-NESS

COPY CONTENT AND EXECUTION

Lab test ——→ $ X - - - → 2%

2-city field test ——→ $ 5X - - - → 3%

5-city field test ——→ $ IOX - - - → 5%

ON

PRODUCT TRIAL

PRODUCT PERFORMANCE

Lab test ——→ $ Y - - - → 5%

Panel test ——→ $ 2Y - - - → 15%

In-home test ——→ $ 4Y - - - → 1%

PRODUCT USAGE

Figure 10.5 Performance testing.

manager insight into the opportunities afforded by this 'on' decision.

There are many possible ways of reaching a 'go' decision by arranging a better marketing programme. A better plan refers to reduced risk, increased profit, or both. Profit depends in part upon the way each element in the marketing programme performs in the market-place. Risk depends in part upon the accuracy of measuring that performance. The selection of which element of the marketing programme requires improvement is .based upon their individual leverage on profit. The extent of that leverage is measured by market research which contributes better data, reducing uncertainty. Both these tasks must be accomplished in the least costly fashion.

These notions can be illustrated by referring to Figure 10.5. The 'on' decision has been specified. One or more of the three marketing elements illustrated in the example in Figure 10.5 may be selected for improvement. As previously pointed out, the conversion of consumers from being aware of the advertising to trying the brand is due to the effectiveness of the creative content of the advertising. The conversion of consumers from triers (first purchase) to users (second purchase) depends upon the product's performance. It is the market-place performance of this advertising or the

product that must be improved, then verified through market research. There are clearly many ways of verifying the performance of each element. One market research tool may be more or less accurate and costly than another. Inaccuracies in the market research contribute to risk, while improved performance of the marketing element contributes to profit. The choice of which marketing element to alter is based upon the likely increase in profitability of the entire programme.

In the case of this drug product, the 'on' analysis selected copy content and product performance as the marketing elements to be improved. Both elements were selected for parallel development and testing, because their profit opportunity and risk reduction per research dollar were virtually equivalent. The advertising agency developed advertising content, which was subsequently tested by measuring the proportion of television viewers who could recall the advertising message (awareness) for each of three alternative advertising approaches.

While this creative development and copy research were being completed, the product group arranged an in-home product-use test of two alternative product formulations. This project determined the proportion of persons in the test who purchased the brand after trying each formulation. In this manner, then, performance of the advertising and performance of the product were

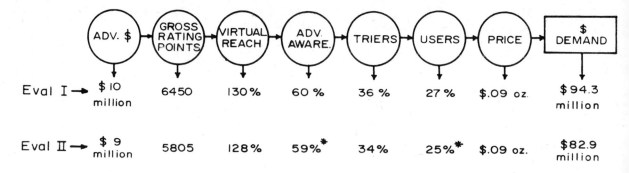

	ADV. $	GROSS RATING POINTS	VIRTUAL REACH	ADV. AWARE.	TRIERS	USERS	PRICE	$ DEMAND
Eval I →	$10 million	6450	130%	60%	36%	27%	$.09 oz.	$94.3 million
Eval II →	$9 million	5805	128%	59%*	34%	25%*	$.09 oz.	$82.9 million

Figure 10.6 DEMON case-study: optimum marketing programme

measured under realistic conditions. These actual field measurements of advertisement awareness and product usage were up to date replacements for the now-obsolete benchmark averages for these two marketing elements.

These new data were used as the starting-point for the second DEMON evaluation. The managerial policies were reviewed to assure that such factors as payout and profit requirements continued to reflect current management viewpoints. DEMON computations then adjusted the advertising and promotion expenditures to obtain a new maximum profit marketing plan. Figure 10.6 illustrates this optimum marketing programme. The asterisks identify the current measured values for the two newly developed marketing elements.

Inspection of Figure 10.6 shows that $9 million spent on advertising over the five-year planning period produces slightly over $21 million of profit. This is in contrast to the first evaluation which shows $24.8 million of profit resulting from a $10 million advertising expenditure. A comparison of Table 10.1 and Figure 10.6 shows that the main difference in the composition of the two marketing plans lies with the advertising appropriation. It is also quite apparent that the target values for the revised media plan are somewhat lower than those for the benchmark plan. The advertising awareness accomplishment, however, is virtually the same as that of the benchmark evaluation. This apparent discrepancy points out that the introduction of actual advertising content, in place of assuming average content, produced virtually the same advertising awareness for $1 million less cost.

Table 10.2 shows the effects of the advertising and product development sequence completed prior to the development of the second evaluation DEMON marketing plan. It is quite apparent that the maximum expected maximum profit of $21.2 million is far in excess of the $6.4 million required profit target. Because

we now deal with verified information (performance of the advertising and the product), the uncertainty or risk associated with the achievement of MEMP has been reduced to about $8.5 million. This risk reduction markedly increases the assurance of achieving the objective and is reflected in the increased confidence of achieving the $6.4 million profit target, which has jumped to 90 per cent, thus satisfying that management requirement.

The rate of profit accumulation results in achieving the break-even point at three years with odds of seven chances out of ten. This result exceeds the requirement laid down by management that pay-out should occur within 3.5 years with odds of seven out of ten. Obviously, if the pay-out odds are seven out of ten in three years, the odds will be even greater in favour of breaking-even in 3.5 years.

On the basis of management requirements for profit, pay-out, and confidence, the results of the second DEMON evaluation indicate that 'go national' is the best decision alternative. Though a 'go' decision has been reached and the marketing plan to implement this decision has been developed, numerous other diagnostic insights into the sensitivity of the marketing plan to changing circumstances can be explored.

For example, Figure 10.7 shows the relationship between gross income and gross profit as a function of various amounts of advertising expenditure. It is quite apparent that beyond $9 million the revenue and profit curve part markedly from one another. So too, under normal circumstances, do the financial officer and marketing officer part company when discussing which plan to implement. Historically, marketing performance has been measured on the basis of market share. This criterion is in clear conflict with the objective of maximum profit, as illustrated in Figure 10.7. Sometimes, there are sound and good reasons for trading-off

Table 10.2 DEMON case-study: effects of advertising and development sequence prior to second evaluation.

	Evaluation 1	Results policies	Evaluation 2
Profit	$24.8 million	$6.4 million	$21.2 million
Risk	±$62.0 million	—	±$8.5 million
Confidence of 'go' profit	43%	70%	90%
Pay-out period	3.5 years	3.5 years	3.0 years
Confidence of pay-out period	36%	70%	70%
	12 yrs @ 70%		

decreased profits against larger market shares. If, for example, the company had a variety of line extensions under development, a larger market share might provide a better platform for launching these other new products. Management might then be willing to sacrifice a relatively short-term profit in order to build up the market share so that the launch of the line extensions could take advantage of established products with a similar brand name.

The sensitivity of success odds to the sales forecast can be seen by referring to Figure 10.8. This graph shows sales volume increasing at a disproportionate rate, along with the odds of achieving the 'go' profit. This

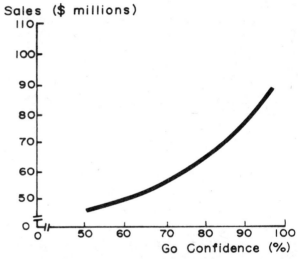

Figure 10.8 DEMON case-study: sensitivity of success odds to the sales forecast.

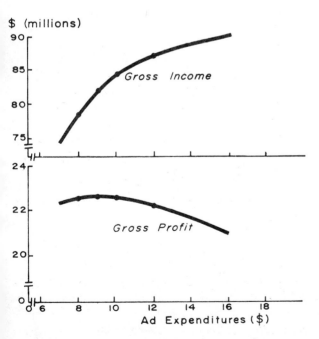

Figure 10.7 DEMON case-study: relationship between gross income and gross profit.

result is surely in line with the intuition most marketing men have held: If the sales volume is bigger, you can have more confidence in achieving the profit target. Once again DEMON shows how much the odds of achieving the target rise with an increase in sales volume.

The initial management decision requirements were 70 per cent confidence in achieving the 'go' profit target. Evaluation 2 results in a marketing plan that exceeds this 70 per cent level, providing 90 per cent confidence of achieving $6.4 million profits. It is apparent in Figure 10.8 that the 90 per cent confidence is associated with the $83 million sales estimate. The 70 per cent confidence level was adequate in management's initial judgement, and the curve in Figure 10.8 shows a sales volume of $55 million associated with the 70 per cent confidence level. Thus, the difference between $55 million and \$83 million (\$28 million) provides the additional 20 per cent confidence.

From another viewpoint, the profit forecast of \$83 million can be in error by as much as a \$28 million overestimate and still be within the original confidence requirement of 70 per cent. Thus, it is quite apparent that the sales forecast might be in error, but exactly the same management decision would be made on the basis of the implications of the total marketing plan. It is also quite apparent from examining these data that, if management's confidence requirements are altered from time to time, so too must the plan accomplishments be altered to maintain pace with expectations or requirements.

As a final illustration of the diagnostic capability of DEMON to examine the sensitivity of the marketing plan, Figure 10.9 shows the relationship between profit and the odds of exceeding such a profit. Thus, \$6.4 million profit can be exceeded with odds of nine out of ten. The odds are better than eight out of ten of exceeding \$12 million, but merely 50-50 of exceeding \$18 million. Extending these results, it is apparent that there is virtually no assurance of exceeding \$21.8 million, because that is the maximum profit level. It is appropriate to point out that, if the odds of exceeding \$18 million look attractive to management, then a new DEMON evaluation ought to explore the profit potential, if management's original requirement was 50-50 odds of exceeding \$18 million. It is quite possible that because of some presently unforeseen circumstance such a profit opportunity might exist, although it might not be apparent under the policy conditions stipulated at the beginning of evaluation 2. In this manner, then, DEMON has the potential to uncover profit opportunities that

may not previously have existed and capitalize upon them via an optimum marketing plan. This type of flexibility is important, especially when overall policies and immediate marketing conditions must be jointly considered to allow further exploration of opportunities that might not have been apparent when planning was started.

A Versatile Tool

System validity

In this case-study, we have shown that the objective of maximum profit can be used to improve the profit status of an initially stipulated pay-back requirement. All parts of the system have been considered and evaluated when a change in a marketing component is effected. It is two years since DEMON was first implemented, and so it is appropriate to raise the issue of whether such a planning system is valid. This question of validity can be answered from three different viewpoints. At the simplest level the system does indeed appear to look correct. It has face value. Knowledgeable marketing men working with the system use it and react in much the same way they would to other kinds of managerial control information. The system has produced no anomalous results, at least insofar as this is attested to by acceptance on the part of marketing people.

The question of whether the component relationships of the marketing planning system are valid can also be examined. In such a validity test, the relationships developed on the original 200 or so cases were projected to forecast marketing achievement in new circumstances. In total more than 3,000 measurements in over 36 different product categories were analysed. The relationships developed on the original data were used to predict results in a completely new setting. These predictions proved quite accurate. About 88 per cent of the brand to brand variability in the new situations was accounted for by the predictions from the old relationships. This statistical evidence shows that the properties of these marketing relationships are quite stable.

In addition, marketing data were collected in the UK and West Germany. Although those data were not originally collected for use in the development of the DEMON system, similar marketing relationships were found. Clearly, there were differences in the size of the economies involved, but the same structural relationships existed both in the UK and West Germany as previously found in the US. This result also makes sense

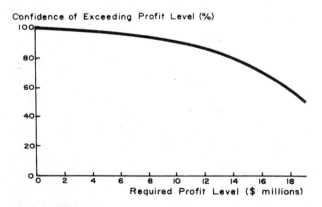

Confidence of Exceeding Profit Level (%)

Figure 10.9 DEMON case-study: relationship between profit and the odds of exceeding such a profit.

from a marketing point of view. For in these foreign countries, marketing managers use no different marking tools and techniques than are used in the US. Since these approaches work equally well (or equally poorly) in Europe, there is no reason to believe that basic differences in marketing exist.

The results of DEMON look right, and the components have the appropriate statistical validity when used in new situations, but the question remains whether the system as a whole has value. There is, of course, no unequivocal way of evaluating whether a DEMON-derived marketing plan might alter the way in which the world behaves, producing more or less profit than some other marketing plan. The nearest approach to turning the world back and replaying it is to set up a parallel test in which the DEMON plan and a conventionally derived marketing plan were implemented and evaluated.

Such a test took place during the 18-month interval between January 1965 and June 1966. Two alternative marketing plans, one derived by DEMON and the other derived in a conventional manner, were implemented in two pairs of evenly matched test markets. The sole difference in the two marketing plans reflected advertising expenditure of the DEMON plan at half the amount of conventional plan. (Recall that the DEMON objective is maximum profit and not market penetration, market share, etc.) All other marketing costs and programmes were identical.

During the 18-month test period, records of consumer sales were gathered, and various categories of costs were subtracted from the respective total sales volume to arrive at an approximate profit in each pair of test markets at the end of the test period. The cost in the two pairs of test markets were virtually identical. Thus, any resulting difference in profit could be attributed only to the difference in the two marketing plans (advertising expenditure level) in each pair of markets. At the end of the accounting period the DEMON plan resulted in 134 per cent of the profit of the conventional marketing plan. This means that $1.34 million in profit accrued from the DEMON markets for every $1 million in profit from the conventional markets. This 34 per cent profit premium points out that the advertising budget in the conventional markets was substantially beyond the optimum level. The performance discrepancy was so great that there was less than one change in 100 that the difference could have been recouped over the course of the five-year planning period. The 34 per cent gain is further enhanced by the fact that the 50 per cent overspent on advertising would

have been available for other ventures, which might have provided significant return in their own right.

It is thus quite apparent that on an overall systems basis there is a substantial premium to the DEMON marketing plan. No matter how optimistic these results may be, it is quite appropriate to point out that the system considers the odds of success, and it is indeed quite possible that in another application the DEMON system might not provide the optimum profit, for there is always some chance the system will be in error. However, on the basis of system results at the present time, it does appear that the promise of DEMON to provide maximum profit in a new product venture can be realized.

A variety of other results have accumulated in the course of utilizing this procedure. DEMON planning has pointed out the critical nature of integrating distribution coverage with the release dates of advertising. Although this point seems rather obvious, many managements either advertise in an area where they have no distribution or do not advertise in areas where distribution has been achieved. This timing of the distribution achievement with the release of advertising is critical for the accomplishment of the plan's sales objectives.

Another aspect of distribution planning that has come into sharp focus via the use of DEMON is the need for integrating the sales forecast with distribution coverage. In many cases marketing management assumes, through the normal sales forecast calculations, that distribution will be achieved virtually instantaneously in all sectors of the country, and the full market potential will immediately be available. In contrast to this assumption, DEMON clearly relates the sometimes agonizingly slow pace of distribution coverage to consumer availability. If only 50 per cent distribution has been achieved, DEMON considers that a maximum of only 50 per cent of the consumers will be able to purchase the brand, and so brand share targets may have to be doubled, if sales and profit targets are to be met on time. Although this example oversimplifies the case, the notion is that conventional sales forecasts do not account for the market not provided by lack of distribution. This discrepancy has a substantial impact on the likelihood of accomplishing the planned objective.

In the course of working with a number of manufacturers, differing organizational structures have evolved as a result of using DEMON. The integrated team approach, where representatives of production, finance, marketing, and R & D are responsible for carrying the new product through its entire commercialization phase, has proved to be quite feasible and thoroughly desirable when using DEMON as a management system. A further side benefit that was entirely unexpected indicates that DEMON acts as a personnel multiplier on the skills of scarce product managers. Put simply, a product manager using DEMON to introduce a new product is quite capable of dealing with many more new product assignments.

Although the results of DEMON applications show it to be a versatile management tool, there are a variety of applications that would be inappropriate and of marginal value. As the system is currently structured, it cannot deal with consumer durable goods. Nor, for that matter, is it appropriate for packaged goods that have a long purchase cycle. Product categories such as anti-freeze, automobile wax, and other low use-up rate goods are inappropriate for DEMON application.

In a similar vein, many capital goods products such as aircraft and many industrial products are also out of bounds for DEMON at this point.

A Total System

Conclusion

By a case example, by diagrams, and by discussion, we have exhibited how the DEMON model operates when applied to marketing a new product. The machinery of DEMON relies heavily on new mathematics developed from research that was directed specifically to improving management methods for marketing new products. It would be a mistake, however, to regard this system solely in terms of mathematical research. The marketing aspects of this development played an important role, as did overall guides and controls obtained by reference to managerial requirements and considerations.

We have indicated how the model was developed so that pay-back and profit could both be accommodated. Overall corporate considerations as well as market behaviour in its various dynamic and uncertain aspects are explicitly accommodated in DEMON. Information feed-back is utilized to alter objectives or evaluate established corporate policies and controls whenever significant new marketing opportunities are uncovered. The planning and risk implications of inaccurate and insufficient data are enumerated. In conclusion, we have also noted certain areas (e.g., consumer durables) where the current version of DEMON does not appear to be applicable. Of course, this does not preclude such

extensions or other possibilities for further research since the basic DEMON concepts appear to be applicable to these areas also.

The need for each of these features was verified by extensive consultations with managers and marketers at various stages in the development of DEMON. With this in mind, we can now summarize the salient dimensions of DEMON as follows:

1 The model is composed of a planning sub-system and a decision sub-system.

2 Within the alternatives provided by these sub-systems, the model determines a best way to proceed and systematically exploits all available data to this end.

3 DEMON brings all results together for review, examination, and exploration in a form suitable for managerial consideration.

Figure 10.1 provides a synopsis of these aspects of DEMON. Each box labelled 'Evaluation' represents the planning system, i.e., planning review and evaluation. These evaluations, it should be noted, are guided by the light DEMON can shed on future marketing alternatives. In short, any evaluation which is currently being undertaken is connected to all future evaluations, because each one is a step in an integrated and changing total planning system. Similar remarks apply to the 'go', 'on', and 'no' decisions which result from each evaluation. That is, each decision makes available new alternatives, which in turn are connected to still other decisions. Thus, again, it is the purpose of DEMON to supply a best course of action relative to the total new product system as well as to optimize at each stage where a decision must be made. The decision system and the planning system are, in addition, connected to other parts of a corporation's policies and objectives, and thus there, too, are accommodated or evaluated by the methods that DEMON supplies.

References

1 *Business Week*, April 29, 1961, pp. 33-34.
2 *Management of New Products* (Booz, Allen and Hamilton, New York, 1960, rev. 1963, 1965).
3 James K. DeVoe, 'Profits, Plans and the Marketing Program', in F.E. Webster, Jr., ed., *Proceedings of the 48th National Conference of the American Marketing Association* (June 1965). See also D.B. Learner: 'A Management Framework for New Product Decisions', in *Proceedings of the Market Research Council* (1964); 'DEMON: A Management Planning and Control System for Successfully Marketing New Products,' in R.M. Kaplan, ed., *Proceedings of the 47th National Conference of the American Marketing Association* (June

1964); and 'DEMON: New Product Planning: A Case History', in F.E. Webster, Jr., ed., *Proceedings of the 48th National Conference of the American Marketing Association* (June 1965).

4 Charnes, Cooper, DeVoe, and Learner: 'DEMON: Decision Mapping Via Optimum GO-NO Networks – A Model for Marketing New Products', *Management Science*, XII:11 (July 1966); 'DEMON Mark II, An Extremal Equation Approach to New Product Marketing', *Management Science,* XIV:9 (May 1968); 'DEMON Mark II: Extremal Equations Solution and Approximation', *Management Science*, XIV:11 (July 1968); and 'Some Recursive Relations Developed as Com-

ponents for Estimating Marketing Strategies', *Management Science* (forthcoming).

5 Chance-constrained programming, itself a recent development in management mathematics, also required further extension for use in DEMON. See Charnes, A. and Copper, W.W. 'Chance-Constrained Programming', *Management Science*, VI:1 (Oct. 1959); 'Deterministic Equivalents for Optimizing and Satisficing under Chance Constraints', *Operations Research*, XI:1 (Jan.-Feb. 1963), 18-39; and *Management Models and Industrial Applications of Linear Programming*, 2 vols. (New York: John Wiley and Sons, Inc., 1961).

11.

Decision Trees in Practical Marketing
by B. K. Chesterton

Reprinted from the IMRA Journal Vol. 7 (3), August, 1971 with permission.

Introduction

This article is a case-study description. The case-study is disguised but everything is true, except for names and detailed data. I have always felt in my reading of journals that when all the work has been nicely tidied up for publication, most of the interesting work has been eliminated. So I've tried to say what did happen as it happened, with the mistakes that we on retrospect now think we have made.

We have been using decision trees and decision theory over three years or so in Unilever in the Economics and Statistics Department for various parts of the Unilever enterprise. We have worked in a number of fields — not just marketing — but this particular example I have chosen is a marketing one, partly because it was easier to use it and to disguise it reasonably, but also because an audience of industrial market researchers might be more interested in a marketing example than others. However, we have used decision theory in other areas, particularly in investment, disinvestment and in decisions on research policy. It is still, however, not a line management routine piece of work at all. It is being used by us, but we have a very large number of reservations about having it as a standard technique used by managers throughout the company on their own, until we have much more experience of the snags. Indeed, even then, I feel that the major problems would probably be better dealt with by a central group.

Before writing this article I noticed a fairly early reference to the use of subjective probabilities. I was reading a book which concerned a corpse that had been left in a deed box in a lawyer's office for some time and it was rather crucial to determine the time of death, or in this particular case, the week of death. An autopsy was performed and the gentleman who did the autopsy examined about 20 separate indicators, such as the degree of separation of the finger-nails from the fingers and toe-nails from the toes and such things. For each of these he produced a subjective probability curve with the likelihood of death at various times before the autopsy, from say four to eight weeks before. He then combined these to obtain a probability distribution for when death was likely to have occurred and narrowed

the time down to two weeks. He was thus able to be of great help in finding the murderer. Unfortunately, he didn't give many details as to the practical method of combining the separate probability distributions, especially when there's very clearly a correlation between very large numbers of them.

In 1965, we were called over to Gallica to help them with the problem of their deodorant soaps. We were told, 'Come over and have a preliminary chat with us, see what our problems are, and see if you think you might be able to help us.' We thought this would be an initial visit and that we would come back later to do the job, if needed. However, when we arrived, we discovered that the problem was urgent and we had to get to work straight away. This forced a very quick decision by us on the structure of the model we used and a lot of hard work to get a satisfactory analysis quickly. This I suppose, is perhaps the first difference from the leisurely textbook situation.

Background

We asked for the background of what was going on. The problem was what to do with the two products, *Fresh* and *Zephyr*. Soaps had been going along quite nicely and suddenly people had found that deodorant in soap seemed as if it might be a winner. We weren't sure yet, and wanted to know whether to add deodorants or not, if so by how much and which product to concentrate on.

Table 11.1 Gallican Deodorant Soaps, April 1965.

Company X	A	New product, introduced nationally January 1965 at a discount; 0.1% deodorants — good start.
	B	Relaunch, national, March 1965; 0.2% deodorants.
Company Y	C	Relaunch with deodorant in test market. September 1964; 0.3% deodorants, inconclusive result.
	D	New product in test market January 1965; 0.5% deodorants.

Unilever   *Fresh* Relaunch with deodorant in test market in South Gallica; 0.05% deodorants, some success.

Zephyr New product in test market in North West Gallica; 0.3% deodorants, very bad.

At the time the situation was as set out in Table 11.1. We had several products on the market. Our competitors, X had product A (a deodorant soap) on the market. It was an entirely new product and was introduced nationally about three months before with 0.1 per cent deodorant, and had done quite nicely. They also had product B which had been selling without deodorants.

It had been re-launched nationally a month earlier with 0.2 per cent deodorants. It was far too early for us to be able to know what was going to happen to it. Then we had a second weaker competitor, Y, with a product C, which they re-launched with deodorants in test market September 1964. At that stage even if the competitor were clear what he should do with this product, we certainly were not. Having examined his results fairly closely, we had no idea whether he would launch it nationally or not — it was totally inconclusive as far as we could see.

Then there were our own products. *Fresh* was our major product and was the one that we were keen on. Its sales were slipping slightly without deodorant. It looked as if it was going to need deodorant in it, so had a test market where we had relaunched it with deodorant in it, so had a test market where we had relaunched it with deodorant. However, we weren't too sure about the actual marketing benefit of deodorants so it had a very small percentage included. In fact, it had the lowest on the market — 0.05 deodorant. And it's having some success.

Lastly, there was *Zephyr*, intended to be a new international product which was in test market in North West Gallica. This was obviously the favoured product. It had a high deodorant content, but unfortunately was doing very badly indeed. Initially, the problem we were to discuss was whether we should launch *Zephyr* nationally or not and when.

Constraints

We went over and had various chats to try and see what the situation was. First of all we found out there were various constraints on our actions. From the time we decided to launch the new product it would take three months before it would be launched, by the time we had labelled it, got the stocks built up and the advertising arranged. This applied to *Zephyr*. *Fresh*, which is the relaunched product would take longer and we were told it would take five months, from the time the decision was taken, before we could relaunch that nationally. It would take longer because we had to allow time for the stocks already in distribution to run through. The second constraint was in advertising. It was not really practicable to advertise both products simultaneously. We could advertise one or the other and had to have a gap in-between. For various reasons the earliest date, therefore, that we could launch or relaunch a product nationally was about October, that year. Thereafter we could operate at what can be considered as three monthly intervals. If we did not launch in October we certainly could not try again till January — we had to allow all the Christmas rush to vanish before we tried getting space in the shops for new soaps! Thereafter, we have opportunities at about three-monthly intervals, basically because of difficulties about advertising allocations.

1st Decision Tree

We now have our first attempt at drawing a decision tree (Figure 11.1).

Mr Anderson: 'How are the probabilities on the tree estimated? Are they probabilities estimated at the beginning? Are there criteria for success or failure? Do you say a product is a success or failure by certain sales criteria if, e.g., sales go ahead by a certain amount or go below a certain level?'

Mr Chesterton: 'The probabilities given were probabilities estimated at the start. They were executive opinions of what might happen. If you were an experienced marketer, you could say you were able to assess these types of things. Alternatively, you could have a whole range of results of test markets in the past and draw up a probability distribution from these. You could assess each test market and say, for example, that 25 per cent were "successful" by your criteria, 40 per cent were "moderate" on your own criteria and 35 per cent were "unsuccessful" on past history. Because you've seen that this particular one was a typical product no better, no worse, than many others you have tested and the probability of its outcome would be like that. This is how these probabilities were obtained.

'The criteria that you were talking about in the second half of your question — how do you know

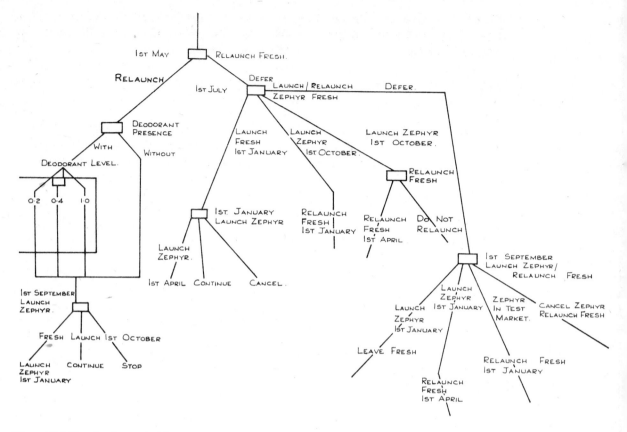

Figure 10.1 First deodorant decision tree.

whether a product is successful or not — are totally different altogether. Depending on the particular products, you might define "successful" as meaning having kept a market share of more than 12 per cent for a period of three months consecutively. The definitions must be appropriate to the particular circumstances. Certainly, I agree, it's very important in doing decision trees, at the very start to define precisely what you will interpret as being successful, unsuccessful or moderate. Otherwise when you actually come to the time for which you have made forecasts, you will then change your mind as to what you mean by successful. There will be a strong temptation for the marketing man concerned, to say, "Well I admit that I said that it needed 12 per cent to be a success, it's only got 10 per cent, but that's really good".'

Back to this deodorant decision tree (Figure 11.1). The first one was our attempt to write down in a formal decision tree exactly what decisions this company was faced with. That's all its attempting to do. It has no probabilities in, nothing like that at all. It was based on

what executives said and was drawn after one day's discussion.

They appeared to have the option on May 1, either (a) to relaunch *Fresh* or (b) not to relaunch *Fresh* — this is shown at the very top. As shown on the left-hand side, if they decide to relaunch, this relaunch would take place on October 1, because of the five month gap.

They can decide either to have it with deodorant or without deodorant. Because it's already on the market, without deodorant, they can amend the packet and add an appropriate advertising slogan. If they decide to launch it with deodorants there are various percentages that could be put in — 0.1, 0.2, 0.4 per cent. Having decided on relaunching *Fresh* (coming down the left-hand side) there is also a decision on September 1 whether to launch *Zephyr* or not. If it's decided on September 1 to launch, *Zephyr* will be launched on January 1 (following the *Fresh* relaunch on October 1).

Alternatively executives may decide they have insufficient information and defer the decision on *Fresh*. The next decision point is then July 1. On that date they can decide either (*a*) to launch *Fresh* on January 1 (in which case again they can decide to launch *Zephyr* on April 1), or (*b*) they may decide to launch *Zephyr* on October 1, and re-launch *Fresh* on January 1.

Or again, coming down the other way, it can be decided to launch *Zephyr* on October 1, and then take a decision whether to re-launch *Fresh* on April 1.

Difficulties

Now, to us, this tree looked rather complicated because our next step should be (according to the textbooks) to ask what the probability is of various events connected with this particular tree. What is the probability that, if you add 0.4 per cent deodorants to *Fresh*, launch it on October 1, and launch *Zephyr* on January 1, you will be successful in the national market? And what's more, you should ask this question for each deodorant level and for each set of decisions here.

We decided this would be rather complicated and that we would have to simplify this tree. That's the first, most important point of all; having laid out your set of possible decisions, you have to try and simplify it in some way. This is common in all mathematical or other models where you must eliminate some of the complexities of the real world before you can do anything with the problem. The art is to make sure you don't eliminate too much but eliminate as much as you can get away with. How to decide this is not clear. You can do a sensitivity analysis in some circumstances and eliminate those items which have a small effect on the answer. It would certainly have been beyond the capabilities of our marketing manager and brand manager to be able to answer questions on probabilities on the number of events in the first tree. You have to ask a set of people for a set of probabilities about what they think is going to happen in a large number of hypothetical circumstances.

Two things happen if you try to ask too many questions; one, suddenly executives become unavailable because of lots of other work to do, and second, their answers become essentially frivolous. They just get fed-up, they get tired of it, they can't answer too many of these questions. The other difficulty they have, we've found, is putting themselves in a hypothetical situation. We might ask, 'Suppose this product is a fantastic success, suppose it reaches 20 per cent of the test market and all your competitors fail, what will you do then?' The marketing manager is tempted to reply, 'Go out and have a fantastic booze-up.' He never thought this would

happen. His product now has a market share of 5 per cent and shows no signs of going up. You just don't get useful answers if you ask too many hypothetical questions. So we had to cut it down. The result is the second decision tree (Figure 11.2).

2nd Decision Tree

If we look at Figure 11.2 we'll notice some startling differences from the one we had before. One of them is that *Zephyr* is no longer in it. Remember we were asked to go over there and analyse the prospects of *Zephyr*'s success and what we should do with it. I'm afraid that we very quickly came to the conclusion that the prospects looked so unpromising that it was not worthwhile deferring any decision on *Fresh* for the benefit of *Zephyr*. Its market shares since the test started had been roughly 5, 6, 5, 4 and 1 per cent. Its target level of success was 8 per cent. The test was vitiated because of a number of unfortunate events including very soon after, another product being launched very similar to it, with a price 20 per cent lower. So we felt that its prospects looked remarkably unpromising and even if the brand were modified, the time this would take would be (with the uncertain results even then) so long that we could ignore it at this time.

Estimation of Probabilities

With *Zephyr*, we had another of the little troubles that can beset the decision analyst. We asked the brand manager of *Zephyr* what he thought the probabilities were that it would reach 8 per cent which was the target level. He said he thought it had about an 80 per cent chance of reaching an 8 per cent level. Remember its last market shares were 4 and 1 per cent.

So we took him to one side and said, 'Are you sure you mean that?' He said, 'Yes, our company's marketing plan says that this will achieve 8 per cent so the product must be very likely to achieve 8 per cent.' We said, 'Look, we want your real answer, not what it says in the marketing plans, not what you planned to do but what you think will actually happen.' Unfortunately, it's very common for people to give to managers higher up the hierarchy what they think the boss wants to hear, rather than what they really think is going to happen. The marketing director certainly did not want this attitude but he had found it difficult to get this over to all his staff. However, after taking the brand manager aside,

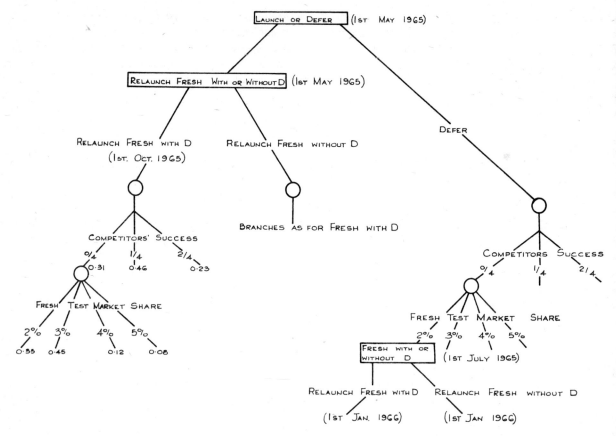

Figure 11.2 2nd Deodorant decision tree.

questioning him privately, and making it clearer that we wanted his personal views, he said the probability of the product reaching 8 per cent was about two in 100, as opposed to his original 80 in 100. The moral of this is – (laughter) – be very careful indeed when you're questioning people that they're really thinking along the right lines; and be careful to give as many questions as possible to cross-check the answers. Of course, you should avoid the opposite danger; pressing so much that the brand manager gives *your* probabilities rather than his. If you want to use your own you should do so, but not pretend they are somebody's else's!

We're still very much at the learning stage in the area of how exactly to phrase all these questions. After these estimates, which his marketing director agreed with, we obviously left *Zephyr* out of the decision tree.

We're now left with re-launching *Fresh* with or without deodorants. Again, you notice, another drastic simplification, we now do not have a deodorant percentage in it. Our scientists tell us in fact that a low percentage deodorant is certainly as effective as a high

percentage, thus, because of the expense, we do not have a high percentage. On the other hand we're not going to have the lowest percentage, so we decide to have 0.2 per cent.

We then tried to deduce what factors were likely to affect the probability of success of *Fresh*. An obvious one is our competitors' success. In Figure 11.1 we have four competing products. We asked our marketing staff first to estimate the probabilities that these would be successful and, second, the effect of their success on us. The reasoning was: if all the deodorant products are successful, it is a very strong indication that the public really appreciate deodorants in soap, and so the likelihood that our brand of deodorant soap will succeed, is increased. But, on the other hand, if all our competitors are successful they may have taken all the market away, so although the market might be bigger, our share might be smaller.

The reverse of this happens if we were to try to relaunch *Fresh* without deodorants. There would be a strong indication that if all our competitors failed the public was not keen on deodorants in soap and we would be more likely to be successful if we relaunched without deodorants. We asked our marketing people to give estimates of the probability of success of our competitors' products and we have the estimates here; no competitor successful 0.31, one successful 0.46, and two successful 0.23. Of course, we do not ask our people to give probabilities accurate to 1 per cent. These are arithmetical combinations of the probability of success of the individual products.

Questioner: 'How much evidence did you require from the marketing people as to why they took these views, or rather what evidence did they produce?'

Mr Chesterton: 'The evidence they had was the traditional market shares, analyses of the products, i.e., the formulations. A few blind test results in laboratories.'

Questioner: 'In most cases products had not been going for very long? So it was largely guesswork?'

Mr Chesterton: 'Yes, that is so. However, these "guesses" incorporate their feel for the market, their experience in similar situations and various intangible indicators, very difficult to put into words, which mean a lot to the experienced manager. In a large number of situations you don't have any hard evidence but still have to make a decision now (even if only to wait for more information). You must rely on what evidence you have. This particular situation was one such. They had to rely on their feel for the market and these results that we've given, to give estimates as to how likely it was to succeed or not. The danger is obvious; that when they are not in this situation, where there are marketing results lying around or comparable situations, which they could analyse, instead of actually analysing them and trying to get information out of them, they use their subjective probabilities instead. This danger makes me very wary of having this method in universal uninstructed use with people who allow their keenness for the product to overcome their analytical abilities.'

Questioner: 'How do you cope with this?'

Mr Chesterton: 'I'm always aware of this danger. If I'm doubtful as to people's opinion and I can see evidence which seems to me to controvert it, I will bring the evidence to their attention and say, "Have you taken account of this", and, "Surely this can't be so, with this information." If, in the end, they stick to their opinion, however misguided I might think this opinion to be, their probability goes down as given. I would try to convince them of my view but our position is that these are the marketing people. They are appointed to do that

job and they have to take the responsibility. So, if they insist on these probabilities, they will be used. A safeguard is these probabilities will go before their marketing manager, their marketing director or even higher up depending on how important the decision is. They will say, 'What on earth are you playing at, giving that probability. We've launched this product in five separate countries and it's been a unanimous failure (or success), why is it going to be a failure (or a success) here?' And then they alter it. This greater ease of communication is a great advantage of decision trees. In addition, if we do disagree, we will bring this to the attention of these higher-ups and also the dependence of the pay-off on these disputed probabilities.'

Pay-offs

Continuing with the problem and turning to Table 11.2 we have the estimates for expected sales from re-launch of *Fresh* with deodorant. There are two factors influencing the estimates, competitors' success, and, of course, our own performance in the test market. On the left-hand side of the table, we have competitor success for 0, 1 or 2 out of 4. On the top we have columns labelled +2, +3, +4, +5 per cent. Those mean 2 per cent better performance in test market than it had done nationally, taking into account the differences in average performance between the test market area and nationally just before re-launching. You will see, from the table, that as more competitors are successful the more tonnage you think your own product will gain, i.e., the market as a whole expands. Simultaneously of course, the more our own product gets in test market the more likely it is to be successful. So the tonnages are continuously increasing from the top left-hand corner to the bottom right-hand corner.

Table 11.2 Expected sales from re-launch *Fresh* with deodorant.

Competitive success	Fresh share in S. Gallica test market			
	+2%	+3%	+4%	+5%
0/4	650	1,200	1,250	1,300
1/4	850	1,300	1,500	1,600
2/4	900	1,350	1,550	1,650

However, if we look at Table 11.3, which is the expected sales from the re-launch of *Fresh* without deodorant, it doesn't show that simple pattern at all. It veers about a bit, for example, if our product does very successfully in test market with deodorant, if you actually launch it without deodorant it may do worse. If it does badly in our test market it may do better without deodorants than with. This time the more our competitors' are successful the less likely it is that our product will be successful. Thus, by asking many questions and looking at the pattern of the answers, we cross-check for self consistency.

We have this reasonably simple decision tree. We can either re-launch *Fresh* on October 1 with deodorants or without deodorants. Alternatively we can defer the decision for more information.

Table 11.3 Expected sales from re-launch *Fresh* without deodorant

	Fresh share in test market			
Competitive success	+2%	+3%	+4%	+5%
0/4	800	1,200	1,220	1,250
1/4	700	1,000	970	850
2/4	600	900	800	550

We had our expected sales as shown on Tables 11.2 and 11.3. In addition, we have Table 11.4 which gives the pay-offs for various outcomes and shows the preferred action.

At the stage at which we are talking (the end of April) we have to take this decision on July 1. We were trying to draw-up the table for the decision to be taken on July 1.

There are the probabilities for 0 out of 4, 1 out of 4, 2 out of 4 competitors' success of 0.31, 0.46, 0.23. There are the probabilities of success in our test market of 0.35, 0.45, 0.12, 0.08, and then we have the results in the pay-off table. As an example, if one out of our competitors is successful, and *Fresh* test market has 5 per cent share, then the table says we expect to gain £1,722 thousand if we launch without deodorants, and £2,883 thousand with deodorants. In this case we should launch with deodorants. The lower matrix in Table 11.4 gives a summary of the decisions to take in various eventualities, on July 1.

In addition, we have to decide whether to wait till July 1 anyway to see which position we're in (i.e., defer), or do we take the decision now? If we take the decision now do we re-launch it without deodorants or do we launch it with deodorants? The pay-offs are very close: deferring £2.10 million; launching without deodorants in October £2.18 million; launching with deodorants in October is £1.80 million.

In other words, if you're going to decide to launch

Table 11.4 Pay-off table for decision on July 1.

The upper figure of each pair refers to re-launch of *Fresh* without deodorant and lower figure refers to re-launch of *Fresh* with deodorant (0.2), in the eventualities set out in respect of the row and column in which the figures are located.

	Fresh share in test market (£'000)			
Competitors' success	+2%	+3%	+4%	+5%
0/4	1,724	2,590	2,698	2,807
	237	1,586	1,845	2,105
1/4	1,345	2,157	1,995	1,722
	808	2,105	2,495	2,883
2/4	1,080	1,886	1,616	1,266
	1,068	2,364	2,754	3,142

Decision to be taken on July 1
(X indicates 'select *Fresh* with deodorant (0.2)';
0 indicates 'select *Fresh* without deodorant')

	Fresh share test market			
Competitors' success	2%	3%	4%	5%
0/4	0	0	0	0
1/4	0	0	X	X
2/4	0	X	X	X

Note: (a) Pay-off from deferred decision is £2.10 million.
(b) If decision is taken now (May 1) pay-offs are:
launch without D on October 1 £2.18 million.
launch with D (0.2) on October 1 £1.80 million.

now you launch without deodorants. It's a fairly close tie between that and deferring the decision.

Results

What did they do, as opposed to what the table suggests they should do? The marketing staff were very interested in all this. They were quite analytically-minded people, particularly the marketing director. He was quite impressed. But what in fact happened was that he did not take the decision on July 1 at all, but in the middle of June. And what's more, he decided in the middle of June to re-launch on October 1, and did not have this five-month gap that was mentioned earlier. They found they could cut down this gap which they'd originally said was necessary for production reasons. Also, in the middle of June they decided they then had as much information as they would have if they waited till July 1. It was pretty clear that our *Fresh* test market had been very successful and was in the 5 per cent class. What's more, two out of our four competitors were successful as well.

In other words, we were right at the bottom of the right-hand corner, of the pay-off table and the correct decision was to launch with deodorants as soon as possible. By bringing the time delay down from five to four months he was able to launch on October 1.

What was the actual outcome as opposed to the decision? Now remember, this is only an academic point. We are interested solely in producing good decisions. We hope for good outcomes. If we say this is the best decision that we could possibly have taken even if the outcome were disaster, ideally we should promote the man concerned! All we can hope to do by use of any technique is take the best decision possible with the information available at that time. If at that time we say on the odds there's a two to three chance that this is going to be successful we take that decision (assuming we have the money and there are no better policies). There's a one in three chance that you may be wrong. Now, if a particular decision maker is always unfortunate and always gets the one in three chance you would still get rid of him. Either because you suspect that his decisions were wrong and he could have got more information or, alternatively, just because he's sheer unlucky (this process can be formalized in terms of prior probabilities of the existence of defective marketing men). Don't employ people who have severe known jinxes, in the marketing field anyway.

The whole object of decision tree analysis is to try and get the best decisions not to try and get the best outcomes. In the long-run, by taking the best decisions, you will however get the best outcome! It is important to get this over to the people for whom you're working.

Comments

How useful did the marketing director find this technique? His answer was a bit vague but can be roughly summarized as, 'I found it very helpful indeed having all my thoughts clarified, being cross-questioned by a set of intelligent observers with no experience in this particular field, having all my assumptions questioned, and having them all rigorously laid out and put down on paper so that I could see exactly what it was

that I was talking about. As far as actually calculating the outcomes is concerned, I'm a little more dubious. I'm not quite sure whether I'm willing to carry it that far. I think I am on this particular case. I think it worked quite well, but my judgement is rather suspended in general.'

Objections were raised by some marketing staff. The chief objection was that the marketing situation changed too quickly. If you drew-up a decision tree like this, the whole market would have changed in three months' time and it would be no use to you. You would have to do it all over again, and we couldn't spare the time.

However, to us if the market generally were changing this rapidly, you still have to take decisions and must make the best estimate you can of the future for this. If you say that the market is changing too rapidly for you to be able to do this kind of analysis, the conclusion is that you take all your decisions by tossing coins. Perhaps in certain circumstances this might be the best decision-making practice, but it was not the method that this objector used. At any rate he didn't confess to using that decision-making method.

Questioner: 'What was the method he used?'

Mr Chesterton: 'This was not wholly explained. Traditional methods used by marketing staff.'

Questioner: 'Tossing coins?'

Mr Chesterton: 'Unkind people might allege that this is the method, but I think they're better than that. I think too, that decision theory is generally gaining a bit more acceptance.'

We have undertaken several marketing examples like this. We think we have learned a lot from doing them. We've certainly learned how to draw-up decision trees more easily and much more realistically from the start. We've become much more experienced at asking questions and trying to assess whether the answers are realistic or not. We have used this technique in, as I said, a large disinvestment decision. (In one instance the decision to set-up a manufacturing enterprise was linked with the probability of success of research.) The whole point of my talk was to try to explain how it actually happens, what the difficulties are when you're doing it, and what the reactions were of the people to whom we were talking, without going into too much theoretical background.

12.

Product Testing Methodology in Relation to Marketing Problems - A Review

by J.C. Penny, I.M. Hunt and W.A. Twyman

Reprinted from the Journal of the Market Research Society, Vol. 14 (1), January 1972 with permission.

1.0 Background, review of concepts and underlying processes

1.1 Background

Considerably more money is spent on product testing than on media research and yet by contrast product testing is scarcely mentioned in the market research literature. The reasons for this public neglect are probably that:

1 Product testing is very much under the control of marketing companies and the individual results are highly confidential. It is often carried out within marketing companies, sometimes in non-conventional ways on employees or expert panels.

2 There is less scope for the entrepreneurial research company to offer syndicated services through some unique technique. No instrument will magically test all products in a way which competitors cannot match (except perhaps a large testing panel).

3 Individual experience in the area is usually narrowly confined to single or closely related product fields which prevents the building-up of generalizable knowledge.

The rare published discussions of product testing have often been either on the seemingly elementary level of presenting the case for studying product qualities as a component in the marketing mix, perhaps a salutary re-statement in some fantasy worlds of marketing, or alternatively a mention of one aspect of product testing methodology or data analysis. The thinness of the published material is adduced not in order to suggest that this article is triumphantly providing the comprehensive review that everybody needs, but to explain why it is considered of value to publish even scanty evidence on some issues where so little exists at present. Some available reviews are listed at the end of the article.[1,2,3]

1.2 The nature of the product-testing task

What kinds of behaviour are under study at the research stage and in real life and how may these be described?

Product testing in this review refers to the situation where some specimens of the product exist and are to be exposed to the experience of respondents. The testing of ideas, propositions or concepts is not under discussion. Following some experience of a product the respondent can be asked various questions relating to:

1 Overall disposition to the product in terms of evaluation or intention ratings.

2 Perception of product attributes in terms of ratings or reasons for 1 above.

3 Comparative discrimination or preference judgement against a product previously experienced or currently experienced in 'real life'.

4 Comparative discrimination or preference judgement against a product previously or currently experienced as part of the test.

Thus, the test can vary between reporting characteristics of an experience either absolutely or comparatively with another experience whose distance in time is another test variable. The experience to be reported upon can vary greatly in indirectness and can include:

1 Simple sensations like taste or smell.

2 A complex of sensations, as when a whole dish is under test.

3 A complex of sensations observed in oneself and others, as with a food product tested on a family.

4 The observed quality of some process carried out by the observer, such as handwashing.

5 A mixture of observing the quality of a process and reporting on sensations, as with food requiring preparation.

6 The observed quality of a process going on in a machine, such as the running of a car.

Situations vary greatly according to how far previous experience has been consistent enough to build-up a stable frame of reference on which to base perception.

Tasting food, for example, usually takes place in a context of visual and maybe verbal cues which make it clear what tastes are likely. Peas always taste of peas whereas nowadays the last thing which soap will smell of is soap. Smell in products therefore has a far less stable frame of reference to back perceptions.

It seems likely that the more stable the experiential frame of reference has been for a product experience, the less it will be affected by differences in test procedure and the more decisive a role the product quality element will play in the marketing mix.

This kind of distinction breaks down at the point where the experience is so indirect that objective aids can be used to record its properties, such as keeping records of car mileage per gallon or the use of light-meters for washing. Clearly, where the market uses objective measures to judge products, product tests should also. This article is concerned with trying to assess subjective experience in the product test.

1.3 Discrimination and preference

A complication in product testing is that the task is often compounded of two factors; whether the product quality experience is different from some other experience and whether it is preferred. It is often not known how far individuals can discriminate between two products. Thus, 'no preference' may be 'no discrimination' or 'discriminated' products liked equally. Also, a stated preference may be allocated by chance. In some cases the measurement of discrimination is the object of the test, but the use of the term 'discrimination testing' is sometimes confusing. It can refer to procedures where the test is presented in terms of whether a difference can be detected. The term is also used where preference is asked on repeat tests and discrimination deduced from consistent responding. Such a procedure could better be called 'consistent preference discrimination testing'. Consistent preference implies discrimination, but perhaps with an added criterion leading to the concept of 'discrimination that matters'.

In tests where discrimination by all respondents is not assured, the question arises as to how to allow for guessing, i.e., estimating the true level of discrimination.

Triangular tests for discrimination testing have been discussed enthusiastically and subsequently dismissed by Greenhalgh.[4,5] These tests take the form of trying to pick the odd product out of three and assume a one-third guessing level. Recorded preferences of those failing to identify the odd product were, however, not random and were similar to those who had demonstrated

discrimination. Greenhalgh interprets this as the complexity of the test suppressing some discrimination but other interpretations are possible. We have also found that, following triangular discrimination tests, those classed as 'discriminators' and 'non-discriminators' both gave similar preferences. Other kinds of sorting procedures using more items than three are also referred to by Greenhalgh.

Sorting procedures of this kind can also be used in the preference context. For example, Gruber and Lindberg[6] report presenting triads with two items the same, asking for the product liked best and least. Respondents giving the same product for both these were regarded as insensitive and a repeat provided a further basis for classifying the inconsistent, here referred to as 'insensitive' and 'unreliable'.

The basic paired comparison procedure whereby two products are tried and a preference stated can also be repeated to provide an estimate of guessing. Greenberg and Collins,[7] using this procedure, point out that of those giving a preference, chance would yield 50 per cent preferring inconsistently and 25 per cent consistently preferring each product. They show that a number of tests which they have analysed show results close to this chance performance. Reporting a further similar beer-tasting test they showed that neither the 'inconsistent preferers' half of respondents nor the two 'consistent preferers' quarters could, in fact, perform at much better than chance on a rather strict discrimination test on the same products. They tentatively advanced the law that the greater the number of inconsistent preferers (presumably rising to a maximum of 50 per cent), the more likely it is that products are non-discriminable and that preferences will be evenly divided, presumably by chance.

Whilst their evidence shows that in some cases this can be so, it is not proven. The demonstration with the beer test is relatively meaningless since it is always possible to set up discrimination tests which are too difficult.

A contrasting vein in the literature is evidence that individually inconsistent preferers when aggregated together do sometimes yield a consistent overall preference not unlike that of consistent preferers as reported by Greenhalgh above. This has sometimes been our experience but not always. An experimental study which repeated a paired comparison test for washing-up liquids four times gave an opportunity to look at preferences by varying degrees of consistency (Table 12.1).

As will be seen, the totally consistent prefers show

the most marked preference but are a small proportion of the sample. The other groups all show smaller net preference in the same direction. This illustrates the probabilistic nature of these judgements made clearer by having four repeat tests instead of two.

How is it possible to make sense of discrimination and preference findings? It is proposed here that many of the difficulties of interpretation arise from the view that individuals discriminate and prefer in an entirely deterministic way, that two items are either always discriminable for an individual or never discriminable and that if discriminable one must always be preferred to the other. This model implies that there are thresholds above which discrimination or preference must occur. It is proposed on the contrary that consumer decisions of this kind are probabilistic, a possibility referred to by Day.[8,2]

In the area of psychophysics where relationships between stimuli and experience are studied, the idea of a threshold of detection where the totally indiscriminable suddenly becomes totally discriminable has been long since abandoned. The model most widely applied for some time is 'signal detection theory' which is an application of statistical decision.[9] This model could be adapted conceptually to aspects of the product-testing situation, although it would be difficult in many cases to collect data suitable for this form of analysis. It is not possible to develop this theme further here. It is mentioned to indicate that there is an immense background of findings and techniques from related areas on which to base a probabilistic view of discrimination and preference.

Table 12.1 Net preference* by consistency in four repeat comparison tests

Group	No. in group	Net preference for product A by group (%)
4 x consistent	47	+57
3 x consistent 1 x no preference	43	+30
3 x consistent 1 x reversed preference	45	+24
2 x consistent 2 x no preference	36	+39
2 x consistent 1 x reversed preference 1 x no preference	69	+33
1 x preference 3 x no preference	27	+11
Either no preference or equally divided	50	−
	317	+29

* Net preference is defined as the difference in percentage preferring the two products

1.4 Implications of a probabilistic model

A probabilistic model would imply that an individual in a particular set of conditions has an average probability of between 0 and 1 of seeing a difference between two test products or a test product and that which is normally used. To this may be added the proposition that an individual will have a probability of making a preference in one direction when stimuli are discriminated, between 0 and 1. Thus a number of possible product test situations may be illustrated.

1 Discrimination is very low, say at a probability of around 0.1 for nearly all respondents. Whatever the preference situation this will produce consistency in repeat testing at about the chance level and results like those discussed by Greenberg.[10]

2 A substantial proportion of respondents may have a probability of discrimination well below 1. They will appear to be guessing but maybe 0.4 of the time they do make a true discrimination. On top of this they may be asked to give a preference, this will be for A rather than B, say 0.8 of the time. Thus, on 0.4 of occasions these non-discriminators will make mostly consistent preferences. This can give rise to the phenomenon of inconsistent responders apparently having a meaningful preference when averaged together, as in the results of Greenhalgh.[4]

3 Virtually all respondents may have a probability of discrimination near 1. This is a 'pure' preference testing situation. In such circumstances a clear preference may be established, say that 60 per cent prefer A, 30 per cent B and 10 per cent have no preference. These results could mean either that 60 per cent of respondents prefer A all the time, i.e., have a preference probability for A of 1, or that at any one time 60 per cent of all respondents prefer A because each respondent has a preference probability of 0.6. This could arise from the complexity of the preference situation and the validity of the preference decision process. Repeat testing could help to separate these two possibilities but more sophisticated procedures and forms of analyses have to be devised than are currently published.

It is clear that the degree of preference possible among inconsistent preferers will vary from case to case. Thus, articles based on a small number of cases which suggest that inconsistent preferers do or do not exhibit meaningful average preferences cannot provide a basis for generalization.

There is also the problem of how to deal with

no-preference judgements. There is no clear guidance in the literature although a number of procedures are discussed.[10,11,12]

Throughout this section discussion has been as if all product tests were comparative in nature. In practice procedures vary in the overtness of comparison. However, any act of identifying and labelling an experience involves some sort of comparative judgement. 'Is this experience more like the image I have of what I like than my memory image of what I normally have or of the previous experience in this test?' This covers comparisons and single presentations. The conceptual framework of signal detection theory, suggested above, could be developed to cover this range of situations.

1.5 Terminology

The variable degree of comparison involved in product tests is often confused terminologically. For the purposes of this article the following terms will be used:

1 Monadic presentation: the respondent experiences only one test product.
2 Comparative presentation: the respondent experiences more than one test product.
a) Simultaneous: all at once.
b) Separated: one at a time (elsewhere sometimes called monadic comparative).

Within either the monadic or comparative format respondents may be asked to rate products or to rank them. Ranking can include a comparison with some experience outside the test such as with the brand usually brought and this can occur within a monadic presentation.

1.6 Matching product tests to the real-life situation

The major determinant of test procedure is the marketing problem for which the research is intended to provide guidance. Designing a test procedure therefore depends on:

1 Formulating a testable proposition which is relevant to the marketing decision.
2 Testing this proposition in accordance with what is known about the consumer behaviour.

The next section analyses the range of possible marketing problems to which product testing can be usefully applied.

2.0 Product testing related to marketing decisions

Testing products in some form can aid decisions at many different stages in the development of a brand. The life-cycle of a typical frequently purchased consumer product will include the stages of choosing a concept, evolving a formulation, developing a marketing mix, evaluating and predicting the potential for complete products (i.e., brands), test marketing and launching a new brand and improving, modifying and re-launching an ongoing brand.

These stages present very different problems to which product testing is applied to aid decision-taking. The stage of the development of the product will also affect the amount of the marketing mix which can be incorporated in the test and the information which the consumer will already have about the product.

Thus, there are unlikely to be universal rules for choosing product testing methods. The choice must depend on the marketing decision and upon the product field. These choices will be based on experience and judgement. The object of the present article is to present some experience as an aid to making judgements about which method to use in particular marketing situations and product fields.

3.0 Problem areas in product testing practice

Many factors can and should be considered before deciding on the appropriate testing methodology for a specific problem in a particular product field at an acceptable level of cost. The following list, while not claimed to be exhaustive, covers the main factors and variants. It is suggested that one particular component underlies many of these factors – its closeness to the conditions under which the product is used in the 'real market' situation as opposed to strictness of experimental control and expertness of the measurer.

On some factors, choice of a particular variant largely determines the choice of variant on other factors. However, many combinations remain possible, and this is evidenced by the number of different methods that have been tried over the years and are still being used. This section examines some of the issues involved in choice of an appropriate method for a particular problem, and presents experimental evidence to support the views expressed.

Table 12.2

	Realism		Control/precision
Environment	At home, place of work in own car		Mobile van, testing centre, scientific laboratory
Nature of exposure	The whole product		Some elements only e.g., perfume/colour/shape
Length of exposure	Full product units (giving one or more consumption acts according to product)		Instant assessment-tasting, sniffing, etc.
Product dress	Full 'mix'	Branded	Blind
Test design	Monadic	paired comparison	Multiple
Sample representation	Target groups		Expert assessors
Recruitment method	Random sample	Consumer test panel	Expert panel
Test instructions	Normal use		Controlled or directed
Response form	Spontaneous		Structured and prompted
Responding method	Without interviewer		With interviewer

3.1 Testing panels v. ad hoc samples

A permanent postal testing panel and the more traditional face to face placement and response technique, can both provide a realistic environment for 'in-use' testing. They differ, however, in recruitment method, response form and responding method. The particular aspects of postal panels causing the concern about their possible 'conditioning' effects are:

1 The opportunity for studying the questionnaire before response is given.

2 The repetition of testing in the same product fields.

These issues have been studied experimentally.

At the time of this study, the RBL Postal Testing Panel totalled 10,000 housewives (now 25,000) who during the two to three years of their membership had participated, on average, in 17 tests per year over a range of product fields. Care had been taken to ensure a clear interval of at least a month between tests of similar or inter-related product types, so that these were at a maximum of six per year. There was, however, growing concern lest this testing frequency should be conditioning the preference responses of panel members. (There was already evidence that usage of new products which had been subject to frequent testing before their introduction to the market had been stimulated to a

higher level than in the general population.) Two product fields were chosen for study, washing powder (with a high volume of testing) and margarine (a low volume of testing). In each case, three basic testing methods were examined:

1 600 panel housewives giving their responses to the products after use by self-completed postal questionnaire.

2 300 freshly recruited housewives – response by self-completed postal questionnaire.

3 300 freshly recruited housewives – response by face to face interview.

The second of these methods, while sometimes used as a basic testing method in its own right, approximates closely to the circumstances under which newly recruited members of a panel will be operating and, therefore, can throw light on the conditioning aspect.

In both product fields, the preference results did not vary significantly between the three testing groups (Table 12.3).

The methods agreed in both product fields on:

1 The attributes definitely thought different about the products and therefore contributing to the preference choice.

2 Which product was the most criticized.

3 The attributes more criticized for one product than the other.

In addition, there was agreement between methods in the washing powder test on the variations in preference between sub-groups, such as brand usership, age and washing machine ownership. In the margarine test, all three methods showed a consistent preference for the experimental 'Summer County' in all sub-groups with its superiority least marked among refrigerator owners.

Table 12.3 Comparison of test methods.

	Postal testing (%)	New sample Self-comp. (%)	Face to face (%)
Washing powder:			
Net preference for non-soap detergent over soap formulation	+22	+28	+26
1 standard error of net preference	4.7	6.1	5.8
Margarine:			
Net preference for experimental over standard 'Summer County'	17.4	+17.8	+18.0
1 standard error of net preference	5.3	7.4	6.6

The marketing recommendations made from the two tests would therefore have been the same, whichever testing method were used. The results did, however, differ on certain points of detail.

1 The proportion expressing preferences between products was lower for the regular panel than for the new samples more especially for the face to face interview group.

2 The levels of criticism of both products in the washing powder test were higher among the new recruits than the regular panel.

3 Housewives in the margarine test, when asked the open question why they preferred the product chosen, gave an average of two reasons in the face to face interview as against 1.5 for the regular panel and 1.7 for the mixed method.

These points of difference are inter-related. The underlying explanation is suggested to be that the regular panel members by virtue of their previous experience of testing products and filling in self-completed questionnaires develop a greater critical faculty which reduces the tendency to give spurious preferences or non-considered judgements about differences between products. The newly recruited housewives will on the other hand enter the test with a greater enthusiasm and willingness to please, because they have less frequently experienced the pleasure of receiving two free samples to test; these attitudes are reinforced by the subtle pressures of the face to face interviewing situation.

Our overall conclusion was that these points of difference would have little effect on the decisions taken from product tests, and that the two to three years testing experience of the panel members had not conditioned their preference responses in any major way. This evidence on representativeness relates to panels of the general public. Panels of expert tasters are often employed, but can have problems of representativeness, some of which are discussed by Watts.[13]

3.2 In-use testing v. instant assessment

Instant assessment of products can be carried out in the environment where they are normally used, but much of the saving in cost and time which this method offers is then lost. Consequently, instant assessments usually differ from in-use tests in terms of testing environment, as well as in the nature and length of exposure to the product; they also provide greater opportunity for flexibility in test design, since it is possible, though not necessarily valid, to increase the number of products assessed by the individual participant with much less effect on costs and reporting dates than for the in-use test. Evidence on the situations for which instant assessment can be appropriate has been obtained over a range of toiletry, household and food products.

3.2.1 Toilet soaps

Results are available from four experiments, each involving from three to five soaps differing only in perfume. The in-use tests consisted of full round-robin paired comparisons, each pair being tested in a separate sample drawn from the RBL Postal Testing Panel with computerized matching for region, social class, age and brand usership; each soap was used in the home for up to one week; response was obtained from a self-completed questionnaire returned postally. The 'instant assessments' were made by sniffing three differently-perfumed tablets of the same soap and ranking them for perfume; all possible sets and orders of three were ranked by separate samples of housewives in a test centre with investigator-completed questionnaire.

The paired and triple comparisons were equated by the use of appropriate scoring procedures. The difference in score between any pair of products gives an estimate pooled from all the data of how one product would compare with another in a direct test between them, i.e., a difference in score of 10 is equivalent to a preference of 55 per cent for one product and 45 per cent for the other. It should be noted that at the time this work was carried out, the 'in-use' test was the standard method for assessing consumer response to possible change in the formulation of toilet soaps. Hence, the sample sizes used were much larger than for the experimental 'instant assessments', and the theoretical standard errors were correspondingly smaller.

The results are illustrated in Table 12.4 for the two tests which gave the best and worst correspondence between methods.

Generalizing from all four tests, we found that the two methods gave more or less the same basic product ordering. In only one case, where the order of the two highest scoring perfumes was reversed, was there any difficulty in identifying the most preferred perfume; but for both methods the difference between their scores was non-significant (less than a half of a standard error). One of these perfumes was more expensive than the other, so that the decision between them could be taken on cost grounds. In all four tests, therefore, the same recommendation would have been made to the client from each method.

Table 12.4 In-use testing *v.* instant assessment: toilet soaps

		In-use test Overall	In-use test Perfume	Sniff test
Lifebuoy:				
Perfume	A	+12.0	+16.8	+25.0
	B	+10.4	+14.8	+19.4
	C	− 2.0	− 5.6	+ 5.6
	D	− 7.8	− 9.6	− 9.4
	E	−12.6	−16.4	−40.6
1 standard error of difference between any pair		± 2.9	± 3.0	±12.2
Rexona:				
Perfume	F	+ 9.2	+14.2	+20.6
	G	+ 6.2	+ 8.4	− 5.0
	H	− 2.2	− 3.6	−15.5
	I	− 2.8	− 4.4	0.0
	J	−10.4	−14.6	0.0
1 standard error of difference between any pair		± 4.4	± 4.4	± 12.2

In the 'in-use' tests, the perfume net preferences cover a wider range of scores than the overall net preferences. This is a standard finding in tests of soap differing only in perfume. More unexpected, perhaps,

was the fact that in all four tests the instant (sniff) assessments showed a still wider differentiation between the scores. There seems no valid reason for supposing that the triple comparison method would in itself improve sensitivity. From a total sample of equal size, it offers the possibility of greater statistical efficiency than the paired comparison method in T-test terms, provided that the 50 per cent gain in numbers assessing each product is not offset by a reduction in the sensitivity of their assessments due to the greater complexity of testing three rather than two products. In our view the more likely source of the increased differentiation is the sniff method which focusses the tester's attention solely on the perfume. Be this as it may, the triple comparison sniff test appears to have the important practical advantage that the sample necessary for equal statistical precision to that from an in-use paired comparison is smaller in size − and in cost.

3.2.2 Toothpaste

Seven toothpastes, six of which differed only in flavour, were tested in-use under conditions similar to those described for toilet soap, and by instant assessment in a test centre (the latter involved one brushing of the teeth with each of two toothpastes).

The sample in each case was confined to users of two major brands. Since one of the products tested was a competitive brand, the results are shown in Table 12.5 in rank order form.

The correspondence between methods is clearly less than with the toilet soap results. Many of the preference scores which led to the rankings are not, in fact, significantly different, but discussions with the client company indicated that different marketing decisions would have been taken on the basis of the two sets of data.

Table 12.5 In-use *v.* instant tests: toothpaste

Tooth-paste	Brand X users In-use test Overall	Brand X users In-use test Flavour	Brand X users Instant test	Brand Y users In-use test Overall	Brand Y users In-use test Flavour	Brand Y users Instant test
A	1	1	2	5	5	1
B	2	3	6	1	3	5
C	3	5	4	2	1	4
D	4	4	7	6	6	2
E	5	2	1	3	4	3
F	6	6	5	4	2	6
G	7	7	3	7	7	7

Some technical difficulty in matching the test centre

and in-home samples may have contributed to the lack of similarity in their results. The more likely explanation, however, is that the two methods are, in effect, measuring different things. In the test centre situation, the subject assesses the initial impact of each flavour at a time of day when toothpaste is not normally used; the in-home test allows each paste to be used over a period of time on normal teeth-cleaning occasions. Perception of flavours and their consequent evaluations are likely to vary considerably through time. Fatigue effects, or conversely a gradual habituation to a flavour initially disliked can operate for this type of product, since a single tube may take some time to finish.

3.2.3 Washing-up liquids
In-use and 'instant assessment' procedures were used to test three types of perfume each at two different concentrations (in other respects the liquids were identical). With this product, the impact of the perfume may be experienced at different points in the washing-up process: the 'instant assessments' were carried out by sniffing directly from the open bottle, and from solutions representing four situations in the washing-up cycle.

In addition, separate sets of paired comparisons and triple comparisons were made for the in-use method and for the five 'instant assessments'.

Results revealed a poor correspondence between the triple and paired comparisons both for the in-use and 'instant assessments'. Moreover, the five forms of 'instant assessment' did not agree well with each other when the triple comparison method was being used. We concluded from this that washing-up liquids, for which perfume is at a much lower concentration than in toilet soaps and usually plays a less important role in the overall assessment of a liquid's performance, are not suitable for the triple comparison method. This appears

to be the case where the potential contribution to improving statistical efficiency is more than offset by loss of sensitivity of the respondents. The triple comparison results were therefore not used further in the analysis.

Considering therefore the paired comparison results only, all five 'instant assessments' showed the higher concentrations of the perfumes to be more preferred than the lower concentrations. Furthermore, three of the methods (from bottle and test situations two and three) revealed the same preference order between the perfume types while the other two showed them as being equally preferred (Table 12.6). The paired comparison in-use tests agreed with the preference order of the three perfume types but showed no difference in preference between the concentration levels.

In the in-use tests, the preference differences between the test perfumes are small and non-significant. Previous tests have shown that it is more difficult to obtain significant differences in overall preference from perfume variations in washing-up liquids than in toilet soaps. The 'instant assessments' show, as in the toilet soap results quoted earlier, a much wider differentiation between the products than was obtained from the in-use tests. The reasonably close agreement between the five 'instant' situations leads us to the conclusion that their results are a genuine expression of preference between these perfumes. It is felt, however, that the 'instant' method may tend to exaggerate the gain in overall preference likely to be obtained from an improved perfume (Table 12.6).

3.2.4 Foods
Several tests of food products have been conducted in which the same housewives participated in the two types of assessment. After a housewife had completed her 'instant assessment', usually at a test centre, she was

Table 12.6 In-use v. instant tests: washing-up liquids

In-use		Mean net preference scores instant				
		From bottle	1	Test situation 2	3	4
Perfume	A Low	−3.5	−18.2	−5.0	−24.4	−15.0	−10.7
	B Low	0.0	− 1.2	−5.0	−13.0	− 1.4	−10.7
	C Low	+3.5	+ 4.4	−5.0	− 1.6	− 4.6	−10.7
	A High	−3.5	+ 5.2	+5.0	+ 1.6	+ 4.6	+10.7
	B High	0.0	+ 1.2	+5.0	+13.0	+ 1.4	+10.7
	C High	+3.5	+ 8.6	+5.0	+24.4	+15.0	+10.7

given the products to test in-home. These tests were not originally designed as methodological studies, but rather in the expectation that the two assessments would measure different things:

1 Preference in an exclusively tasting situation, under controlled cooking and serving conditions.

2 Overall preference in the context of a family meal, when cooking might be variable, when the products might be served with other differing foods, and when the opinions of other family members might influence the housewife's own judgement.

Housewives knew that they were being given the same two products to test in-home, but the codings were changed so that they could not readily identify each with what they had already tried. These tests can therefore legitimately be taken as further evidence on the issue of 'instant' v. in-home assessment.

In general, the results indicate that the evaluation of the products in the test centre did not differ markedly from their in-home evaluation. The same marketing conclusions would have been drawn from both. This can be demonstrated by two examples.

Table 12.7 In-use v. instant tests: food

		Test centre taste test	In-home use test
Beefburgers – experimental v standard			
London:	Product preferred	A	A
	Net preference	17%	8%
	Significance level	1/20	n.s.
Manchester:	Product preferred	B	B
	Net preference	10%	21%
	Significance level	n.s.	1/20
Peas – Type A v Type B			
London:	Net preference for A	46%	47%
	Standard error	±6.3%	±6.2%
Manchester:	Net preference for A	28%	39%
	Standard error	±6.3%	±7.6%

In the second test, a major difference in the method of preparing and cooking the peas may have been responsible for type A obtaining a stronger preference in the home situation in Manchester. These and other similar examples suggest that the taste testing situation does *not* enhance the preference difference obtained from in-use tests – contrary to our finding for perfume differences in toilet soaps and washing-up liquids. It seems possible that for certain products in the food area flavour is the

dominant criterion of evaluation and cannot perhaps be much affected by the change in testing situation.

3.2.5 Conclusion

To summarize, 'instant' tests would seem to have been validated for perfume assessment in toilet soap and washing-up liquids, and this can probably be extended to other types of product in which perfume is an important factor. They would also be appropriate for evaluating foods where eating qualities are the only variables. In-home tests are judged preferable for:

1 Products whose assessment must be made over a period of time (because of multiple uses; build-up effects, etc.).

2 Products for which a heavy fatigue element may be involved (e.g., highly spiced foods, strong toothpaste flavours etc.).

3 Products for which an in-home factor (e.g., preparation of foods) may be crucial in the overall assessment.

4 Products where usage instructions are followed with varying consistency.

3.3 Testing on target groups

The differences between groups of individuals in their response to products has a number of implications for product testing. The naive view of product testing is that it selects the 'most popular' product. As has been frequently pointed out,[1,14,15] if everybody followed this policy then a number of identical products share the market equally and many customers whose tastes were not modal would be dissatisfied. That products are rarely designed to appeal to the whole population is now a commonplace of marketing and segmentation is the norm.

There are a number of approaches to dividing the population into groups who will have special product requirements. Products designed for a target group should clearly be tested on such a group. But it may also be worth finding out to *which* groups some new products appeal.

Division according to different existing purchasing habits. Where there is an established product field existing loyalties will condition the perception of blind tests, but particularly grossly affect preferences in branded tests. An example is shown in a later section (Table 12.14) where the differences in preferences between loyal users of brand A and brand B are apparent and massively influenced by branding. Mixing clearly defined usership groups in a product test can easily produce a bipolarity of response which renders the data unanalysable. In some marketing situations purchasing groups may define appropriate target groups.

Division by demographic characteristics or other single dimensions. The need to test a washing powder for automatic washing machines on owners of automatic machines is self-evident. Other product markets can be similarly defined in terms of children, young housewives, housewives with children, experimental housewives, girls with dry hair, etc. Such target markets may differ from existing buying groups because they are designed to cut across such alignments to meet needs inadequately satisfied by existing brands. When this approach is developed in a more sophisticated way it merges into that of the next heading.

Division into groups defined by multi-variate analysis. The notion that important marketing groups might be defined by the interaction of several needs or attitudinal characteristics has been much developed in recent years with the growing use of multi-variate analysis techniques. These developments in the mapping of consumer needs have been much discussed elsewhere.[16,17] The testing of products in groups defined by methods such as cluster analysis is a natural outcome but creates problems for some of the conventional rather casual approaches to product testing. Obtaining data on which to base a multi-variate analysis may be a long and elaborate process, although valid short-cut methods are being sought. It is here, however, that very large product testing panels are at an advantage in that such data can be obtained on recruitment and held in records or obtained separately from testing in the case of special requirements. Testing within target groups also creates problems for any reference to normative rating data unless norms within these target groups are available.

Division by preferences for specific values of a product attribute. One approach to segmentation reported in a number of articles[13,14] uses a series of product tests to establish a distribution of preferences across a range of values for some product attribute. Thus, one may find that preferences are bi-modal for some characteristics and market two products, a 'sweet' and a 'dry' for example, or launch a product at the value where there is a gap in the market. This approach is well documented and it is not proposed to deal with it further here, except to comment that it relates to fairly early on in

product development and is suitable for products which have gradually variable dimensions of considerable but unknown importance. In many product fields it is the interaction of many qualities, physical and psychological (from the marketing story) which provide the successful product/marketing mix. Multi-variate techniques can again be used here to provide a product map[19,20] but derivation of such optimum mixes is often less readily done along continua and development often veers more to trial and error testing.

Division by the results of a product test. Another approach which has been used is to test one or more products on a population about whom a great deal of classification information is known or is specially obtained. The characteristics can then be examined for groups defined in terms of likers on non-likers based on the product test results. This approach pinpoints those to whom the product *does* appeal. It contrasts with some of those above which can be used to define groups to whom subsequently developed products are intended to appeal. These contrasting approaches are most likely to apply to different product development strategies rather than appear at different stages of development. In one case a market gap is defined, and if this work is sound, testing should be against the criterion of satisfying this gap, i.e., testing on a target group. The approach in this section is more applicable where a product or idea is already developed and the need is to establish the best marketing strategy (and whether to market it).

3.4 Comparative v. monadic testing

3.4.1 Conventional arguments
Except where the use of one product will clearly affect the evaluation of another product these have often been seen as alternative product testing strategies.[21,22] The relevant arguments are:

	Monadic presentation	Comparative presentation
Realism	More like real-life where products are usually used one at a time.	Products are sometimes used in parallel or overlappingly in real life. If more appropriate, can always present the products one at a time.
	Can be used realistically with an absolute rating (uninfluenced by other test products) which reflects market-place performance. Can additionally ask for a comparative judgement against a known brand.	Comparative judgement against another possibility sometimes corresponds to marketing decisions. Otherwise, one of the test products can be one in the market-place giving a known reference point for the test product. Ratings can always be asked additionally to rankings.
Sensitivity	Sensitivity believed to be more like market sensitivity (i.e., more directly valid) and this is more useful for some marketing decisions.	Sensitivity believed to be magnified and therefore more readily detectable with smaller samples (i.e., indirectly valid for some decisions).
Validity	On the *a priori* grounds of greater realism, assumed more like the market-place in direction and extent of portraying product differences.	Validity of size of differences questioned. Also, possible doubts as to whether direction of preferences could be distorted sometimes.

3.4.2 Realism

The argument that one procedure more closely represents real-life product experience is largely an *a priori* one (in the absence of detailed data on validity) and it can only be assessed as a matter of judgement in a given situation. That real-life product usage conditions and test usage conditions should be carefully studied and as closely matched as possible seems indisputable, but assessing the gain in realism against cost can be difficult. No economically viable routine product testing method can be wholly realistic anyway.

We have found particular value in a close investigation of how test conditions operate in practice, particularly in less controlled testing conditions such as in-home testing. Interviewing housewives who had taken part in a number of in-home separated comparison tests, we found a number of things happening which were obviously making conditions less like real life and we were consequently able to improve procedures, e.g.:

1 Respondents believed that there *must* be a difference between products and could go to unnatural

lengths to find one in order to be helpful (over-co-operation). This can be remedied by making the possibility of no difference between products more explicit and plausible.

2 Various detailed findings from this study enabled instructions subsequently to be made more 'realistic' in relation to opinions of other household members, price, reference to other brands and the meaning of attributes.

3.4.3 Sensitivity

A number of studies confirm that product differences are reported more readily from comparative than monadic presentation. Bengstron and Brenner[23] demonstrate comparison, simultaneous, more sensitive than comparison separated, in turn more sensitive than monadic presentation (Table 12.8). This was summarized as showing that different testing methods give different results meaning that the monadic results gave the products as equally rated whereas the others showed a difference. Greenberg[24] reports similar results from different methods used on the same subjects but this meant only that in all cases there was no significant difference between the products and thus gave no evidence on sensitivity.

We can report briefly two experiments comparing the sensitivity of techniques. One yielded similar results to Greenberg: there were no statistically significant differences between two products rated monadically, rated comparatively or ranked comparatively with equal sample sizes throughout. There were, however, small non-significant differences on virtually all measures used in the same directions and appearing across all six conditions. There was therefore the statistically unsupportable suggestion that monadic ratings were here just as sensitive as comparative rankings. A much larger experiment used different sample sizes for different techniques which makes the results hard to present. In one part of the experiment the variety of techniques was used to assess three toilet soap formulations. Techniques were tried both with the RBL postal testing panel and by direct field placement.

The comparison of results shown in Table 12.8 demonstrates the greater sensitivity of comparative testing methods in the field setting and results similar to those from the monadic tests were obtained with smaller sample sizes by comparative tests using panels. Unfortunately, the technique used as a possible validation involving 'real life' sampling was employed on too small a scale to yield significant differences. Whilst this failure appeared to support the monadic findings in the field it is all too easy to achieve this by using inadequate samples and cannot be regarded as evidence either way.

In conclusion, the generally-held view that comparison testing is more sensitive than monadic testing is confirmed by published evidence and our own experiments with one somewhat dubious exception.

We have also experimented with ways of further increasing sensitivity in the comparison situation. One such approach was to direct attention through the testing instructions to the particular performance attributes on which the products were intended to differ. This did indeed sharpen sensitivities to product differences compared with an unprompted group. This approach could be realistic where product advantages are likely to be conveyed clearly by marketing activity.

3.4.4 Evidence on validity

Published examples never seem to have included different techniques showing a reverse order of preference. The greatest conflict is difference *v.* no difference. In our own major comparative experiment all techniques impressively showed either the same rank order on both overall preference and attributes or the differences failed to reach significance – there were no reversals. Different product test methods appear therefore to be measuring the same kind of thing but to differ in degree of magnification of effect. Validity therefore depends on correspondence to the market-place choice in direction and degree. Little has been published on validity and little systematic evidence is likely to be forthcoming. Companies do not systematically market the products which fail in product tests.

Comparative preference results are in particular unlikely to be validated where the decision was a choice between new variants. Even if the comparative test is a new versus an old product the marketing conditions of the two are then unbalanced and make the comparison difficult. Monadic test ratings can also be compared with real life market performance and will give some indication of the relevance of the whole product testing

Table 12.8 Comparative sensitivity of methods.

Measure	Paired comparison	Triple comparison separated		Triple comparison simultaneous		Monadic	
		Results significant at the 0.05 level or better					
	Panel	Field	Panel	Field	Panel	Field	Panel
Overall preference	A>C B>C	NS	A>C B>C	B>C	A>C B>C		
7-pt rating scale	–	B>C	A>C	B>C	B>C	NS	A>C B>C
5-pt scale	NS	NS	NS	NS	NS	NS	A>C
Sample sizes	267 per pair	350 per triple	350 per triple	350 per triple	350 per triple	400 per product	400 per product

operation to marketing decision-making.

Our basic findings are that the relative importance of elements of the marketing mix, of which the product quality is one, varies with product field. Where the product is all-important, as in certain food fields, the product alone can be tested and its acceptability assessed monadically. In other fields more components of the marketing mix have to be tested together and here prediction varies with the degree to which these elements can be simulated in the test situation. In Table 12.9 we show the results for the easiest case – a food field where product quality is important. All 15 new products launched in recent years are arranged in rank order of monadic rating. The subsequent market-place assessment by the brand manager is given. The correlation is very good, better in fact even than it appears, when changes in formulation and price between test and launch, and distribution problems are taken into account.

Table 12.9 New food product test results and market success.

Product	Intention to buy 5-pt scale indexed to 100%	Marketing company assessment
A	86	Good success
B	81	Moderate success
C	80	Moderate success
D	76	Good success
E	76	Moderate success
F	75	Moderate success
G	73	Neither success nor failure
H	72	Good success
I	71	Moderate failure
J	69	Moderate success
K	68	Moderate success
L	68	Moderate failure
M	66	Moderate failure
N	62	Bad failure
O	62	Moderate failure

What is missing is published evidence on whether the differences from comparative testing can be misleadingly large for those marketing decisions where accuracy matters. Greenhalgh suggests that they are misleading for level of discrimination although the one case which he quotes gives comparative testing results very like his 'real life' semi-validation. This he attributes to compensatory errors.[5]

3.4.5 Conclusion

Given that the sensitivity of product tests can be manipulated by presenting them comparatively, and

through instructions and timing, it is clear that a range of answers is possible for any marketing question, and it becomes crucial to define precisely what information is needed for the decision concerned. If the direction to the answer only is required then there is a case for magnifying sensitivity. If some kind of market acceptability rating is required then the best strategy appears to be to make the test conditions as much like real-life usage as possible which may mean monadic testing, and to rely upon past experience or other research to indicate the meaning of any rating obtained.

3.5 Scaling methods

Scales commonly used in product tests for Unilever include a series of five-point scales concerned with product trial, adoption as a 'usual' brand, variations on frequency of use (adapted to product field) and willingness to pay the price. It is one of these scales which was shown to correlate so well with market-place performance in section 3.4.4. Used in conjunction with these are five-point agree-disagree scales for product attributes. These were reliable across all techniques in our larger comparison of techniques study mentioned above.

Table 12.10 Probability of switching to the brand, by scale rating of intention to buy averaged across three fields.

Germany: sample size 500 housewives	
Scale point	Probability of switch
1	0.015
2	0.015
3	0.033
4	0.040
5	0.077
6	0.126
7	0.207

Research International companies also use a seven point intention-to-buy scale. This has been subject to validation work in both West Germany and the UK.

In West Germany, the amount of switching to a brand between two checks 15 days apart was related to product assessments on the seven-point scale, for three fields. Table 12.10 shows the probabilities of a switch (i.e., having the brand on the second check but not on the first), associated with each scale point across the three fields.

The UK study established purchases for a previous week in an interview and measured them with a diary for a week subsequent to obtaining product ratings for two product fields. Table 12.11 shows the probability of buying on the second week among those not buying on the first by rating-scale point. The UK study probably uses a cruder measure of market-place buying than the West German study.

Most published reports give some indication of scales used in product tests. Of particular interest is Eastlach's article[25] which shows product attributes rated on a version of the differential scale with ideal product attributes as the centre point in each case.

In a test in the UK of the five-point intention-to-buy scale, people who had tested and rated new products were followed up and their early purchasing measured. About 1,000 housewives were interviewed for each of three products. The average percentage buying sub-sequently is shown above for each scale position averaged for all three products.

Table 12.11 Probability of switching to the brand by scale rating of intention-to-buy averaged for two fields.

UK: sample size 734 housewives	
Scale point	Probability of switch
1	0.01
2	–
3	–
4	0.01
5	0.02
6	0.12
7	0.28

Table 12.12 Percentage of respondents who subsequently bought test products by intention-to-buy scale position.

Position	Buying (%)
1	12
2	16
3	24
4	31
5	35

It is clear that purchasing increases with scale position. What is surprising is the overall high level of purchase for new products. This was higher than in an untested control sample, suggesting that all experimental purchasing levels were raised by a sales effect from the product test.

As well as which scale to use there is also the question of how to use scales. It is dangerous to rely on mean scores from rating scales (despite their preponderance in this article for illustrative purposes). Not only does the mean lose information such as whether there is a bi-polarity of response, but also taking a mean implies giving equal values to the interval between each scale point. The evidence on the seven-point scales above, Tables 12.10 and 12.11, shows that this is inappropriate. In general, distributions should always be examined. It is only meaningful (and often only statistically feasible) to compare means when the distributions are similar in form.

3.6 Order of testing effects

That preference may be biased by the order in which products are tried is well-known.[26,27] References in the literature are often to single cases and sometimes show a favourable bias towards the first product tested, and sometimes towards the second the disparities being noted with surprise. Some time ago we examined order effects in 463 paired comparisons tests with the results shown in Table 12.13.

These results show first that overall both kinds of order effects are equally likely and that they can be large. Second, that there appear to be differing tendencies in different product fields. The need to balance for order effects in all comparative testing is clear, but whilst this eliminates bias the order effects still reduce the sensitivity and meaningfulness of the results. Some knowledge of what order effects are likely in a given situation is therefore of value in interpreting results. It is also worthwhile to investigate ways of reducing order effects.

3.7 Blind v. branded v. mix research

The distinction between testing products in an apparently unidentifiable form compared with labelling them with a brand name and product claims is well-known. With some products the surrounding aura of the marketing story is a stronger element than the 'pure' product qualities, and preferences may be completely reversed as between the 'dressed' and 'naked' product. This kind of finding is absolutely in line with more general work in the perception area where it is often shown that how things are perceived depends both on sensory input and also upon expectations and preconceived image. The motto of modern research in perception could also be 'believing is seeing'. For a full discussion of perception as a cognitive process see Neisser.[27a] Arndt[28] quotes a US study of blind and branded preferences for six beers, three American, three imported. Ratings for all save one of the beers improved when tested and labelled, but more so for the imported and/or more expensive ones, producing some big changes

Table 12.13 Variations due to order of testing.

	No. of tests									Summary		
	Over −17%	−17% to −12%	−12% to −7%	−7% to −2%	−2% to +2%	+2% to +7%	+7% to +12%	+12% to +17%	over +17%	1st pref.	No diff.	2nd pref.
All House-hold products	6	7	35	97	153	107	39	15	4	145	153	165
Food products	6	6	23	48	68	31	6	2	–	83	68	39
Toilet-ries	–	1	12	47	72	68	31	12	4	60	72	115
	–	–	–	2	13	8	2	1	–	2	13	11

in the rank order of preference. Watts discusses some related problems[13] and Clarke also makes a blind *v.* branded comparison.[3] That test results can be sensitive to details of information was shown by Pettit[29] and also that times have changed since 1958, since two possible descriptive phrases which did *not* affect results then were 'chemically treated' and 'has been exposed to rays'.

Generally-speaking, branded products are rated higher in tests than unbranded samples, but there appear to be some exceptions in highly psychologically segmented markets were branding can suggest a narrower appeal. Comparisons between blind tests and tests with varying additional information can provide evidence of the strengths and weaknesses of elements of the marketing mix. Interactions can be important, however, and these can only be checked by testing as much of the total mix as is feasible.

One possible interaction which can be investigated is that between the product itself and its own and other brand images. In the example which follows two entirely different brands of toothpaste were tested under three conditions, blind so that preferences for merely the formulations were under investigation, branded so that the current brand images could be compared and finally using only the formulation for one product (the most popular) but comparing it branded as itself with it branded as its competitor (Table 12.14).

The results are particularly interesting in the usership groups. They show that the naked information for A is the most popular, being heavily preferred by extensive users of B (there is possibly some novelty effect here but it does not operate on users of A). Correctly labelling the brands shows a majority of each usership group favouring their own brand (and reversing the blind preferences for users of B). When testing *A labelled as B* against *A labelled as A*, the preference for the A label

Table 12.14 Preferences according to branding.

Net (preferences for brand A for those giving a preference sample size about 1,000 for each condition)

	Formu-lation A v. Formu-lation B	Brand A v. Brand B	Formulation A branded as v. Formulation A branded as
	(%)	(%)	(%)
Total sample	+12	+ 6	− 2
Exclusive users of A	+ 6	+42	+28
Exclusive users of B	+22	−29	−22
Users of A and B	+18	+ 2	−12
Users of neither	+ 8	+ 2	− 4
(Percent giving a preference total sample)	(80)	(83)	(74)

against B label among users of A was weakened, suggesting that the product qualities were important to them. Changing the product labelled product B to formulation A did not, however, improve its appeal to regular users of B, despite the fact that formulation A was preferred blind, suggesting that their branded preferences were dependent on brand image. Changing the formulation of brand B to A would improve its standing with the other two usership groups. There are a number of fascinating marketing implications from these and related results depending on which of the two brands one is marketing.

When should products be tested blindly, branded and with the marketing mix? Ideally, all mix elements may need testing, but this may be uneconomical. Consider ation of the nature of the decision the product test is supposed to assist will often suggest the appropriate strategy. This approach of *a priori* reasoning from marketing problems will, however, suggest that the

Table 12.15 Indexed intention-to-buy scores according to mode of testing for new products.

	Monadic testing		(sample sizes 200 in each condition)	
	Blind	Branded	Branded with press ad.	Branded with tv ad.
Product P (an easily understood food product) 5-pt scale indexed to 100%	82	83	82	84
Product Q (a toilet product) 7-pt scale indexed to 100%	58	60	64	64

maximum product mix should be tested whenever the aim is to predict total in-market success.

Testing the total mix is often costly and impracticable, particularly for new products. How far can one rely on early non-mix tests? Does 'the mix' always matter? Two examples (Table 12.15) suggest as a working hypothesis that for some fields it does more than others, but we do not really know the possible interaction with quality of advertising. In the first case, P, there are no significant differences. In the second, Q, conditions with an advertisement, yield significantly higher scores than those without. The lower scores for Q are partly because of the scale used, but there are also lower norms for that field.

Notice that the press advertisement has a similar effect to the television commercial. Perhaps relatedly, we have found that the mini-test market has given accurate predictions for a product supported in the market-place by a heavy television campaign on the basis of only a press advertisement in the mini-test market.[30] Whilst we have only looked at this in situations where advertising has a strong informational value, these findings suggest that, where acceptability may be influenced by a marketing story, then this effect may be created for the test by press-type advertisements if television commercials are not available.

Other mix relationships may also be tested. For example, a marketing story may be tested on its own

and then with a product trial. This then provides a basis of comparing expectations created by advertising with how the first trial lives up to these expectations. It is on such a basis that anticipated in-market trial and repeat purchase can be investigated. Table 12.16 shows for a new class of food product the kind of result which occurs when trial does not match up to expectations.

When marketing failures occur the reasons can be diagnosed sometimes by this kind of analytic approach, breaking out the effects of marketing mix components, using some region where the product had not been sold.

Decisions as to when mix testing is important remain based on judgement and experience rather than the impossible level of experimental product testing necessary to prove rules. Nevertheless, the examples above support the view that mix testing is less important to the degree that true product qualities are readily discriminable and dominate the consumer response to the product. Whilst this appears almost a truism it is nevertheless a useful framework into which findings can be fitted to produce general rules about how far testing different levels of product will predict market-place acceptability.

4.0 Adapting product-testing methods to different product fields

Most manufacturers use some means of exercising quality control over their products, and in a sense product-testing on the consumer is an extension of these methods in a marketing orientated situation where objective (e.g., instrument) measures no longer provide the whole story. The need for subjective (e.g., consumer) measures has always been most clear for food products[31] where not only are product qualities important but many are difficult to measure objectively. If there is a product-testing tradition it has probably developed by increasing extensions into fields where perception of

Table 12.16 Indexed intention-to-buy for a new food product.

	Response 5-pt scale indexed to 100%
Test of product description and television advertisement only	65
Test of product description and television advertisement followed by in-home trial	56

product qualities is less direct and more influenced by the marketing story. The 'obvious' fields of product testing have been foods, drinks, household cleaners, toiletry products and cosmetics. Are there any limits beyond these? We have so far adapted product-testing methodology to cover a variety of alcoholic drinks, tobacco products, home decorating products, publications (whole and parts), prams, vacuum cleaners, kitchen utensils, cutlery, painting reproductions, travel, investment portfolios and motoring products. Motor cars too are discussed in the literature.[32] The main problem is to achieve appropriate test situations for products requiring extended use, perhaps in special environmental conditions. This has so far always proved possible. BP has used 'real-life' product-testing techniques among representative motorists to test alternative formulations of petrol. The major problems encountered were of an operational and procedural nature. The technique used, the repeat paired comparison method, worked well and yielded meaningful results.

The conclusion offered, therefore, is that product-testing methods can be extended to a wide range of fields, but clearly not in any stereo-typed way. Indications have been given already as to how far differences of methods have to be used even between fields more traditionally associated with product-testing.

5.0 Conclusion

This article has proposed a probabilistic view of discrimination and preference and suggested that further theoretical development could be derived from signal detection theory.

Choice of product-testing method must depend on fitting the procedure to the consumer behaviour whose prediction is relevant to the marketing decision concerned. Methodological developments are concerned with conducting tests more economically as well as trying to make them more predictive of the market-place.

In the pursuit of economy we have presented evidence showing that postal panels give results similar to newly recruited samples and that some product classes, but not others, can be tested through 'instant trial' at testing centres.

Our evidence, on balance, confirms a greater sensitivity for comparative testing. We have suggested that comparative methods can be used where such comparative judgements would be made in real-life usage or where only the direction of difference is important,

since the degree of sensitivity which is valid in each situation is largely unknown. Monadic tests can be used to predict market acceptability and we have shown that ratings from such tests can predict market outcome, and individual scores will relate to future probability of purchase.

We have shown the interaction of other marketing variables with product qualities, determining the outcome of a product test.

The formulation of exact rules whereby marketing problem and product class can be related together to provide the optimum testing conditions depends on having feedback from marketing experience and also occasional use of validation methods. We feel that the mini-test market[30] provides us with one method whereby alternative outcomes of product tests can be marketed cheaply to test prediction. Another possibility is the measurement of sales following a 'real-life' placement such as is discussed by Greenhalgh.[5]

We already have evidence that product-testing works in differentiating marketing successes and failures with a usable certainty. All future progress reduces to improving the quantification of such predictions, at economic costs.

References

1 Kuehn, Alfred A. and Day, L. 'Strategy of product quality'. *Harvard Business Review'*. (1962) **40**, November-December, pp. 100-110.
2 Day, L. 'Preference tests and management of product features'. *J. Marketing.* (1968) **32**, July, pp. 24-29.
3 Clarke, T.J. 'Product testing in new product development'. *Commentary* (now *Journal of the Market Research Society*). (1967) 9, 3, pp. 135-146.
4 Greenhalgh, C. 'Some techniques and interesting results in discrimination testing'. ESOMAR Conference and *Commentary* (now *Journal of the Market Research Society).* (1966) 8, 4, pp. 215-236.
5 Greenhalgh, C. 'Discrimination testing: further results and developments'. ESOMAR Conference. (1970), pp. 181-90.
6 Gruber, A. and Lindberg, B. 'Sensitivity, reliability and consumer taste testing.' *J. Marketing Research.* **III**, (1966) August, pp. 235-238.
7 Greenberg, A. and Collins, S. 'Paired comparison taste tests: some food for thought'. *J. Marketing Research.* **III**, February, pp. 76-80.
8 Day, R.L. 'Systematic paired comparisons in preference analysis'. *Journal of Marketing Research.* (1965) 11, November, pp. 406-412.
9 Green, D.M. and Swets, J.A. *Signal detection theory and psycho-physics.* (1966) New York: John Wiley and Sons Inc.
10 Greenberg, Marshall G. 'A modification of Thurstone's Law of Comparative Judgement to accommodate a judgement

category of "equal" of "no different".' *Psychological Bulletin*. (1965) **64**, August, pp. 108-112.

11 Odesky, S.H. 'Handling the neutral vote in paired comparison product testing'. *J. Marketing Research*. (1967) **IV**, May, pp. 199-201.

12 Ross, I. 'Handling the neutral vote in product testing'. *J. Marketing Research*', (1969) **6**, May, pp. 221-222.

13 Watts, G. 'Flavour tests on beer'. *The Statistician*, (1969) **18**, 2, pp. 149-156.

14 Benson, P.H. 'Fitting and analysing distribution curves of consumer choices'. *J. Advertising Research*.(1965) **5**, March, pp. 28-34.

15 Thurstone, L.L. 'The prediction of choice'. *Psychometrika*, (1945), **10**, pp. 237-253.

16 Hill, P.B. 'Multi-variate analysis – what pay-off for the marketing man?' *J. Market Research Society*, (1970) **12**, 3, 169-180.

17 Lunn, J.A. 'Perspectives in attitude research: methods and applications'. *J. Market Research Society*. (1969) **11**, 3, pp. 201-213.

18 Peryam, D.R. and Gutman, N.J. 'Variation in preference ratings for foods served in meals'. *Food Technology*, (1958) **12**, January, pp. 30-33.

19 Morgan, N. and Purnell, J.M. 'Isolating openings for new products in multidimensional space'. *J. Market Research Society*. (1969) **11**, 3, pp. 245-266.
Moss, M.G. 'What the marketing men require from research'. MRS Annual Conference (1967).

20 Lunn, J.A. in Worcester, R. (Ed.). *Handbook of consumer market research*. (1971) London: McGraw-Hill.

21 Blankenship, A.B. 'Let's bury paired comparisons'. *J. Advertising Research*. (1966) **6**, 1, pp. 13-17.

22 Haller, T.P. 'Let's not bury paired comparisons'. *J. Advertising Research*. (1966) **6**, 3, pp. 29-30.

23 Bengstron, R. and Brenner, H. 'Product test results using three different methodologies'. *J. Marketing Research*. (1964) **1**, November, 49-52.

24 Greenberg, A. 'Paired comparisons vs. monadic tests'. *J. Advertising Research*. (1963) **3**, 4, pp. 44-47.

25 Eastlach, J. Jr. 'Consumer flavor preference factors in food product design'. *J. Marketing Research*. (1964) **1**, February, pp. 38-42.

26 Berdy, D. 'Order effects in taste tests'. *J. Market Research Society*. (1969) **11**, 4, pp. 361-371.

27 Mitchell, J.W. 'Time errors in the paired comparison taste preference'. *Food Technology*. (1956) **10**, May, pp. 208-210.

27a Neisser, U. *Cognitive psychology*. (1967) New York: Appelton-Century-Crofts.

28 Arndt, J. 'A beer testing experiment'. *The European Marketing Research Review*. (1970) **5**, 2, pp. 10-22.

29 Pettit, L.A. 'Information bias in flavour preference testing'. *Food Technology*, (1958) **12**, January, pp. 12-14.

30 Pymont, B.C. 'The development and application of a new micro-market testing technique'. ESOMAR Conference, (1970) pp. 201-222.

31 Harper, R. 'Fundamental problems in the subjective appraisal of foodstuffs'. *Applied Statistics*. (1955) **4**, 3, pp. 145-161.

32 Leyshon, A.M. 'Product testing in the automotive industry'. *J. Market Research Society*. (1968) **10**, 2, pp. 111-118.

13.

A Method for Effective New Product Decisions by Supermarket Buyers

by P. M. Doyle and C. B. Weinberg

Reprinted from the Operational Research Quarterly, Vol. 24, (1), March, 1973 with permission.

Effective New Product Decisions for Supermarkets

The supermarket buyer is a neglected link in the new product development chain. Research on product development has focused on the decisions of the new product producer and the final consumer, virtually ignoring the retailer's role. But most new consumer products must be distributed in retail outlets. Supermarkets, in particular, play a large and growing part in this area. A manufacturer meets a major hurdle in getting the supermarket to stock his new grocery product. For the supermarket, the decision to stock is an allocation of resources offering both significant problems and substantial profit opportunities.

This article proposes a method for supermarket buyers to select the products to stock from the many new products offered to them. Interviews with the buyers for several large UK supermarkets suggest that current procedures are lacking in careful analysis. A method of selection is proposed which helps overcome these inadequacies. It views the buying function as a classification problem and uses a Bayesian extension of discriminant analysis to achieve a fruitful and practical solution. The parameters used depend explicitly upon observed attributes of past successful products and opportunity costs of the supermarket buyer's decision. The value and economy of this method are illustrated and discussed.

Current Buying Procedures

We first investigated how supermarkets in the UK select new products to stock. Three features of the decisions are significant here: their volume, their informality, and their speed.

In the US, 50 to 100 items may be presented to a buyer in one week[1] (p. 19). This volume reflects the general level of new product activity among manufacturers. Failure rates appear particularly high among grocery products; of 3,700 new products considered by one supermarket's buying committee, 78 per cent were rejected[1] (p. 7). Even when accepted, many new products are discontinued by supermarkets before they provide a return to the manufacturer. Thus, one survey in the UK showed that 53 per cent of all new products launched had failed after four years.[2] Because of the number of products offered therefore, the store must make frequent, rapid, and routine decisions about which to stock.

Supermarket selection processes are also informal. The manufacturer's representative meets the buyer responsible for the particular product group who, in most instances, makes the effective decision with little deliberation. He determines whether the product will be distributed nationally, tested in selected stores, or rejected. Little paperwork enters into the evaluation. No relevant internal operating data, such as sales, margins or experience with existing items, is systematically collected and considered. Nor did the supermarket buyers interviewed use new product forms to record data conveniently and uniformly. The only written information which commonly affects decisions appears to be the manufacturer's literature.

Buying decisions are speedy because of the volume of new products requiring decisions and because of the lack of analysis which takes place. The typical buyer makes no quantitative estimate of a product's expected contribution. Nor, despite electronic information processing equipment, are there comparative evaluations of product performance or promotional budgets. The buyer makes these continual decisions from his experience. The new product is judged by the knowledge and attitudes built up in the multitude of prior decisions the typical buyer has made.

Limitations of Current Procedures

The disadvantages of this approach to decision-making stem from the lack of an analytical framework. Estimates of the return from a product are rare; nor are alternative criteria explicit. Selection is often based upon one or two manifest product dimensions such as, package appearance or the size of the advertising budget, to the neglect of other factors. Previous data which would aid decision-making, though easily obtainable, is not considered. This lack of sophistication contrasts with the methods used in other areas. Most supermarkets have, for example, computerized warehouse and stock control systems. Site location decisions and financial analysis also exhibit considerable planning and research.[3]

There are a number of reasons for this lack of progress. First, little research has taken place. Despite the vast literature on new product decisions, very little treats the buyer's problem. Second, buyers generally have had neither the time nor the training to devise satisfactory alternatives. Their workload is heavy. Not only are they responsible for new products, but typically also for regular re-orders, promotions, and often pricing and distribution control. Only the most rudimentary analysis concerning the dozen or more new products which each sees weekly is possible. Third, buyers do not appreciate the costs of incorrect decisions. If a rejected product is successful elsewhere, then buyers regard it as easy to order subsequently. Products which are tried or accepted can be discontinued if they fail to move. Because opportunity costs do not figure in the financial statements, poor buying decisions are generally not revealed. Finally, buyers believe that more analytical procedures would increase costs without providing compensating benefits. They are confident of their own judgements, experience, and methods.

A Screening Alternative

We suggest a method of product selection which avoids some of these limitations. It is based upon a screening procedure. The buyer's purchasing decision is seen as a problem of classification: with certain data on the product, and experience of previous decisions and outcomes, the buyer needs to classify it as likely to be successful and to be accepted, or as likely to be unsuccessful and to be rejected. The buyer also has a third class for equivocal risks, products whose outcomes are not clear and which should be tested in selected stores.

Screening devices or checklists have received considerable attention in the literature.[2,4,5] Their main advantage is that they force buyers to adopt a multi-dimensional approach. This prevents them taking a decision on the basis of one or two obvious attributes to the neglect of other important factors. Also, used correctly, such a procedure permits management to use directly past experience in the analysis, and allows decisions to be evaluated later so that learning takes place.[4]

A screening procedure for supermarkets requires four steps. First, product characteristics important in indicating the profit potential of products must be identified. Second, the products must be evaluated along the selected characteristics to build a profile of the product. After completing these two steps, the supermarket will have a data file of successful and unsuccessful products with each product rated on the relevant characteristics. Third, weights must be placed on these characteristics according to their significance in the classification. These then provide a 'score' for a given product. This score corresponds to its probability of success or failure. Finally, standard scores are set by considering the potential costs and revenues. Comparison of a product's score to the standard score is the basis of discrimination.

Opportunity Costs of the Buying Decision

In a pioneering study of supermarket operations McKinsey recommends that direct product profit should be the basis for decisions on the individual products carried by the supermarket.[6] This is computed by deducting directly attributable product costs, such as warehousing, delivery and shelving, from gross margins.

This concept can be extended to the decision of whether to stock a new product; the decision should be one of trying to find products which will return a greater direct product profit than is obtained on the average in the space allocated to the product line. This higher profit can result either from higher volume or from greater profit per unit sold. Thus, a product which is called a success is one which generates a return which is significantly above the average in the product class; similarly, a failure is one whose return is significantly below the average. Let these deviations from the average be C_1 and C_2 respectively. In addition to the variable revenues and costs, there is also a one-time set-up cost involved in the initial stocking of a product. Denote this cost by C_3.

By using such opportunity costs, we can see what happens when the buyer makes a wrong decision. As shown in Table 13.1, this can occur in either of two ways: (a) he accepts a failure or, (b) he rejects a success. Central to this issue is the time before the buyer knows that he has made a wrong (or a right) decision.

From interviews with buyers, it appears that each firm has a period of between three to six months after the product's introduction into the stores after which in general, its sales are checked. At this time, the buyer feels that its success or failure can be evaluated and, in the latter case, the product is removed from the stores. This review period is taken as the basic period of analysis and all time based costs, such as C_1 and C_2, will be expressed in terms of it.

Table 13.1 Opportunity costs: choice of two acts.

Event	Act	
	Accept	Reject
Success	0	$C_{R/S}$
Failure	$C_{A/F}$	0

If an accepted product is a failure, this is known to the manager within one time period. On the other hand, it takes considerably longer for the buyer to determine that a rejected product is a success in other stores. Buyers' estimates of this time vary considerably but it is usually considered to be at least one year. For the sake of generality, it will be assumed that it takes T periods beyond the initial one for the buyer to become aware of the success of a new product. T usually lies in the range of one to four.

It is now possible to construct the opportunity costs necessary for Table 13.1. The opportunity cost of accepting a failure, $C_{A/F}$, is the one period loss of profit compared to the average profit plus the set-up cost of stocking the new product, i.e.,

$$C_{A/F} = C_2 + C_3$$

On the other hand, the opportunity cost of rejecting a success, $C_{R/S}$, is the profit lost over the $T + 1$ periods before the buyer becomes aware of his error less the set-up cost, i.e.,

$$C_{R/S} = (T + 1) C_1 - C_3$$

Buyers, however, have a third option — the product can be tested in a fraction r of their stores. The results of this test indicate whether the product is, in fact, a success or failure. In other words, provides the buyer with what may be regarded as perfect information. The opportunity cost of choosing the course of action 'test' depends upon the outcome of the event. If the product is a failure, the cost is $rC_{A/F}$. If it is a success, the opportunity cost is the profit lost in the $(1 - r)$ stores which were not in the test, i.e., $(1 - r) C_1$. A full listing of the opportunity costs is given in Table 13.2. These provide the basis for the development of characteristic

weights and the following analysis of the buyer's decision.

Table 13.2 Opportunity costs for supermarket buyer (over $T + 1$ periods).

Event	Act			
	Accept	Reject	Test	
Success	0	$(T + 1) C_1 - C_3$	$(1 - r) C_1$	
Failure	$C_2 + C_3$	0	0	$r (C_2 + C_3)$

Assignment of Characteristic Weights

The conventional approach to the problem of finding weights which minimize the costs of mis-classification[1] (pp. 126 to 152) needs to be modified to apply to the supermarket situation. Here, the buyer may not only accept or reject products, but he may also decide to test them. The cost of this option depends upon the outcome.[7] The approach can be outlined briefly. Each new product is regarded as an observation on an n-dimensional vector. There are two probability distributions of these vectors, one of scores of successful products and one of scores of unsuccessful products.

Let the two likelihood functions be $f_s(x)$ and $f_u(x)$ respectively, where x is the observed vector. For a given x the probability of a mis-classification is minimized by assigning the group with the higher conditional probability. Therefore if

$$\frac{f_s(x)}{f_s(x) + f_u(x)} \geqslant \frac{f_u(x)}{f_s(x) + f_u(x)} \qquad (1)$$

we choose to assign the product to the successful group; i.e., we accept it. Since the probability of mis-classification is minimized at each point, it is minimized over the whole space; equation 1 can be simplified to the rule

$$f_s(x)/f_u(x) \geqslant 1 \qquad (2)$$

This rule is particularly useful when the two distributions can be taken to be multi-variate normal with equal covariance matrices.[1] Then after taking logarithms and some simplification, equation 2 can be written

$$z = 1 \left(\frac{f_s(x)}{f_u(x)} \right) = [x - \tfrac{1}{2} (\mu_s + \mu_u)] \sqrt{}^{-1} (\mu_s - \mu_u) \geqslant 0 \qquad (3)$$

which is the familiar classification function[7] (pp. 133 to 7). Here, $= \Sigma$ is the covariance matrix and μ_s and μ_u are the mean vectors of the two distributions.

However, the aim is to minimize the costs of mis-classification rather than simply the probability of mis-classification. Given the dichotomous choice situation represented in Table 13.2, the decision will be to accept the new product if

$$\frac{f_s(x)}{f_u(x)} \geqslant \frac{C_{A/F}}{C_{R/S}} \qquad (4)$$

Again, assuming observations on products are normally distributed equation 4 can be written as

$$z = \log \frac{f_s(x)}{f_u(x)} \geqslant \frac{C_{A/F}}{C_{R/S}} = z^* \qquad (5)$$

where z is as defined in equation 3.[8] New products are accepted if the observed z score exceeds some value z^*.

Buyer Decision Criteria

In the problem of the supermarket buyer, however, this analysis must be extended. There are three courses of action – accept (A), reject (R) or test (T) – despite there being only two possible outcomes – success or failure of the product in the supermarket. In this case, three breakpoints z_1^*, z_2^* and z_3^* need to be established such that for any value of z, the optimal course of action can be specified.

Table 13.2 shows the opportunity costs associated with any course of action. Using equation 5 to specify the decision rule which minimizes expected costs the following results hold

$$E(T) \leqslant E(R) \text{ when } z \geqslant \log \pi_1 = z_1^*$$
$$E(A) \leqslant E(R) \text{ when } z \geqslant \log \pi_2 = z_2^* \qquad (6)$$
$$E(A) \leqslant E(T) \text{ when } z \geqslant \log \pi_3 = z_3^*$$

where $\pi_1 = \dfrac{r(C_2 + C_3)}{(T+1)C_1 - C_3 - (1-r)C_1} = \dfrac{r(C_2 + C_3)}{(T+r)C_1 - C_3}$

where $\pi_2 = \dfrac{C_2 + C_3}{(T+1)C_1 - C_3}$

where $\pi_3 = \dfrac{C_2 + C_3 - r(C_2 + C_3)}{(1-r)C_1} = \dfrac{C_2 + C_3}{C_1}$

The relative ranking of the cost ratios π_1, π_2, and π_3 depends upon the relationship between the costs C_1 and C_3. However, if $(T+1)C_1 \leqslant C_3$ then even a successful product will not return its costs and the optimal course of action is to reject. Now if $(T+1)C_1 > C_3 \geqslant TC_1$, then $\pi_1 > \pi_2$ and it is never economical to test. In the usual case, $TC_1 > C_3$ and $\pi_1 < \pi_2 < \pi_3$ and any one of the three acts may be optimal according to the value of z. That is, when $z \geqslant \pi_3$ the optimal act is to accept, when $z \leqslant \pi_1$ the optimal act is to reject, and otherwise, to test. These results are summarized in Table 13.3.

An Illustrative Application

Adoption of this method may offer real advantages over

Table 13.3 z-Score breakpoints.

Cost	z score range to		
	Reject	Test	Accept
$C_3 \geqslant (T+1)C_1$	Always	Never	Never
$(T+1)C_1 > C_3 \geqslant TC_1$	$z < z_2^*$	Never	$z \geqslant z_2^*$
$TC_1 > C_3$	$z < z_1^*$	$z_1^* \leqslant z < z_2$	$z \geqslant z_3^*$

current procedures. It allows the buyer to quantify his judgements along the dimensions he considers important and his previous experience is directly incorporated into the decision. In addition, the data needed to use this procedure is readily available to the buyer.

The first step is to determine the important dimensions. In our survey, we found that the buyer's decision is generally based upon how the product is rated along some or all of the following eight characteristics:

1 Potential opportunities in relevant product class.
2 Marketing reputation of the manufacturer.
3 Price of the brand compared to competitors.
4 Quality of the brand compared to competitors.
5 Contribution margin.
6 Rating of proposed product launch.
7 Expected volume compared to others in product class.
8 Potential profitability to the supermarket if launch successful.

In practical application, the method is envisaged to operate as follows: when a new product is offered to a buyer, he rates it on these eight factors. This is the basic information input on the new product. The store will have on a computer file a record of past products offered together with whether they turned out to be successful or not. To decide on a new one, the scores from the buyer's rating sheet are read in and the computer, by calculating the z-score, classifies the product as likely to be successful, unsuccessful or worth testing. This requires an on-line computing facility. Alternatively, the file can be periodically updated and a standard set of weights developed for each product class.[4] Given this function, the product can be quickly classified by the buyer substituting into the function, hand-calculating the score, and then comparing the z-score to the break-points established for the product class.

An application of the proposed scheme may be illustrated in the following hypothetical situation. In this example, there is on the store's computer file a sample of 60 products of which 33 were known to be successful and 27 unsuccessful. Each has been rated on eight 5-point bi-polar scales (+2 to −2). The means of these two groups are given in Table 13.4.

Table 13.4 Group means along eight dimensions.

	(i)	(ii)	(iii)	(iv)	(v)	(vi)	(vii)	(viii)
Successful	0.82	1.02	0.27	1.24	1.18	0.76	1.06	1.06
Unsuccessful	−0.92	−1.04	−0.04	0.18	−0.15	0.29	−0.63	−1.29

To decide on a new product, the scores from the rating sheet are read in, and after substituting the sample estimates for the parameters in equation 6, the product is classified. Suppose the profile vector x is (0, 1, 1, 1, 0, 1, 1, 1); how should it be classified?

Using equation 3, the classificatory z value is computed as 0.2. The decision will then depend upon the appropriate costs. Suppose these and other relevant statistics are $C_1 = 4$, $C_2 = 4$, $C_3 = 6$, $r = 2$, and $T = 2$. Since $TC_1 > C_3$, only π_1, and π_3 need to be calculated. From equation 6, $\pi_1 = 0.8$ and $\pi_3 = 2.5$ so that,

$$z_1{}^* = -0.2$$
$$\text{and, } z_3{}^* = +0.9$$

In this case, since $-0.2 < z < 0.9$ the new product should be tested.

Of the 60 products used in the initial sample, 27 of the 33 successful products would have been correctly accepted with these costs, four would have been tested and two rejected. The complete classification is shown in Table 13.5.

Table 13.5 Classification of initial sample.

	Accept	Test	Reject
Successful (33)	27	4	2
Unsuccessful (27)	2	3	22

Assumptions and Extensions

As with regression analysis, the classification procedure outlined above assumes the underlying relationship is linear. In general, this ought not to be too restrictive as appropriate transformations can usually be found to satisfy this requirement. A further criticism might be that it treats the buyer's ratings as interval scales when in fact they are properly only ordinal. There are a number of approaches to this problem. In most situations,

however, the solutions will not be too sensitive to particular scaling assumptions. Alternatively, the problem can be avoided by using the device of dummy variables.[8]

Also in common with multiple regression, observation vectors are taken to be drawn independently from a common covariance matrix. If the groups' covariance matrices are not equal (or approximately equal) the difficulty arises that the procedure leads to non-linear classification boundaries. In this case, some care is necessary in the interpretation of the results.[9]

Another problem frequently mentioned with this type of procedure is obtaining representative past data. To obtain the classification function, the analyst has a choice of using only those products actually accepted by the buyer, or, to use these products plus those originally rejected. The latter choice may appear more representative in that a far larger proportion of all new products are included in the population sampled. On the other hand, this is likely to mean including in the unsuccessful group some which were, or could have been, successful. For this reason, it has been preferred to include only those products accepted by the buyer, and consequently, for which the outcome was known. While the sample is not strictly representative, the classification itself should not be biased systematically.

The analyst needs also to be aware of the fact that ratings may reflect not only differences between the products but also differences among the evaluators. This will be more of a problem where they are evaluated by a buying committee rather than an individual. It could also cause difficulties if buyers changed jobs frequently. In both situations efforts would need to be made to standardize ratings across buyers. This is not an infrequent problem when dealing with scaling exercises.

One difference between the present screening process and devices offered by other writers is the number of dimensions considered. Wilson,[5] for example, suggests some 40 to 50 attributes need to be rated, O'Meara[10] has 17. Standard multi-variate procedures cannot usually deal effectively with so many variables partly because of the number of degrees of freedom used up, and partly because of the multi-collinearity which will occur in such a situation. Statistically, we could handle the problem by factor-analysing the data first and using the resultant factors in our classification function. In the supermarket situation, such a refinement appears unnecessary. Because the problem is fairly well defined it appears more efficient to carefully design the questionnaire and so avoid including redundant data. In other situations, where decisions are more irregular and less well defined (e.g., manufacturers screening new product ideas at the early development stage, cf. O'Meara,[10]) there are greater advantages in considering a large number of attributes and handling the problems through either factory analysis or a step-wise procedure.

Finally, there are a number of other extensions which can easily be made. One is that the buyer's prior probabilities of success or failure can be included. Instead of taking prior probabilities to be equal, it might be more appropriate to give a higher prior to products failing since it is known that the majority of new offerings do not succeed. This means in effect that the right-hand side of equation 5 is multiplied by the logarithm of the ratio of the prior probability of success to the prior probability of failure.[3] In general, if prior probabilities are made to reflect variations in the two sample sizes, there will be fewer misclassifications, but at the same time, it will be less clear how well the independent variables discriminate.[9] Another extension for classificatory analysis suggested by Freimer and Simon is to develop the Bayesian context further by calculating the expected value of perfect information about the product profiles.[4] Such a refinement would probably not be worthwhile operationally in the supermarket situation because perfect information about factor values would never be available even after the stocking of the product. The logical testing procedure appears to be the one described above.

Concluding Observations

With free and perfect information, the supermarket buyer would find it optimal to choose those products offering the highest rate of return to the store. Since information from market research is inevitably imperfect and also costly and time consuming to obtain, buyers adopt rules of thumb and 'satisficing' approaches to these decisions. The method outlined here has attempted to systematize such decision rules through a screening procedure. It presents an effective tool because it allows the buyer to quantify his judgement along the dimensions he considers to be important. It also uses past experience directly and presents a decision rule which minimizes the costs of mis-classification. The data needed to use this procedure are readily available to the buyer. Thus, adoption of the systematic approach to supermarket buying developed here can be readily done and offers significant advantage over the present subjective and informal methods.

References

1 Borden, N.H. Jr., *Acceptance of New Food Products by Supermarkets*, Boston: Harvard University, 1968.
2 Krauser, Andrews and Eassie Limited. *New Products in the Grocery Trade 1971: A UK Study*, London 1971.
3 National Economic Development Office, *The Future Pattern of Shopping*, London: Her Majesty's Stationery Office, 1971.
4 Freimer, M. and Simon, L., 'The Evaluation of Potential New Product Alternatives', *Management Science*, 13, Feb. 1967, 279-292.
5 Wilson, A. 'Industrial Market Research in Britain', *Journal of Marketing Research*, 6 Feb. 1969, 15-27.
6 McKinsey – General Foods Study, *The Economics of Food Distributors*, New York: General Foods Corporation, 1963.
7 Anderson, T.W. *An Introduction to Multivariate Statistical Analysis*, New York: John Wiley & Sons, 1958.
8 Chatterjee, S. and Barcun, S. 'A non-parametric Approach to Credit Screening', *Journal of the American Statistical Association*, 65, Mar. 1970, 150-154.
9 Morrison, D.G. 'On the Interpretation of Discriminant Analysis', *Journal of Marketing Research*, 6, May, 1969, 156-163.
10 O'Meara, J.T. 'Selecting Profitable Products', *Harvard Business Review*, 39, Jan.-Feb. 1961, 83-99.

Notes

[1] This is unlike the situation discussed by Freimer and Simon;[4] there the cost of the decision to test is independent of the outcome and test information is imperfect.
[2] The data can be transformed if necessary to approximate this assumption.
[3] Note that differences in prior probabilities, say q_s and q_u, can easily be taken into account. In this case equation 5 becomes accept if

$$z \geqslant \log\left\{\frac{c_{A/F}}{c_{R/S}}\frac{q_s}{q_u}\right\}$$

[4] The authors have written a short program which carried out the classification procedure.

Exercises & Study Questions

New Products

1. 'Our best source of new product ideas is our research department. They keep up to date with scientific progress and tell us what is technically possible.' What other sources of new product ideas exist? What sort of ideas are they likely to generate?

2. Given that ideas for new products come from many different places, what system is needed to make sure that each idea is properly evaluated?

3. What factors have to be considered in the evaluation of new product ideas?

4. What are the responsibilities for new product development, testing and marketing of the following departments: marketing, sales, production, top management, finance, new products, research.

5. You have been given responsibility for taking an idea for a new product from the initial research stages through to market launch. Draw-up an outline critical path network for this process. You will find this question easier to answer if you refer throughout to a company or industry which you know well.

6. What are the pros and cons of the following possible strategies for launching a new product: launch nationally straight away, launch in a regional market first and gradually extend the market coverage, carry out a test market then launch nationally?

7. You are contemplating the launch of a new fruit juice, to sell at 7p per tin. The market for this sort of product has been fairly steady for some years now at 100 million tins per annum. Your market research manager has given you his estimates of the share you might achieve within a year of launch. These are:

Market share	Probability of achieving this
0	0.05
2	0.1
4	0.2
6	0.3
8	0.2
10	0.1
12	0.05

The fixed costs of production, advertising and distribution, etc. will be £200,000 per annum and variable costs will be 3p per tin. Should you go ahead? A market research firm has offered to carry out a survey which will enable you to predict your market share accurately. How much can you afford to pay for this?

8. Your company has just completed preliminary tests on a preproduction batch of a new line of mechanical diggers. If you start selling them now, there is a 30 per cent chance that you will make very few sales and will lose most of the £100,000 the project has cost so far. There is an equal chance that sales will take off and the project will make a clear profit of £200,000, and a 40 per cent chance that it will make only £50,000. One of your customers is prepared to do a year's field trials of the digger, at a cost to you of £5,000. If the trials turn out well, you will make at least £200,000 clear profit. If they turn out badly you will probably abandon the project. You don't know what the result of the test will be. What should you do, and why?

9. What methods are there for testing products? What are the pros and cons of each one?

Part IV
Product Line Management

Introduction

The methodical analysis of an organization's existing product line has not been a popular topic for management writers, nor, apparently, for practitioners. Innovation and growth have been the fashionable slogans, but new grafts will not 'take' and develop if their way is blocked by dead and decaying wood. One reason for the lack of progress is that the problem is a very difficult one. It is easy to say that unprofitable products should be dropped, but how does a firm with a thousand different products on the market allocate costs to each individual product? Any cost breakdown will be arbitrary, as will the resultant profit figure. In many cases it is not even possible to allocate variable costs with any accuracy, and so contribution cannot be used as the criterion. Nor is it easy to isolate products in a marketing sense. Nuts may be unprofitable, but if nut manufacture is stopped, this will make it much more difficult to sell bolts. Many firms carry loss leaders or a 'fighting brand' to attract customers or maintain a position in the market.

It can also be expensive to discontinue a product. Customers may lose confidence in the firm's ability to supply them in the future, obsolete spares will have to be stocked and existing machinery may become redundant. Inertia and sentiment also play a part. Change involves risk, and it may appear more attractive to prolong the life of an existing product by what is, in effect, cosmetic surgery than to court danger with something new.

In this context Glen Urban's article, the first in this section, is a notable pioneering effort. He constructs an equation for a product's sales as a function of product class marketing variables, product class interdependencies and intragroup competitive brand effects. By combining this with a cost equation, it is possible to measure the profitability of a product. Unfortunately, to be useful, this model requires that an enormous amount of data be collected, as it involves a number of cross elasticities. Urban lists thirty in an example involving only three products.

In the second article John Winkler discusses the broader issues of product line management. Signposts of an inadequate product mix are declining sales or profits, highly seasonal sales, or an unbalanced range, where a few products account for almost all the sales. The problem facing management is how to allocate a limited amount of marketing resources to the greatest effect, instead of, as is usually the case, putting too much effort behind the failures. Winkler also lists ways of upgrading the product line, by improving such things as style, quality or service.

Elton & Mercer measure the interdependence of products by estimating the probability of a sale being lost because a suitable model is not available. It is then possible to estimate the trade off between increased variety (less sales lost through unavailability) and reduced service level (greater likelihood of being out of stock). They use, as an example, a retail chain, with limited storage, but the method could be used for a manufacturing concern, with limited capacity. J.T. Rothe tackles the most difficult problem, that of deciding when to drop products. Basing his questionnaire largely on a decision model proposed by Philip Kotler*, he has surveyed a number of firms to find out what procedures they used.

* Philip Kotler, 'Phasing out Weak Products', Harvard Business Review, 107, Mar.-Apr. 1965.

14.

A Mathematical Modelling Approach to Product Line Decisions

by Glen L. Urban

Reprinted from the Journal of Marketing Research, Vol. VI, February, 1969 published by the American Marketing Association.

Introduction

Most firms market several somewhat similar products called a product line. Policies of product diversification and new product introduction have been implemented by widening the product line. Depth in the product line has emerged as firms attempt to meet competition and satisfy the needs of the market's subsegments. Although the multi-product firm has grown in importance, there has not been a corresponding growth in model-building and research to help solve the marketing problems of firms with a product line.

Product line decisions are difficult because the products in the line are not usually independent. Products cannot be optimized individually and then added to the line to produce optimum product line results. The marketing mix established for one product may affect the sales of another product; inter-dependency is the key consideration in product line decision-making. This article develops a mathematical product line model that analyses the marketing strategy implications of product interdependency. The model will be developed by *a priori* reasoning and will be subjected to a preliminary test based on empirical market data.

A Mathematical Model of the Product Line Decision

Model Development Criterion

In developing a model of product line effects many approaches are available ranging from micro-analytic simulations and its potential for a highly disaggregated consideration of the consumer choice process [1] to a highly aggregated model that might be represented in a simple linear regression model. Between these extremes there are several other levels of aggregation such as complex single equation and multiple equation models.

In developing the model proposed in this article, two criteria were established. The first was decision relevance, i.e., the model should encompass the major

factors and market phenomena affecting the problem of finding the best marketing mix for a product line. The second criterion is reflected in the doctrine of parsimony and requires that simple models be preferred whenever possible. These criteria suggest the development goal that the product line model should be the simplest model that encompasses the relevant market phenomena and is useful in decision-making.

To specify the relevant phenomena the basic consumer choice process should be examined. [2] For example, consider the purchasing process for four classes of goods related to shaving: electric shavers, safety razors, aerosol shaving cream, and after-shave lotion. The consumer choice process originates with the development of an awareness of these classes of goods and the particular brands in these classes. Awareness may be produced by advertising, personal selling, word of mouth, or post-buying experience.

The consumer also forms attitudes about each product class, the relationship between these classes, and the brands in the classes. These attitudes may be directed toward product characteristics or advertising appeals. For example, consumers will form attitudes about electric shavers and their advertising appeals. They will also form attitudes about electric *v.* safety razors, and electric razors *v.* after-shave lotion. These consumer attitudes become prime factors for developing a perceived need for the products. When the level of perceived need is sufficient, a search effort — a shopping trip in this example — is conducted and a purchase decision is made. In the store the consumer is influenced by point of purchase communication, and he integrates this new information with existing attitudes. The consumer will choose the product with the greatest perceived utility per dollar, assuming a satisfactory alternative is present. It can be expected that the consumer's willingness to buy a product at a given price will depend on his attitude toward the product's characteristics and appeals. This implies a marketing mix effect between price and advertising since price response will depend on the level of advertising.

In examining the purchase decision the effects between and within product classes should be considered. Since the proneness to purchase from a group is a function of the perceived need for that group, the combined advertising of all brands in the group may influence the attitudes and utility ascribed to the product class. For example, if all brands of after-shave lotion increase their advertising, the attitudes and sales of the group may increase. The same product group phenomena could occur for other product classes, such as safety razors and electric razors. However, in these cases the additional sales generated by a group may be obtained from a related product group. For example, if all safety razor brands increase their advertising, consumers may develop attitudes that suggest substitution of safety razors for electric shavers. Substitution is not the only possible intergroup effect; some groups may be complementary. If advertising of safety razors increases, the perceived need for shaving cream and perhaps after-shave lotion may increase.

An intragroup phenomenon, the competition of brands within the group, also exists. If consumers choose a brand because of relative utility per dollar, the selection reflects a combination of attitudes and price and implies that the relative marketing mix effects of brands are significant. For example, the in-store choice of Schick over Gillette would probably reflect the combined advertising, promotion and price advantage of Schick over Gillette as perceived in the customer's utility assessment.

From this brief and simplified consideration of the process, an *a priori* specification of the most important phenomena can be derived. For the model three factors were identified as having high behavioral and decision relevance: (*a*) aggregate product class marketing mix effects, (*b*) product class interdependencies, and (*c*) intragroup relative competitive brand effects. The goal was to design a simple model of these phenomena for aiding product line decisions.

Aggregate Product Class Marketing Mix Effects

For a simple model of the combined effects of price and non-price marketing activity, an aggregate sales response function will be postulated. This function should include three basic marketing variables: advertising, price, and distribution. Distribution may be measured by the percentage of outlets carrying the product, the number of salesmen selling the product, the middleman's margin

on the product, or a combination of these. The simplest form would be a linear equation of these variables, but this has two disadvantages. First, it does not allow marketing mix effects since the sales response to a variable is not affected by other variables. Second, the linear form would imply a linear response to advertising which can lead to unreasonable decision implications since it usually implies extremes of large or small levels of advertising. A linear form would also not allow for decreasing effects on advertising expenditure.[3] The next most appropriate form for representing the mix effects is a linear log function. In unlogged form the formulation would be:[4]

$$X_{jI} = a\, P_{jI}^{EPI}\, A_{jI}^{EAI}\, D_{jI}^{EDI} \tag{1}$$

X_{jI} is industry sales of product j

a is a scale constant

P_{jI} is average price level of all brands in product group j

A_{jI} is total advertising of all brands in product group j

D_{jI} is total distribution level for all brands in product group j

EPI is industry price elasticity for product j

EAI is industry advertising elasticity for product j

EDI is industry distribution elasticity for product j.

This function captures marketing mix effects and allows nonlinearity in response to marketing variables. The nonlinearity is reflected in the parameters EPI, EAI, and EDI. For example, if $0 < EAI < 1$, the marginal sales response to advertising would be constantly decreasing as advertising increases. If $EAI = 0$, total group advertising does not affect the group's total sales. In general, EAI and EDI should be expected to fall between 0 and +1. The price parameter EPI should be negative because as price increases, sales should decrease. The parameters EAI, EDI, and EPI are elasticities and reflect the proportionate changes in the product group's sales resulting from a proportionate change in one variable.

Equation 1 reflects marketing mix effects since the sales response of one variable depends on other variables as established, for example, by differentiating equation 1 with respect to price. The marginal response to price changes (dX_{jI}/dP_{jI}) depends on the level of advertising and distribution. Differentiating equation 1 with respect to the other variables will yield similar results.

Equation 1 is appropriate for this model since it satisfies the twin criteria of decision relevance and simplicity; that is, it includes non-linear marketing mix effects in a simple form.[5] In addition, equation 1 can be estimated by linear logarithmic regression.

Product Class Interdependencies

Two basic kinds of interdependencies exist, complementarity and substitutability. Substitutability implies an introspective consumer attitude of substituting one product for another under certain conditions; complementarity implies that one product will be purchased along with another product. Substitution or complementary effects of one product group with other product groups are essential to a product line model. To include nonlinearity and marketing mix effects in the consideration of interdependency, the general form of equation 1 seems applicable. In considering intergroup effects the variables would relate to other groups, and a reasonable form would be:

$$b \ P_{IM}^{CPjM} \ A_{IM}^{CAjM} \ D_{IM}^{CDjM}, \qquad (2)$$

b is scale constant
P_{IM} is average price of product group M
A_{IM} is total advertising level for product group M
D_{IM} is total distribution level for product group M
CP_{jM} is cross price elasticity for products j and M
$CAjM$ is cross advertising elasticity for products j and M
$CDjM$ is cross distribution elasticity for products j and M.

The equation's parameters — cross elasticities of price, advertising, and distribution — have theoretical economic content; they measure product interdependency. The cross price elasticity between products 1 and 2 is:

$$CP12 = \frac{dx_1/x_1}{dP_2/P_2}$$

x_1 is sales of product 1
P_2 is price of product 2

In general if the cross-price elasticity is positive, the products are substitutes and if negative, the products are complements.[6] Since price is not the only appropriate variable for monitoring interdependencies, promotion and distribution cross elasticities should be considered. The cross advertising elasticity is:

$$CA12 = \frac{dx_1/x_1}{dA_2/A_2}$$

x_1 is sales of product 1
A_2 is advertising for product 2

If this elasticity is positive, the goods demonstrate complementarity and if negative, substitutability. The same implications are true for distribution. Interdependencies should be monitored through several variables since a product may be a substitute with respect to one and a complement with respect to another.

Notation 2 is a good model choice since it allows non-linear interdependency effects and considers the marketing mix effects between products as it retains a simple form for log-linear regressions.

The group marketing mix and intergroup product interdependencies can be combined to specify the total sales of one product class as:

$$X_{jI} = kP_{jI}^{EPI} \ A_{jI}^{EAI} \ D_{jI}^{EDI} \ (II_M P_{IM}^{CPjM} \ A_{IM}^{CAjM} \ D_{IM}^{CDjM}) \quad (3)$$

where II_M is product sum over M, $M \neq j$ and k is scale constant.

Intragroup Competitive Brand Effects

The market share a brand gets will reflect that brand's relative marketing effectiveness compared with that of other brands in the product group. Relative effectiveness was pre-specified as relevant for the theoretical presumption that the consumer-buying process entails comparing the perceived utility of competing products. A simple form for representing relative market share effects would be by a firm's advertising expenditure compared with the total industry's advertising. However, this does not include the marketing mix effects of each brand. Since the consumer judges each product by its overall utility, brand choice could be formulated by representing each brand's mix effects and adding the relative effectiveness. A form for representing mix effects of a product was developed in equation 1. A market share expression using this format and including relative mix effects is:

Market share for product j in firm 1 =
$$\frac{P_{1j}^{SP1} \ A_{1j}^{SA1} \ D_{1j}^{SD1}}{\Sigma P_{ij}^{SPi} A_{ij}^{SAi} D_{ij}^{SD1}} \qquad (4)$$

P_{ij} is price of product j by firm i
A_{ij} is advertising level for product j by firm i
D_{ij} is distribution level for product j by firm i
SP_i is competitive price sensitivity for firm i and product j
SA_i is competitive advertising sensitivity for firm i and product j
SA_i is competitive distribution sensitivity for firm i and product j.

Equation 3 seems complicated, but it is the simplest equation that captures the pre-specified relevant phenomena of marketing mix and the relative brand choice.[7] The parameters of the equation reflect the market share sensitivity of each brand's marketing variables.[8] These parameters are individualized to allow the consideration of product differentiation within each product group.

Given equation 3, the effects of various strategies and counter-strategies can be related to the market share a firm will receive. For example, if firm 1 is the price leader for a homogeneous product market ($EP1 = EPi$), price lowering by that firm would be followed by price lowering of other firms with no change in market share. However, industry effects described in the previous section may be produced. Given a strategy and set of counter-strategies, this expression could be used to consider intra-product group competitive brand effects.[9]

Demand, Cost and Profit Models for a Firm

The sub-models developed in the previous three sections can be combined into one equation to describe the sales of one brand of a product class. The sales of firm 1's brand in product j class is:

$$x_j = kP_{jI}^{EPI} A_{jI}^{EAI} D_{jI}^{EDI} [\Pi_M P_{IM}^{CPjM} A_{IM}^{CAjM} D_{IM}^{CDjM}] \quad (5)$$

$$\begin{bmatrix} P_{Ij}^{SP1} A_{Ij}^{SA1} D_{Ij}^{SD1} \\ \sum_i P_{ij}^{SPi} A_{ij}^{SAi} D_{ij}^{SDi} \end{bmatrix}$$

where Π_M is product sum over M, $M \neq j$, and other notations as previously defined. Given constant direct and cross elasticities and sensitivities, this equation represents the demand for one product of a firm's product line. This formulation could be extended to include more than three marketing variables by specifying the appropriate direct and cross-elasticities and sensitivities.

A firm's total revenue is the sum of each product's price times its sales. To calculate profit, costs must be specified. The costs may be in the simple form of fixed plus variable costs, but if the products share common production resources, this is unlikely. If there are production interdependencies, a linear programming model designed to minimize the cost of producing specified quantities of the products could be used. Successive runs of this model or cost records could provide the data for estimating an interdependent cost function such as:

$$TVC_j = AVC_j(x_j) \Pi_M (X_M)^{CCjM} \quad (6)$$

TVC_j is total variable cost of producing the firm's brand of product j

AVC_j is average variable cost function for the firm's brand of product j, if produced independently of other products

x_j is quantity of brand of product j produced

x_M is quantity of brand of product M produced, (M $\neq$ j)

$CCjM$ is cross cost elasticity of firm's brands products j and M, (M $\neq$ j)

Subtracting the variable cost and fixed production, advertising and distribution costs from the total revenue will yield total profit.

Combining the cost and demand equations in the calculation of profit results in a simple model that includes the phenomena that were considered *a priori* to have high decision relevance.

Output of Model

Assuming the firm's problem in the short-run is to maximize the total profit subject to existing technical, managerial, financial, and production constraints, the output of the model should be the best marketing strategy for each brand in the firm's product line. This requires the optimization of the model's profit function which is difficult since the model is not amenable to mathematical programming or other analytical techniques. However, it may be solved by an iterative search routine.[10]

The feasibility of gaining the described output from the model rests on the ability to generate meaningful input and on the presence of a practical solution method. The direct and cross-elasticities could be estimated on a subjective basis that reflects the decision-maker's best judgement. This approach might be justified since the decision must be made and if the model is not used, a simpler and perhaps less accurate decision procedure would be used. However, subjective inputs should be used only after all empirical information relating to the problem has been considered.

The model developed could be especially useful to firms using brand managers since it can be a basis of allocating resources to each brand in the product line. The brand manager concept artificially imposes independence between specific products in the line by delegating products to competing brand managers. But if resources are allocated on the basis of product interdependencies at the top marketing management level, the motivational advantages of the brand manager concept and the use of product line resources to maximize total line profits can be compatible.

Table 14.1 Product group elasticities and cross-elasticities separated by producer and competitors[a]

Elasticity	Class	Product 1 (j = 1)	Product 2 (j = 2)	Product 3 (j = 3)
Price elasticity of	Us	−3.83[b]	−1.86[b]	−2.64[b]
product j (EPI)	Them	−[e]	−1.01[d]	0.26
Facing elasticity of	Us	−0.173	0.113	0.157
product j (EFI)	Them		0.837[b]	0.038
Cross-price elasticity between products j & 1 (CPj1)	Us		0.266	1.28
Cross-facing elasticity between products j & 1 (CFj1)	Us		−0.081	0.162
Cross-price elasticity between products j & 2 (CPj2)	Us	−0.91		1.67[c]
	Them	−0.55		−1.61
Cross-facing elasticity between products j & 2 (CFj2)	Us	0.24		−0.105
	Them	0.38[d]		0.41[d]
Cross-price elasticity between products j & 3 (CPj3)	Us	−0.29	−1.55[b]	
	Them	0.207[c]	0.136[b]	
Cross-facing elasticity between products j & 3 (CFj3)	Us	0.11	−0.42[d]	
	Them	−0.301[d]	0.09	
R^2		0.52[b]	0.61[b]	0.51[b]

[a] Significance is based on one tail test for direct elasticities and two tail tests on cross elasticities.

[b] Significant at 0.01 level.

[c] Significant at 0.05 level.

[d] Significant at 0.10 level.

[e] There was no competition in product 1's market.

Note: 'Us' is our brand in product group j; 'them' is all other brands in product group j.

CPiN > 0 ⇒ substitutes	CFiN > 0 ⇒ complements
CPiN < 0 ⇒ complements	CFiN > 0 ⇒ substitutes

An Empirical Application

To test the descriptive adequacy and usefulness of the proposed model in a real product line problem, 100 grocery store audits of a three-product line of related frequently purchased consumer goods were used.[11] These product line data were used to estimate the parameters of the product-line model, and an on-line computer search programme derived the optimum marketing mix for each product in the producer's line.

The audited product line contained three classes of products that served the same food need but had different product features. Product group 1 was a new product and only the firm to be examined offered a brand in this class. The competitors in product groups 2 and 3 were aggregated into one competitor in each market. The aggregation resulted in a firm with a three-product line and brands which faced no competitors in product group 1, one competitor in product group 2, and one competitor in product group 3.

In each product class the brand, shelf price, number of facings, deals, and special displays were recorded in the audits. Over 95 per cent of the data were recorded with cents-off or bonus-size deals. Hence, dealing was not considered a separate variable since it could be reflected in the price per unit. Special displays occurred so infrequently (less than 1 per cent of the data) that they were not considered in the analysis. The audits did not monitor national or local advertising in the test area. It was assumed that none of the brands received a disproportionate amount of local advertising at any of the audited stores, and advertising was not considered as a variable in the testing.

Model Parameter Estimation

Product Class Marketing Effects and Product Interdependency

The product group elasticities and cross-elasticities for each product class were obtained by linear logarithm regressions of equation 3 where distribution is represented by the number of total facings of the product group and where advertising is omitted. All the direct price elasticities obtained from this regression were negative, and all facings' elasticities were positive as expected and significant at least at the 0.05 level. The significant cross elasticities of price and facings for the products indicated that the three product groups were basically complementary. This complementarity did not agree with *a priori* feelings and past studies that indicated these kinds of products could be competing for the same buyers in the general product class.[12] This finding implies that the pre-specification of the model's product interdependency section was not satisfactory.

To explore alternative forms for updating the model, the interdependencies between our brand in a product group and other product groups were postulated to be different from other brands in the group. To evaluate this updated model structure, the industry price and facing data for each product group were subdivided into 'us' and 'them' classes. 'Us' was our brand price and facings and 'them' was the average price and facing for all other competitors. The elasticities and cross-elasticities for the firm us and the competitors them in each product are indicated in Table 14.1.

An examination of cross elasticities for product 1 indicates that product 1 was complementary to both our brand and other competitive brands of product 2. Cross-elasticities for product 3 indicate that product 1 was complementary to our brand of product 3 but shows substitution effects with other brands in product 3. Product group 2 was complementary to our brand in the product 3 group but was a substitute for competitive brands in product 3's market. Although the initial regression showed products 1 and 2 to be complementary to product 3, the new regressions (Table 14.1) indicate that complementarity was with our brands of product 3, and that products 1 and 2 were competitive with other brands of product 3. This is the interdependency pattern a marketing manager would desire.

Product group 3 showed no significant interdependencies with product 1 but displayed some interesting relationships with product group 2. $CP32_{us} = 1.67$ indicates our brand of product 2 was a substitute for product 3. But $CP23_{us} = -1.55$ indicates product 2's sales were complementary to our brand of product 3. The asymmetry in the interdependency is significant at the five per cent level and the elasticities are large, i.e., greater than one.[13]

That product group 3 felt substitution effects from our brand of product 2 is understandable. As the price of our brand of product 2 increased, our brand buyers substituted product 3. That product group 2 felt complementary effects from our brand of product 3 is more difficult to explain. $CP23_{us} = -1.55$ so that a ten per cent reduction in the price of our brand of product 3 caused a 15.5 per cent increase in the sales of product 2. This could have occurred if buyers of our brand of product 3 had also bought product 2 when they perceived low prices for this class of goods. If the perception is based on the price of product 3, lowering our brand's prices of product 3 could have caused a perception of low prices for these buyers. They might have bought more of product 2 with little sensitivity to its price. The income effect caused by lower prices in brand 3 also indicates complementarity. This increase in real income might have led to additional purchases of product 2.

Except for the asymmetry, the new regressions

indicate that the products within the firm's product line are complementary but are substitutes for products in other firms' product lines. The split product group regressions explained 30 per cent more of the variance in the data than the earlier regressions so updating the model for split interactions is advisable.

Intragroup Competitive Brand Sensitivities

The estimation of the competitive sensitivities to be used in describing market share effects (see equation 4 with facings representing D and omitting A) was carried out by a computer program to minimize the total variation between the actual market shares and the market shares predicted by equation 4 given a set of sensitivities, observed prices, and observed facings. The estimation was executed on the MIT computation centres compatible time-sharing system. The interactive ability of an on-line system was used in a conversational program that asks the researcher or manager to supply initial estimates of the price and facing sensitivities for the firm and its competitors. These initial sensitivities are incremented by an amount prescribed by the manager. The number of incremental steps to be taken for each sensitivity is also an on-line input supplied by the manager. All combinations of the initial and incremented sensitivities are evaluated; the set of sensitivities producing the minimum total variation for the audit data points is recorded.

Then the manager is asked to supply a new increment and number of steps for the search. The next evaluation uses the best past estimates as initial values. By continuing this process the manager can guide the search until it has reached a prescribed level of accuracy. This procedure does not guarantee that the optimal fit has been achieved; rather, it is a heuristic procedure based on the manager's best judgement and the computational power of a high speed computer.[14]

The minimum variation estimates for the two competitive product markets are shown in the tabulation. The estimates explain 24 per cent of the variance of the market shares in product 2 and 54 per cent of product 3's market shares. This empirical success adds confidence to the *a priori* specification of the competitive phenomena.[15]

Producer	Product 2		Product 3	
	Price	Facing	Price	Facing
Our firm	−0.27	1.31	−0.855	1.13
Competitor	0.00	0.75	−1.24	1.20

Table 14.2 Search results

Variable	Reference	No interaction	Product group interaction	Split product-group interaction
Price of product 1	20.5	.16.8	16.8	16.8
Price of product 2	17.0	22.0[a]	22.0[a]	22.0[a]
Price of product 3	21.0	26.0[a]	26.0[a]	16.0[a]
Facings of product 1	2.00	0.75[a]	0.75[a]	0.75[a]
Facings of product 2	4.00	3.50	6.25	6.50
Facings of product 3	2.00	3.75	1.00	0.75[a]
Total profit	382,600	594,500	585,180	908,700
Profit of product 1	107,100	128,000	158,700	154,000
Profit of product 2	184,600	299,800	324,400	704,800
Profit of product 3	90,900	166,700	102,000	49,900
Sales for product 1	1,500,000	3,083,200	3,722,200	3,625,600
Sales for product 2	2,500,000	2,421,700	2,611,100	5,537,100
Sales for product 3	1,000,000	1,167,400	762,200	1,165,200
Market share for product 1	100%	100%	100%	100%
Market share for product 2	29.64%	28.76%	31.01%	31.1%
Market share for product 3	74.79%	70.03%	72.03%	80.37%

[a] These values are at the upper or lower limit of the data used for estimation.

The competitive sensitivities in product 2 indicate that the competitor has little or no effect on market share by his change in prices while changes in our price have a negative sensitivity. The facings sensitivities of product 2 indicated our firm's facings were 1.5 times as effective as the competitor's in producing market share changes. The product 3 competitive estimates indicated our firm's price and facing variables were less effective in changing market share than the competitor's.

The estimation of the competitive sensitivities completes the parameter estimation for the model's demand equation (see equation 5). The remaining demand input is the strategy competitors were expected to use; they were expected to be non-adaptive with respect to the number facings and price for product 2 and be followers with respect to product 3. The final input to the model is the cost function (see equation 6). In this test application the costs for each product were independent, and the marginal costs were considered constant over the meaningful range of production.

Optimization of Product Line Profit

The maximization of the model's product line profit was carried out by an on-line computer search routine.[16] The trial and error routine began by evaluating a reference set of prices and facings for each of the three products and then examining a range of values on each side of the reference values in discrete steps. The range and steps were specified from the remote computer console. Given the increments and ranges all combinations of the trial values were run, and the best total product line profit based on equations 1 to 6 with the estimated parameters was recorded. After the first series of trials have been reported, the manager can respecify the step intervals and ranges. By continuing this process he can achieve the desired level of accuracy. One constraint was placed on the search — the total facings had to be less than eight for our product line. This constraint forces the search routine to allocate the shelf space between the products in the line.

The search programme results are shown in Table 14.2. The first column gives the price per unit, facings weighted by package size, profit, sales, and market share for our brand of each product at the reference level. The reference results are based on the average price and facings for each group as observed in the audits.

The next question was whether the interdependencies between products should be considered at the aggregate product group level or at the split-product group level. The empirical estimation indicated that the model should be updated for the split, but if the decision were insensitive to the added complexity of the split, it might be omitted. A sensitivity analysis determined if the optimum marketing strategy was different under varying interaction assumptions.

To establish a reference base in evaluating decision sensitivity, the most profitable programme with no interactions was found. It was considerably different from the reference programme. The price of product 1 was decreased but the prices for products 2 and 3 were increased. The facing's allocation was also altered. Products 1 and 2 received fewer facings but product 3 received more. The result of an improvement in profit of over 50 per cent and an increase in the sales of each product implies that on the basis of the model the existing strategy was nonoptimal.

The best programme with aggregate product group interaction led to the same price structure as the no interaction case. The facing allocation was changed, however (see Table 14.2). The facings were concentrated in product 2 because of the complementarity between the facings of product 2 and sales of products 1 and 3 in the regressions.

The next phase of the sensitivity analysis was to determine the maximum profit for the most empirically valid case — split-product-group interactions. In this case a different pricing strategy should be used. The price of product 3 is lower than even the reference price primarily because of the complementarity of the price of our brand of product 3 and the sales of product 2 (see Table 14.1). The product line profits in this analysis were 50 per cent greater than in the no interaction or group interaction cases. Additional profits occurred in product 2, but the profits in product 3 decreased almost 70 per cent because of the asymmetric product interdependencies between our brands of products 2 and 3. The decision output is sensitive to the splitting of the interactions; since this is the most empirically viable model structure, the model should be updated to reflect the differences in the product interdependencies between our brands and other brands in other product groups.

The output of the optimization and sensitivity testing can be summarized in the recommendations that the price of product 1 be lowered, the price of product 2 be raised, and the facings allocation be more concentrated on product 2. The price of product 3 should be lowered if the asymmetric interdependency between products 2 and 3 is real as it appears to be. Additional study is necessary to ascertain the underlying behaviour that generates the asymmetric condition, but updating the model for split interactions is recommended since application of the model identified significant product interdependencies and recommended changes in the marketing mix of the products in the line so that the interdependencies could be exploited for additional profit. The updated model possesses reasonable descriptive adequacy and decision relevance.

Summary and Extensions

This article presented an *a priori* product line model for finding the best marketing mix for each product in a line. The model includes aggregate product group marketing mix, product interdependency, and competitive brand effects. The initial testing of the model suggests that the basic structure is appropriate and the model deserves additional consideration, testing, and development.

The model analysis could be extended in several ways. First, the model was a static one period model; the analysis could be extended to include carry-over effects and the problem of multiperiod marketing mix determination. Second, the model test application examined only three related products; it would be useful to expand the test product definitions to include other classes of products or to narrow the product definition to consider package sizes in each product. A hierarchy of interdependencies exists, and a sequential application of the model to increasingly more specific product definitions would be appropriate. Third, the multiple regression and iterative search routines used to estimate the model's parameters were applied to a limited data base of 100 store audits. Although reasonable descriptive adequacy was found, it would be useful to have an information system that builds a data bank on the products' performances to obtain more accurate input estimates and test more complex response forms. And consideration of the effects of adding or dropping a product from the line and the effects of this action on the marketing mix would extend the analysis.[1][2]

References

1 Amstutz, E.A. *Computer Simulation of Competitive Market Response*, Cambridge, Mass.: MIT Press, 1967.
2 Benjamin, B. and Maitland, J. 'Operational Research and Advertising: Some Experiments in the Use of Analogies', *Operational Research Quarterly*, 9 (Sept. 1958), 207-17.
3 Benjamin, B., Jolly, W.P. and Maitland, J. 'Operational Research and Advertising: Theories of Response', *Operational Research Quarterly*, 11 (Dec. 1960), 205-18.

4 Douglas, P.H. *Theory of Wages*, New York: The Macmillan Company, 1934.

5 Henderson, P.L., Hind, J.F. and Brown, S.E. 'Sales Effects of Two Campaign Themes', *Journal of Advertising Research*, 1 (Dec. 1961), 2-11.

6 Kotler, P. 'Competitive Strategies for New Product Marketing Over the Life Cycle', *Management Science*, 12 (Dec. 1965), 104-19.

7 Kuehn, A.A. and Weiss, D.L. 'Market Analysis Training Exercise', *Behavioral Science*, 10 (Jan. 1965), 51-62.

8 Massy, W.F. and Frank, R.E. 'Short Term Price and Dealing Effects in Selected Market Segments', *Journal of Marketing Research*, 3 (May 1965), 171-85.

9 Nicosia, F.M. *Consumer Decision Processes*, Englewood Cliffs, N.J.: Prentice-Hall, Inc., 1966.

10 Shakun, M. 'A Dynamic Model for Competitive Marketing in Coupled Markets', *Management Science*, 12 (Aug. 1966), 525-30.

11 Urban, G.L. 'Sprinter: A Tool for New Product Decision Makers', *Industrial Management Review*, 8 (Spring 1967), 43-55.

12 Urban, G.L. 'A New Product Analysis and Decision Model', *Management Science*, 14 (Apr. 1968), 490-517.

13 Urban, G.L. 'An On-Line Technique for Estimating and Analyzing Complex Models', in Reed Moyer, ed., *Changing Marketing Systems*, Winter Conference Proceedings, American Marketing Association, 1967, 322-7.

14 Wilde, D. and Beightler, C.S. *Foundations of Optimization*, Englewood Cliffs, N.J.: Prentice-Hall, Inc., 1967.

Notes

[1] See [1].

[2] This brief description is consistent with Nicosia's basic structure. See [9].

[3] For empirical consideration of decreasing returns to advertising, see [2, 3].

[4] This is similar in form to the Cobb-Douglas production function used by many authors in marketing, see [4]. For theoretical uses see [6, 7]. For empirical support see [8].

[5] For a discussion of more complex response forms, see [11]. If equation 1 is not empirically viable, more complex forms should be investigated.

[6] This reasoning is not valid for a product that violates the law of demand (e.g., a Giffin good) because as price increase sales increase.

[7] For a discussion of a more complex form including advertising interdependency in the consideration of competitive effects, see [10].

[8] The sensitivities appear to be similar to elasticities, but they are not elasticities. They do not represent proportionate changes in market share as the result of proportionate changes in the variable. However, they do represent the sensitivity of the market share to changes in the marketing mix for each firm. Equation 4 is similar to Kotler[6] except the sensitivities are subscripted to allow the possibility of differentiated products and response.

[9] For game theoretic considerations of this form, see [6, 10].

[10] See the application section of this article and ref[14].

[11] The author thanks Samuel G. Barton and I.J. Abrams of the Market Research Corporation of America for use of these data. The product line is not identified to protect the interests of the producer and MRCA.

[12] See [5].

[13] This asymmetry was difficult to accept, so step-wise multiple regressions were run for our brand sales in markets for products 2 and 3. The asymmetry again appeared at the five per cent significance level. Analysis of the correlation matrix showed little multi-colinearity between the variables. Since the data was taken at one point in time, auto-correlation in the data was not suspected. If there had been multi-colinearity in the auto-correlation, this might have caused the asymmetry. The elasticity of store size averaged 0.08 for the relevant brands. This appeared reasonable and supported the assumption that the stores represented a simple sample with respect to market responses to the variables.

[14] For details of the search technique, see ref [13]

[15] The pre-specified structure was also reinforced since simple log-linear regressions of the two firms' prices and facings against sales produced low R^2 values and unreasonable coefficients in the two products. This suggests that the proposed form is a relevant level of detail.

[16] See [13].

5.
Product Planning
by John Winkler

This article originally appeared as Chapter 10 of Winkler on Marketing Planning, J. Winker, Cassell/Associated Business Programmes Ltd, London, 1972 and is reprinted with permission.

A company's product mix sets the upper limit for its potential profitability. The quality of the company's marketing programme determines how far this limit is reached. Therefore there are two factors to adjust constantly in order to optimize profits. One is the product range, and the other is the marketing programme to support the product range. The term 'product planning' embraces both of these factors at the same time. This subject is at the core of company profitability.

The composition of the range of products which a company offers for sale is called the product mix. There are three aspects to this mix, which shall be discussed here. The first is the width of product range, referring to the number of different items offered for sale. The second is the depth of the mix, which relates to the number of products offered within each group of similar products. The third is the consistency of the mix, which refers to the degree to which products within the range are similar to each other in terms of their end-use, their distribution channels, or their production requirements.

Products within the range are being modified continuously; more often by managers outside the marketing function. For example, different classes of raw materials are purchased from time to time, yielding different quality levels. Alterations in production systems, or in control, provide different product results. Changes in distribution systems may affect product quality, in terms of freshness, or breakage. Countless pressures are exerted on all products every day and strictly these should result in only marginal changes. These changes should be within the levels of tolerance agreed by the marketing function as being acceptable in relation to competitive standards.

Products have intangible characteristics also, which are recognized by the customers as being part of the product's 'personality'. Products are known for their sales appeal, for their colour, for their advertising, for their packaging, for their shape and size, for their after-sales service; and they are known as belonging to the general family of products sold by the organization. Marketing men change these factors directly, constantly, and usually without knowing the true end result of changes they make.

The truly profit-oriented marketing manager is recognized primarily by his ability to increase the total profitability of the product mix he handles. There are only three points of attack – an attack on costs, an attack on price levels and discounts, and an attack on sales turnover.

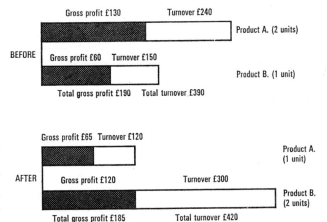

Figure 15.1 How an increase in your sales may result in a reduction in your profits.

Product A outsells product B by 2 to 1.
Product A sells for £120 and earns a gross profit of £65.
Product B sells for £150 and earns a gross profit of £60.
Product B is easier to sell than product A. A new sales campaign, concentrating on this product increases sales turnover by just over 7½ per cent. At the end of the campaign product B is outselling product A by 2 to 1 having substituted sales of product A.
What happens to gross profit?
As a result of the campaign the turnover has therefore increased but the gross profit margins have been reduced by just over 2½ per cent.
If there are no savings in overheads or marketing costs flowing from the change in product sales mix, then this loss of gross margin must be paid out of *net profit*. There is nowhere else for it to come from.
If the company normally makes a 10 per cent net profit rate, then as a result of these increased sales it could be losing up to one-quarter of its net profits.

Seven possible alternatives present themselves when modifying products. The use of each technique is dependent upon the circumstances of the product in relation to the buyer, and matched with the product objectives.

Quality improvement

Most managements seek to improve product quality constantly, in the belief that this will strengthen their competitive position. However, the deliberate and sustained effort to build-in extra 'quality' as perceived by the engineer, through the use of, say, higher-grade materials, may not achieve the desired effect of increasing 'quality' as perceived by the buyer.

There are four levels of quality improvement in descending order of relevance to the market. The first, and most important, is the quality improvement which is perceived as such by a significant number of buyers, in both the appearance of the product and in its performance.

The second is the improvement which is not visually observable by a significant number of buyers, but is one which they detect in improved product performance once they try it.

The third is the improvement in quality which is aimed at a specialized end use, and only of significance to a proportion of the buyers.

The fourth is the improvement to the product which not only cannot be perceived visually, but cannot be easily detected in the product function; the existence of which the buyers must take for granted. Many proprietary medicines come into this category.

Feature improvement

This aims at increasing the number of real or imagined product benefits. The first cameras were bulky, heavy things. With an improvement in lenses and shutters, a series of alternative speeds was made available, and miniature versions were developed. This led on to built-in range finders: then built-in exposure meters; and flash connections. Such feature improvements are designed to increase the range and scale of the product's use. They can be adapted to appeal to special segments of the market. They are flexible, and here the problem may lie, for it is often fairly easy for a competitor to copy a successful new feature.

Style improvements

This aims at improving the aesthetic appeal of the product, rather than its functional performance. In certain classes of goods, it may be the critical factor governing the buyers' choice, and excellent styling may even outweigh some functional disadvantages. For example, very fine glassware needs to be handled with extreme care (one disadvantage), and it is expensive (another disadvantage). But it appeals to our sense of fashion or taste nevertheless.

Colour, shape and texture are the three most common variables when building style improvements. Style improvements often may be limited to packaging or pack design. Nearly all buyers, including industrial companies, respond to good, clear, presentation. Even when tendering for contracts, companies using glossy presentations have been known to edge out bids from companies which present them poorly.

The importance of having a high level of presentation in marketing products cannot be emphasized strongly enough. The presentation must be appropriate to the market, and to the product function. In competitive situations buyers often make decisions about products which they have never used before, or about products which other people will use. They operate in a situation of ignorance and must therefore rest their judgement of quality upon three factors alone. First, they judge by what the salesman, or other personal information source tells them about the product. Second, they judge by their regard for the company and its reputation. Third, they judge by the look of the product, the sample, and the literature. The product which looks good will always beat the one which does not inspire confidence.

Style improvements need not be exclusive of other product improvements. And they can often be introduced with little additional expense at the new product stage, provided that thought and care is devoted to the problem.

Value Analysis

This seeks to change the formulation of the product in such a way as to improve the performance, or at the least to hold it constant, while reducing the cost. Value engineering seeks the same end, through the examination of the production process. A series of formal value analysis techniques has been developed, often involving the building of mathematical models, and the creative application of development techniques. The intrinsic worth of each component part of a product and the function it has to perform is questioned and analysed. Many products are made of some materials which are scarce or costly. The replacement of these materials by a lower grade or cheaper alternative, may horrify the ngineers or production executives, but if it does not affect the performance of the product in relation to the customers' expectations, then the company has little cause to worry about the change. The value analysis technique has been developed to great lengths in the past few years while inflationary pressures have been felt on company profit margins. A little care needs to be exercised over the continuous application of the technique, since one small modification may not be felt, but the cumulative effect of a series of modifications may be detectable within the product performance over time.

Product degradation

One of the effects of price wars, rapid inflation, and declining markets is to reduce the product quality. In order to stay in business, a company will trim quality from the product, to cheapen it in price, or to maintain its profitability. Bit by bit it goes, until the product performance is affected, and noticed by the buyers. Industry-wide, all the products which are under profit pressure may be produced down to the lowest level of quality that the law allows — and some will go lower than that, through widening their specification tolerances. This is what everyone fears when quality levels are reduced. However, product degradation may be a desirable manoeuvre and may not have harmful effects on the market. Most basic quality standards are set by the production function — whatever marketing may say. The production men are the only ones who are expert enough to nominate the alternative levels of quality in a new product from which marketing can choose. They build in quality safety levels. And so products are often made to quality standards which are not desired by the market but are there to shore up production risks.

Therefore, in most products there are wasteful components and materials which are of peripheral interest to the buyer. Packaging often comes into this category. These items can be altered and the products 'degraded' safely.

In consumer product markets, a triangular panel test is usually used to check on the consumer perception of such changes. Two test samples of buyers are drawn — matched in their characteristics. Before each tester is placed three samples of the product; say, two standard products and one modified version. The panel is asked to pick out the odd one of the three. The matched sample is given the reverse order, say, two modified versions and one standard product. If the changes cannot be detected then there will be a more or less even distribution of answers between the two product types across the two samples. A standard preference test can take place after the tester's choice of the odd one out has been made.

Service improvement

A technique of service improvement is often employed by smaller companies competing with large organizations. Service may mean technical advice, more frequent delivery, faster supply, breaking bulk, consultancy help, and after-sales support. The problem with service improvement is that if it works, then competitors tend to copy. It may be expensive to apply. Service improvements usually appeal only to a sector of the market; and work best where the chosen service is the outstanding weakness in competitive organizations. When service standards are already high in a market, it pays to look elsewhere for product improvement.

Promotional benefits

Some companies, particularly those operating in price competitive markets, usually those with undifferentiated products, seek to add value to their products through the addition of promotional benefits. Giveaways, competitions, collector premiums, invitations to the company's sponsored gold competition, all serve primarily as short-term inducements to buy. But some product fields have become so inundated with promotion activities that they have become a regular part of the product offerings. Incentive schemes have a tendency to make buyers switch brands more — and in undifferentiated product fields a significant number of them will often switch primarily for the special offer.

The question of which combination of these seven factors of product improvement to select must be matched against the responsiveness of the market. In order for the selection to be considered successful the buyers must respond in significant numbers. This will largely depend upon the level of the buyers' interest in the product. The greater the risk of the purchase being a bad one, the less likely the buyer is to respond to any product change except that of increased quality. The buyer will perceive his risk as being related to the cost of the product matched against his resources available; or to the importance of the function of the product to him. Material suppliers cannot move far from the basic quality levels of their products simply because materials are usually central to the buyer's need, and they are costly to him. However, low-price consumer durable products can move easily in any direction of product improvement, provided that basic quality standards are met — that is product function, and safety.

The approach to product planning

The general approach to product planning is to identify first those products which are earning the bulk of the company's current profit contribution. Place alongside these the products of the future, which may be unprofitable today, but which can be expected to enter the mainstream of profitable products some time. Finally, isolate those products, with their turnover and profit contributions, which are acting as a drain on the company resources.

The main profit earners must be given their due weight of marketing attention, in order to defend the current profits of the business, as shown in Figure 15.2. Tomorrow's profit-earners must be given more than their fair share of marketing resources, including time, skill and energy. Development areas of the business are always demanding these resources.

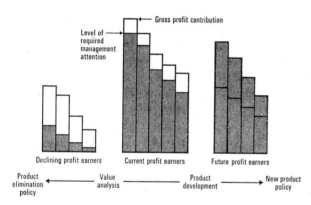

Figure 15.2 Product planning.

This will only leave a light level of activity to support the weak areas of the business. By weak areas we mean to include those new products which were once produced with great hopes but did not turn out well. We include also those products which used to sell well, but where the market has drifted away; or those products which are becoming steadily more costly to produce and which have pricing constraints applied, and so on. It is logical to provide low support to these areas. After all, a company has only scarce resources to allocate as best it can between every competing demand — and something has to give.

This argument may be logical, but it is rare to find it being applied in practice. Companies actually work in the reverse way. Because these declining product areas

represent the 'problems' of the business, they get *more* than their fair share of time, attention and money no less. Most managers worry and meddle with these products to try to 'get them going again'. They also spend a great deal of time and energy on tomorrow's profit-earners. This means that the current profit producers within the organization, those slightly dull products which everyone knows about, but is bored with, receive less than their due share of the resources. Certainly, production departments concentrate their energies here in trying to reduce the cost and increase the productivity of the manufacturing process. But the marketing department often leaves them until they turn into a problem. Even sales forces become bored with pushing the same old products, especially those big ones which are less responsive to sales pressure. Sales forces would rather be faced with a 'challenge' and new products.

Having identified these three groups of products, further analysis is now required in some detail. This will identify specific product problems, starting with the high priority items. A number of quantification techniques may be required at this stage.

Value analysis may be required with those products which appear to be capable of cost reductions of some substance, and which will not harm product quality as perceived by the customer. A skew analysis technique may be required to position the profitability of the products in relation to the markets' resources they currently command. This will show the familiar fact that 20 per cent of the products produce 80 per cent of the results, and vice versa. Sensitivity analysis may be used

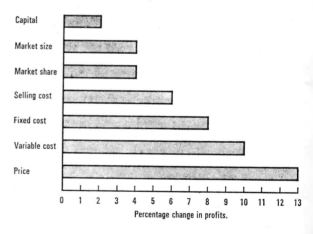

Figure 15.3 The effects on profits of a 1 per cent change in various major parameters. (*Source:* Ivan J. Goldberg, 'Quantification Techniques in Marketing'; *Marketing*, June 1969, p. 37.)

to assist management in assessing those key areas of the product operation which must be carefully controlled. (Figure 15.3.) By the use of consumer attitude studies, it can be seen that some aspects of product quality may affect purchasing habits. Not all the product features are regarded with equal favour by purchasers. How, then, do such features rank, in order of importance? The price/quality/size/style relationship can be investigated in this way.[1]

Signs of an inadequate product mix

Figure 15.4 shows, in diagram form, a number of problems which occur constantly in the product mix. Each problem has a distinct character; and most of them require marketing activity of a strategic kind spread over a long time period.

Sales decline

A product group or single line may have been dropping in sales consistently over a period of time. The nature of the problem will often be easy to identify, and this will determine the technique to be adopted. However, when companies are faced with this situation they usually make the initial assumption that the fault is internal, that they are doing something wrong in their advertising, selling, or pricing operation. They often believe that they are not 'pushing' it hard enough. Consequently, the first line of attack is upon the marketing activity. This approach is also the easiest to develop, and should be the quickest in response.

If this does not work, then the problem might lie within the product, and more careful analysis of the cause is required. This may result in a product modification programme, or new variety introduction. This is more expensive, and takes longer.

Beyond this, the market may be topping-out and at the point of maturity. In this case, a marketing segmentation approach is required, leading to new markets and new uses for the product. If the market is in decline, or if some external factor means the product cannot be revived, then it is best to cut the losses as swiftly as possible through a profit-stripping policy, leading to the phasing out of the product. Otherwise an expensive waste of time and money will go on for a long time.

Profits may decline, while sales hold steady. There are three moves to counter this, which may be used together. The first is to raise prices, the second is to apply value analysis techniques, and the third is to modify the product, usually by splitting it into

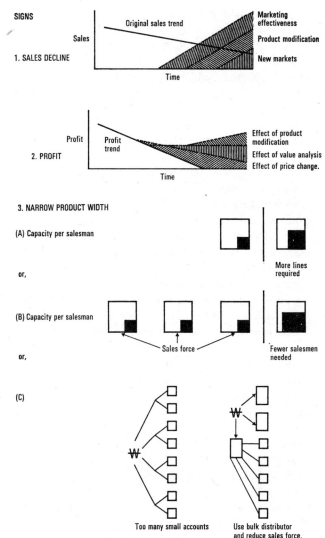

Figure 15.4 (1st half)

varieties – an expensive, large, or high-quality version, and a cheap, small, or low-quality version. Each new variety is designed to operate on a higher gross margin platform than before.

Under-utilizing marketing resources

Some companies have marketing resources which they are not fully utilizing. A narrow product range company often regrets that its salesmen are not selling more products at each call; that its advertising is expensive. The obvious solution is to have more lines, or fewer salesmen. The problem may lie in distribution with too many small accounts. Here the answer may be to split the system and introduce a distributor for the small customers.

A less obvious solution is to carry 'merchandise' products which may be made by another organization, possibly packed under the company brand name, and sold to the company's customers. The company will not obtain the prime manufacturing profit from these products, but they will assist the marketing costs. The danger lies in letting this activity form too high a proportion of the total company business. Then capital resources will be applied to it, inevitably, salesmen will be hired essentially because of the demands of the 'merchandise' products, advertising programmes increased, and so on. The company will become a distributor, and will require a distributor's skills and management outlook. This is a danger to any company which is indulging in this activity merely in order to increase its marginal contribution. The long-term strategy may be for the company to engage finally in the manufacture of the bought-in products. In this case the move takes on an experimental marketing role.

High seasonal sales pattern

Figure 15.4 also shows an annual sales curve for the turkey market. There are three small sales periods for turkeys, Easter, Whitsun and the August Bank Holiday – and one enormous sales period at Christmas. Not many companies face the turkey producers' problem that 80 per cent of their annual output is consumed in 1½ hours every year. This is an intractable seasonal sales problem.

The seasonal problem breaks down into two kinds: extending the 'shoulder' of the season, and filling up the off-season slump. The first problem of extending the shoulder often lends itself to some artificial market forcing technique involving sales promotion. By adding value to the purchase, a few marginal users might be encouraged to buy. The sales cost of this approach might be very high, particularly if the offer must be spread across all the normal users of the product at the time. Special price offers sometimes help, but the total cost of the price reduction must be set against the profits earned only on the marginal extra sales. Price deals to clear end of season stocks are also self-defeating in the long-run. Buyers begin to realize, after a time, that special prices are normally offered at the end of a season, and they hold off some of their main purchases until this time.

To resolve the central problem of lifting sales in the off-season slump can be one of the most difficult tasks in marketing. If the market is not there and does not

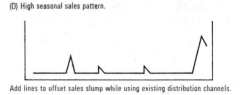

(D) High seasonal sales pattern.

Add lines to offset sales slump while using existing distribution channels.

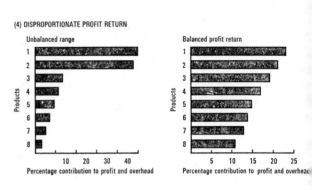

(4) DISPROPORTIONATE PROFIT RETURN

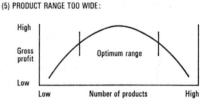

(5) PRODUCT RANGE TOO WIDE:

Figure 15.4 Inadequate product mix.

want to buy, sometimes nothing can shift it. For example, a company making antihistamine products has no market to sell to once the season for hay fever allergies is over. It may move into the development of cough and cold cures to employ its sales force, and to keep its channels of trade busy. But these are major new products operations in their own right.

Filling-in off-season sales slumps can be done sometimes – but the successes are rare. The ice-cream manufacturers now sell a range of varieties for desserts during the winter, to balance their peak demand in the summer. This meant a major move for them into developing new markets, and required radical new product development.

The problem, if it can be solved at all, needs a product diversification move. The essential characteristics of such a move are that it should use the same marketing skills and resources as the company possess say, the same sales force and distribution channels

Preferably it should not require the input of heavy development capital, because there is a high risk that the move will not be successful. The more a company attempts to 'educate' the market to a new way of behaviour, the greater needs to be its capital resources, the more dominant it needs to be in its market, and the higher the rate of potential profit return. The real solution may be to acquire a going and profitable concern with the right product range, selling through the same channels, but with an inverse seasonal sales problem. The resources can then be meshed together, particularly the sales forces, economies taken, and the problem partially solved. Strong seasonal sales problems are seldom solved perfectly and always remain a planning difficulty.

Unbalanced product range

Some companies producing a range of products find that their profits are dependent upon the sales of only one or two lines. This puts them at risk, because all markets change in time, and without these key products the company might not survive. This is the classical product planning problem, because it requires every single development opportunity to be located and exploited. It is also a difficult problem to deal with unless there is a profit squeeze exerted on the company. The reason is that companies in this situation are often very profitable indeed, and find that profit opportunities in the development areas are nowhere near as high. Consequently there is a lack of the necessary corporate stimulus.

There are three lines of approach to the problem. The first is the defence of the existing product markets. This is carried out by splitting the key products, adding new varieties and developing new uses, so far as possible, for the key products. The profit return from these activities will be lower than is earned at present, but it will keep the product markets going, and it will buy the company some time.

The second line of approach is upon those other products in the existing range which might have some future, allied with other new products which can be developed into markets or channels of trade with which the company has experience. This requires product and market segmentation analysis. It may take a considerable time before these new markets can be exploited to their full profit potential. Five years or more is not unusual, from the time of starting development work. The third line of approach requires long-term planning, using the 'gap profit analysis' technique. This will show how far

the company needs to go, compared to how far its existing moves can take it. The difference must be made up through merger and acquisition. The acquisition of a profitable organization with a complementary product range may be the cheapest and fastest way of solving this problem.

Product-clutter

This is one of the most difficult problems to analyse. Theoretically, one can imagine that the total marketing resources represented by salesmen, advertising, promotion funds and the like can be set against too few products, thereby under-utilizing some of these resources. Alternatively, the marketing operation may have to support too many products, so that the general level of marketing power applies to each product is too small. For example, the salesman with too many products to sell, becomes an order-taker, and can only promote two or three products at each call. There is then going to be a lack of sales drive behind some of the products. Theoretically there is an 'optimal' size of product range. But its precise measurement is difficult.

Allocating marketing resources to products

The basic choice for allocating resources between the products in the range lies between some notion of incremental profits, and the concept of net profits over full cost.[2] Incremental profits refer to the difference in the firm's profits with, and without, the addition of the product or activity in question. By adding a new product to existing facilities which are under-utilized, all the cash earned above the cost of materials and other direct costs is treated as a contribution to the company's net profit. As any management accountant will explain, this is a dangerous costing approach to use except in the short-term, and one which will ultimately drive the company out of business, if practised continuously.

This is because these additional products or activities which are designed to mop up overheads will in time produce new overheads. They also incur new untraceable costs, such as the drain on management time. The extra gross margin does not all flow through to net profit therefore.

The alternative idea, that of full costing, means that some of the fixed and semi-fixed overheads are loaded on to the new product or new activity, and the cost burdens of existing products are correspondingly lightened. But as any product development executive will explain, the full cost system makes new products look particularly unattractive, because they bear their full burden of overhead charge against low volume production and high manufacturing cost.

The concept of incremental costings and marginal pricing works well under two circumstances. First, it may be useful for short-run activities, such as sales promotion, where the incremental profits are simply the difference between price and the short-term marginal cost. Because the activity will finish distinctly, and because it is run over a short time-period, overheads do not have much chance to drift upward. It is fairly safe, therefore, to treat any returns above material costs and other direct costs, such as discounts, as a contribution to net profit. In this way the existing organization is squeezed to produce the extra profit.

The second circumstance where it may be useful to use incremental costing is in new product development up to the point at which the product breaks even. The new product forecast will therefore show several levels of break-even. First, there will be a break-even point on materials and other direct costs, which should occur immediately. The second stage allows for breaking-even on semi-variable costs, such as physical distribution, sales and advertising. The third is the break-even on full cost. The fourth is the break-even point allowing for full cost plus required profit objective. This treats the new product fairly, without discouraging the executive team responsible for it. And it still leaves the management accountants secure in the knowledge that the product will pay an increasing share of the running costs of the business.

The most difficult allocation problem in marketing is between existing products with differing rates of profit return and varying degrees of sensitivity to promotion. Take, for example, the question of allocating promotion funds between three different products, A, B, and C. (Figure 15.5.) Assume that the differences in sales response to every unit of promotion from each product can be estimated. (This information is not normally available. Most product ranges are much wider than this, with greater competition for existing resources. Furthermore, there are different types of allocation to make — sales, advertising, promotion and so on. In this example the allocation problem has been reduced to its bare components.)

Some companies will assume that their gross margins on each product are similar, and will allocate the promotion units simply according to the turnover on each product. This is a major error in assumption, but it is often committed by sales-oriented managements, particularly when the accounting information on pro-

Figure 15.5 Question

You have three units of promotion funds to allocate across three product groups. You can allocate one on each, but you must support at least two product groups. Product group A outsells product group C by 3 to 1. Its market is sensitive to each unit of promotion by + 10 per cent. (For one unit of promotion the sales will go up by 10 per cent, for two units of promotion the sales will go up by 20 per cent.) Product group B outsells product group C by 2 to 1 and its market is sensitive to + 20 per cent for each unit of promotion. Product group C is sensitive to + 30 per cent for each unit of promotion.

Question. Given only the turnover information above how would you allocate funds?
Answer.

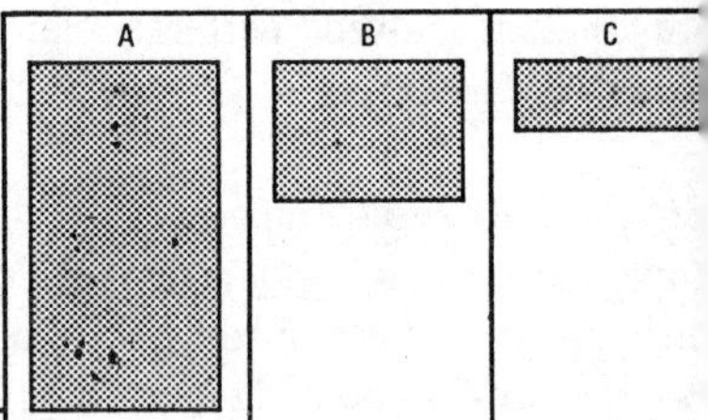

	A	B	C
Original turnover	£500	£200	£100
Percentage increase in turnover per unit of promotion	10%	20%	30%
Actual increase in turnover per unit of promotion	£50	£40	£30
Unit allocation based on turnover	2 units	1 unit	0 units

Question. Given also the following information on gross margins for each group, would you change your decision? If so, how?

Product group A: 30 per cent gross margin
Product group B: 40 per cent gross margin
Product group C: 50 per cent gross margin.

	A	B	C
Original turnover	£500	£200	£100
Gross margin as a % of turnover	30%	40%	50%
Gross margin	£150	£80	£50
Percentage increase in turnover and gross margin per unit of promotion	10%	20%	30%
Actual increase in gross margin	£15	£16	£15
Unit allocation based on gross margin	Either 1 unit	2 units	Or 1 unit

This demonstrates three factors:
1. Allocating funds based on turnover will always be wrong while there are varying rates of gross margin.
2. That using gross margin *percentages* only, as a guide, can be equally mistaken.
3. That the factor which really matters is the total amount of money earned as company contribution to running costs and profit after direct costs have been met.

Figure 15.5 Allocating funds between products.

duct line profits is inadequate. Inevitably it will lead to a poor decision. In the case of the problem set, two units will be spent on A and one on B if allocated in this way.

As soon as the gross margin figures on each product are known the allocation will change. Allocating funds according to the total earning power of the product after direct costs have been met is a standard practice. But mistakes are often made by executives who focus upon the percentage return on the product, and not upon the total cash return. It is the total amount of money which is available to pay for the business which matters and not an index figure, which is what a percentage really is.

The answer to the problem if based on gross margin calculations will allocate two units of promotion on product B (a change from the previous decision based only on turnover), and the problem of spending the third unit either on A or on C.

The problem of which product A or C to allocate this final promotion unit now requires other information before the decision can be made. For example, the attitude of the responsible marketing executive is likely to be concerned with the prospects for products A and C in the years to come. Which one has the greater growth potential? Which of the two products will help others in the range to sell? These are questions that should be asked. The production executive's view is likely to be concerned with the production planning process; will a higher rate of labour productivity or material utilization be achieved with one product compared to the other? The attitude of the management accountant is likely to be different again. He will be concerned with the problem of 'scarce' resources. He will ask, at what point will the growth of either product push the company into the provision of extra facilities – say in plant, or in physical distribution?

Alternatively, he may ask for the various levels of capital employed behind each product to be measured, and for the decision to be based upon the product which shows the highest return. The difficulty here, as in most multi-product companies, is to measure the element of capital employed in supporting each product. It is usually only possible to calculate where discrete plant and equipment is used to manufacture each line. Even in this case the total capital employed is often a matter of judgement.

It is not often that allocation problems are as distinct as this, but by reducing this one to its essentials, the natural conflicts in management attitude emerge.

A mathematical model involving linear programming can be developed to solve the problem. But the total of all the allocation problems of this kind are extraordinarily complex, and the factors are changing constantly. The answers turn upon information which is not generally available and which must be guessed at – i.e., how responsive are the various products to different levels of promotion?

Allocating the resources according to the gross margins earned from each sector of the business will be better than allocating simply according to turnover. But without further thought given to the likely net profits earned from each sector, the allocation will still be wrong. Some products which show a low gross margin may still show a high net profit. This is a feature which wholesalers and retailers know from their experience, but which is not so evident to manufacturers. Many manufacturers find it very difficult to calculate the net profit returns from different products; and when they do, they often feel reluctant to be guided by them.

Some products may require little investment in sales or distribution; private label products, packed under the customer's brand name and delivered in bulk with no investment in sales or advertising, may show a high net profit despite earning a low gross margin.

Figure 15.6 describes the difficulty. Product A shows a high gross margin (60 per cent) but with high sales, advertising and distribution costs which bring the net profit to 20 per cent. This could be, for instance, the company's brand which it markets itself. Product B shows a low gross margin (40 per cent) but with the same net profit of 20 per cent. This could be the private label product, packed especially for the customer.

If both products have an equal opportunity for

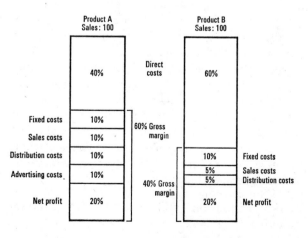

Figure 15.6 *Question.* Given equal opportunity for each product, which one do you select for additional marketing resources?

growth then nearly every manager will allocate extra resources to the high gross margin product. If pressed for a reason, they will probably use an argument based upon marginal profit return. They will assume that if all the fixed costs and overheads are being borne by the current earnings from sales, then most of the additional gross margin on each extra sale of product A will flow through to net profit. Therefore every extra sale of product A will earn at the rate of 60 per cent net profit. In the long run this argument is clearly absurd. As the product sells more it will require more sales, distribution and advertising resources. If the marginal profit argument were valid, then we could expect to find products which sell in increasing quantities producing ever-increasing rates of net profit. Such economies of scale are very hard to find outside production costs. In fact, most products earn successively lower rates of net profit as they sell more.

There may be a more substantial case for putting extra marketing resources behind product B despite its lower gross profit return. After all, the company can only earn its net profit out of its gross margin. The direct costs are 'dead'. On product B a net profit return of 100 per cent is earned for every unit spent in the marketing and overhead area. (20 per cent costs produce 20 per cent net profit.) But product A earns a net profit of only 50 per cent for every unit spent on marketing and overhead. (40 per cent costs produce 20 per cent net profit.)

No one is suggesting that companies should promote automatically their low gross margin lines; but gross margin calculations by themselves are not sufficient to resolve allocation problems. An idea of the net profit returns is required, matched with a view of the future growth of the markets and matched with the capacities of the company in terms of sales and physical distribution as well as production resources.

Product planning is one of the most fascinating aspects of marketing. It is also one of the least researched areas, where subjective judgement based upon 'experience' and 'feel' is used in preference to formal techniques. It is an area of marketing where good or bad decisions are seldom traceable in the short-run. And the sin of omission, that is, the decision not to do something, is never found out.

Market Situation and attitudes to Product Planning

Package Goods: Consumer
The problem in multi-product companies rests exactly upon the question of resource allocation which we have just discussed. One of the primary motivations is the selection of those products which can act as 'leaders' in the range, and which can carry other products with them. This is a critical question for the allocation of advertising support. The greatest doubt exists about the true nature of net profits earned from individual products in the range.

Consumer Durables
Product planning in these companies is often less difficult than it appears. Each product is often discrete in its manufacture and allows for the accountant to calculate the rate of return on capital employed. Each market is often discrete, and the future performance of the product over its 'life-cycle' is easier to estimate. Therefore complete profitability analyses over the life of the product can be estimated. Product modification often operates in the area of additional features, or in styling.

Plant and Equipment
Market and customer planning is more the rule in these companies. The capital intensity of the industry makes a long product life-cycle inevitable. Short-term incremental costing and pricing practices are common, in order to use up production facilities. Product modification is usually concentrated in the area of quality improvement, and of service development.

Components
Most product modification problems are concerned with quality improvements, but features and styling changes may be effective in some markets. Value analysis is often a feature of this kind of company. The traditional product planning dilemma is whether to allocate all the marketing and sales resources behind a small group of products which are planned to 'lead' the sales of the rest or whether to promote across the range.

Materials
Material manufacturers concentrate their product modification policy in the product quality and value analysis areas. They often search to find ways in which customers can achieve better utilization from lower quality grades of material, giving them a price advantage over competition. Advertising resources are often concentrated behind the consumer versions of the product they sell, in order to use the 'carry over' effect of this promotion to influence industrial buyers.

Differentiated Products

These are the companies to whom product planning and the allocation of resources present the greatest difficulties. The problem for them is to get out of the general run of competition supplying the identical product as competition. They search for pockets of markets which will respond to some kind of specialist package of products. Frequently this will drive them into the production of a 'system' or a group of products which, taken together, may form a neat parcel for a particular type of use. In allocating their resources, they will be concerned to support their leading lines. They will also try to develop those products which, having a certain distinction about them, are able to mark the company out from its competitors.

Custom-built Products

Here the planning process will concentrate on separate tenders and will be directed towards making each order profitable. The allocation of advertising resources is more likely to be spent in promoting the general reputation of the company, and the corporate image. The promotion and sales resources will be directed at soliciting enquiries for tender.

Fragmented Markets

Here companies will be quick to copy features and modifications introduced by competitors and which look as if they will be successful. The interest will lie with what the distributive trade will be prepared to buy. Service development often forms a major part of their planning programmes.

Concentrated Markets

The leaders will be concerned with their own performance. They will usually seek to close up parts of the market which might let competitors in, by developing small product modifications. The accent will be on keeping productivity high, and servicing costs low.

Example: Product Planning

Background

Broads Builders' Merchants Ltd is a private company centred in London. They sell building and decorating materials to the building trade and householder. The product lines vary from paints and water taps to manhole covers. Broads specialize in the provision of heavy-duty ware, such as bricks and drainage materials for trade users, e.g., building contractors.

Initially the company were merchants, but gradual reorganization of the company and its activities resulted in a holding company (Broad & Co., Ltd) being formed and two subsidiary companies, thus there were now two branches of the company – manufacturing (Broads Manufacturing Company Ltd) and merchanting (Broads Builders Merchants Ltd). It is the latter which is dealt with in this case-study.

The Problems

Originally the company had developed in the traditional fashion of builder's merchants, that of having a poor consumer image and uninteresting showrooms other than to builders and architects.

Gradually the company was restructured to place emphasis on the various depots, in this way depots increased their individual buying power and responsibility to meeting market needs. By rationalizing the stocks over all the depots and tying the whole organization to a stocklist the advantages in buying and selling gradually gained momentum. During this time the first moves were made by the company towards the establishment of a self-service department and more professional displays in the showrooms.

Whilst the new policies were beginning to work the various departments lacked cohesion and more impetus was required in sales. The ROI was still too low. It was decided, therefore, to appoint a marketing manager.

Solution

With the identification of the new appointment a new division was formed – the marketing division.

The division was able to build results on the work that had already been initiated in three main areas.

1 Stocks were geared to minimum stock turn levels.
2 The Marketing Division became responsible for overall buying policy; thus the assessment and satisfaction of demand became a continuous process.
3 The sales force became totally involved with the product range carried by the individual depots.

The traditional market with the builder, lacked immediate growth potential. Expansion was achieved by:

1 Taking the self-service department that had been started in 1967 and widening its stock range to appeal to the 'do it yourself' customer. Colourful decoration and up to date merchandizing assisted this aim.
2 Introducing associated products such as fitted

bedroom and kitchen furniture, tiles, timber and own-brand products, thereby widening the product range.

3 The showroom was turned into a 'Bathroom and Kitchen Design Centre' with improved displays. A consultancy service was also added to advise customers of kitchen layout, with a service to design their kitchen, if they wished.

Advertising was stepped up. This aimed at the Londoner especially, by advertising on the underground. Direct mail shots became a standard form of publicity to customer and potential customer.

Results

In the 18 months following the implementation of the new policy the following results have been observed.

1 For the latter ten months of 1970 'the budgeted figure was beaten by 3 per cent and for 1971 the present trends show that the results will be 19 per cent up on 1970'.

The average rate of growth since reorganization is 12 per cent per annum.

2 They are more marketing oriented.

3 Personnel are working as a team towards common objectives.

4 The company is able to recognize and profit from changing demand patterns.

Reference

1 I.J. Goldberg, 'Quantification Techniques in Marketing'; *Marketing,* June 1969, pp. 36-38.
2 J. Dean, 'Product Line Policy'; *U.S. Jnl. of Business,* Oct. 1950, pp. 248-258.

16.

Estimating the Effect of Variety on Sales
by M.C.J. Elton and A. Mercer

Reprinted from the Operational Research Quarterly, Vol. 20 (3), September 1969 with permission.

Introduction

One of the greatest problems facing a selling organization is that of deciding how much variety should be offered to its customers. For example, a shirt manufacturer must decide how many colours and sizes to produce. The retailer must also decide how many different brands of shirts to sell. Whilst size is functional in the sense that nobody will buy a shirt of the wrong size, the brands, styles and colours are alternatives from which a purchaser may choose. A manufacturer or retailer will incur unnecessary costs if the range is too large and sales are likely to suffer when there is too little variety. Attention to the need for methodology in this area has been drawn by authors such as Baumol and Ide,[1] but the only paper of any operational significance appears to be that by Schaffir,[2] who was mainly concerned with the problems of garment manufacturers. This article compares two different methods which were used to determine how the sales of a large chain of stores selling branded consumer durables varied with the number of models sold. It is one aspect in the study of a stocking, distribution and retailing system. The organization is currently decentralized with warehouses in different regions. If a centralized system were introduced, then stocking a larger range becomes less costly. However, if the variety were reduced, then the manufacturers of the retained products could be expected to give larger discounts but some sales would inevitably be lost.

The aggregate statistics usually kept within an organization are inadequate for a study of the sales-variety problem because they give no information on lost sales. Moreover, the true contribution of a model to a range will be larger than its actual sales if it makes the whole range more attractive. Equally, a model serves a less useful purpose if it simply draws sales from the other models of the range. The most reliable results would be given by experiments but these were not practicable because of the large variances in the retail outlets' sales about their forecast values. Consequently all the shop assistants filled in questionnaires whenever sales were either made or missed for a period of a week. The 3,500 questionnaires were analysed extensively for bias, including that due to any delay in completing the

questionnaires, but none was found.

The optimum variety to sell will be dependent on the organization's other marketing policies. For example, a customer is more likely to purchase from a limited range if the prices are lower than elsewhere. Consequently, numerical answers can only be regarded as relating to one retailing chain at a particular point in time.

Lost Sales and the Number of Models available

The shop assistants noted on the questionnaires when a sale was lost because a suitable model was not available. Thus the probability of losing sales was obtained for the retail outlets served by each regional warehouse. During the period when the questionnaires were being completed, the number of models available in each warehouse was noted. This information was obtained for six products, and for each product the probability of losing sales because of non-availability was plotted as a function of the number of models available. The maximum and minimum number of models available are given in Table 16.1 for each product. Within these limits the relationships were all linear but they implied a probability of much less than 1 if extrapolated to zero models available. This is illustrated in Figure 16.1 for product code 2, for which the observed linear range is from six to 16 models and the probability for zero

Table 16.1 Observed ranges and extrapolated values of the number of models available.

Product code	No. of models		
	Observed maximum	Observed minimum	Extrapolated minimum
1	38	11	7
2	16	6	5
3	20	5	4
4	8	4	2
5	14	3	2
6	11	4	3

models is 0.301. This extrapolation was clearly incorrect so that it was assumed that the linear relationships were only valid to the values given in the last column of Table 16.1, which involved extrapolating only slightly outside the observed range. For each product, the extrapolated limit of the probability of losing a sale was joined by a line to a probability of 1 for losing a sale when there is no model available. For product code 2, the extrapolated probability of 0.209 for five models given in Table 16.1 is therefore joined to a probability of 1 for zero models available. Thus, the whole relationship consists of a pair of lines which initially appears to be a linear representation of a negative exponential curve. However, the relationship decreases more quickly than an exponential for low variety and less quickly when the range is large.

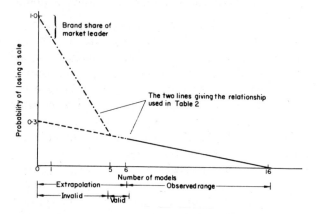

Figure 16.1 The calculation of the probability of losing a sale of product code 2 as a function of the number of models available.

It was subsequently observed that for all the products except code 6, the probability of losing a sale with one model available was within 0.02 of 1 minus the market share of the brand leader. This is intuitively very reasonable for it implies that if a retail outlet is going to sell only one model, it will sell the brand leader which can readily be identified. Then the proportion of demand satisfied will be the market share of the brand leader, which varied between 10 and 42 per cent for the six products considered. Now the extrapolated minima in Table 16.1 were determined subjectively to be one model less than the observed values except for product codes 1 and 4. It was felt that the extrapolated minima for product codes 4 and 5 should be the same and that 7 was a more reasonable value for product code 1 than 10 would have been. Thus, there is no reason why the

extrapolated minimum for product code 6 should not be changed from 3 to 2. If this is done, then the probability of losing a sale with one model available differs from 1 minus the market share of the brand leader by only 0.01.

Hence a pair of straight lines gives a good approximation to the relationship between the probability of losing a sale because of the availability and the number of models. One of the lines is obtained from observed data whereas the second has a slope equal to minus the brand share of the market leader and has an intercept of 1 on the probability axis. Obviously, the approximation will underestimate the probability of losing a sale for a small number of range sizes in the region where the lines meet, but this difference will normally be of little operational significance because such low variety is unlikely. The probabilities for the six products considered are given in Table 16.2 for up to 20 models.

Table 16.2 The probability of losing a sale because of the availability as a function of the number of models

No. of models	Product code					
	1	2	3	4	5	6
1	0.877	0.842	0.791	0.555	0.683	0.593
2	0.753	0.683	0.583	0.110	0.366	0.186
3	0.630	0.525	0.374	0.091	0.335	0.167
4	0.506	0.367	0.165	0.073	0.305	0.147
5	0.383	0.209	0.161	0.055	0.274	0.127
6	0.260	0.190	0.157	0.037	0.243	0.107
7	0.136	0.172	0.153	0.018	0.212	0.088
8	0.134	0.153	0.149		0.181	0.068
9	0.131	0.135	0.145		0.150	0.048
10	0.128	0.116	0.141		0.119	0.028
11	0.126	0.098	0.137		0.088	0.008
12	0.123	0.079	0.133		0.057	
13	0.120	0.061	0.129		0.026	
14	0.118	0.042	0.125			
15	0.115	0.024	0.121			
16	0.113	0.005	0.116			
17	0.110		0.112			
18	0.107		0.108			
19	0.105		0.104			
20	0.102		0.100			

There are many more than 20 models on the market for product codes 1 and 3 so that the probability of losing a sale with 20 models available is significant. At the other extreme, no sales of product code 4 will be lost if eight models are available.

Model switching with subjective probabilities

The reaction of customers to the product range will depend on whether or not they knew what they wanted before entering the retail outlet. Of those who had decided what to buy, some would be returning to the shop after one or more exploratory visits whilst others would have been influenced by such factors as the manufacturers' advertising and friends' advice, so that the behaviour of these two groups of customers will be different. This situation is illustrated in Figure 16.2, where the possible flow of customers through the retail outlets is given. The figures given in the parentheses are the probabilities derived from the questionnaires. Therefore the customers are divided into three classes, which will be referred to as the U, DF and DS classes. The U customers are undecided when they enter a shop. The DF customers have decided at the time of their first visit, whereas the customers in the DS class who have decided are on at least their second visit. Only a negligible number of customers will return to an outlet of the organization concerned if they know what they want at the time of the first visit but find that the required model is out of stock.

Now let p_{ij} be the probability that a customer who actually brought model i would have bought model j instead if i, and only i, had been unavailable given the present range in stock. Denote $\Sigma_j \, p_{ij}$ by p_i and thus if p_{ik} is zero, then p_i is the probability that a buyer of model i will buy something else if i is unavailable, irrespective of whether or not model k is available. It was found from a subsequent survey that if customers would have been satisfied with an alternative model, the latter was almost always one of the high-demand models. Thus, if the range were reduced, it was most unlikely that both a customer's first and second choice would be eliminated. In other words, the assumption that p_{ik} is zero is valid for all pairs i and k which might be removed from the range. Hence p_i is the probability that a customer who actually bought model i would still have made a purchase if i was not stocked. It is not important to consider what the alternative purchase would be and the need to estimate all the probabilities p_{ij} is avoided. There will be different values of p_i for all the three classes.

One of the questions to be answered by the sales assistant after a sale had been made was what chance there was of switching the customer to another model if that purchased had not been available. The alternative answers were 'fairly certain', 'possible' and 'poor'. It was assumed that the customer would have switched if the answer were 'fairly certain', and that the customer would not have switched if the answer were 'poor'. The information in the 'possible' answer was ignored. Thus, the probability of switching a customer in the Bernouilli process which arises when the first choice is not available may now be obtained as the ratio of the 'fairly certain' answers to the sum of the 'fairly certain' and the 'poor' answers. However, for every product a model was sold under the organization's own brand name and the management was prepared to estimate a subjective probability distribution of the switching probability for each of these models. Therefore, the prior probability of switching was assumed to have the same beta distribution for all the models of a product. Then the questionnaire answers were used to obtain the posterior distribution of the probability of switching, which was obviously different for the various models of the same product and for the three classes of customer. These distributions were not obtained for the DS class, who had partly chosen their model in terms of what was available at the time of the previous visit. If the range had been smaller at that time, then they might not have decided on the particular model to which they were committed. However, there was no means of determining what they might have chosen. On the other hand, the DS class are more likely to switch than the DF class

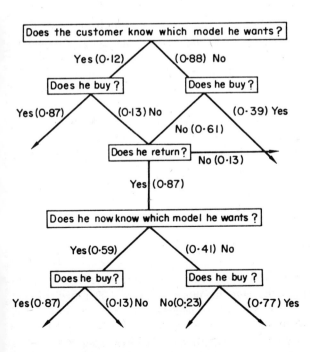

Figure 16.2 Decision tree for a customer.

when less variety is available because they did not feel sufficiently strongly disposed towards their choice to make a purchase on the first visit. Consequently if the expected probabilities of switching by DF and DS customers are denoted by p_i^1 and p_i^2 respectively, then it is assumed that p_i^2 is equal to $p_i^1 + k(1 - p_i^1)$, where k is a constant between 0 and 1. Since only about 20 per cent of buyers belong to the DS class, the value of k is of little operational significance.

For each class of customer, the expected number of lost sales when a model is removed from the range is the product of its annual sales and the expected probability that a customer will not switch to another model. Then after summing over the three customer classes, the models may be listed in order of decreasing potential lost sales. Thus, the relationship between sales and variety is obtained by successively removing models from the range in the order of increasing lost sales. Because the method depends on sales assistants' impression of customer behaviour, it is unreasonable to continue the process to product ranges which are smaller than any experienced previously. Therefore, in Figure 16.3 the results for product code 1 are compared with those given in Table 16.2 for the regional availability method for product ranges between 10 and 20. Similarly the results for product code 2 are given in Figure 16.4 for product ranges between 5 and 15. For both products, these ranges reflect the observed values given in Table 16.1. The value of k was arbitrarily chosen to be a half, but if it were taken to be either a quarter or

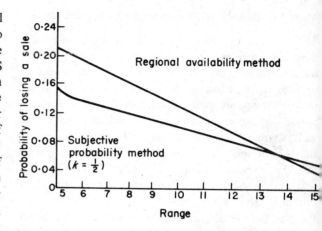

Figure 16.4 Lost sales for product code 2.

three-quarters, the maximum change in the probability of losing a sale would be 0.02, which occurs for low product ranges.

The prior distribution was found to be comparatively unimportant for models purchased by at least eight customers of each of the U and DF classes. Thus, it reduces the effect of the sampling fluctuation of models with a small market share.

Variety and Inventory Control Policies

One of the uses for the relationship between sales and variety is to determine how many models should be stocked. However, this decision cannot be taken without also considering the service levels for each model because the two jointly determine the proportion of demand which is lost. Let q_j be the probability of losing a sale conditional on j brands being available and define β to be the unconditional probability of losing a sale. Suppose that b brands are normally stocked with the same service level, α, for each. Then:

$$\beta = \sum_{r=0}^{b} \frac{b!}{r!\,(b-r)!}\, \alpha^r (1-\alpha)^{b-r} q_r$$

This expression assumes that stock-outs of different models occur independently and no evidence was found to the contrary. If in other studies, different brands from the same manufacturer were replenished together or there was a large demand for a second choice brand when the first choice was out of stock, then stock-outs might not be independent. The expression also appears to ignore the identities of the brands in stock. However,

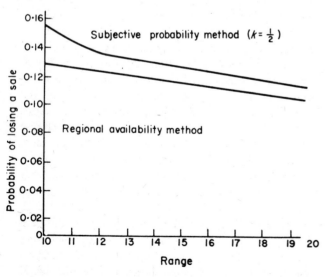

Figure 16.3 Lost sales for product code 1.

Table 16.3 The probability of losing a sale as a function of the number of models stocked and the service level

Product code	No. of models stocked	Service level			
		0.60	0.80	0.90	0.99
1	10	0.286	0.153	0.133	0.129
	15	0.148	0.123	0.119	0.116
	20	0.124	0.112	0.107	0.103
2	5	0.525	0.367	0.288	0.216
	10	0.223	0.154	0.135	0.118
	15	0.136	0.079	0.051	0.026
3	5	0.390	0.232	0.182	0.161
	10	0.171	0.149	0.145	0.141
	15	0.145	0.133	0.127	0.121
4	5	0.133	0.076	0.064	0.056
	10	0.038	0.009	0.002	0.000
5	5	0.363	0.306	0.289	0.275
	10	0.243	0.181	0.150	0.122
6	5	0.205 (0.274)	0.150 (0.164)	0.137 (0.139)	0.128
	10	0.108 (0.111)	0.068	0.048	0.030

the subjective probability method should be used to ensure that the best combination of brands is stocked. The probability of losing a sale will depend on which brand is temporarily out of stock, but to a first approximation the expression is justifiable to illustrate the argument unless the number of brands stocked is small compared with the total number on the market. The work described in this article is part of a wider study by Elton and Mercer[3] to locate warehouses for consumer durables. In a practical inventory control study, it might be desirable to use a more complex expression for β which takes into account the identity of the brand out of stock and also assigns different service levels to different brands. Values of β are given in Table 16.3 for service levels of 0.60, 0.80, 0.90 and 0.99 for each of the six products with the probabilities of losing a sale given in Table 16.2. Those for product code 6 based on the original values of q_r with an extrapolated minimum of three models are given in parentheses. They only differ appreciably for a small product range with a very low service level and then the operational implications are unchanged.

At the lower service levels, the probability of losing a sale is less than the probability that a particular model will be out of stock, but this is not true at the 90 per cent service level or higher for five of the six products. This is the obvious effect of customers not purchasing if they feel that there is limited choice of models. The probability of losing a sale decreases as the range increases and Table 16.3 clearly suggests that it may be better to increase the range at the expense of the service level. Indeed there would appear to be no advantage to be gained from having a service level higher than 80 per cent if it were possible to increase the range by five models. Obviously the effects of other factors such as purchase discounts from manufacturers would have to be considered before finally making such a decision. The inferences drawn from Table 16.3 were confirmed when all the costs in the wider study were taken into account.

A critique of the two methods and conclusions

Whilst the data used by the two methods were collected during the same time period, they are essentially very different. The regional availability method only required the total sales and the total demand lost because of non-availability for each region. Any bias in the data would be due to potential customers attributing a non-purchase to lack of availability when they were really dissatisfied with some other factor such as price. This would result in the probability of losing a sale because of the availability being overestimated. The subjective probability method was based on the questionnaire answers relating to customers who had purchased. In this case, sales assistants are likely to optimistically overestimate their ability and con-

Table 16.4 A comparison of the probability of losing a sale for inventory policies determined with the two estimation methods

Product code	No. of models stocked	Estimation method	Service level			
			0.60	0.80	0.90	0.99
1	10	Regional availability	0.286	0.153	0.133	0.129
		Subjective probability	0.302	0.184	0.163	0.155
	15	Regional availability	0.148	0.123	0.119	0.116
		Subjective probability	0.174	0.140	0.132	0.126
	20	Regional availability	0.124	0.112	0.107	0.103
		Subjective probability	0.142	0.123	0.117	0.112
2	10	Regional availability	0.223	0.154	0.135	0.118
		Subjective probability	0.190	0.113	0.100	0.091
	15	Regional availability	0.136	0.079	0.051	0.026
		Subjective probability	0.104	0.070	0.055	0.041

sequently the probability of losing a sale will be underestimated. However, for product code 1, the postulated upper bound given by the regional availability method is less than the postulated lower bound given by the subjective probability method. This appears to be unimportant because the two bounds in Figure 16.3 are close together, so that it may be concluded that both methods give an unbiased estimate of the relationship between sales and variety. For product code 2, the bounds are close together for ranges greater than 12 and indeed they intersect. For lower variety levels, the true relationship will lie within the limits given in Figure 16.4, which are reasonably close together. The differences between the results for the two methods are not numerically significant and are operationally unimportant. For example, the probability of losing a sale has been calculated as a function of the range and service level using the subjective probability method for ranges above the extrapolated minima given in Table 16.1. The values are given in Table 16.4 together with the comparable probabilities from Table 16.3, which are obviously identical for five models of product code 2.

The advantages of the regional availability method are that it is simple and quick to use and requires little subjective data. However, it is necessary for the different regions to adopt different policies or for experiments to be carried out. This is less important for the subjective probability method, which provides an explanation of the behaviour of the different customer classes towards the different models. Indeed it identifies which, if any, models should be dropped from a product range. This is important because such models are not necessarily those with the lowest sales. Because the subjective probability method can be used for individual shops, it is well suited to taking account of local competitive situations.

Advertising by manufacturers will influence both the proportion of customers who decide on their purchase before entering a retail outlet and the strengths of their predispositions. Thus, the subjective probability method might enable manufacturers to obtain a better understanding of the effectiveness of advertising.

The problem studied is essentially the short-term one. Variety also has a long-term effect because it contributes to an organization's image. For example, a customer may visit a retail outlet which he expects to offer a large choice. If the range has been reduced, the customer might still buy, but he would not return to that shop the next time he wished to make a purchase. This is a problem which needs to be studied.

References

1 Baumol, W.J. and Ide, E.A. Variety in Retailing, *Management Science*, (1957) 3, 93.
2 Schaffir, K. The Economics of Non-functional Variety *Ops Res. (1963)* 11, 702.
3 Elton, M.C.J. and Mercer, A. The Stocking, Distribution and Retailing of Consumer Durables. In *Large Scale Provisioning Systems*, (1968) English Universities Press, London.

17.
The Product Elimination Decision
by James T. Rothe

MSU Business Topics, pp. 45-52, Autumn 1970. Reprinted by permission of the publisher, Division of Research, Graduate School of Business Administration, Michigan State University.

Introduction

The management of products throughout their life-cycles is of great and growing importance in our economy. In less developed economies, functions are performed by the same physical means over such extended periods of time that the life-cycle of products can hardly be observed and certainly is not of major concern to the businessman. In our economy, particularly since 1945, rapid technological advancement and high levels of income have induced such frequent shifts in customer preferences for products that the management of products over their life-cycles is becoming one of the high priority managerial concerns.

While an enormous amount of attention has been paid to new product development efforts, little thought has been devoted to product elimination efforts.[1] This neglect is unfortunate because a planned and systematic product elimination programme may contribute substantially to the firm's profitability and future growth. Profits can be enhanced by eliminating certain costs associated with products in the later stages of their life as well as by increasing the productivity of the resources released from the older products.

Most contributions to the product elimination issue have been theoretical in nature. Articles published by Kotler, Alexander, Berenson, and Kline develop a theory of product elimination, but little research has been done on this aspect of business.[2] Consequently, factual knowledge is extremely limited in an area where it could be quite useful to management.

This article reports on a study which surveyed the product elimination decision as it is currently being made by management. The study focused on: the importance of elimination decisions to firms, organization for and participation in product elimination decisions, the structure of elimination decisions, the degree of formality in elimination programmes, and typical management problems with elimination programmes. The study was limited to manufacturers of consumer products since consumer products tend to have shorter life-cycles than industrial products. On the basis of buying habits, consumption patterns, distri-

bution similarities, product similarities, and price similarities, a five category industry classification was developed: drugs, major appliances, food, clothing, and minor appliances. A sample of 100 firms was selected systematically for each of the five categories and two mailings of the questionnaire were used. Responses to the questionnaire were classified by industry type and by the degree of formality of their product elimination programmes. These responses, where practicable, were then converted to means per industry and formality categories on a 100-point basis. The equality of these means was then tested statistically.

Product elimination proved to be of interest to respondents. More than 40 per cent of firms contacted responded to the study and approximately 30 per cent of these responses were usable. The minor appliance category reported the largest product lines as well as the shortest life-cycles for their products. For each industry category, the mean number of new products introduced annually exceeded the mean number of products eliminated yearly. This apparent proliferation of product line accentuates the need for improved total product management including product elimination efforts.

Firms rated product elimination activities approximately one-third as important as new product activities of the firm. Table 17.1 shows how different industry respondents rated each of the product planning and development activities. The respondents were asked to note the relative importance on a scale 0 to 100, 100 being most important; their average scores are shown in the table.

An interesting pattern of response is indicated in Table 17.1. Each industry rates new product activities as most important, changing or revitalizing existing products second most important, with the development of new uses and product elimination activities about equally valued and ranking third in importance. However, the drug industry rates new product activities higher than other industries while product elimination activities were rated most important by the appliance categories.

Table 17.1 Importance of product planning and development activities.

Activity	Drugs	Major appliances	Food	Clothing	Minor appliances
Planning for new products[a]	51	40	40	37	40
Developing new uses for old products	15	12	17	16	14
Changing and/or revitalizing existing products	24	32	31	35	31
Eliminating products from the product line[a]	10	16	12	12	15
Other	Few observations				
Total points	100	100	100	100	100

[a] Significant statistical differences were found among the means at the δ level of 0.05, using the one way analysis of variance, fixed effects model. Specific hypotheses were tested for all possible combinations of two means by the student t ratio at the same level of significance. This was done without added risk of type I error because the within group variance provided an unbiased estimate of the variance of the treatment population. The results of this statistical analysis are interpreted as: (a) the drug industry respondents placed more value on new product activities than other industries, and (b) the drug industry respondents valued product elimination activities less than the major appliance and minor appliance industries while both appliance categories rated elimination activities higher than other categories.

Table 17.2 Organizational participation in elimination programmes

Functional Group	Most important Participant		Second most important participant	
	Number	Percentage	Number	Percentage
Accounting	1	*	14	8
Engineering	1	*	12	7
Finance	3	2	17	10
Marketing	130	75	27	15
Production	4	2	41	24
Purchasing			4	2
Corporate management	27	16	48	28
Committee	8	5	11	6
Total	174	100	174	100

* Insignificant Fraction

Marketing and corporate management executives dominate the elimination activity. Table 17.2 shows responses related to organizational participation. The lack of financial executive participation in the decision was not expected and suggests an imbalance which should be corrected.

Professor P. Kotler recommended the three stage approach to product elimination decisions, as represented below in Figure 17.1. The approach was purely normative and represents an excellent starting point from which data can be generated to substantiate the framework offered. Modelling this part of the study after Kotler's approach, respondents were asked to indicate how they handled each stage of the process.

Creation stages

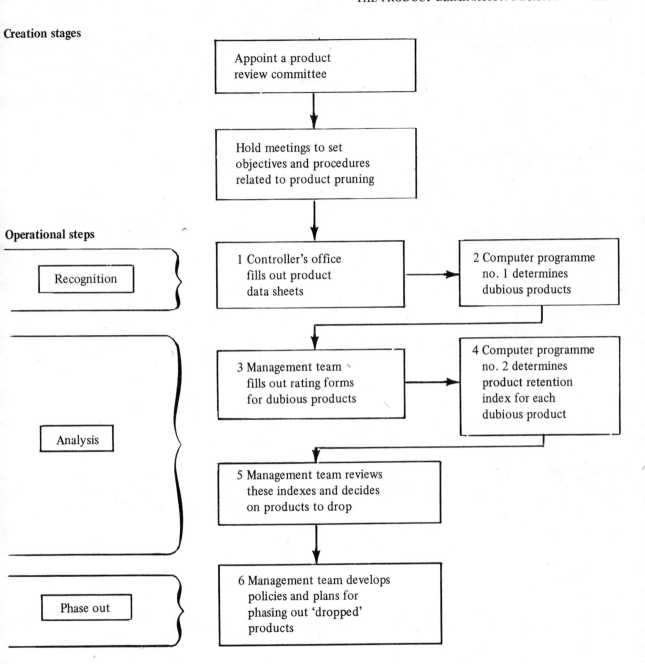

Figure 17.1 Structure of elimination decisions.

Recognition

Responses to the recognition state of the decision (see Table 17.3) show that minimum sales volume proved to be the most popular variable in recognizing products for possible elimination. Respondents again were asked to note the relative importance on a scale 0 to 100, with 100 being most important. The average scores are shown in the table. Surprisingly, little attention was given to product profitability at this stage of the analysis. Life-cycle theory would suggest that profitability analysis would be vital at this stage of the process because profitability figures tend to lead sales figures. This may represent a serious flaw in the recognition phase of elimination programmes.

Table 17.3 Recognition of Weak Products.

Variable used	Drugs	Major appliances	Food	Clothing	Minor appliances
A minimum sales volume	36	33	29	32	29
A minimum product volume	15	22	19	12	19
A minimum market share percentage	13	13	13	12	13
Some percentage figure of actual divided by fore-cast sales volume	14	7	7	11	10
Some comparison of today's market share with previous years	10	10	13	12	10
A percentage figure of actual divided by projected production	3	6	7	5	7
Percentage of total company sales this product contributes	9	9	12	16	12
Other			Few observations		
Total points	100	100	100	100	100

Table 17.4 Factors used to analyse weak products.

Major factors	Drugs	Major appliances	Food	Clothing	Minor appliances
Product profitability[a]	45	31	45	31	36
Product costs[a]	11	17	13	16	14
Product investment	16	14	16	13	15
Company alternatives[a]	10	15	12	19	13
Market position[a]	18	23	14	21	22
Others			Few observations		
Total points	100	100	100	100	100

[a] Denotes significant statistical differences among the means, as explained in footnote in Table 17.1.

Table 17.5 Phase-out strategies.

Elimination strategy	Drugs (%)	Major appliances (%)	Food (%)	Clothing (%)	Minor appliances (%)
Drop immediately	44.4	53.0	53.1	78.3	61.8
'Milk' or slow phase-out	33.3	41.7	34.0	15.0	28.7
Both drop and 'milk'	21.2	5.3	12.9	6.7	9.5
Total percentage	100.0	100.0	100.0	100.0	100.0

Analysis

Five factors were used by the respondents to analyse products previously recognized as potential candidates for elimination. Table 17.4 shows these factors and their relative importance; respondents again were asked to note the relative importance on a 0 to 100 scale, and the table shows the average scores.

The pattern of responses shown in Table 17.4 can be interpreted several ways. A general pattern emerges with respondents rating profitability first in each industry and market position second in four of the five industries. A wide degree of significant statistical variation exists among the industries with respect to how they rate a given factor. Four of the five factors employed by respondents were rated significantly different in importance for this phase of the elimination process.

Phase Out

Respondents were asked which phase out strategy they most often used. Surprisingly, the quick drop strategy was preferred to the slower phase out often suggested as a better strategy; the answers are categorized in Table 17.5.

Formality in Elimination Programmes

Much of the literature dealing with product elimination dwells on the formality issue. An almost universal appeal

Table 17.6 Formality in elimination programmes.

Highest formal development

Type	Number	Percentage of highest	Percentage of total industry category
Drugs	6	15	18
Major appliances	10	26	26
Food	6	15	19
Clothing	5	13	17
Minor appliances	12	31	28
Total	39	100	—

Intermediate formal development

Type	Number	Percentage of intermediate	Percentage of total industry category
Drugs	12	17	36
Major appliances	16	23	42
Food	9	13	29
Clothing	16	22	53
Minor appliances	18	25	43
Total	71	100	—

Lowest formal development

Type	Number	Percentage of lowest	Percentage of total industry category
Drugs	15	23	46
Major appliances	12	19	32
Food	16	25	52
Clothing	9	14	30
Minor appliances	12	19	29
Total	64	100	—

for formal systems is readily apparent. Part of the purpose of this study was to look more closely at the formality issue. To do this, respondents' programmes were placed in one of the three categories: highest formal development, intermediate formal development, or lower formal development. Results of this classification are shown in Table 17.6.

The data in Table 17.6 suggest that the drug and food industry respondents were less formal in their elimination decisions while both appliance categories were more formal. This is consistent with each industry's rating of the importance of elimination activities as shown in Table 17.1. The drug industry rated elimination activities significantly lower than the four other industries, while the appliance categories rated elimination activities higher than the other categories.

The most important issue is whether or not the degree of formality influences the factors used in the decision. An analysis of the responses to this study suggests that formality does not influence choice and rating of importance of factors used in elimination decisions. This is shown in Table 17.7.

The pattern of responses shown in Table 17.7 is similar to that of Table 17.4 in that the general pattern of results is the same. In each category, product profitability is rated most important while market position is rated second. However, at this point, one very real difference is apparent. When the responses to the analysis stage of elimination decisions were categorized by type of industry, widespread statistical differences were noted in how firms rated factors (4 of 5 cases in Table 17.4). Note that in Table 17.7, no significant differences were found. This type of finding was evident throughout this part of the study.

It seems evident that elimination decisions vary with industry category. That is, the relative importance of factors used shows significant statistical variation across industry type not found when responses were classified by degree of formality.

Does formality matter? This question can be answered by scrutinizing the industry category with the greatest percentage of 'highest formal development' responses — minor appliances. Minor appliance firms also had the largest product lines, the shortest life-cycles, and rated elimination activities as very important. In short, formality of elimination programmes is related to need rather than structure or content of programmes. As such, it is not correct to assert that more formal programmes are necessarily better programmes, but that formality as an ingredient of the firm's elimination programme should be tempered by need.

The responses suggested that several typical problems affected the management of elimination programmes. The most common of these problems were: lack of top management interest and participation, resistance to elimination of products by sales personnel, lack of interdepartmental co-ordination in elimination programmes, and lack of a regular routine for the programme. These problems do not seem insurmountable, but the lack of recognition by top management of the importance of life-cycle management at this end of the cycle would seem to be dangerous.

Conclusions and Implications

If management becomes more aware of opportunities afforded by product elimination programmes, the purpose of this study will have been achieved in part. While it is to be expected that the contributions of product elimination programmes to the operations of a firm will vary, the proper performance of the programme should result in increased profitability for the

Table 17.7 The influence of formality on decision factors in the analysis state.

Major factors	Highest	Intermediate	Lowest
Product profitability[b]	38	37	36
Product costs[b]	13	16	14
Product investment[b]	15	15	15
Company alternatives[b]	14	14	13
Market position[b]	20	18	22
Total	100 pts.	100 pts.	100 pts.

[b] No significant differences. (See note to Table 17.1 for explanation of methodology)

firm, through an improved growth rate since resources will be reassigned to more productive uses, and through the enhancement of the planning function in the firm through better exploitation of the life-cycle concept. This study has attempted to show how a number of firms are currently making the product elimination decision. Unfortunately, it is not possible to prescribe an elimination programme or system with numerically specified variables for all firms. Variation does and should exist in elimination programmes since individual firm needs vary. In addition, it is not as easy to develop an index of effectiveness for product elimination programmes as it is for new product programmes (for example, the percentage of new product programmes expenses devoted to successful new products). Rather the findings of this study with respect to the organization, structure and management of elimination activities can be used by firms to design elimination programmes which will fit their individual needs. In doing so, management will increasingly recognize that product elimination efforts are a normal and necessary part of product planning and development activities. Certainly as increased competition and improved technology place more and more emphasis on managerial competence for success in the market place, the product elimination decision will demand more attention.

References

1 Clifford, D.U. 'Managing the Product Life Cycle', *Management Review*, June, 1965, p. 137; and Drucker, P.F. 'Care and Feeding of the Profitable Product', *Fortune*, March, 1964, p. 133.
2 Kotler, P. 'Phasing Out Weak Products', *Harvard Business Review*, March-April 1965, pp. 107-18. Alexander, R.S. 'The Death and Burial of Sick Products', *Journal of Marketing*, April 1964, pp. 1-7. Conrad Berenson, 'Pruning the Product Line', *Business Horizons*, Summer 1963, p. 63. Charles H. Kline, 'The Strategy of Product Policy', *Harvard Business Review*, July-August 1955, p. 100. Kotler, P. 'Phasing Out Weak Products', p. 257.

Exercises & Study Questions

Product Line Management

1. 'The brand manager type of organization only works for firms selling fast moving consumer goods.' Is this true, and if so, why?
2. How many ways are there of discontinuing a product? In what circumstances would you use each one?
3. What can be done to prolong a product's life? In what circumstances would you wish to do this?
   How would you measure the contribution made by an individual product to the profitability of a company?
5. 'Twenty per cent of our products contribute 80 per cent of the profits.' Why is this said so often? What would you do if the ratio was 10/90 rather than 20/80?

6. Describe a process for periodically reviewing the performance of individual products. Discuss the decisions which have to be made after such a review, and the decision rules which would be used.
7. Should a manufacturer produce a full range of products to appeal to every market segment? If he does not do this, what alternative policies are open to him?
8. Salesmen often claim that obsolete products should be kept on as they are the 'calling cards of the business'. How would you answer this claim?
9. Comment on the product lines carried by: British Leyland Motor Corporation, your local supermarket, British Rail, Tube Investments.

18.

Josiah Doncaster & Co Ltd

Prepared by Mr Hugh Murray, London Business School, 1973.

On March 4 the Board of Josiah Doncaster met for the second time in three weeks. Its brief, as before, was to decide what action to take, if any, on a consultant's report, commissioned by the marketing director. The consultant's report investigated the feasibility of extending their product base into in-line compressed air filters, using the company's ceramic know-how.

Established in 1740, the company had built a world-wide reputation for fine household china, and it carefully preserved all its traditions. Management was paternalistic and financially very conservative. Nevertheless, the firm had become well-established in industrial porcelains for high voltage insulation over the last ten years.

Bill Hawkins, the newly appointed marketing director, opened the discussion with an aggressive presentation. At 35 he was a good 15 years younger than anyone else on the board. A Harvard MBA man, he was also the only board member with any formal management training.

'I hope certain members of the board have reconsidered their positions since our last meeting three weeks' ago. Because as far as I am concerned my recommendations still stand. Let's go through them once again, shall we? What are the pertinent facts from the consultant's report? Let's tick them off, one by one ...

1 At £4.50 per filter unit, and 1 million units annually, the market value is £4.5 million.

2 One company, Western, has 85 per cent of the market.

3 The market doesn't like operating under a monopoly, particularly since Western rarely, if ever, give bulk order discounts.

4 The number of buying points worth going after is about 20,000, of which 150 in London, 220 in Birmingham, and 70 in Manchester take 55 per cent of the total.

5 There are 35 key manufacturers of machinery powered by compressed air, who fit filters as part of their machine package.

6 Western don't make a thing; they assemble bought-in parts. So could we.

7 The estimated out-of-pocket cost of their filter unit is £2.50. It sells at £4.50. So there's a nice fat gross margin of over 55 per cent.

8 Their sintered-bronze filter core costs 60p, selling at £1.20. Our ceramic filter core costs ½p! So on the filter as a whole we have a 59½p cost advantage, i.e., our costs are only 76 per cent of theirs.

9 We have a technological edge, because their filter core can only filter down to 64 microns; we can quickly and cheaply tailor our ceramic core to filter down to any required micron filtration.

10 Finally, everybody knows our name, its a household word, and we've got a 200-year quality reputation.

So I say let's go. Look here!' He went over to the new flip chart, mounted on an easel by the Adam fireplace. Pointing, he said:

'Page 1 – strategy. Exploit anti-monopoly feeling of the market, our cost advantage, and product superiority by launching our complete product against Western.
Page 2 – tactics. Prices 10 per cent below Western. Give 25 per cent bulk purchase discount. Personal selling to key buying points and equipment manufacturers. Sell to the rest by direct mail and trade magazine promotion.
Page 3 – targets. 10 per cent of market in year 1, 25 per cent of market in year 2, 40 per cent of market in year 3.
Page 4 – contribution (revenue – variable costs). Year 1 £113,500, year 2 £283,750, year 3 £454,000.
Page 5 – additional costs per annum. Three representatives to cover London, Birmingham, Manchester. Salaries, etc., £15,000, support staff and services £10,000, advertising and promotion £25,000.
Page 6 – estimated gross profit. Year 1 £63,500, year 2 £233,750, year 3 £404,000.
Page 7 – conclusions. Enter the market!

If we're to do our duty to the shareholders, our action is clearly indicated. No more hesitation. Move in on Western.'

'The implication that this board needs reminding of

its duty to its shareholders is neither necessary nor just,' said Paul Doncaster, the managing director.

'Sorry Paul. I guess my enthusiasm ran away with me.'

'It's my function to see it doesn't run away with all of us. The proposition as made is too one-sided, too easy. No account has been taken of the risks involved. When you've had more experience you will realize that taking on a market leader, as dominant as Western is, is no easy thing. Filtration is their business, and they do a good job. There is no complaint anywhere in the report about their product performance, their service or their price. Only what amounts to a feeling that it would be nice if they weren't quite so dominant. What good is that? There are 11 other makers of filters and they share 15 per cent of the market between them. They've made no impression on Western's position. Yet you assume we will, with ease.

'No account has been taken of Western's competitive reaction. And react they will. And quickly. All we know of this market is in the report. They know it backwards. They have the original equipment manufacturers sewn up, and get automatically all the re-orders from the factories. I doubt if any buyer focuses on these as a significant cost centre. Take the 440 chief users. In total they spend £2.475 million i.e., about £5,600 per annum. The replacement units are bought as required over the year, i.e., expenditure averages about £470 per month. To a large company buyer this is small beer. And remember these are safeguards to extremely expensive machinery. The incentive to save pennies at the risk of £1,000's of machinery is very low.'

'Well, the engineer user notices these filters', Bob McGregor, a dour Scot in his mid-sixties, and works director, went on, 'There's a point barely mentioned in the report. The life of these units is about six years. We find that like everyone else we have to clean the sintered bronze core on average once every three months. We use caustic soda solution, then neutralize with weak acid. It's a costly operation both in cleaning, and in machine down-time. When you have to clean the filters you have to stop the machine. Why don't we say that with our filter unit. you throw away the core and replace it with a new one?'

'If we did that we'd have to really lower the filter core price. And that would give the game away. The only difference between our product and Western's is the filter core, and you're asking us to indicate how cheaply we produce it!' John Davies, longest serving member of the board, and financial director, went on, 'I must say again that I don't like the product idea. The report says we must have a clear plastic bowl like Westerns so that people can see the water, oil and dirt rejected by the filter. But I remembered (and my people have looked it up) that there was a court case in 1962 when one of these plastic bowls exploded under pressure. There was a lot of publicity about it, and heavy compensation had to be paid out to workers who were injured. Don't let's forget that household china last year amounted to £1.2 million, 80 per cent of this company's profits. Anything that could harm that side of the company is not worth the risk. If we go into this field we can't risk using plastic bowls, we must use something stronger.'

'But that will affect the entire marketing strategy and tactics. You must give the market what it wants.'

'No Bill, we don't have to in this case,' said Paul Doncaster. 'I think we would be well advised to commission a more general survey into potential new products that don't involve risk to our main product line and that don't involve taking on a monopolistic producer. I propose we take no action on this report but commission a more general survey into completely new products, and formally propose this to the board. Could I have your votes please.' Hawkins jumped to his feet. 'This is crazy. We're passing up an opportunity of a lifetime. Where else am I supposed to find an alternative new product strategy with half the potential of this one? As for some of the objections, they're so bloody feeble they amaze me. There's a way to make a killing in the filter market and I've outlined it. What else do you need? What else can I do to convince you?'

19.
Cork Products Company Limited

Prepared by Mr. Baxter English, 1970

The Cork Products Company Limited (CPC) with a factory and offices in a London suburb has been in the cork closure business for 50 years, and has supplied the bottling trade throughout the UK.

The company has been interested in widening the scope of its activities for some years, and as an outcome of development activities has produced a new type of floor covering which is considered suitable for light industrial flooring. The product is cork-based, and can be laid by any artisan with experience of surfacing by means of a trowel.

It is supplied as a ready mixed paste in five gallon drums which will cover an average of five sq. yds. It is suitable for installation over new or old concrete, or composition floors. Though cork-based, it is high-density, and the finished surface can, therefore, be from 2 mm upwards in thickness – depending on the use to which it is to be put.

It compares quite favourably with the floor tile in being dust-free and resistant to mild acids and alkalis. It stands up to the wear of small fork-lift trucks and stiletto heels, while retaining the resilience of cork.

Accelerated 'ageing' tests have been carried out and the development staff believe that it should have the same life expectancy as vinyl floor tiles.

CPC have considered plans for marketing this product but they have no experience or organization appropriate to the floor covering market.

Plant has been modified to produce 300,000 drums annually (at full capacity). CPC realize that they cannot expect to reach this figure in the first year of marketing, but would like to do so by the end of the third year of the product's life. At 20p per gallon for material, and 25p for the drum, CPC would cover direct production and packing costs, and factory overheads attributable to the product.

As it is not their intention to involve the present organization in the project, beyond the production point, CPC regard £1.25 per drum as a 'transfer price' to a separate, new marketing division for flooring products only. To avoid complications, this transfer price would obtain at all levels of output, up to capacity.

Further production capacity of 200,000 drums annually could be made available, if necessary, at about three months' notice and would justify the cost of plant modification if the transfer price remained at £1.25p per drum.

CPC have an easy cash position, and do not envisage problems in providing working capital for marketing activities, but would like to break even or preferably see a positive cash flow by the end of the second year.

They have decided, therefore, to ask one or two firms of marketing consultants to present them with complete plans for marketing this product. They propose a fee for each consultant firm and a premium for the firm whose plan they select, and further, to retain that firm to recruit and train marketing staff to implement the plan. The terms on which this further activity will be undertaken, are for discussion with the successful firm after the presentation of plans.

CPC have collected a certain amount of data about the market, and this is attached. Any requirement for extra information should be written in to the plan, and it should be made clear to what extent detailed elements of the plan depend upon such information, and the effects this will have upon outcomes.

© VBE 1970.

Report produced for management on the industrial floor-covering market.

The market

13 million sq. yds of new industrial building area was approved, by the issue of Industrial Development certificates in 1969. This was double the equivalent figure for 1961. 260 million sq. yd. is stated to be the total area of industrial building, but one estimate quoted 100 million sq. yd. of light industrial flooring composed of cement or composition suitable for treatment with CPC's new product.

It was believed that in the last year something like five million sq. yd. of new industrial flooring had been laid with competitive products.

Total sales of smooth floor coverings, other than carpets, were 85 million sq. yd., for a value of £28.3 million in 1969. Sales of thermoplastic and vinyl tiles and floorings represented 41 million sq. yd., and almost £14 million of this total; one source estimated that perhaps a quarter of these sales were to industrial users. However, it was impossible to distinguish between sales to industry and sales to domestic users with any accuracy since the distribution channels supplied both markets.

Competition

Main competitors are Marley, Nairn Williamson, Armstrong Cork, and Dunlop. Market shares are difficult to ascertain.

Advertising expenditures varied from nil to a top figure of £25,000 in 1969 by one firm in the industrial market, and £150,000 in the consumer market.

Distributors

Distribution of floor coverings by manufacturers takes these forms:

1 Direct to the customer as material, or as laid flooring, or both.

2 Via specialist distributors selling at retail, or as laid flooring, and other retailers such as furniture and hardware stores.

3 Via builders' merchants supplying the trade or in some cases providing a laid flooring service for builders.

4 Via floor covering contractors providing a complete laid-flooring service for customers.

Firms concentrating on industrial flooring tend to use methods 1, 3 and 4, as the most effective specialist distributors are a retail chain owned by a major manufacturer. Some have their own teams of floor-laying specialists to give a complete laid floor service to industry.

Builders merchants vary considerably in size. The total number is believed to be 3,500 but 1,500 are members of the Federation of Builders and Plumbers Merchants, and the biggest 220 are generally held to do half the business.

Floor covering contractors number about 1,300 but they vary greatly in size. The Floor Covering Contractors' Association has been set up to maintain standards of performance for the industry. It has 85 members who believe that they lay about 70 per cent of the flooring in the UK. Some of the members are manufacturers.

Price Schedules

Retail prices vary from over £1.50 per sq. yd. for the best 'domestic' covering to less than 50p per sq. yd. for industrial or institutional use.

Manufacturers' net realization for a high quality industrial product comes to 53p per sq. yd.; for the cheapest industrial type it is 25p. The average over the range, excluding the cheapest felt, is 44p.

A typical price schedule would be roughly as follows:

average net realization	45p
manufacturer's trade price	
(to a retailer or small	
merchant)	50p
purchase tax (13¾%)	7p
margin for trader say . . .	
(RPM has been abolished)	25p
'Retail' price to a user	82p

Manufacturers, retailers, and merchants will of course 'shade' their 'retail' prices according to the size of an industrial contract. Moreover, where a floor-laying service is offered, the customer is often quoted an 'all in' price, for material and laying. The price generally quoted for laying as a separate service is 30p per sq. yd.

Cork based flooring – a technical report

Introduction

This report describes a series of tests that have been carried out on 'cork base' and comparable products. The details of the results are given fully below, and can be summarized by saying that our product is comparable in most respects and better in others. The tests are listed below.

Comparable Products

Marketing department supplied samples of the products on which to base the tests. There are a large number of makes and some classification and selection had to be made. The resulting categories for testing depend on the thickness required.

Category 1 (normal household usage)

No.	Description	Specification
A1	Lino tiles (1)	2.00 mm th, 3.75 kg/sq.m
A2	Thermoplastic tiles (4)	2.10 mm th, 3.60 kg/sq.m
A3	CORK product (1)	2.00 mm th, 2.75 kg/sq.m
A4	Resiliant black vinyl (3)	2.6 mm th, 3.90 kg/sq.m
A5	Cushioned vinyl laminate (4)	2.7 mm th, 4.20 kg/sq.m

th = thickness*, kg/sq.m = kilogrammes/square metre including the backing material, where applicable.

Category 2 – Institutional
(Useful where extra durability is necessary, e.g., schools, business premises, and public buildings.)

No.	Description	Specification
B1	Plain linoleum (2)	3.2 mm, 6.0 kg/sq.m
B2	Thermoplastic tiles (4)	3.2 mm, 5.5 kg/sq.m
B3	CORK product (1)	3.2 mm, 4.4 kg/sq.m
B4	Resiliant back vinyl (3)	3.2 mm, 4.8 kg/sq.m
B5	Cushioned vinyl laminate (4)	3.0 mm, 4.7 kg/sq.m

Category 3
(Useful for sports halls, etc.)

No.	Description	Specification
C1	Cork carpet (1)	4.5-6.00 mm, 5.0 kg/sq.m
C2	CORK product (1)	4.5 + mm, 6.2 kg/sq.m
C3	Linoleum (1)	4.5 mm, 8.4 kg/sq.m

* The figures in brackets refer to the number of products tested.

Category 4
(Light industrial)
(Not tested to date)

Tests

A series of tests were carried out to compare:

1 Resistance to indentation.
2 Resistance to wear.
3 Resistance to chemicals.
4 Electrical properties.
5 Colour stability.
6 Resistance to fire.
7 Water absorption.
8 Dimensional stability.
9 Thermal insulation properties.

As well as the above tests, some research has been done to compare sub-floor preparation, and maintenance characteristics.

The results of these tests are fully reported as follows.

Resistance to indentation

All the samples concerned were tested for compliance with BSS 3261 for residual identation. The tests were carried out using a cylindrical steel rod of 4.52 mm (0.178 in) diameter through which a load of 26.286kg (80 lb) was applied for 10 minutes giving a pressure of approximately 2.268 kg/mm^2 (1.44 tons/sq.in.). The load was then removed and the residual indentation monitored. BSS 3261 allows a maximum residual indentation of 0.152 mm (0.006 in.).

The tests were carried out on all the specimens provided by marketing department, each sub-category being tested 20 times. The average and standard deviations of the residual indentations are presented below. Individual manufacturers' products have not been isolated e.g., all thermoplastic tiles are placed in a single sub-category.

Category 1

No.	Gauge (mm)	Initial indentation after 10 min.	Residual indentation after 30 min.	60 min.
A1	2.0 (0.1)	0.28 (0.06)	0.10 (0.05)	0.071 (0.009)
A2	2.1 (0.1)	0.32 (0.05)	0.13 (0.04)	0.025 (0.006)
A3	2.0 (0.1)	0.26 (0.04)	0.09 (0.03)	0.023 (0.008)
A4	2.6 (0.1)	0.27 (0.04)	0.18 (0.04)	0.031 (0.008)
A5	2.7 (0.1)	0.25 (0.05)	0.17 (0.04)	0.032 (0.008)

The figures in brackets are the standard deviations of the readings.

Category 2

No.	Gauge (mm)	Initial indentation after 10 min.	Residual 30 min.	60 min.
B1	3.2 (0.1)	0.92 (0.21)	0.53 (0.13)	0.42 (0.10)
B2	3.2 (0.1)	0.87 (0.20)	0.51 (0.11)	0.32 (0.09)
B3	3.2 (0.1)	0.56 (0.09)	0.32 (0.06)	0.23 (0.05)
B4	3.2 (0.2)	1.01 (0.18)	0.64 (0.12)	0.32 (0.08)
B5	3.2 (0.2)	1.02 (0.19)	0.49 (0.13)	0.28 (0.11)

Category 3

No.	Gauge (mm)	Initial indentation after 10 min.	Residual indentation after 30 min.	60 min.
C1	4.5 (0.3)	1.63 (0.57)	0.97 (0.38)	0.81 (0.31)
C2	4.5 (0.1)	0.72 (0.10)	0.31 (0.07)	0.22 (0.06)
C3	4.5 (0.2)	0.94 (0.19)	0.62 (0.13)	0.43 (0.11)

The results indicate that the Cork product gives better resistance to indentation than all other products tested, and is well within the limits set by BSS 3261.

Resistance to Wear

An ageing test giving the equivalent of ten years' wear over a period of six months has been performed on all the samples. The test simulates the effect of normal shoe wear over long periods of time. The effect of wear on the material was monitored. Two separate trials have been carried out. In one case no maintenance is carried out (unless a hole appears in the material) and in the other, polish/cleaner is applied equivalent to weekly attention. The results are presented below and should be self-explanatory.

Category 1

Case 1 No maintenance

No.	Initial thickness	Resulting thickness	No of times attention required	Condition Poor	Fair	Good	V. good
A1	2.0 (0.1)	1.6 (0.2)	2	6	9	4	1
A2	2.1 (0.1)	1.7 (0.2)	1	7	8	3	2
A3	2.0 (0.1)	1.8 (0.2)	5	9	5	4	2
A4	2.6 (0.1)	2.2 (0.4)	4	7	6	5	2
A5	2.7 (0.1)	2.1 (0.4)	3	8	5	4	3

Category 2

No.	Initial thickness	Resulting thickness	No. of times attention required	Condition Poor	Fair	Good	V. good
B1	3.2 (0.1)	2.4 (0.2)	3	7	8	3	2
B2	3.2 (0.1)	2.5 (0.2)	2	6	8	4	2
B3	3.2 (0.1)	2.8 (0.3)	4	6	6	5	3
B4	3.2 (0.2)	2.7 (0.4)	2	8	8	3	1
B5	3.2 (0.2)	2.8 (0.2)	3	7	8	4	1

Category 3

No.	Initial thickness	Resulting thickness	No. of times attention required	Condition Poor	Fair	Good	V good
C1	4.5 (0.3)	3.0 (0.3)	3	5	6	5	4
C2	4.5 (0.1)	3.8 (0.3)	4	4	5	6	5
C3	4.5 (0.2)	3.7 (0.3)	3	6	7	5	2

Case 2 Regular maintenance   **Category 1**

No.	Initial thickness	Resulting thickness	No. of times attention required	Condition			
				Poor	Fair	Good	V good
A1	2.0 (0.1)	1.9 (0.2)	1	4	3	7	6
A2	2.1 (0.1)	1.8 (0.2)	0	6	6	5	3
A3	2.0 (0.1)	1.9 (0.2)	0	7	5	4	4
A4	2.6 (0.1)	2.4 (0.3)	1	3	4	7	6
A5	2.7 (0.1)	2.2 (0.4)	0	5	6	6	3

Category 2

No.	Initial thickness	Resulting thickness	No. of times attention required	Condition			
				Poor	Fair	Good	V good
B1	3.2 (0.1)	2.5 (0.2)	0	4	6	8	2
B2	3.2 (0.1)	2.7 (0.2)	0	4	5	7	4
B3	3.2 (0.1)	3.0 (0.2)	0	2	4	7	6
B4	3.2 (0.2)	2.9 (0.3)	0	5	6	7	3
B5	3.2 (0.2)	2.9 (0.3)	1	4	4	7	5

Category 3

No.	Initial thickness	Resulting thickness	No. of times attention required	Condition			
				Poor	Fair	Good	V good
C1	4.5 (0.3)	4.1 (0.3)	0	3	2	9	6
C2	4.5 (0.1)	4.2 (0.3)	0	2	2	9	7
C3	4.5 (0.2)	4.2 (0.3)	0	3	4	8	5

The results indicate that the cork product appears to wear at the same rate as the other samples. Further tests are required over the next six months if 20-year life is to be tested. One point to note is in the case of no maintenance the cork-based product required attention more times than the other products in categories 1 and 2. This may be due to wearing characteristics of the product, or this may be due to the sampling error, but at present no conclusion may be drawn without further tests being carried out.

Resistance to chemicals

The results of various chemical tests are presented below.

Chemical/category	Category 1					Category 2					Category 3		
	A.1	A.2	A.3	A.4	A.5	B.1	B.2	B.3	B.4	B.5	C.1	C.2	C.3
Water	N	N	N	N	N	N	N	N	N	N	N	N	N
Butter	N	N	N	N	N	N	N	N	N	N	S	N	N
Paraffin	N	N	N	N	N	N	N	N	N	N	S	N	N
Milk	N	N	N	N	N	N	N	N	N	N	N	N	N
Domestic bleach	S	S	N	N	N	S	S	N	N	N	S	N	N
Hydrogen peroxide	S	S	N	N	N	S	S	N	N	N	S	N	N
Soap solution	N	N	N	N	N	N	N	N	N	N	N	N	N
Detergent solution	N	N	N	N	N	N	N	N	N	N	N	N	N
White spirit	N	N	N	N	N	N	N	N	N	N	N	N	N
Washing soda	S	S	N	N	N	S	S	N	N	N	S	N	N
Cooking fats & oils	S	N	N	N	N	S	N	N	N	N	S	N	N
Beer	N	N	N	N	N	N	N	N	N	N	N	N	N
Blood	N	N	N	N	N	N	N	N	N	N	S	N	N
Fruit juices	N	N	N	N	N	N	N	N	N	N	S	N	N
Methylated spirits	N	N	N	N	N	N	N	N	N	N	S	N	N
Diesel oil	S	S	N/S	S	S	S	S	N/S	S	S	S	N/S	S
Ketones	S	S	S	S	S	S	S	S	S	S	S/C	S	S
Chlorinated solvents	S	S	S	S	S	S	S	S	S	S	S	S	S
Acetate solvents	S	S	S	S	S	S	S	S	S	S	S/C	S	S
Benzene	S/C	S/C	S	S/C	S/C	S/C	S/C	S	S/C	S/C	C	S	S/C
Toluene	S/C	S/C	S	S/C	S/C	S/C	S/C	S	S/C	S/C	C	S	S/C
Hexane	S	S	S	S	S	S	S	S	S	S	C	S	S
Petrol	S	S	N	S	S	S	S	N	S	S	S/C	S	S
Various hairdressing preparations	S/C	S/C	S	S/C	S/C	S/C	S/C	S	S/C	S/C	C	S	S/C
Various photographic chemicals	S/C	S/C	S	S/C	S/C	S/C	S/C	S	S/C	S/C	C	S	S/C
Boot polish	S	S	S	S	S	S	S	S	S	S	S	S	S
Ink	S	S	S	S	S	S	S	S	S	S	S	S	S
Caustic soda	C	C	C	C	C	C	C	C	C	C	C	C	C
Concentrated acids	C	C	C	C	C	C	C	C	C	C	C	C	C

N: Negligible effect   S: Slight staining and surface marking   C: Corrosion

From the table it is seen that the cork product is equal to the
other products as to staining, and in some cases more resistant to corrosion.

Electrical properties

All samples were tested accordingly to BSS 903 Part 33 (1950) using 9.5 cm electrode and 500 v, DC, the volume resistivity being measured in ohm cm of product. The resistivity was measured after 1 min., 2 min., and 10 min., respectively. The agreement between the readings taken at different times is close and so only one result is present below for comparison.

Volume resistivity (ohm/cm)

Category 1

A1	1.5×10^{10} (0.4×10^{10})
A2	2.0×10^{13} (0.8×10^{13})
A3	2.0×10^{11} (1.0×10^{11})
A4	1.1×10^{13} (0.8×10^{13})
A5	1.6×10^{10} (0.8×10^{10})

Category 2

B1	1.7×10^{12} (0.3×10^{12})
B2	3.1×10^{13} (0.8×10^{13})
B3	3.2×10^{12} (0.7×10^{12})
B4	1.7×10^{13} (0.4×10^{13})
B5	3.2×10^{11} (0.6×10^{11})

Category 3

C1	1.5×10^{9} (0.5×10^{9})
C2	3.4×10^{12} (0.6×10^{12})
C3	1.8×10^{12} (0.3×10^{12})

Colour stability

During initial trials of the cork product it has been noticed that the lighter coloured specimens are slightly affected by ultra-violet light, and after a few months, a plain coloured floor sometimes takes on a mottled effect. Research is being carried out at the moment into the causes of this effect and it is felt that it is only a matter of time before a more stable pigment is found. No such effect has been found in the darker coloured specimens, and in any of the other samples supplied by marketing department.

(It has not been possible to produce a pattern floor using the cork product, but a mingled effect has been produced using different non-mixable pigments. This variety has not been tested to date.)

Resistance to fire

All the samples submitted will neither support combustion nor burn unless exposed continuously to a naked flame. Burning cigarettes scarred all the samples, and to a greater extent in the cork based products.

The cork based products also appear to give off more smoke when exposed to a naked flame than other products, although this difference has not been measured accurately.

Water absorption

The surfaces of the samples were completely covered with water for 24 hours and their increase in weight noted. The results are presented below under heading test A.

Increase in weight
(%)

	Test A	Test B
Category 1		
A1	0.5 (0.3)	1.2 (0.4)
A2	0.4 (0.2)	1.1 (0.3)
A3.	0.5 (0.3)	1.1 (0.4)
A4	0.4 (0.3)	NA
A5	0.6 (0.5)	NA
Category 2		
B1	0.5 (0.4)	0.9 (0.3)
B2	0.5 (0.3)	1.1 (0.4)
B3	0.4 (0.3)	1.0 (0.3)
B4	0.6 (0.4)	NA
B5	0.5 (0.4)	NA
Category 3		
C1	6.2 (1.4)*	NA
C2	0.5 (0.3)	1.1 (0.3)
C3	0.4 (0.3)	0.9 (0.3)

Another test was also performed by completely immersing the samples (where applicable), for 24 hours, and the results are presented under heading test B.

NA: Not applicable

Dimensional stability

A common cause of flooring failure arises out of expansion, and contraction due to temperature changes. Various samples were taken of equal length and placed in a constant temperature at 0°C and 65 per cent relative humidity. Length measurements were then taken again. The samples were then placed at a constant temperature at 22°C and 65 per cent relative humidity. After leaving for 24 hours the lengths were remeasured. The resulting changes are given below:

*   This test was abandoned when the heavy absorbency was discovered.

Average change in length (%)	
Category 1	
A1	0.62
A2	0.51
A3	0.29
A4	0.36
A5	0.47
Category 2	
B1	0.65
B2	0.50
B3	0.36
B4	0.38
B5	0.46
Category 3	
C1	0.61
C2	0.35
C3	0.64

The cork product has greater dimensional stability than any of the other products tested.

Thermal insulation

The thermal conductivity of the samples is given below in Btu/in/ft^{2}h$^\circ$F).

A1	A2	A3	A4	A5
.6 (0.3)	3.4 (0.8)	4.5 (1.0)	3.2 (0.8)	0.1 (0.007)

B1	B2	B3	B4	B5
.7 (0.5)	3.6 (0.7)	4.6 (1.3)	3.4 (0.7)	0.12 (0.00)

C1	C2	C3
.5 (2.1)	4.6 (2.0)	1.7 (0.6)

This factor has to be taken into account when considering underfloor heating systems. Research is proceeding into this area and the results will be published in a later report.

Sub-floor preparation

Cork product has been laid on solid sub-floors and timber floors with great success. Little preparation is necessary and only a trowel is necessary. It is relatively easy to get a horizontal surface, but difficulties may occur when the floor is not horizontal. For floors between 2 and 4.5 mm, thick the drying period is between 24 and 48 hours, depending on the relative humidity and ambient temperature. Two minor difficulties have arisen (a) it is often difficult to gauge the usage on uneven floors (b) the laying tools are difficult to clean.

Maintenance characteristics

Cork product is as easy to maintain as all other products tested and the same cleaning materials are appropriate. One benefit that cork product has over the other products is that severe damage can be repaired by refilling the cavity and allowing to dry.

An attempt has also been made to get some indication about customer preference by carrying out a small experiment. The results are presented in Appendix 3.

Conclusions

It is felt that the product is a worthwhile product, and passes all the standard tests. Even though there are slight difficulties at present e.g., colour these will be overcome very shortly. No production problems are envisaged.

Appendix 3

Customer preference test

Results of tests carried out with our own staff (58 women, 18 men); Speedy Mail Order warehouse staff (84 women, 6 men); Longlife Insurance Company office staff (26 women, 20 men), and Electronic Light Industries Ltd (62 women, 14 men).

Nine sq. yd. of our own, and competitive flooring were laid in canteens, and staff were asked to complete a questionnaire, on a voluntary basis. These are the conclusions:

'Which of the products you have tested would you rate best for these qualities?'

No.	1	2	3	4	5
Comfortable to walk on	6	81	102	70	20
Springy	2	40	120	102	12
Safe – not slippery	20	70	85	87	21
Pleasing appearance	20	84	30	89	60
Easy to keep clean	32	48	42	68	47
Quiet	18	85	96	65	24
Easy on the feet	15	85	71	78	14

Code: No. 1 = lino tiles
2 = cushioned vinyl laminate
3 = Cork product
4 = resilient backed vinyl
5 = thermoplastic tile

Suggested product description – Corkbase: a new advance in floor covering

Description
The product is supplied as a ready mixed paste which can be laid on almost any surface. ·

Specification
Available in 5-gallon drums and is manufactured in a range of colours, medium brown, dark brown and dark grey, all having colour fastness to daylight to the level required by BSS 3261. The thickness required varies according to the usage required.

Uses
For household usage (2mm thick), schools, business premises, shops and public buildings of all kinds (3.2 mm thick), light industrial (4.5 mm thick).

Indentation resistance
The resistance to indentation is outstanding and is well within BSS 3261. Tests were carried out using a cylindrical steel rod of 4.53 mm (0.178 in) diameter through which a load of 26.286 kg (80 lb) was applied for ten minutes giving a pressure of approximately 2.268 kg/mm^2 (1.44 tons/sq.in). The load was then removed and the residual indentation measured. The table below shows the exceptional results obtained.

Thickness of material (mm)	Initial indentation after 10 minutes	Residual indentation after	
		30 minutes	60 minutes
2.0	0.26	0.09	0.023
3.2	0.56	0.32	0.230
4.5	0.72	0.31	0.220

Chemical resistance
Corkbase has good all-round resistance to most chemicals in general use.

Electrical properties
Corkbase has poor electrical conductivity properties, and consequently can be used for most floors with complete safety.

Dimensional stability
The product is extremely stable to temperature changes, and at 22°C change in temperature produces only a 0.29 per cent change in dimension.

Maintenance
The flooring is extremely easy to maintain, and better wearing is obtained by regular use of any of the recommended propriety cleaners. If by some unusual chance the floor does become damaged, this can be easily repaired by the application of more material and allowing to dry overnight.

Sub-floor preparation
The product can be laid on solid sub-floors or timber floors. Little preparation is necessary, and only a trowel is required for the laying.

Appearance
The flooring has a pleasant appearance and an extremely kind effect on the feet, having more spring in it than conventional flooring. This quality coupled with its hard wearing characteristics make an excellent floor covering for households, schools, offices, and light industrial premises.

Appendix 5

Miscellaneous Government Statistics

1. EXTRACT FROM BUSINESS MONITOR, PRODUCTION SERIES, P.40 FLOOR COVERINGS

Reproduced by permission of HMSO.

Summary

In the second quarter of 1970, manufacturers' sales of smooth floorcoverings, at £7.9 million, were 7 per cent less than in the corresponding period of 1969. Sales to the home market fell by three per cent and exports by 25 per cent.

Sales in terms of volume were 23.1 million sq. yd, a decrease of 12 per cent when compared with a year earlier. On the home market, where sales fell by 12 per cent, the only items to show any improvement over the previous corresponding period were calendered inlaid tiles and spread vinyl on felt. Exports were also down, by 16 per cent. Sales of printed linoleum on textile, thermoplastic and the thinner type of vinyl asbestos tiles, calendered inlaid tiles and spread vinyl on textile bases other than needle-loom felt all increased over a year earlier but exports of all other items fell.

Table 1.1   Floor coverings. Quarterly manufacturers' sales by volume (000 sq.yd)

	1969						1970			
	April-June		July-September		October-December		January-March		April-June	
	Total	Export	Total	Export	Total	Export	Total	Export	Total	Export
Printed felt base	8,067	2,885	8,002	2,707	9,565	3,586	6,769	2,997	6,915	2,515
Linoleum in sheet and tile form										
On a paper or paperboard base	163	21	112	6	108	5	119	35	94	12
On a textile base										
Printed	3	1	1	1	–	–	–	–	2	2
Inlaid and plain	2,531	642	2,388	459	2,454	598	2,382	450	1,985	258
Rigid and semi-rigid tiles										
Thermoplastic tiles:										
BS 2592	3,680	25	3,792	30	3,950	29	3,158	51	3,236	30
Vinyl asbestos tiles:										
BS 3260	2,344	441	2,342	386	2,335	395	2,121	465	2,301	421
BS 3260 but less than 0.06 in thickness	985	62	883	96	875	128	688	61	883	105
Calendered vinyl floorings										
Printed (sheet and tiles)	4,993	878	4,920	908	4,401	842	3,710	701	4,272	823
Inlaid Sheet	710	145	658	146	639	91	593	113	598	98
Tiles: BS 3261, including those less than 0.06 in thickness	1,734	82	1,640	103	1,665	141	1,593	72	1,779	90
Spread vinyl floorings										
On needleloom felt	771	151	720	149	833	169	701	132	797	132
On other textile bases	66	3	72	7	67	5	101	33	72	13
High quality vinyl floorings	108	34	91	28	75	14	74	17	80	24
Other floor coverings	100	14	84	3	75	4	95	6	83	10
Total	26,256	5,386	25,705	5,029	27,042	6,007	22,103	5,132	23,097	4,533

Table 1.2   Floor coverings. Quarterly manufacturers' sales by value (£ 000)

Printed felt base	892	323	881	301	1,078	410	781	350	811	296
Linoleum in sheet and tile form										
On a paper or paperboard base	55	5	46	3	42	2	44	9	37	4
On a textile base										
Printed	1	–	–	–	–	–	–	–	–	–
Inlaid and plain	1,462	341	1,347	241	1,391	287	1,448	240	1,236	156
Rigid and semi-rigid tiles										
Thermoplastic tiles:										
BS 2592	944	9	967	9	997	9	830	16	870	9
Vinyl asbestos tiles:										
BS 3260	1,155	310	1,143	141	1,155	169	1,061	191	1,179	172
BS 3260 but less than 0.06 in thickness	269	20	249	35	238	50	199	23	257	37
Calendered vinyl floorings										
Printed (sheet and tiles)	1,773	299	1,738	300	1,566	277	1,344	216	1,557	293
Inlaid Sheet	451	110	386	74	373	62	352	66	385	64
Tiles: BS 3261 including those less than 0.06 in thickness	895	50	877	64	864	87	851	48	974	53
Spread vinyl floorings										
On needleloom felt	314	56	286	54	315	63	292	47	320	50
On other textile bases	38	2	37	33	3	3	42	11	37	8
High quality vinyl floorings	129	39	113	30	102	16	106	19	126	31
Other floor coverings	71	6	61	2	51	2	86	4	70	5
Total	8,449	1,570	8,131	1,257	8,204	1,438	7,437	1,238	7,859	1,178

These figures represent sales by all UK firms known to be manufacturing floor coverings in sheet or tile form. Rubber and cork floor coverings, mats, matting and carpet underlays are excluded. Printed felt bases excludes vinyl surfaced material. High quality vinyl floorings exceed BSS 3261.

Values are not selling prices; purchase tax, trade discounts and commissions have been excluded. Exports are goods exported directly or known to be destined for export.

Table 1.3   Annual sales

	(000 sq. yd)						(£000)					
	1967		1968		1969		1967		1968		1969	
	Total	Export	Total	Export	Total	Export	Total	Export	Total	Export	Total	Export
Printed felt base	42,722	11,682	39,042	12,686	32,718	11,387	4,427	1,241	4,169	1,376	3,628	1,278
Linoleum in sheet and tile form												
On a paper or paperboard base	1,483	346	848	174	512	42	465	95	294	48	193	13
On a textile base												
Printed	142	80	34	27	11	6	30	17	8	5	2	1
Inlaid and plain	14,493	3,561	12,494	2,649	10,036	2,276	7,208	1,601	6,830	1,291	5,708	1,154
Rigid and semi-rigid tiles												
Thermoplastic tiles: BS 2592	15,378	103	16,018	149	15,046	116	3,696	32	4,108	46	3,827	37
Vinyl asbestos tiles:												
BS 3260	8,781	1,206	9,341	1,507	9,073	1,590	4,131	406	4,561	534	4,514	740
BS 3260 but less than 0.06 in thickness	3,473	313	3,561	254	3,502	319	957	105	968	85	959	116
Calendered vinyl floorings												
Printed (sheet and tiles)	25,374	4,243	22,774	3,688	19,433	3,524	8,495	1,299	7,894	1,235	6,776	1,177
Inlaid												
Sheet	1,833	447	2,086	428	2,665	498	1,023	280	1,175	260	1,592	315
Tiles: BS 3261, including those less than 0.06 in thickness	6,113	471	7,054	409	6,666	421	3,222	281	3,677	226	3,503	233
Spread vinyl floorings												
On needleloom felt	2,329	648	2,670	655	3,085	624	1,061	281	1,190	251	1,239	232
On other bases	349	26	259	16	268	19	215	15	138	9	142	11
High quality vinyl floorings	276	21	308	56	364	95	325	26	392	64	462	106
Other floor coverings	6,357	2,335	592	74	358	35	1,106	308	292	33	259	18
Total	129,101	25,481	117,081	22,771	103,738	20,954	36,360	5,987	35,692	5,456	32,802	5,433

2. INDUSTRIAL BUILDING

Table 2.1 Industrial Building 1961 to 1969.

million sq. ft

	Total	Great Britain Development areas	(1)	Great Britain Rest	North	Yorkshire and Humberside	East Midlands	East Anglia	South East	South West	Wales	West Midlands	North West	Scotland
1961	56.5	15.0 ..	(1)	41.5	6.5	4.2	3.5	1.8	18.1	2.8	2.5	5.0	7.4	4.3
1962	37.3	9.1 ..		28.2	3.0	2.4	2.2	1.8	11.8	2.4	2.1	3.7	4.4	3.7
1963	39.2	12.2 ..		27.0	4.2	3.7	2.5	1.5	9.6	2.4	1.6	3.5	5.3	4.9
1964	59.0	20.2 ..		38.7	8.2	6.0	3.7	2.5	11.9	4.4	3.2	5.0	8.2	5.9
1965	61.7	24.6 ..		37.1	6.2	6.2	3.4	1.8	11.2	3.1	4.5	5.1	9.2	11.0
1966	68.8	28.6 ..		40.2	8.2	6.4	4.4	3.8	10.8	3.6	9.3		9.0	6.2
1967	87.2(59.7)	28.9(26.5)	33	58.3(33.2)	7.5(7.5)	8.7(4.6)	6.4(3.9)	3.6(2.1)	20.6(11.1)	6.3(3.3)	5.7(5.7)	7.1(4.0)	11.3(7.5)	10.1(10.1)
1968	110.3(78.9)	37.9(35.7)	34	72.4(43.1)	11.9(11.9)	9.0(5.8)	7.3(4.2)	4.8(2.8)	21.0(11.1)	6.3(3.9)	8.8(8.8)	11.6(6.6)	17.8(11.9)	11.8(11.8)
1969	115.9(80.6)	33.0(30.6)	29	82.8(49.9)	9.9(9.9)	15.4(10.7)	6.7(4.1)	6.3(4.0)	26.3(13.9)	6.8(4.1)	8.3(8.3)	10.4(5.9)	16.8(10.6)	9.1(9.1)
1967 1st qtr	27.2(18.6)	9.8(8.9)	36	17.4(9.7)	2.6(2.6)	3.4(1.6)	1.7(1.0)	0.8(0.5)	5.4(2.9)	1.9(0.9)	1.6(1.6)	2.2(1.2)	3.5(2.2)	4.1(4.1)
2nd qtr	21.2(14.5)	6.9(6.5)	32	14.3(8.0)	1.4(1.4)	2.0(1.2)	0.9(0.6)	0.8(0.4)	5.3(2.9)	1.7(0.9)	1.5(1.5)	1.9(1.1)	2.9(1.9)	2.7(2.7)
3rd qtr	20.6(14.0)	6.0(5.5)	29	14.6(8.5)	0.9(0.9)	1.8(1.0)	2.2(1.4)	0.9(0.5)	5.6(3.1)	1.4(0.9)	1.3(1.3)	1.7(0.9)	2.9(2.3)	1.8(1.8)
4th qtr	18.3(12.5)	6.3(5.7)	34	12.0(6.8)	2.6(2.6)	1.5(0.8)	1.6(0.9)	1.1(0.8)	4.3(2.2)	1.2(0.7)	1.3(1.3)	1.3(0.8)	2.0(1.1)	1.5(1.5)
1968 1st qtr	24.6(18.0)	8.9(8.4)	36	15.6(9.6)	2.6(2.6)	2.0(1.5)	1.8(1.0)	1.6(1.0)	4.0(2.0)	1.4(0.8)	1.7(1.7)	1.8(1.0)	3.8(2.6)	3.8(3.6)
2nd qtr	27.2(19.5)	8.2(7.9)	30	18.9(11.6)	3.4(3.4)	3.0(1.9)	1.4(0.8)	0.9(0.5)	5.3(3.3)	2.0(1.3)	1.3(1.3)	3.9(2.1)	3.6(2.5)	2.4(2.4)
3rd qtr	31.1(22.3)	12.6(11.8)	40	18.6(10.5)	4.4(4.4)	2.2(1.3)	1.6(1.0)	1.3(0.7)	6.4(3.2)	1.5(0.9)	3.0(3.0)	2.8(1.7)	5.1(3.3)	2.8(2.8)
4th qtr	27.5(19.1)	8.2(7.7)	30	19.3(11.4)	1.6(1.6)	1.9(1.2)	2.5(1.3)	1.0(0.7)	5.3(2.6)	1.3(0.8)	2.8(2.8)	3.1(1.9)	5.3(3.5)	2.7(2.7)
1969 1st qtr	33.3(22.5)	9.5(8.7)	28	23.8(13.8)	2.6(2.6)	3.6(2.3)	2.2(1.3)	2.0(1.4)	8.2(4.0)	2.3(1.3)	2.4(2.4)	2.7(1.6)	4.6(3.0)	2.5(2.5)
2nd qtr	29.9(20.5)	9.9(9.0)	33	20.0(11.5)	3.8(3.8)	2.1(1.2)	1.7(0.9)	1.7(0.9)	6.9(3.5)	1.7(1.1)	2.1(2.1)	2.8(1.7)	5.1(3.1)	2.0(2.0)
3rd qtr	25.8(18.1)	6.8(6.5)	26	19.0(11.6)	1.9(1.9)	3.6(2.2)	1.4(1.0)	1.4(0.9)	5.8(3.4)	1.5(0.9)	2.2(2.2)	2.6(1.3)	3.3(2.1)	2.1(2.1)
4th qtr	26.9(19.5)	6.9(6.5)	26	20.0(13.0)	1.5(1.5)	6.0(4.9)	1.3(0.9)	1.3(0.8)	5.3(2.9)	1.3(0.8)	1.6(1.6)	2.3(1.3)	3.8(2.3)	2.4(2.4)

NOTES: The figures relate to schemes, mainly over 5,000 sq. ft., for both manufacturing and non-manufacturing industry approved during the periods stated: New Buildings, extensions to existing premises and existing buildings turned to industrial use are included.

( ) The figures in brackets are estimates of the floor area which would have been approved on the basis in use before the introduction of the Industrial Development Act in August 1966. The area of industrial development certificates was then extended to include all ancillary space for storage, canteens, etc. In Scotland, Wales and the North of England ancillary space was already being included in areas approved before that date but not in the other regions; because of the lack of comparability the percentage share of development areas is not shown prior to 1967.

(1) The figures in this column are development area approvals as percentages of UK totals. The places designated as development areas under the Industrial Development Act, 1966 are the whole of the northern region, most of Scotland and Wales, and parts of the North West and South West regions.

3. EXTRACT FROM MONTHLY DIGEST OF STATISTICS, AUGUST 1970, HMSO
Reproduced by permission

Table 3.1   Manufacturers sales of floor coverings

Carpets and rugs

Quarterly averages or totals for quarters(1)

('000 sq. yd.)

| | All types | | Woven carpets | | | | Tufted carpets | | Coir mats, matting and matting rugs (2) | Imports(3) |
| | | | Faced with wool | | Faced with man-made fibres | | | | | |
	Total	Of which for export	Total	Of which for export	Total	Of which for export	Total	Of which for export	Total	
1966	28,168	2,217	9,439	1,003	4,528	384	10,750	665	23	96,100
1967	30,014	2,385	8,522	970	5,107	368	13,167	901	28	81,820
1968	34,047	3,822	9,651	1,474	5,573	541	14,887	1,453	15	85,320
1969	36,423	5,088	9,440	1,704	5,543	642	15,830	2,347	15	61,940
1967 1st qtr	26,496	2,204	8,177	966	4,543	345	10,736	743	19	27,560
2nd qtr	29,994	2,314	8,426	901	4,982	367	13,285	878	51	20,380
3rd qtr	27,858	2,192	7,404	892	4,731	334	12,732	836	31	18,900
4th qtr	35,707	2,829	10,079	1,121	6,173	426	15,914	1,150	14	14,980
1968 1st qtr	34,929	3,237	10,113	1,189	5,985	485	15,398	1,336	18	19,360
2nd qtr	32,712	3,564	9,655	1,579	5,278	475	14,554	1,306	14	21,860
3rd qtr	31,738	3,927	8,274	1,379	4,839	538	13,917	1,340	17	20,620
4th qtr	36,811	4,560	10,563	1,748	6,190	666	15,678	1,829	12	23,480
1969 1st qtr	33,727	4,434	8,993	1,572	4,940	386	14,554	1,911	17	14,500
2nd qtr	36,160	4,858	9,227	1,549	5,331	606	15,904	2,343	19	11,780
3rd qtr	33,269	4,747	8,351	1,652	5,128	638	14,382	2,091	14	15,580
4th qtr	42,537	6,311	11,188	2,044	6,766	737	18,482	3,044	8	20,080
1970 1st qtr	33,736	4,917	8,442	1,397	4,840	561	15,165	2,511	7	16,750

1 Before 1967 figures relate to years ending November and to quarters ending February, May, August and November. From 1967 figures relate to calendar quarters, i.e., ending March, June, September and December. 2 The import figures have been revised to include coir mats and matting rugs. Import figures published in this table up to 4th quarter 1969 were for coir matting only. These separate figures are no longer available. 3 Hundredweights.

Linoleum, vinyl and other synthetic materials

Quarterly averages or totals for quarters

('000 sq. yd.)

Table 3.2 Manufacturers sales of floor coverings

	Printed felt base		Linoleum in sheet and tile form		Rigid and semi-rigid tiles		Calendered vinyl floorings in sheet and tile form		Spread vinyl floorings		Other (1)	
	Total sales	For export	Total sales	For export	Total sales	For export	Total sales	For export	Total sales	For export	Total sales	For export
1966	11,903	3,480	4,998	1,515	6,510	420	8,344	1,499	570	206	1,477	621
1967	10,681	2,921	4,030	997	6,908	406	8,330	1,290	658	164	1,670	593
1968	9,761	3,172	3,344	713	7,230	478	7,979	1,131	732	168	225	33
1969	8,180	2,847	2,640	581	6,905	506	7,191	1,111	838	161	181	33
1968 1st qtr	11,174	4,537	3,854	799	6,829	527	7,870	1,261	640	147	181	27
2nd qtr	10,260	2,528	3,451	726	7,511	486	7,603	835	675	174	243	31
3rd qtr	8,293	2,487	3,043	635	7,451	424	8,565	1,312	769	169	267	52
4th qtr	9,315	3,135	3,028	692	7,129	473	7,876	1,118	845	181	209	20
1969 1st qtr	7,084	2,209	2,799	591	6,434	433	7,404	1,108	824	159	189	33
2nd qtr	8,067	2,885	2,697	664	7,009	528	7,437	1,105	837	154	208	48
3rd qtr	8,002	2,707	2,501	467	7,018	512	7,218	1,157	792	156	175	31
4th qtr	9,565	3,586	2,562	603	7,160	552	6,705	1,074	900	174	150	18
1970 1st qtr	6,769	2,997	2,501	485	5,967	577	5,986	886	802	165	169	23

1 Excluding carpets, matting and underlays and rubber or cork flooring.

Courtesy: Ministry of Technology

Table 3.3 CONSTRUCTION Industrial building in Great Britain[1]

New Standard Regions. Area approved during period[2]

million sq. ft.

	UK	North (3)	Yorkshire and Humberside	East Midlands	East Anglia	South East	South West (3)	Wales (3)	West Midlands	North West (3)	Scotland (3)	Development areas million sq. ft.	Percentages of UK
Old basis (4)													
1965	61.8	6.2	6.2	3.4	1.9	11.2	3.1	4.5	5.0	9.2	11.0	24.7	...
1966	69.7	8.2	6.4	4.4	3.8	10.9	3.6	9.3	5.8	9.0	8.2	28.6	...
1967	59.8	7.5	4.5	3.7	2.1	11.4	3.3	5.7	4.0	7.5	10.1	26.4	...
1968	78.9	11.9	5.8	4.2	2.8	11.1	3.9	8.8	6.6	11.9	11.8	35.7	...
1969	80.7	9.9	10.7	4.1	4.1	13.9	4.1	8.3	5.9	10.6	9.1	30.5	...
1968 1st qtr. ...	18.0	2.6	1.5	1.0	1.0	2.0	0.8	1.7	1.0	2.6	3.8	8.4	...
2nd qtr. ...	19.5	3.4	1.9	0.8	0.5	3.3	1.3	1.3	2.1	2.5	2.4	7.9	...
3rd qtr. ...	22.3	4.4	1.3	1.0	0.7	3.3	0.9	3.0	1.7	3.3	2.8	11.8	...
4th qtr. ...	19.1	1.6	1.2	1.3	0.7	2.6	0.8	2.8	1.9	3.5	2.7	7.7	...
1969 1st qtr. ...	22.6	2.6	2.3	1.3	1.4	4.0	1.3	2.4	1.6	3.0	2.5	8.7	...
2nd qtr. ...	20.5	3.8	1.2	0.9	0.9	3.6	1.1	2.1	1.7	3.1	2.0	9.0	...
3rd qtr. ...	18.1	1.9	2.2	1.0	0.9	3.4	0.9	2.2	1.3	2.1	2.1	6.5	...
4th qtr. ...	19.5	1.5	4.9	0.9	0.8	2.9	0.8	1.6	1.3	2.3	2.4	6.5	...
1970 1st qtr. ...	18.5	1.9	1.1	1.0	0.6	3.1	0.9	2.1	2.0	4.1	1.7	6.7	...
2nd qtr. ...	19.5	3.6	1.2	1.4	0.6	3.1	1.0	2.9	1.2	2.2	2.4	9.2	...
New basis (4)													
1967	87.3	7.5	8.7	6.4	3.6	20.7	6.3	5.7	7.1	11.3	10.1	28.8	33
1968	110.4	11.9	9.0	7.3	4.8	21.1	6.3	8.8	11.6	17.8	11.8	37.9	34
1969	115.9	9.9	15.4	6.7	6.3	26.3	6.8	8.3	10.4	16.8	9.1	33.0	28
1968 1st qtr. ...	24.6	2.6	2.0	1.8	1.6	4.0	1.4	1.7	1.8	3.8	3.8	8.9	36
2nd qtr. ...	27.2	3.4	3.0	1.4	0.9	5.3	2.0	1.3	3.9	3.6	2.4	8.2	30
3rd qtr. ...	31.2	4.4	2.2	1.6	1.3	6.5	1.5	3.0	2.8	5.1	2.8	12.6	40
4th qtr. ...	27.5	1.6	1.9	2.5	1.0	5.3	1.3	2.8	3.1	5.3	2.7	8.2	30
1969 1st qtr. ...	33.3	2.6	3.6	2.2	2.0	8.2	2.3	2.4	2.7	4.6	2.5	9.5	29
2nd qtr. ...	29.9	3.8	2.1	1.7	1.7	6.9	1.7	2.1	2.8	5.1	2.0	9.9	33
3rd qtr. ...	25.8	1.9	3.6	1.4	1.3	5.8	1.5	2.2	2.6	3.3	2.1	6.8	26
4th qtr. ...	26.9	1.5	6.0	1.3	1.3	5.3	1.3	1.6	2.3	3.8	2.4	6.9	26
1970 1st qtr. ...	25.9	1.9	2.0	1.7	0.9	5.8	1.3	2.1	3.0	5.6	1.7	7.1	28
2nd qtr. ...	27.0	3.6	2.1	2.3	1.0	5.7	1.6	2.9	2.0	3.3	2.4	9.8	36

Table 3.3. (continued)

New Standard Regions. Area approved during period[5]

million sq.ft.

	GB	North (3)	Yorkshire and Humberside	East Midlands	East Anglia	South East	South West (3)	Wales (3)	West Midlands	North West	Scotland (3)	Development areas
1965	38.3	4.3	3.2	2.1	1.1	8.1	2.3	1.4	4.0	7.5	4.3	14.3
1966	37.4	4.6	3.3	2.4	1.4	5.5	2.0	2.0	4.3	5.6	6.3	13.9
1967	34.9	3.8	4.0	2.7	1.5	5.9	1.8	2.1	2.9	4.2	6.0	13.6
1968	39.2	3.9	4.6	3.0	1.4	6.3	3.0	2.7	4.1	6.0	4.1	13.5
1969	46.4	4.9	4.6	2.8	2.4	8.7	2.8	5.5	3.1	4.9	6.9	19.5
1968 1st qtr. ...	9.5	1.1	0.8	0.8	0.3	1.3	1.2	0.7	0.7	1.5	1.1	3.7
2nd qtr. ...	9.1	0.5	1.0	0.7	0.3	1.2	0.5	0.6	1.1	1.8	1.2	3.3
3rd qtr. ...	9.8	1.1	1.1	0.8	0.4	1.8	0.8	0.4	1.2	1.4	0.9	2.8
4th qtr. ...	10.7	1.2	1.6	0.7	0.4	2.0	0.5	0.9	1.1	1.4	1.0	3.6
1969 1st qtr. ...	8.8	1.1	0.8	0.7	0.5	1.6	0.4	1.2	0.4	1.0	1.1	3.7
2nd qtr. ...	13.0	1.5	1.3	0.8	1.2	2.2	0.9	1.0	1.0	0.9	2.3	5.3
3rd qtr. ...	12.1	1.5	1.2	0.5	0.3	2.6	0.9	1.2	0.8	1.2	1.8	5.1
4th qtr. ...	12.6	0.8	1.2	0.8	0.5	2.3	0.6	2.1	0.9	1.8	1.7	5.4

Courtesy: Ministry of Technology

1 The figures relate to schemes mainly over 5,000 sq. ft. 2 For all projects (new buildings, extensions to existing premises and buildings converted to industrial use) for which industrial development certificates were issued. 3 These regions take in the places designated as development areas under the Industrial Development Act, 1966: the aggregate figures for the development areas are shown separately. 4The area of industrial building has, since the introduction of the Industrial Development Act in August 1966, been extended to include all ancillary space for storage, canteens, etc. Prior to that date ancillary space was not counted, except in Scotland, Wales and the northern region; the figures since that date on the old basis of measurement are estimates of the area which would have been approved under the pre-August 1966 definition. 5 For manufacturing industry only (new buildings and extensions to existing premises).

4. EXTRACT FROM ANNUAL ABSTRACT OF STATISTICS, 1969, No. 106. HMSO.
Reproduced by permission

Table 4.1 Construction: Value of output in the UK.

(£ million)

Building and construction

	1958	1959	1960	1961	1962	1963	1964	1965	1966	1967	1968
Total by all agencies	2,177	2,399	2,581	2,845	3,011	3,110	3,614	3,851	4,039	4,307	4,569
Output by contractors:											
New work: Total	1,405	1,514	1,653	1,881	2,006	2,051	2,467	2,631	2,734	2,906	3,090
New housing: Total	518	568	629	689	738	784	995	1,051	1,064	1,172	1,256
For public sector......	254	245	240	252	293	323	424	466	511	586	633
For private sector ...	264	323	389	437	445	461	571	585	553	586	623
Other new work: Total ...	887	946	1,024	1,192	1,268	1,267	1,472	1,580	1,670	1,734	1,834
For public sector	416	444	432	498	560	585	708	739	801	902	984
For private sector:											
Total...............	471	502	592	694	708	682	764	841	869	832	850
Industrial	271	282	341	408	370	336	383	433	466	425	441
Non-industrial.......	200	220	251	286	338	346	381	408	403	407	409
Repair and maintenance ..	415	462	493	522	548	586	625	671	716	748	791
Public sector:											
Output by direct labour- [1].............	357	423	435	442	457	473	522	549	589	653	688

1 Output of operatives employed directly by government departments, local authorities and public utilities (British Railways, Central Electricity Generating Board, etc.). The figures from 1959 cover a somewhat wider field than the earlier series.

Courtesy: Ministry of Public Building and Works

Table 4.2 Construction: Value of new orders obtained by contractors for new work in UK

(£ million)

	1958	1959	1960	1961	1962	1963	1964	1965	1966	1967	1968
New work: Total	1,441	1,723	2,023	2,107	2,243	2,535	2,993	2,912	2,878	3,394	3,221
New housing: Total	518	690	733	742	808	980	1,204	1,203	1,154	1,421	1,258
From public sector	219	255	257	273	343	454	465	510	564	709	636
From private sector	299	435	476	469	465	526	739	693	590	712	622
Other new work: Total	923	1,033	1,290	1,365	1,435	1,555	1,789	1,709	1,724	1,973	1,963
From public sector	411	448	513	584	678	784	927	894	939	1,227	1,137
From private sector[1]											
Total	512	585	777	781	757	771	862	815	785	746	826
Industrial	291	323	457	418	348	374	406	431	427	447	484
Non-industrial	221	262	320	363	409	397	456	384	358	299	342

1 Figures for private sector include work to be carried out by contractors on their own initiative for sale.

Courtesy: Ministry of Public Building and Works

Published Market Information

1. EXTRACT FROM IPC MARKETING MANUAL 1970, B.6.5. FLOOR COVERINGS
Reproduced by permission

Table 1.1 Annual Size/value of the market

Manufacturers' sales of floor coverings – million sq. yd.

	1964	1966	1967	1968	export (%)
Linoleum	34.9	20.0	16.1	13.4	(32)
Printed felt base	64.5	47.6	42.7	39.0	(21)
Rigid/semi-rigid tiles	26.7	26.0	27.6	28.9	(7)
Calendered vinyl	23.4	33.4	33.3	31.9	(14)
Other	4.6	8.2	9.3	3.8	(15)
Total, lino, vinyl etc.	154.1	135.2	129.0	117.0	(19)
Coir matting	0.2	0.1	0.1	0.1	(n)
Carpets and rugs:					
Woven wool	43.2	39.2	35.7	39.9	(15)
Tufted	33.3	43.0	52.7	59.5·	(10)
Other	19.3	21.0	21.8	23.9	(10)
Total, carpets, etc.	96.0	103.3	110.3	123.4	(11)

It would seem as though UK *consumer* expenditure on flooring materials is in the area of £200 million. EIU *Retail Business* No. 128 suggests a figure of £150 million for the carpet market.

Within the smooth coverings, note the downward trend for lino and printed felt base and the upward trend for vinyl. In the carpet sector, note the upward trend for tufted which has, however, slowed down considerably in the late 1960s, leaving excess production capacity in this field.

Table 1.2 Principal Advertisers and Brands (those spending £75,000 or more in 1969)

Advertiser/brand	Press and TV advertising (£'000)					
	1968		1969			
	TV	Press	Total	(%)	TV	Press
Allied Carpets	(n.a.)		124	(6)	–	124
BMK Carpets	163	3	136	(7)	134	2
British Carpet Centre	–	75	195	(10)	–	195
Crossley Carpets	–	77	88	(5)	–	88
Kosset Carpets	1	136	124	(6)	4	120
Mayman Carpets	–	52	75	(4)	–	75
Total for groups, 'Carpets/rugs, flooring'	602	2,115	1,929	(100)	229	1,699

In the flooring group the main advertisers in 1969 were Armstrong (£50,000), Marley (£22,000), Nairn (£50,000), Vynolay (£35,000).

Channels of Distribution

Furniture stores, departmental stores, carpet specialists, mail order and flooring specialists.

Indications of brand shares

1 *Types:* In terms of money, it appears that carpets probably account for about 75 per cent of the market, other types about 25 per cent although in square yardage the proportions seem to be much closer to 50:50. Within the carpet sector tufted is reported to account for 52 per cent — presumably in yardage.

2 *Makers:*

(*a*) Carpets: EIU in *Retail Business* No. 128 suggested that in the woven sector John Crossley was the leading maker, followed by Brintons, BMK and Birstall Homfray. These four accounted for about 40 per cent and, apart from Carpet Manufacturing Company (5th on EIU's list), the remainder (about half) was divided between numerous manufacturers. Recent mergers in the industry mean that Carpets International is now the largest group including the Carpet Manufacturing Company, Crossley and Kosset Carpets.

In the tufted group, Lancaster was put ahead of Shaw, Cyril Lord and Kosset but in this case the four makers account for 80 per cent of sales.

The Cyril Lord assets have been acquired by Viyella which subsequently has been the subject of an ICI bid.

(*b*) Other: principal individual shares are likely to go to Nairn, Semtex and Marley.

Other points of interest

1 In carpets wool is no longer the major fibre—cellulosic has now an equal or slightly larger share.

2 Tufted is expected to continue to gain from woven — mainly on price — but at a reduced rate.

3 In its 1967 'Furniture and Furnishings' Survey, Odhams Press found that in the last five years:

(*a*) 15 per cent of housewives had bought carpet (Last 2 years: 7 per cent).

(*b*) 8 per cent of housewives had bought tiling or linoleum (4 per cent).

(*c*) 2 per cent of housewives had bought other floor covering (1 per cent).

These recent (last five years) purchasers of carpet tended to be biased towards the younger age groups, C class and in Midlands and North West.

Although tiling or lino seemed to be more 'down-scale', the same age and area emphasis existed as for carpet.

TGI (1969) found that 36 per cent of housewives had bought carpet(s) *or rugs* and 22 per cent had bought lino or vinyl. (The differences are almost certainly due to difference of definition rather than to real growth.)

Courtesy: Annual Abstract of Statistics 1969 — Monthly Digest of Statistics — National Income and Expenditure (HMSO); IPA: 'Total Market Sizes'; EIU *Retail Business* No. 128; Odhams Press 'Furniture and Furnishings', 1967; MEAL 1968 and 1969 Digests; BMRB Target Group Index, 1969; *Financial Times* March 3, 1970.

2. EXTRACT FROM RETAIL BUSINESS 128, Oct. 1968 – CARPETS AND FLOORCOVERINGS
Reproduced by permission

Development of the industry

Plastic floor-coverings have fairly recently succeeded the rather poor products of the immediate post-war period. With technical advance, a wide range of colours and materials have now entered the market. Plastic floor-coverings are based on the product PVC which is highly flexible, and from which an almost infinite variety of end products can be developed.

In the last two years there have been some significant advances, including the introduction of the printed vinyl sheet which has allowed manufacturers to print stone or ceramic patterns on tiles. Recently, too, a market has been established for sound-deadening cork and pvc tiles. (These are simple to install and have great potential for both industrial and domestic uses.)

Floor-coverings are now available in a wide range of styles and prices: for example, at the cheaper end of the scale is 'Contura' by Dunlop Semtex Ltd, which retails at 49p per sq. yd. and is a solid vinyl sheet with an embossed mosaic design. In contrast, 'Hardura 77' (produced by Hardura Ltd) is foam-backed, has a leather grained surface texture, and costs between 99p and £1.19 per sq. yd.

Despite technical advances, the smooth floor-coverings industry would seem to be losing ground to carpet manufacturers; so several firms have now diversified into the carpet industry (e.g., Marley Tiles Ltd, Dunlop and Nairn), and other companies prefer to concentrate on developing new types of smooth floor-coverings, like adhesive tiles.

Leading manufacturers in this industry are Nairn Floors, Dunlop Semtex and Marley Tiles.

Alternative types of floor covering include cork and wood. Cork is at present enjoying increased demand – especially in laminates with plastic in tiling – as flooring in multi-storey buildings where sound-proofing is an important feature. Wood has, on account of its 'quality' appearance, great scope in the luxury market, particularly as a very wide range of colours and patterns has now been developed.

3. EXTRACT FROM IDS REPORT 86, Mar. 1970
Reproduced by permission

Building Industry Wage Agreements

Floor layers are considered as an ancillary group to the building trades. The National Joint Council for the industry determines their wage rates.

A long-term pay and productivity agreement which gives increases in standard hourly rates of 10½p for craftsmen and 9p for labourers (see IDS Report No. 81, p. 22) has been ratified by the Building NJC and approved by the Department of Employment and Productivity. It also provides for three days' additional annual holiday entitlement in 1971. In addition, the NJC has agreed a 'Statement of General Principles concerning Incentive Schemes and Productivity Agreements'.

The pay increases were effective in three stages: craftsmen received increases in standard hourly rates of 4½p on 2 February, 1970; 2½p from 2 November, 1970; and 3½p from 7 June, 1971; and labourers received increases in standard hourly rates of 3½p, 2p and 3p respectively.

Date of last increase: 4 November, 1968; when interim hourly increases of 1½p for craftsmen and 1½p for labourers were paid pending NBPI Reports 91 and 92 (see IDS Report No. 58, p. 26).

Date of last decrease: 30 December, 1968, when decreases of ½p per hour for all workers were agreed following the reports of the NBPI (see IDS Report No. 59, p. 17).

Objectives

The agreement states that the objectives of incentive schemes and productivity agreements are as follows:

1 To increase efficiency, thereby keeping the cost of building at an economic level.

2 To encourage greater productivity thereby providing an opportunity for increasing earnings by increased effort, while maintaining a high standard of workmanship and avoiding a waste of labour and materials. It follows that such agreements must be strictly related to productivity.

Flexibility

Although local arrangements may exist for the recognition of certain operations as the sole prerogative of a particular trade of craft, the agreement states that 'the employer shall not be in breach of that agreement, arrangement or understanding if he arranges to engage on the operation, operatives of another trade or craft who are skilled and qualified to carry it out.

It shall further be accepted that in those districts where there have been understandings about the employment of craftsmen's mates, employers shall not in future be regarded as being in breach of such understandings if mates are not employed on operations which do not require them.

Standard weekly rates
(provincial)

	Old rates 30 December, 1968	New rates 2 February, 1970	New rates 2 November, 1970	New rates 7 June, 1971	Increase (%)
Craftsmen	£15.66½	£17.58	£18.50	£20.00	26.3
Labourers	£13.50	£15.00	£15.75	£17.00	25.9
Hours	40	40	40	40	

London and Liverpool rates are 25p per week higher.

Work Measurement

The agreement also sets out general principles for the issue by management of targets for each operation performed by an individual operative or gang and states that 'according to the extent that performance is better than the target, an additional payment should be made over and above the appropriate standard rate of wages'. Targets are based on BSI standards and are 'dependent on the saving rate adopted in each scheme'. 'The incentive scheme must state the proportion of the saving which is to be paid out as bonus.'

Application of Incentive Schemes

It is accepted that 'The effective application of incentive schemes depends upon willing co-operation between management and operatives to ensure on the one hand that the organization of the job is such as will permit realistic targets to be achieved and on the other hand a genuine effort is made to improve output. Where it is necessary to carry out work study this should be arranged by mutual consent.'

Operation of Target System

1 The target should be stated as a given quantity of work to be done in a number of hours, to the satisfaction of management. (The given number of hours may be expressed as a monetary value where this method is customary.)

2 Where tasks are pre-measured they should be of short duration so that, as far as is possible, they do not extend into a second pay-week.

3 Gains and losses occurring in different pay-weeks shall not be offset; except where a target which has been pre-measured covers work to be done in more than one pay-week.

4 Working targets once fixed may not be altered unless there is a significant change in the job content or in working methods and then only after joint consultation.

5 At the commencement of repetitive work, a jointly-agreed 'learning-curve' allowance is permissible having regard to the improvement in productivity that should subsequently follow.

6 The target will be inclusive for craftsmen and labourers and all hours will be chargeable against the target except where there is an interruption of work beyond the control of the parties.

7 The time of non-working supervision should not be charged against the gang. In the case of part-time working supervision the proportion of time to be charged against the gang should be agreed in advance.

8 The time of first-year apprentices should not be charged against the gang. In the case of apprentices in their later years of apprenticeship, the proportion of their time which should be charged should, as a guide, be the same as the proportion of the craftsmen's rate which they receive under the apprentices' wage for age scale.

9 Overtime premiums, guaranteed time and travelling time should not be charged against targets.

10 Bonus payments, after adjustment in the case of a proportionate scheme, should be made at the standard plain time rate of the operative concerned, including extra payments.

11 The amount of bonus earnings should be notified to operatives not later than the pay-day next following the pay-week in which the work was completed. The bonus should be paid not later than the next pay-day after that.

12 Where work for which bonus has been paid proves defective and has to be re-executed in whole or in part (a) the remedial work shall be carried out by the same operative gang (b) no bonus shall be paid therefor; and (c) the time taken shall be off-set against any savings on subsequent targets. This provision shall not apply where the original work had been carried out strictly in accordance with precise instructions.

Productivity Agreements

The agreement states: 'The objective of a productivity agreement is to make a joint effort to improve efficiency by reducing unit costs through such means as the use of balanced gangs, greater flexibility or the relaxation of specified work practices. Such an agreement should provide an opportunity for higher earnings.'

Disputes – Incentive Schemes or Productivity Agreements

In the event of a dispute or difference arising over an incentive scheme or productivity agreement 'there shall be no restriction of work or withdrawal from operation of the scheme whilst the procedure is being followed'. 'Any settlement of such a dispute or difference shall apply with retrospective effect from the date upon which the dispute or difference was raised officially by the accredited site representative(s) of the operatives.'

Guaranteed Weekly Wage

Under the previous arrangements, an employee was entitled to one week's guaranteed pay in the case of bad weather. Under the new provisions 'as from the end of the pay-week in which he was engaged an operative shall be guaranteed payment at his standard weekly rate of wages for the full normal working hours of each subsequent and complete pay-week of the period of employment, whether work is or is not provided by the employer, and regardless of temporary stoppages through inclement weather or other causes beyond the control of the parties'. 'The guarantee is reduced proportionately for any pay-week in which there is a day or days of locally recognized holiday or of certified absence due to sickness and injury', and suspended in the event of work being unavailable due to industrial action being taken by other employees.

Additional Annual Holiday Entitlement
As and from the 1971/72 holiday season, annual holiday entitlement is increased by three days (making a total of two weeks, three days). The additional three days must be taken over the Christmas/New Year period.

Disputes Procedure
It is agreed that 'no strike, lock-out or other industrial action shall be taken by any party to a dispute before the procedure ... has been exhausted'. The disputes procedure has been amended to provide a single machinery in which the local regional employers and union representatives, together with the NJC are responsible for the settlement of emergency disputes e.g., industrial action. Previously, the NJC was not immediately concerned in emergency disputes procedure and dealt only with items under the normal disputes procedure. Under the new agreement, 'responsibility for the settlement of all disputes and differences arising in the building industry shall be vested in the council'.

Comment:
For background details relating to the agreement (see IDS Reports No. 74, p. 8; No. 77, p. 4; No. 80, p. 6; and No. 81, p. 5).

Appendix 7

Notes on a conversation with an ex-member of a main competitor's staff held subsequent to Report for Management.

One of Cork Products' development team happened to meet an ex-member of a competitor's staff on a social occasion, expressed interest in the flooring market, and obtained the following information.

Market shares are difficult to quantify since 'routes' to the user differ. Four firms, Marley, Nairn, Armstrong and Dunlop are believed to hold 90 per cent by cash, and a variety of smaller companies, and imports make up the remainder. Marley are believed to have about 40 per cent share of the retail sector, and Armstrong lead the industrial contract market.

All except Armstrong operate their own floor-laying service, and are alleged to price all-in work cheaply during downturns in business. Armstrong deal through independent distributors etc., and are, therefore, held in favour by the flooring contractor trade.

The same source believed that in the *tile* market flexible vinyl was on the increase and could double in five years, whereas vinyl asbestos was on the decline. Thermoplastic tiles would show a very slow decline.

Product problems which do not emerge from a study of literature, and which should not occur with our proposed product are:

1 Corners and edges of tiles do not always provide a clean match.

2 Plastic has dimensional stability – a 'memory' as the informant put it – which makes it difficult to correct slight imperfections in the tile, while laying.

Adhesives are not altogether satisfactory, and old or uneven flooring generally needs the prior application of a smooth surfacing agent.

When asked for information on the 'split' of business between retailers and contractors, the source indicated that in sterling value, at manufacturer's net realization, it was about 50/50, but in square yards 40/60.

Later, the following detail on split by product type was provided by telephone.

Table 1

	Contractor (%)	Retailer (%)
Printed calendered; felt-based	–	100
Sheet:		
Vinyl inlaid	90	10
Vinyl cushioned	10	90
Spread feltback	80	20
Foam, corkback	90	10
Linoleum	50	50
Tile:		
Thermoplastic	100	–
Vinyl asbestos	95	5
Flexible vinyl	60	40

Table 2 Resilient Flooring Market

	Volume in million of sq. yd. Value in £million gross sales					
	1965	**1967**	**1969**		**1975**	
	sq. yd	sq. yd	sq. yd	£	sq. yd	£
Felt base & linoleum						
Felt base — Printed with paint or ink	41.4	31.0	20.5	2.2	—	—
Felt base — Vinyl laminate	1.5?	2.0?	3.0	0.5	10.0	1.5
Linoleum	16.7	12.1	8.4	4.8	2.0	1.1
Total felt base & linoleum	59.6	45.1	31.9	£7.5	12.0	£2.6
Tile						
Thermoplastic Tile	13.4	15.3	14.5	3.7	12.0	3.1
Vinyl Asbestos Tile	8.0	7.6	8.3	3.8	6.0	2.7
Flexible Vinyl Tile (inc. hq)	3.3	5.9	7.6	4.3	14.5	8.2
Total tile	24.7	28.8	30.4	£11.8	32.5	£14.0
Vinyl sheet						
Inlaid	0.8	1.4	2.7	1.6	3.0	1.8
Printed Calendered	19.7	21.1	16.6	5.7	17.0	5.8
Fashioned	—	—	3.4	1.8	12.0	6.4
Thread, Felt (Filz) Backed	1.8	2.0	3.8	1.4	5.0	1.8
Foam Backed, Cork Backed, etc.	—	—	0.4	0.3	2.0	2.0
New Product (see notes)	—	—	—	—	0.5	0.8
Other — Corlon, etc.	—	—	0.03	0.05	0.1	0.17
Total sheet vinyl	22.3	24.5	26.93	10.85	39.6	18.77
Grand total	106.6	98.4	89.23	£30.15	84.1	£35.37

Table 2 gives a breakdown of the resilient flooring market based on official published statistics and existing information. A projection of the market by 1975 is also made. Full details of these statistics and projections is given in the appendices. It can be seen that despite the decline in volume the market is expected to increase in value by £5 million, and offers a number of opportunities for growth, upgrading and innovation, particularly for sheet products.

Table 3 Smooth floorings – manufactures in million sq. yd

Courtesy: Board of Trade and Report on the Supply of Linoleum 1956

Vinyl Asbestos and Thermoplastic figures adjusted in view of other information available

Year	Lino	Felt base		Thermoplastic tile	Vinyl asbestos tile	Flexible vinyl tile	Total tile	Flexible vinyl sheet	Other	Total
		Paint	Vinyl							
1933-37 av.	49.5	32.6	—	—	—	—	—	—	—	82.1
1937	52.6	41.6	—	—	—	—	—	—	—	94.2
1944-46 av.	19.0	19.0	—	—	—	—	—	—	—	38.0
1947-54 av.	29.3	48.8	—	—	—	—	—	—	?	?
1954	40.4	61.1	—	10?	Starting	—	—	—	?	111.5
1963	23.9	49.5	—	10.9	7.1	2.6	20.6	10.7	1.4	112.4
1964	21.9	47.3	1.0 ?	15.6	8.7	3.3	27.6	19.2	1.8	118.8
1965	16.7	41.4	1.5 ?	13.4	8.0	3.3	24.7	22.3	2.4	109.0
1966	13.9	33.7	2.0 ?	14.3	6.7	5.4	26.4	22.7	3.2	101.9
1967	12.1	31.0	2.0 ?	15.3	7.6	5.9	28.8	24.5	4.0	102.4
1968	10.5	26.4	3.0 ?	15.9	7.8	6.9	30.6	24.6	0.5	95.6
1969 est.	8.4	20.5	3.0 ?	14.5	7.4	6.6	28.5	24.1	0.3	84.8

Linoleum	: Plain linoleum was included under 'other' until 1965 inclusive. However, the 1963 to 65 'other' totals look suspiciously low and some Plain Line may have been included with lino.
Felt base	: Vinyl surfaced material is excluded. Guessed figures for Nairn's 'Crestabelle' are therefore shown separately.
Thermoplastic	: Production started in 1948.
Vinyl asbestos	: Accoflex was introduced in June 1955.
Flexible vinyl tile	: Includes high quality on assumption that sales refer to Amtico.
Flexible vinyl sheet	: See separate analysis.
Other	: Excludes rubber and cork flooring.

Further Reading

Books, Pamphlets
Most general marketing texts have at least one chapter on product management. Some specialist titles follow.

Berg, T.L. and Schuchman, A. *Product Strategy & Management*, Holt, Rinehart & Winston, 1963.

Booz, Allen and Hamilton *Management of New Products*, Booz, Allen & Hamilton, 4th ed. 1965.

Dominguez, G.S. *Product Management*, American Management Association, 1971.

King, S. *Developing New Brands*, Pitman, 1973.

Kraushar, Andrews and Eassie Ltd *New Products in the Grocery Trade 1971: A UK Study*, Kraushar, Andrews & Eassie Ltd.

Medcalf, G. *Marketing and the Brand Manager*, Pergamon, 1967.

Morley, J. (ed.) *Launching a New Product*, Business Books, 1968.

Offord, R.H. (ed.) *Product Management in Action*, Business Publications, 1967.

Pessemier, E.A. *New Product Decisions: An Analytical Approach*, McGraw-Hill Book Co., 1966.

Phelps, D.M. (ed.) *Product Management: Selected Readings (1950-69)*, Irwin, 1970.

Skinner, R.N. *Launching New Products in Competitive Markets*, Cassell & Associated Business Programmes, 1972.

Ward, E.P. *The Dynamics of Planning*, Pergamon, 1970.

Bibliographies
Fisher, R.W. and Hirst, M. *The Quantitative Approach to Marketing, A Selected Bibliography (1966 to 1971)*, Warwick University, 1972.

Megathlin, D.E. and Schaeffer, W.E. *A bibliography on New Product Planning*, American Marketing Association, 1966.

Michalowska, A. *Etude Bibiographique sur les Nouveaux Produits*, Revue Francaise du Marketing, 4th Trimestre 1971, p. 87.

Sandeau, G. *International Bibliography of Marketing and Distribution*, Staples Press, 1972.

Articles
Adler, L. *Time Lag in New Product Development*, Journal of Marketing, 30(1), 17, Jan. 1966.

Adler, L. *Systems Approach to Marketing*, Harvard Business Review, 45(3), 105 May-Jun. 1967.

Allen, D.H. *Credibility Forecasts & their Application to the Economic Assessment of Novel R & D Projects*, Operational Research Quarterly, 19(1), 25, 1968.

Ames, B.C. *Marketing Planning for Industrial Products*, Harvard Business Review, 46(5), 100 Sep.-Oct. 1968.

Ames, B.C. *Dilemma of Product/Market Management*, Harvard Business Review, 49(2), 66, Mar.-Apr. 1971.

Ansoff, H.I. and Stewart, J.M. *Strategies for a Technology-Based Business*, Harvard Business Review, 45(6), 71 Nov.-Dec. 1967.

Armitage, R.Q. and Muir, A. *How to Plan Products*, Management Today, Jul. 1967, p.92.

Beattie, D.W. *Marketing a New Product*, Operational Research Quarterly, 20(4), 429, December 1969.

Brown, R.V. *Just How Credible Are Your Market Estimates,* Journal of Marketing, 33(3), 46, Jul. 1969 .

Caffyn, J. and Loyd, A. *Predicting Effect of Brand Name Consumer Predispositions on Consumer Purchase Decisions: A Case History*, ADMAP, 4(11), 538, Dec.1968

Catling, H. and Rodgers, P. *Forecasting the Textile Scene: An Aid to the Planning of a Research Programme*, R & D Management, 1(3), 141, Jun. 1971.

Cetron, M.J., Martino, J. and Roepcke, L. *The Selection of R & D Program Content – Survey of Quantitative Methods*, IEEE Transactions on Engineering Management, EM-14(1), 4, Mar. 1967.

Charnes, A., Cooper, W.W., Devoe, J.K. and Learner, D.B. *DEMON, Mark II: An Extremal Equation Approach to New Product Marketing*, Management Science, 14(9), 513, May 1968 and 14(11), 682, Jul. 1968.

Claycamp, H.J. and Liddy, L.E. *Prediction of New Product Performance: An Analytical Approach*, Journal of Marketing Research, 6(4), 414, Nov. 1969.

Corsiglia, J. *The Management Decision in Product Strategy & Pricing*, IEEE Transactions on Engineering Management, EM-12(2), 34 Jun. 1965.

Cox, W.E. Jnr *Product Life-Cycles as Marketing Models*, Journal of Business, 40(4), 375, Oct. 1967.

Cunningham, M.T. *The Application of Product Life Cycles to Corporate Strategy: Some Research Findings,* British Journal of Marketing, 3, 32, Spring 1969.

DeVries, M.G. *The Dynamic Effects of Planning Horizons on the Selection of Optimal Product Strategies*, Management Science, 10(3), 524, Ap. 1964.

Dory, J.P. and Lord, R.J. *Does TF Really Work?* Harvard Business Review, 48(6), 16 Nov.-Dec. 1970.

Dusenbury, W. *CPM For New Product Introductions*, Harvard Business Review, 45(4), 124, Jul.-Aug. 1967.

Ehrenberg, A.S.C. *Predicting the Performance of New Brands*, Journal of Advertising Research, **11**(6), 3, Dec. 1971.

Freimer, M. and Simon, L.S. *'The Evaluation of Potential New Product Alternatives*, Management Science, **13**(6), B-279, Feb. 1967.

Gabor, A. *The Pricing of New Products*, Marketing, Feb. 1971, p. 46.

Goodman, S.R. *Improved Marketing Analysis of Profitability, Relevant Costs, and Life-Cycles*, Financial Executive, **35**(6), 28, Jun. 1967.

Hamelman, P. and Mazze, E.M. *Improving Product Abandonment Decisions*, Journal of Marketing, **36**, 20, Apr. 1972.

Hanan, M. *Corporate Growth Through Venture Management*, Harvard Business Review, **47**(1), 43, Jan.-Feb. 1969.

Hartmann, F. and Moglewer, S. *Allocation of Resources to Research Proposals*, Management Science, **14**(1), 85, Sept. 1967.

Karger, D.W. and Murdick, R.G. *Product Design, Marketing and Manufacturing Innovation*, California Management Review, **9**(2), 33, Winter 1966.

King, S. *Identifying Market Opportunities*, Management Decision, **9**, 7, Spring 1971.

Kotler, P. *Phasing Out Weak Products*, Harvard Business Review, **43**(2), 107, Mar.-Apr. 1965.

Kotler, P. *Competitive Strategies for New Product Marketing Over the Life-Cycle*, Management Science, **12**(4), B-104, Dec. 1965.

Laffy, R. *Applications de la Methode MARSAN pour la Recherche, La Selection et le Lancement de Produits Nouveaux*, Revue Fancaise du Marketing, **22**, 45, 1st Trimestre, 1967.

Learner, D.B. *DEMON New Product Planning: A Case-History*, New Directions in Marketing, AMA 48th Conference, 489, June 1965.

Levitt, T. *Marketing Myopia*, Harvard Business Review, **38**(4), 45, Jul.-Aug. 1960.

Levitt, T. *Exploit the Product Life-Cycle*, Harvard Business Review, **43**(6), 81, Nov.-Dec. 1965.

Longbottom, D.A. *The Application of Decision Analysis to a New Product Planning Decision*, Operational Research Quarterly, **24**(1), 9 Mar, 1973.

Minkes, A.L. and Samuels, J.M. *Allocation of R & D Expenditures in the Firm*, Journal of Management Studies, **3**, 63, Feb. 1969.

Nicholson, T.A.J. and Pullen, R.D. *MAPLE: A Linear Programming System For Product Planning*, Management Accounting, **48**(10), 364, Oct. 1970.

North, H.Q. and Pyke, D.L. *'Probes' of the Technological Future*, Harvard Business Review, **47**(3), 68, May-Jun. 1969.

Oxenfeldt, A.R. *Product Line Pricing*, Harvard Business Review, **44**(4), 138, Jul.-Aug. 1966.

Pearson, A.S. *How to Compare New Product Programs*, Journal of Advertising Research, **11**(3), 3, Jun. 1971.

Pearson, A.W. and Topalian, A.S. *Project Evaluation in Research and Development*, Management Decision, **3**(3), 26 Autumn 1969.

Pengilly, P.J. and Moss, A.J. *Choice of a New Product, its Selling Pattern and Price*, Operational Research Quarterly, **20**(2), 179, Jun. 1969.

Quinn, J.B. *Technological Forecasting*, Harvard Business Review, **45**(2), 89, Mar.-Apr. 1967.

Rutenberg, D.P. *Design Commonality to Reduce Multi-Item Inventory: Optimal Depth of a Product Line*, Operations Research, **19**(2), 491, Mar. 1971.

Schoen, D.R. *Managing Technological Innovation*, Harvard Business Review, **47**(3), 156, May-Jun. 1969.

Silk, A.J. *Preference & Perception Measures in New Product Development: An Exposition & Review*, Industrial Management Review, **11**, 21, Fall, 1969.

Simmonds, K. *Removing the Chains from Product Strategy*, Journal of Management Studies, **5**, 29, Feb. 1968.

Smallwood, J.E. *The Product Life-Cycle: A Key to Strategic Marketing Planning*, M.S.U. Business Topics, **21**(1), 29, Winter, 1973.

Urban, G.L. *Sprinter Mod III. A Model for the Analysis of New Frequently Purchased Consumer Products*, Operations Research, **18**(5), 805, Sep. 1970.

Whaley, W.M. and Williams, R.A. *A Profit-Oriented Approach to Project Selection*, Research Management, **14**(5), 25, Sep. 1971.

Williams, D.J. *A Study of a Decision Model for R & D Project Selection*, Operational Research Quarterly, **20**(3), 361, Sep. 1969.

Wood, J.F. *New Product Development*, ADMAP, Jan. 1967 – Jan. 1968.

Woods, W. *Product Concept Research: Why & How* Scientific Business, **3**(10), 165, Aug. 1965.

Index

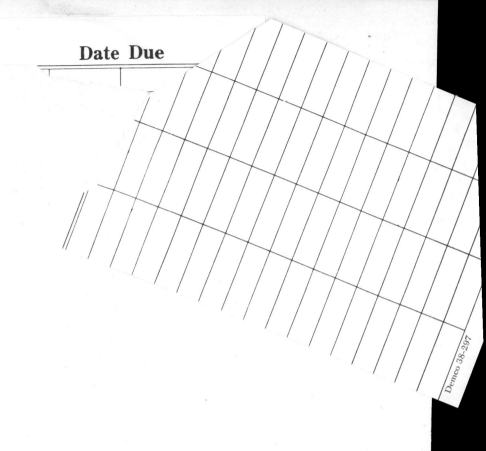

Date Due